D1047952

Not For Tourists Guide to
PHILADELPHIA

Get more on
notfortourists.com

Keep connected with:
Twitter:
twitter/notfortourists

Facebook:
facebook/notfortourists

iPhone App:
nftiphone.com

www.notfortourists.com

Not For Tourists Inc

Skyhorse Publishing

designed by:

Not For Tourists, Inc

NFT$_{TM}$—Not For Tourists$_{TM}$ Guide to Philadelphia

www.notfortourists.com

Publisher
Skyhorse Publishing

Co-Founders
Jane Pirone
Rob Tallia

City Editor
Meg Favreau

Information Design
Jane Pirone
Rob Tallia
Scot Covey

Director
Stuart Farr

Managing Editors
Craig Nelson
Rob Tallia

Sales & Marketing Director
Sarah Hocevar

Production Manager
Aaron Schielke

Printed in China
ISBN# 978-1-61608-566-7 $16.95
Copyright © 2011 by Not For Tourists, Inc.
7th Edition

Every effort has been made to ensure that the information in this book is as up-to-date as possible at press time. However, many details are liable to change—as we have learned.
Not For Tourists cannot accept responsibility for any consequences arising from the use of this book.

Not For Tourists does not solicit individuals, organizations, or businesses for listings inclusion in our guides, nor do we accept payment for inclusion into the editorial portion of our book; the advertising sections, however, are exempt from this policy. We always welcome communications from anyone regarding ANYTHING having to do with our books; please visit us on our website at www. notfortourists.com for appropriate contact information.

Skyhorse Publishing books may be purchased in bulk at special discounts for sales promotion, corporate gifts, fund-raising, or educational purposes. Special editions can also be created to specifications. For details, contact the Special Sales Department, Skyhorse Publishing, 307 West 36th Street, 11th Floor, New York, NY 10018 or kmennone@skyhorsepublishing.com.

www.skyhorsepublishing.com

10 9 8 7 6 5 4 3 2 1

Dear NFT User,

We never get tired of saying "Philadelphia: City of Winners." If you weren't in Philadelphia when the Phillies won the World Series, you missed one hell of a party. Some might report that there were riots in Philadelphia that night, but the truth is that there were parties. The streets swarmed with the young and the old, the smashed and the sober, all cheering and setting off fireworks. Trucks drove slowly through the streets, filled with shouting, happy people. Our baseball team—which, incidentally, is mascoted by a creature that looks like a green, bipedal Snuffleupagus—won.

Of course, Philadelphia is much more than just sports fans and street parties (really, it is), and we here at NFT have worked hard to tell you about it. In this book you'll find hard facts like the location of your bank's ATM or the best way to drive across the city. You'll also find our honest opinions on everything from where to live to where to go to school, what museum is best to take your visiting parents to and where to get drunk on the cheap. If you're new to the city, we'll help you get acquainted. If you've been here a while, hopefully we can point out some places you've never been to, but should definitely check out.

So welcome to NFT's Philadelphia. Besides the book we have a great website (www.notfortourists.com) that features tons of content that we couldn't fit in the book: daily happenings around town, longer musings on the city, photo galleries, editor and neighborhood specific pages, and so much more. And hey, for those of you that have iPhones, we also have an app for Philly. Welcome to the future.

With a Toast,

Meg, Craig, Jane & Rob

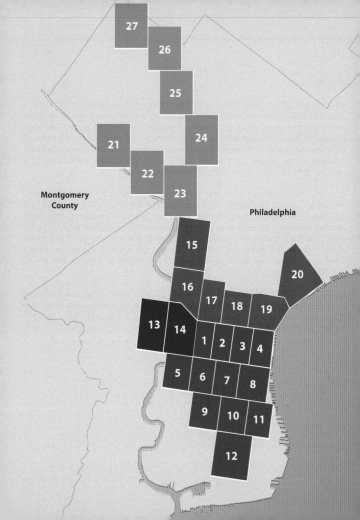

Map 1 · **Center City West**

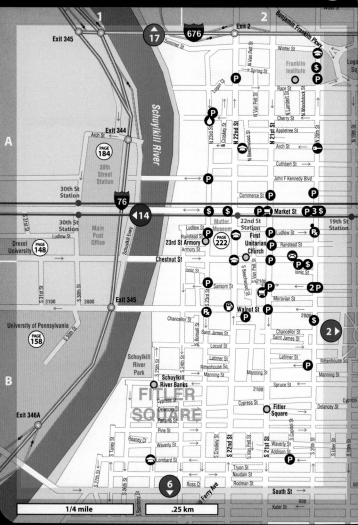

Not quite University City and not quite Rittenhouse, Center City West straddles a strange area of Philadelphia. But it also holds some of our best gems: The Mutter Museum and Franklin Institute are two of the most interesting museums in Philly (beware: the Institute's giant heart smells), and you can always take in an indie rock show at the First Unitarian Church.

 Banks

- **Citizens (ATM)** · 214 S 20th St
- **Citizens (ATM)** · 2200 Market St
- **Conestoga Bank** · 2301 Market St
- **PNC (ATM)** · Wawa · 2002 Chestnut St
- **PNC (ATM)** · Mandell Center · 222 N 20th St
- **Sovereign** · 2000 Market St
- **Wachovia** · 2005 Market St

Car Rental

- **Avis** · 2000 Arch St

Car Washes

- **Executive Auto Care** · 117 N 23rd St

Gas Stations

- **Sunoco** · 2201 Walnut St

Landmarks

- **23rd St Armory** · 22 S 23rd St
- **First Unitarian Church** · 2125 Chestnut St
- **Fitler Square** · 21st St b/w Locust St & South St
- **The Franklin Institute** · 222 N 20th St
- **Schuylkill River Banks** · 2500 Spruce St

Parking

Pharmacies

- **Doctors Pharmacy** · 17 S 20th St
- **Rite-Aid** · 2301 Walnut St ◎

Post Offices

- **Middle City** · 2037 Chestnut St

Schools

- **The College of Physicians of Philadelphia** · 19 S 22nd St
- **Greenfield** · 2200 Chestnut St
- **Moore College of Art & Design** · N 20th St & Benjamin Franklin Pkwy
- **The Philadelphia School** · 2501 Lombard St
- **Science Leadership Academy** · 2140 Arch St

Supermarkets

- **First Food Market** · 116 S 21st St
- **Trader Joe's** · 2121 Market St

Catch a stand up comedy show at Helium (and don't miss the rousing combination of crazies and legitimately good comics on open mic night), discover how hair care can be kind of scary at Julius Scissor, and make sure you're ready for nausea if you take in a not-made-for-IMAX film at the Franklin Institute's IMAX theater.

☕ Coffee

- **Almaz Café** · 140 S 20th St
- **Capogiro** · 117 S 20th St
- **Darling's Coffeehouse & Famous Cheesecakes** · 2100 Spring St
- **Dunkin' Donuts** · 2001 Chestnut St
- **Good Karma Café** · 331 S 22nd St
- **Mochima Café** · 1101 Spruce St
- **Nook Bakery & Coffee Bar** · 15 S 20th St

📋 Copy Shops

- **FedEx Office** · 2001 Market St ⊕
- **Philadelphia Print & Color** · 1900 John F Kennedy Blvd
- **Ridgeway's** · 261 S 22nd St

💪 Gyms

- **Rittenhouse Square Fitness Club** · 2002 Rittenhouse Sq
- **Sweat** · 200 S 24th St

🔧 Hardware Stores

- **Lee's Hardware** · 266 S 20th St
- **Rittenhouse Hardware** · 2001 Pine St

🎬 Movie Theaters

- **Roxy Theatre Philadelphia** · 2023 Sansom St
- **Tuttleman IMAX Theater-Franklin Institute** · 222 N 20th St

🍸 Nightlife

- **The Bards** · 2013 Walnut St
- **Doobie's** · 2201 Lombard St
- **Helium Comedy Club** · 2031 Sansom St
- **Irish Pub** · 2007 Walnut St
- **Medusa** · 27 S 21st
- **Mix** · 2101 Chestnut St
- **Roosevelt Pub** · 2220 Walnut St
- **Tank Bar** · 261 S 21st St

🐾 Pet Shops

- **Pooch's Choice-Woof Woof** · 133 S 23rd St
- **Rittenhouse Square Pet Supply** · 137 S 20th St

🍴 Restaurants

- **Audrey Claire** · 276 S 20th St
- **The Bards** · 2013 Walnut St
- **Bistro St Tropez** · 2400 Market St, 4th Fl
- **Café Lutecia** · 2301 Lombard St
- **Dmitri's** · 2227 Pine St
- **Erawan Thai Cuisine** · 123 S 23rd St
- **Friday Saturday Sunday** · 261 S 21st St
- **Fuji Mountain** · 2030 Chestnut St
- **Mama Palma's** · 2229 Spruce St
- **Mama's Vegetarian** · 18 S 20th St
- **Melograno** · 2012 Sansom St
- **Porcini** · 2048 Sansom St
- **Primo Hoagies** · 2043 Chestnut St
- **Roosevelt Pub** · 2222 Walnut St
- **Tampopo** · 104 S 21st St
- **Thai Singha House to Go** · 106 S 20th St
- **Tinto** · 114 S 20th St
- **Twenty Manning** · 261 S 20th St
- **Vic Sushi Bar** · 2035 Sansom St

🛍 Shopping

- **Bilt Well Furniture Showroom** · 2317 Chestnut St
- **Rejuvalux Body Klinic Day Spa** · 2012 Walnut St
- **Classical Guitar Store** · 2038 Sansom St
- **Dahlia** · 2003 Walnut St
- **Dollar General** · 520 S 23rd St
- **Home Sweet Homebrew** · 2008 Sansom St
- **Julius Scissor** · 2045 Locust St
- **Long In The Tooth** · 2027 Sansom St
- **Pleasure Chest** · 2039 Walnut St
- **Salvation Army Family Store** · 2140 Market St
- **Springboard Media** · 2212 Walnut St
- **Trader Joe's** · 2121 Market St
- **Wonderland** · 2037 Walnut St

📹 Video Rental

- **Video City** · 329 S 20th St

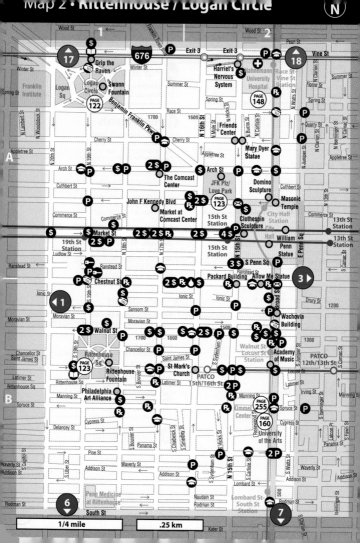

Map 2 • Rittenhouse / Logan Circle

Walnut Street is where the decadent shop and later eat at an array of look-at-me restaurants. Rittenhouse Square sits at the center of the universe, filled with crusty punks, moms, and rich old ladies who refuse to pick up their dog sh*t. Too crowded? Go take a look at the fountain in Logan Square.

$ Banks

- **Bank of America** • 1428 Walnut St
- **Bank of America** • 1600 John F Kennedy Blvd
- **Bank of America** • 1818 Market St
- **Beneficial Savings** • 1600 Chestnut St
- **Citizens** • 1417 Walnut St
- **Citizens** • 1515 Market St
- **Citizens** • 1735 Market St
- **Citizens** • 2001 Market St
- **City National** • 1701 Market St
- **Commerce** • 121 S Broad St
- **Commerce** • 1726 Walnut St
- **Commerce** • 1900 Market St
- **Commerce** • N 15th St & John F Kennedy Blvd
- **Commerce (ATM)** • University of the Arts • 320 S Broad St
- **Conestoga Bank** • 1632 Walnut St
- **Conestoga Bank** • 1835 Market St
- **Firstrust** • 1515 Market St
- **Firstrust** • 1901 Walnut St
- **HSBC** • 1515 Market St, Ste 110
- **M&T (ATM)** • 117 S 18th St
- **Mellon** • 1735 Market St
- **National Penn** • 1617 John F Kennedy Blvd
- **NOVA Savings** • 1535 Locust St
- **NOVA Savings** • 200 S Broad St
- **Philadelphia Federal Credit Union** • 1400 Arch St
- **Philadelphia Federal Credit Union** • 1600 Arch St
- **Philadelphia Federal Credit Union (ATM)** • 1901 Vine St
- **PNC** • 1511 Walnut St
- **PNC** • 1600 Market St
- **PNC** • 230 S Broad St
- **PNC** • S 19th St & Walnut St
- **PNC (ATM)** • Suburban Station • 1617 John F Kennedy Blvd
- **PNC (ATM)** • Liberty Place (Food court) • 1625 Chestnut St
- **PNC (ATM)** • Wawa • 1707 Arch St
- **PNC (ATM)** • Wawa • 226 W Rittenhouse Sq
- **PNC (ATM)** • 235 S 15th St
- **PNC (ATM)** • Allegheny University • 245 N 15th St
- **PNC (ATM)** • 266 S 18th St
- **Prudential Savings** • 112 S 19th St
- **Republic First** • 1601 Market St
- **Republic First** • 1601 Walnut St
- **Republic First** • 1818 Market St
- **Royal** • 30 S 15th St
- **Sovereign** • 1500 Walnut St
- **Sovereign** • 1717 Arch St
- **Sun Federal** • 1735 Market St, Ste C-16
- **TD Bank** • 1607 Walnut St
- **TD Bank** • 1845 Walnut St
- **TD Bank** • N 18th St & Arch St
- **United Bank of Philadelphia (ATM)** • Rite Aid • 1628 Chestnut St
- **Wachovia** • 1500 Market St
- **Wachovia** • 1700 Market St
- **Wachovia** • 1712 Walnut St

Car Rental

- **Hertz** • 31 S 19th St
- **National** • 36 S 19th St

Car Washes

- **Preston's Auto Handwash & Detail Salon** • 1625 Chestnut St

Cheesesteaks

- **Dolce Carini** • 1929 Chestnut St
- **Jake's Pizza** • 201 N Broad St
- **Rick's Steaks** • 200 S Broad St
- **Swann Lounge at Four Seasons** • 1 Logan Sq
- **Tony Jr's** • 118 S 18th St

+ Emergency Rooms

- **Hahnemann University Hospital** • Broad St & Vine St ⏺

Landmarks

- **Academy of Music** • Broad St & Locust St
- **Allow Me Statue** • 1412 Chestnut St
- **City Hall** • Market St & S 15th St
- **Clothespin Sculpture** • 15th St & Market St
- **The Comcast Center** • 1701 Arch St
- **Domino Sculpture** • 1401 John F Kennedy Blvd
- **Friends Center** • 15th St & Cherry St
- **Grip the Raven** • 1901 Vine St
- **Harriet's Nervous System** • 15th St & Vine St
- **Love Park** • N 15th St & JFK Blvd
- **Market at Comcast Center** • 1701 Kennedy Blvd
- **Mary Dyer Statue** • 15th St & Cherry St
- **The Masonic Temple** • 1 N Broad St
- **Packard Building** • 15th St & Chestnut St
- **Philadelphia Art Alliance** • 251 S 18th St
- **Rittenhouse Fountain** • b/w 18th & 19th and Locust & Walnut Sts
- **St Mark's Church** • 1625 Locust St
- **Swann Fountain** • Logan Cir
- **Wachovia Building** • Broad St & Sansom St
- **William Penn Statue** • City Hall, Broad St & Market St

Libraries

- **Central Library** • 1901 Vine St
- **Philadelphia City Institute** • 1905 Locust St

P Parking

Pharmacies

- **Barclay Pharmacy** • 1736 Spruce St
- **CVS** • 1424 Chestnut St
- **CVS** • 1500 Spruce St
- **CVS** • 1826 Chestnut St ⏺
- **Jomici Apothecary** • 273 S 15th St
- **Medical Tower Pharmacy** • 255 S 17th St
- **Pickwick Pharmacy** • 1700 Market St
- **Eckerd** • 1426 Walnut St
- **Rite-Aid** • 1535 Chestnut St
- **Rite-Aid** • 1628 Chestnut St
- **Rite-Aid** • 215 S Broad St
- **Walgreens** • 1617 John F Kennedy Blvd
- **Walgreens** • 245 N Broad St

Post Offices

- **Land Title Bldg** • 100 S Broad St
- **Penn Center** • 1500 John F Kennedy Blvd

Schools

- **City Center Academy** • 315 S 17th St
- **The Curtis Institute of Music** • 1726 Locust St
- **Freire Charter** • 1425 Arch St
- **Friends Select** • N 17th St & Benjamin Frankin Pkwy
- **Peirce College** • 1420 Pine St
- **Pennsylvania Academy of the Fine Arts** • 118 N Broad St
- **Philadelphia Electrical & Tech** • 1420 Chestnut St
- **Roman Catholic High** • 301 N Broad St
- **Russell Byers Charter** • 1911 Arch St
- **Thomas Durham** • S 16th St & Lombard St
- **Tria Fermentation School** • 1601 Walnut St
- **University of Phoenix-Center City Campus** • 30 S 17th St
- **University of the Arts** • 320 S Broad St
- **World Communications Charter** • 512 S Broad St

Map 2 · **Rittenhouse / Logan Circle**

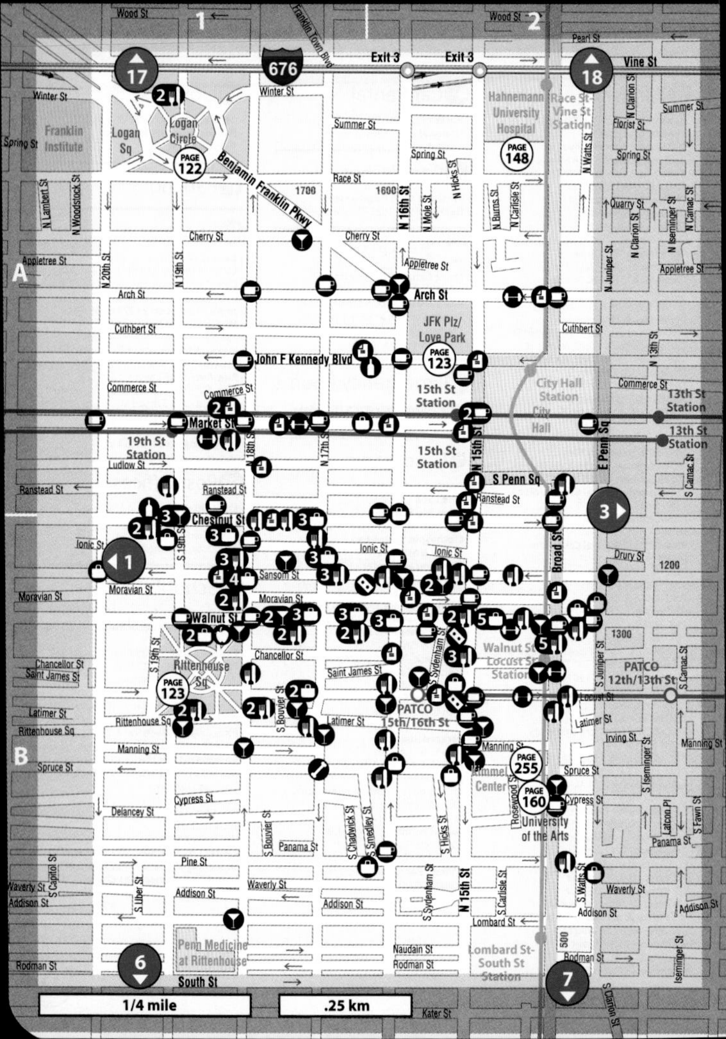

PAGE 122
PAGE 148
PAGE 123
PAGE 123
PAGE 255
PAGE 160

Wood St

Wood St

Pearl St

676

Exit 3   Exit 3

Vine St

17

18

Winter St

Winter St

Summer St

Summer St

Franklin Town Blvd

Hahnemann University Hospital

Race St Vine St Station

Florist St

Spring St

Franklin Institute

Logan Sq

Logan Circle

Spring St

Race St

N Hicks St

N Mole St

N Burns St

N Carlisle St

Quarry St

N Clarion St

N Iseminger St

N Van Pelt St

N 20th St

N Woodstock St

N Lambert St

Benjamin Franklin Pkwy

Cherry St

1700

1600

Cherry St

Appletree St

N 16th St

N Juniper St

N Camac St

Appletree St

Arch St

Arch St

A

Cuthbert St

Cuthbert St

JFK Plz / Love Park

City Hall Station

Commerce St

Commerce St

13th St Station

Commerce St

John F Kennedy Blvd

15th St Station

City Hall

Market St

19th St Station

15th St Station

Market St

13th St Station

Ludlow St

Ranstead St

Ranstead St

Ranstead St

S Penn Sq

S 18th St

Ionic St

Chestnut St

Moravian St

Ionic St

Ionic St

Drury St

1200

1

Moravian St

Sansom St

Broad St

E Penn Sq

Walnut St

Walnut St

Chancellor St

Saint James St

Walnut St Locust St Station

1300

Rittenhouse Sq

Chancellor St Saint James St

Latimer St

PATCO

S Juniper St

PATCO 12th/13th St

Latimer St

Rittenhouse Sq

Manning St

PATCO 15th/16th St

S Camac St

S Iseminger St

Irving St

Manning St

Spruce St

Spruce St

Cypress St

Cypress St

Kimmel Center

University of the Arts

Latona Pl

Delancey St

Pine St

Addison St

Waverly St

S Bouvier St

S Chadwick St

S Smedley St

S Hicks St

S Sydenham St

N 15th St

N Carlisle St

Lombard St

S Watts St

S Fawn St

Waverly St

Latimer St

Chancellor St

Saint James St

Waverly St

Addison St

6

Penn Medicine at Rittenhouse

South St

Naudain St

Rodman St

Lombard St-South St Station

7

Rodman St

Kater St

1/4 mile   .25 km

The restaurant scene around Walnut offers some of Philly's finest culinary experiences, but a sandwich from Good Dog is comparable in its own way. Patronize Buffalo Exchange for hipster-approved used clothing, and then celebrate shopping well done with a $3 22 oz. lager at Oscar's.

Coffee

- **Academia al Caffe** • 1 S Penn Sq
- **Au Bon Pain** • 1625 Chestnut St
- **Au Bon Pain** • N 18th St & Arch St
- **Au Bon Pain** • 2005 Market St
- **Bonte Wafflerie & Cafe** • 130 S 17th St
- **Café Loftus** • 136 S 15th St
- **Capriccio Café** • 110 N 16th St
- **Cosi** • 1720 Walnut St
- **Cosi** • 1720 Walnut St
- **Cosi** • 235 S 15th St
- **Dunkin' Donuts** • 1 E Penn Sq
- **Dunkin' Donuts** • 101 N Broad St
- **Dunkin' Donuts** • 117 S 16th St
- **Dunkin' Donuts** • 1324 Walnut St
- **Dunkin' Donuts** • 1500 Market St
- **Dunkin' Donuts** • 1507 Chestnut St
- **Dunkin' Donuts** • 1600 John F Kennedy Blvd
- **Dunkin' Donuts** • 1617 John F Kennedy Blvd
- **Dunkin' Donuts** • 1500 John F Kennedy Blvd
- **La Cigale** • 113 S 18th St
- **La Citadelle** • 1800 Pine St
- **La Colombe** • 130 S 19th St
- **La Primavera Café** • 1717 Arch St
- **Metro Café** • 100 S Broad St
- **Starbucks** • 1500 Market St
- **Starbucks** • 1528 Walnut St
- **Starbucks** • 1528 Walnut St
- **Starbucks** • 1601 Market St
- **Starbucks** • 1839 Chestnut St
- **Starbucks** • 1900 Walnut St
- **Starbucks** • 200 S Broad St
- **Starbucks** • 254 S 15th St
- **Starbucks** • 337 S Broad St

Copy Shops

- **A-C Reproduction & Copy Center** • 1733 Chestnut St
- **Can Do Service Center** • 1530 Locust St
- **Conant** • 42 S 15th St, 9th Fl
- **Copy Cat Printers** • 42 S 15th St
- **Copy Secure** • 1835 Market St
- **FedEx Office** • 121 S Broad St
- **FedEx Office** • 216 S 16th St
- **IKON Document Services** • 1760 Market St
- **Kelly & Partners** • 1500 Market St
- **Liberty Quick Print** • 2 Penn Centre
- **Medical Copy Services** • 1601 Market St
- **The Printer's Place** • 126 S 16th St
- **Quality Copy** • 1628 John F Kennedy Blvd
- **Reliablecopy Services** • 1818 Market St
- **Replica** • 35 S 16th St
- **Rittenhouse Instant Press** • 1811 Sansom St
- **Service Point USA** • 211 N 13th St
- **Staples** • 1500 Chestnut St
- **Taws** • 1527 Walnut St
- **The UPS Store** • 1229 Chestnut St

Farmers Markets

- **Rittenhouse (Tues, 10 am–1 pm; Jun 5th–Oct; Sat 10 am–3 pm through Nov 17th)** • Walnut St W of S 18th St

Gyms

- **Bally Total Fitness** • 1435 Walnut St
- **Philadelphia Sports Club** • 1735 Walnut St
- **The Sporting Club at the Bellue** • 224 S Broad St
- **Sweat Gym** • 1425 Arch St
- **Weston Fitness** • 1835 Market St

Liquor Stores

- **State Liquor Store** • 1628 John F Kennedy Blvd
- **State Liquor Store** • 1913 Chestnut St

Nightlife

- **The Black Sheep** • 247 S 17th St
- **Boathouse Row Bar** • 210 W Rittenhouse Sq
- **Cadence** • 300 S Broad St
- **Denim Lounge** • 1712 Walnut St
- **Drinker's Pub** • 1903 Chestnut St
- **The Franklin Mortgage & Investment Co** • 112 S 18th St
- **Good Dog** • 224 S 15th St
- **Happy Rooster** • 118 S 16th St
- **Tavern on Broad** • 200 S Broad St
- **Mace's Crossing** • 1714 Cherry St
- **McGlinchey's** • 259 S 15th St
- **Misconduct Tavern** • 1511 Locus St
- **Monk's Café** • 264 S 16th St
- **Noche** • 1907 Walnut St
- **Nodding Head** • 1516 Sansom St
- **Oscar's Tavern** • 1524 Sansom St
- **Raven Lounge** • 1718 Sansom St
- **Ritz-Carlton Rotunda** • 10 S Broad St
- **Rouge** • 205 S 18th St
- **Stir** • 1705 Chancellor St
- **Tangier Café** • 1801 Lombard St
- **Tequila's Bar** • 1602 Locust St
- **Time Restaurant** • 1315 Sansom St
- **Tir Na Nog** • 1600 Arch St
- **VIP Lounge** • 38 S 19th St
- **The Walnut Room** • 1709 Walnut St
- **Whistle Bar** • 40 S 19th St

Pet Shops

- **Doggie Style** • 114 S 13th St
- **Doggie Style** • 1635 Spruce St

Restaurants

- **Alfa** • 1709 Walnut St
- **Alma de Cuba** • 1623 Walnut St
- **Barclay Prime** • 237 S 18th St
- **Bliss** • 224 S Broad St
- **Byblos** • 114 S 18th St
- **Cadence** • 300 S Broad St
- **Capital Grille** • 1338 Chestnut St
- **Chez Collette** • 120 S 17th St
- **Chris' Jazz Café** • 1421 Sansom St
- **Continental Mid-town** • 1801 Chestnut St
- **Davio's** • 111 S 17th St
- **Devon Seafood Grill** • 225 S 18th St
- **Di Bruno Brothers** • 1730 Chestnut St
- **Dolce Carini** • 1929 Chestnut St
- **Fountain Restaurant** • 1 Logan Sq
- **Good Dog** • 224 S 15th St
- **Il Portico** • 1519 Walnut St
- **Jean's Café** • 1334 Walnut St
- **Joe's Pizza** • 122 S 16th St
- **Jose Pistola's** • 263 S 15th St
- **La Creperie** • 1722 Sansom St
- **La Viola** • 253 S 16th St
- **Lacroix at the Rittenhouse** • 210 W Rittenhouse Sq
- **Le Bec-Fin** • 1523 Walnut St
- **Le Castagne** • 1920 Chestnut St
- **Little Pete's** • 219 S 17th St
- **Marathon Grill** • 121 S 16th St

- **Marathon Grill** • 1339 Chestnut St
- **Marathon Grill** • 1818 Market St
- **Matyson** • 37 S 19th St
- **Miel Patisserie** • 204 S 17th St
- **Monk's Café** • 264 S 16th St
- **Moshi Moshi** • 108 S 18th St
- **Nodding Head Brewery & Restaurant** • 1516 Sansom St, 2nd Fl
- **Paolo's Pizza** • 1334 Pine St
- **Parc** • 227 S 18th St
- **Pietro's Coal Oven Pizzeria** • 1714 Walnut St
- **Prime Rib** • 1701 Locust St
- **Rick's Steaks** • 200 South Broad St
- **Rouge** • 205 S 18th St
- **Roy's** • 124 S 15th St
- **Sahara Grill** • 1334 Walnut St
- **Shiroi Hana** • 222 S 15th St
- **Sotto Varalli** • 231 S Broad St
- **Swann Lounge** • 1 Logan Sq
- **Tequilas** • 1602 Locust St
- **Tria** • 123 S 18th St
- **Tuscany Café** • 222 W Rittenhouse Sq
- **Upstares & Sotto Varalli** • 1345 Locust St
- **Warsaw Café** • 306 S 16th St
- **XIX (nineteen)** • 200 S Broad St, 19th floor

Shopping

- **Adresse** • 1706 Locust St
- **AIA Bookstore & Design Center** • 117 S 17th St
- **Anthropologie** • 1801 Walnut St
- **Apple Store** • 1607 Walnut St
- **Barnes & Noble** • 1805 Walnut St
- **Benjamin Lovell Shoes** • 119 S 18th St
- **Boyd's** • 1818 Chestnut St
- **Buffalo Exchange** • 1713 Chestnut St
- **Bundy** • 1809 Chestnut St
- **City Sports** • 1608 Walnut St
- **Coach** • 1703 Walnut St
- **Daffy's** • 1700 Chestnut St
- **David Michie Violins** • 1714 Locust St
- **Design Within Reach** • 1710 Walnut St
- **Frankinstein Bike Worx** • 1529 Spruce St
- **Giovanni & Pileggi** • 256 S 16th St
- **Greenhouse Market** • 1324 Chestnut St
- **H&M** • 1725 Walnut St
- **Halloween** • 1329 Pine St
- **Head Start Shoes** • 126 S 17th St
- **International Salon** • 1714 Sansom St
- **Jacob's Music** • 1714 Sansom St
- **Jos. A. Bank Clothiers** • 1650 Market St
- **Joseph Fox Bookshop** • 1724 Sansom St
- **Knit Wit** • 1718 Walnut St
- **Liquid Hair Salon** • 112 S 18th St
- **Lucky Brand Jeans** • 1634 Walnut St
- **Maron Chocolates** • 1734 Chestnut St
- **Motherhood Maternity** • 1615 Walnut St
- **Nicole Miller** • 200 S Broad St
- **OMOI** • 1608 Pine St
- **Pearl of the East** • 1720 Chestnut St
- **Ritz Camera** • 1330 Walnut St
- **Scoop DeVille** • 1734 Chestnut St
- **Sophisticated Seconds** • 2019 Sansom St
- **Sue's Produce Market** • 114 S 18th St
- **TLA Movies** • 1520 Locust St
- **UBIQ** • 1509 Walnut St
- **Urban Outfitters** • 1627 Walnut St
- **Vigant Inc – Believue Hotel** • 200 S Broad St
- **VIP Food & Produce** • 1314 Walnut St
- **Zara** • 1715 Walnut St

Video Rental

- **TLA Movies** • 1520 Locust St
- **Video Liquidators** • 1632 Sansom St
- **West Coast Video** • 212 S 15th St

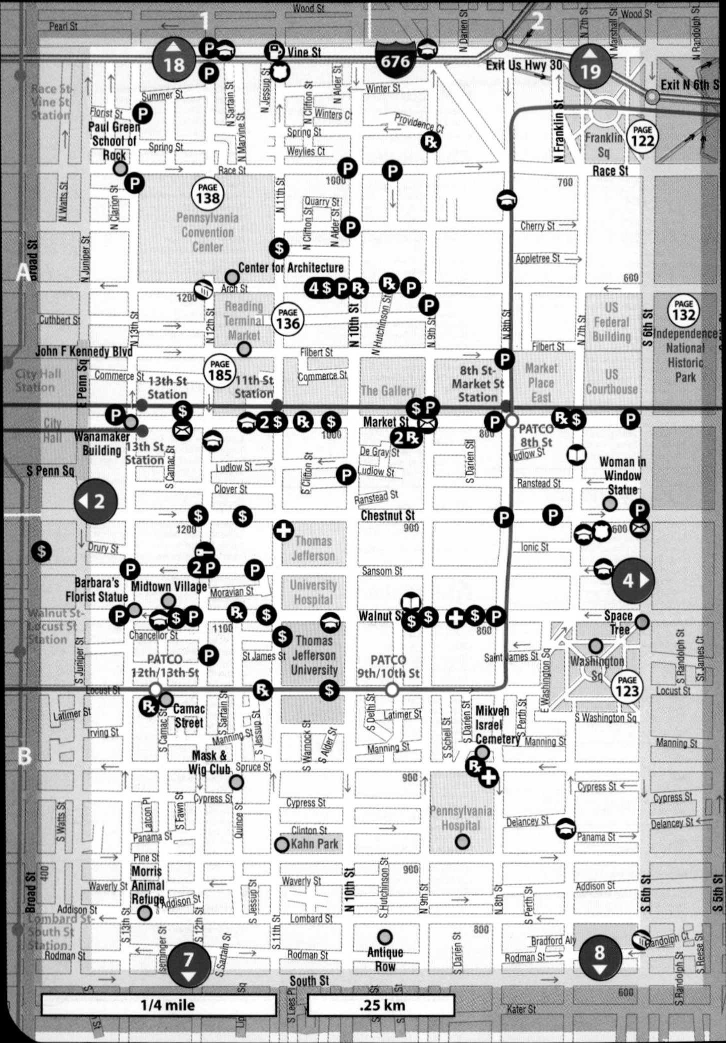

Map 3 · **Center City East**

N

Pearl St

Wood St

1

Vine St

676

Exit Us Hwy 30

2

Exit N 6th St

Summer St

N Randolph St

Wood St

N 2th St

N 13th St

N Marshall St

Race St-
Vine St
Station

Florist Row

Paul Green
School of
Rock

N Clarion St

Spring St

N Watts St

N Juniper St

N 13th St

N 12th St

N 11th St

N Jessup St

N Marvine St

N Sartain St

N Clifton St

N Camac St

Winter St

Spring St

Weylies Ct

Race St

PAGE
138

Pennsylvania
Convention
Center

1000

Quarry St

N 10th St

N Hutchinson St

N 9th St

N 8th St

Providence Ct

N Franklin St

Franklin
Sq

PAGE
122

Race St

700

Cherry St

Appletree St

600

US
Federal
Building

PAGE
132

Independence
National
Historic
Park

A

Cuthbert St

John F Kennedy Blvd

Penn Sq

City
Hall
Station

Center for Architecture

4

Reading
Terminal
Market

PAGE
136

Filbert St

Commerce St

PAGE
185

11th St
Station

Arch St

Filbert St

Commerce St

1200

13th St
Station

Commerce St

The Gallery

Market-
East

8th St-
Market St
Station

Market
Place
East

US
Courthouse

Filbert St

S 7th St

S 6th St

Wanamaker
Building

City
Hall

S Penn Sq

2

13th St
Station

S Camac St

Market St

1000

De Gray St

Ludlow St

Ranstead St

Chestnut St

900

PATCO
8th St

Ludlow St

Ranstead St

S Darien St

800

Woman in
Window
Statue

600

4

B

Barbara's
Florist Statue

Midtown Village

2

Chancellor St

PATCO
12th/13th

S Juniper St

Moravian St

St James St

Thomas
Jefferson
University

1100

Thomas
Jefferson
University
Hospital

Sansom St

Walnut St

Walnut St

800

Ionic St

Space
Tree

Washington
Sq

PAGE
123

S Randolph St

S 5th St

Walnut St-
Locust St
Station

Drury St

1200

Locust St

Latimer St

Irving St

Camac
Street

Mask &
Wig Club

Chancellor St

S Sartain St

S Jessup St

Spruce St

St James St

S 11th St

S 10th St

S Delhi St

Latimer St

Manning St

S Schell St

S Darien St

Mikveh
Israel
Cemetery

Manning St

E Washington Sq

S Washington Sq

Locust St

Manning St

S 8th St

S 7th St

Panama St

Cypress St

Delancey St

Broad St

S Watts St

S Fawn St

Panama Pl

S Iseminger St

Pine St

Morris
Animal
Refuge

Waverly St

Addison St

Quince St

Cypress St

Clinton St

Kahn Park

Waverly St

Lombard St

Rodman St

S 11th St

S 10th St

S Hutchinson St

900

Antique
Row

S 9th St

S 8th St

S Perth St

Bradford Aly

Addison St

Delancey St

Cypress St

S 6th St

S 5th St

8

Lombard-
South St
Station

Rodman St

South St

Kater St

600

7

1/4 mile

.25 km

Chinatown, the Gayborhood, Independence Park—Center City East is stuffed with many tiny, distinct neighborhoods. Washington Square might not have Rittenhouse flair (although it does come close), but it does have a tree planed from a seed that was brought to the moon. Franklin Square, meanwhile, has the only mini-golf in the city, if you feel like dealing with tons of smelly kids.

$ Banks

- **Beneficial Savings** · 1139 Chestnut St
- **Citizens** · 1234 Market St
- **Citizens** · 701 Market St
- **Citizens** · 830 Walnut St
- **Citizens (ATM)** · Walgreens · 901 Market St
- **Commerce** · 111 N 11th St
- **Conestoga Bank** · 1032 Arch St
- **HSBC** · 1027 Arch St
- **Philadelphia Federal Credit Union** · 1206 Chestnut St
- **PNC** · 1111 Market St
- **PNC** · S 9th St & Walnut St
- **PNC (ATM)** · Jefferson Hospital-Alumni Hall · 1020 Locust St
- **PNC (ATM)** · Wawa · 1038 Arch St
- **PNC (ATM)** · Jefferson Hospital · 111 S 11th St
- **PNC (ATM)** · Philadelphia Hospital · 800 Spruce St
- **PNC (ATM)** · Wawa · 912 Walnut St
- **Royal** · 1230 Walnut St
- **Sovereign** · 1101 Market St
- **TD Banknorth** · 1100 Walnut St
- **Wachovia** · 123 S Broad St
- **Wachovia (ATM)** · 1101 Market St

🚗 Car Rental

- **Enterprise** · 123 S 12th St

🥩 Cheesesteaks

- **Blackbird Pizzeria** · 507 S 6th St
- **Rick's Philly Steaks** · 1136 Arch St

➕ Emergency Rooms

- **Jefferson University Hospital** · 111 S 11th St 🏥
- **Pennsylvania Hospital** · 800 Spruce St 🏥
- **Wills Eyes** · 840 Walnut St 🏥

⛽ Gas Stations

- **Shell** · 1135 Vine St

🅾 Landmarks

- **Antique Row** · Pine St b/w S 12th St & S 9th St
- **Barbara's Florist Statue** · 1300 Walnut St
- **Camac Street** · 200 S Camac St
- **Center for Architecture** · 1218 Arch St
- **Kahn Park** · Pine St & S 11th St
- **Mask & Wig Club** · 310 S Quince St
- **Midtown Village** · b/w Spruce & Market Sts & 11th & 13th Sts
- **Mikveh Israel Cemetary** · Spruce St b/w S 8th St & S 9th St
- **Morris Animal Refuge** · 1242 Lombard St
- **Paul Green School of Rock** · 1320 Race St
- **Pennsylvania Hospital** · 800 Spruce St
- **Reading Terminal Market** · 12th St & Arch St
- **Space Tree** · Walnut St & S 6th St
- **Wanamaker Building** · 13th St & Market St
- **Washington Square Park** · Walnut St b/w S 6th St & S 7th St
- **Woman in Window Statue** · Chestnut St b/w S 6th St & S 7th St

📖 Libraries

- **Independence Branch** · 18 S 7th St
- **Library for Blind and Physically Handicapped** · 919 Walnut St

🅿 Parking

🅡 Pharmacies

- **Arch Pharmacy** · 933 Arch St
- **BioScrip Pharmacy** · 1227 Locust St
- **CarePlus CVS Pharmacy** · 1117 Walnut St
- **CVS** · 1046 Market St
- **Franklin Drug Center** · 829 Spruce St
- **KMart** · 901 Market St
- **Neff Surgical Pharmacy** · 222 N 9th St
- **Rite-Aid** · 1000 Market St
- **Rite-Aid** · 730 Market St
- **Walgreens** · 901 Market St

🅟 Police

- **6th Police District** · 235 N 11th St
- **Center City District** · 660 Chestnut St

✉ Post Offices

- **Continental** · 615 Chestnut St
- **John Wanamaker** · 1234 Market St
- **William Penn Annex** · 900 Market St

🏫 Schools

- **Architecture and Design CHS** · 675 Sansom St
- **Holy Redeemer** · 915 Vine St
- **Hussian School of Art** · 1118 Market St
- **Independence Charter** · 105 S 7th St
- **McCall** · 325 S 7th St
- **Parkway--Center City** · 9 S 12th St
- **Student Ed Center & Del Valley High** · 1311 Chancellor St
- **Temple University School of Podiatric Medicine** · N 8th St b/w Race St & Cherry St
- **Thomas Jefferson University** · 1020 Walnut St
- **Wakisha Charter** · 1209 Vine St

Map 3 • **Center City East**

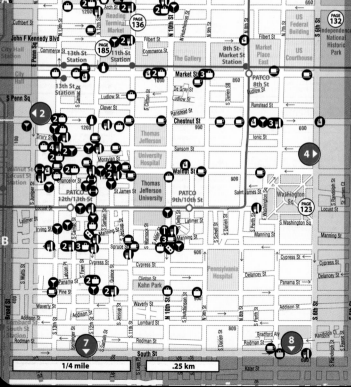

Philly's food scene comes alive with what is perhaps Starr's best candidate for appearance in Ocean's 14, Morimoto, along with a miasma of delectable Chinese, all of which Vietnam seems to trump (although check out Lee How Fook). After eats, get gay at your pick of place—Woody's and Sisters for starters.

☕ Coffee

- **Bonte Wafflerie & Cafe** · 922 Walnut St
- **Cafe Mocha** · 263 S 10th St
- **Cosi** · 1128 Walnut St
- **Cosi** · 833 Chestnut St
- **Dunkin' Donuts** · 1105 Chestnut St
- **Dunkin' Donuts** · 1113 Market St
- **Dunkin' Donuts** · 634 Market St
- **Dunkin' Donuts** · 701 Market St
- **Dunkin' Donuts** · 808 Chestnut St
- **Greenland Tea House** · 210 N 9th St
- **The Last Drop** · 1300 Pine St
- **Old City Coffee** · 1136 Arch St
- **Ray's Café & Tea House** · 141 N 9th St
- **Spruce Street Espresso** · 1101 Spruce St
- **Starbucks** · 1005 Chestnut St
- **Starbucks** · 1201 Market St
- **Starbucks** · 1201 Walnut St
- **Starbucks** · 200 W Washington Sq
- **Starbucks** · 901 Market St
- **Tbar** · 117 S 12th St
- **Tenth Street Pourhouse** · 262 S 10th St

🖨 Copy Shops

- **Centennial Philadelphia Blueprint** · 725 Chestnut St
- **Copy Center** · 615 Chestnut St
- **Creative Characters** · 913 Walnut St
- **FedEx Office** · 1201 Market St ♿
- **Postal Instant Press** · 1420 Walnut St
- **The Printer's Place** · 1310 Walnut St
- **Sir Speedy** · 47 N 9th St
- **Staples** · 1044 Market St

🌾 Farmers Markets

- **Reading Terminal Market** (Mon–Sat, 8 am–6 pm; Sun 9am–4pm) · 12th St & Arch St

💪 Gyms

- **12th Street Gym** · 204 S 12th St
- **Club Body Center II** · 1220 Chancellor St
- **Vigorworks Fitness Center** · 1315 Walnut St

🔧 Hardware Stores

- **Buck's Hardware** · 218 N 13th St
- **10th Street Hardware** · 257 S 10th St

🍾 Liquor Stores

- **State Liquor Store** · 1218 Chestnut St
- **State Liquor Store** · 5 N 12th St

🍸 Nightlife

- **12th Air Command** · 254 S 12th St
- **Bike Stop Inc** · 206 S Quince St
- **Bump** · 1234 Locust St
- **Dirty Frank's** · 347 S 13th St
- **El Vez** · 121 S 13th St
- **Fergie's Pub** · 1214 Sansom St
- **The Field House** · 1150 Filbert St
- **The Irish Pub** · 1123 Walnut St
- **Las Vegas Lounge** · 704 Chestnut St
- **Locust Bar** · 235 S 10th St
- **Lucky Strikes** · 1336 Chestnut St
- **McGillin's Old Ale House** · 1310 Drury St
- **Moriarty's Restaurant** · 1116 Walnut St
- **Sal's on 12th** · 200 S 12th St
- **Sisters** · 1320 Chancellor St
- **Tavern on Camac** · 243 S Camac St
- **Tenth Street Pourhouse** · 262 S 10th St
- **Trocadero** · 1003 Arch St
- **Vintage** · 129 S 13th St
- **Woody's** · 202 S 13th St

🍴 Restaurants

- **Aqua** · 705 Chestnut St
- **Banana Leaf** · 1009 Arch St
- **Basic Four Vegetarian** · 1136 Arch St
- **Bassett's Ice Cream** · 45 N 12th St
- **Bindi** · 105 S 13th St
- **Capogiro Gelateria** · 119 S 13th St
- **Caribou Café** · 1126 Walnut St
- **Charles Plaza** · 234 N 10th St
- **Chickpeas** · 630 South St
- **Delilah's at the Terminal** · 12th St & Arch St
- **Dutch Eating Place** · 1136 Arch St
- **Down Home Diner** · 51 N 12th St
- **Effie's** · 1127 Pine St
- **El Fuego** · 723 Walnut St
- **Gianna's Grille** · 507 S 6th St
- **House of Chen** · 932 Race St
- **Imperial Inn** · 146 N 10th St
- **Jones** · 700 Chestnut St
- **Kanella** · 266 S 10th St
- **Kingdom of Vegetarians** · 129 N 11th St
- **Knock Restaurant** · 225 S 12th St
- **La Buca** · 711 Locust St
- **Lee How Fook** · 219 N 11th St
- **Little Thai Market in Reading Terminal** · 51 N 12th St
- **Lolita** · 106 S 13th St
- **Maccabeam** · 128 S 12th St
- **Maoz** · 1115 Walnut St
- **Mercato** · 1216 Spruce St
- **Mixto** · 1141 Pine St
- **More Than Just Ice Cream** · 1119 Locust St
- **Moriarty's** · 1116 Walnut St
- **Morimoto** · 723 Chestnut St
- **Nan Zhou Hand Drawn Noodle House** · 927 Race St
- **New Harmony Vegetarian Restaurant** · 135 N 9th St
- **New Samosa** · 1214 Walnut St
- **Pho Xe Lua** · 907 Race St
- **Rangoon** · 112 N 9th St
- **Sang Kee Peking Duck House** · 238 N 9th St
- **Shiao Lan Kung** · 930 Race St
- **Singapore Kosher Vegetarian** · 1006 Race St
- **Spruce Rana** · 1034 Spruce St
- **Tai Lake** · 134 N 10th St
- **Tenth Street Pourhouse** · 262 S 10th St
- **Tria** · 1137 Spruce St
- **Union Trust** · 717 Chestnut St
- **Valanni** · 1229 Spruce St
- **Varga Bar** · 941 Spruce St
- **Venture Inn** · 255 S Camac St
- **Vetri** · 1312 Spruce St
- **Vietnam** · 221 N 11th St
- **Vietnam Palace** · 222 N 11th St
- **Washington Square** · 210 W Washington Sq
- **Westbury Bar & Restaurant** · 261 S 13th St
- **Zio's Pizza** · 111 S 13th St

🛍 Shopping

- **AIA Bookstore & Design Center** · 1218 Arch St
- **After Hours Formalwear** · 1205 Walnut St
- **Aldo Liquidation** · 901 Market St
- **Armand Records** · 1108 Chestnut St
- **Baum's** · 106 S 11th St
- **Beaux Arts Video** · 1000 Spruce St
- **Bike Line** · 1028 Arch St
- **Black Tie Formal Attire** · 1120 Walnut St
- **Bridals by Danielle** · 203 S 13th St
- **Burlington Coat Factory** · 1001 Market St
- **Chartreuse** · 1200 Spruce St
- **Children's Place** · Market St & S 9th St
- **Claire's Boutique** · Market St & S 9th St
- **DeCarlo Hair Salon** · 1210 Sansom St
- **De Village in Reading Terminal** · 12th St & Arch St
- **Downtown Cheese** · N 12th St & Arch St
- **Dudes Boutique** · 646 South St
- **Duross & Langel** · 117 S 13th St
- **Giovanni's Room** · 345 S 12th St
- **Greene Street Consignment Shop** · 700 South St
- **Grocery 13 Inc.** · 105 S 13th St
- **I Goldberg Army & Navy** · 1300 Chestnut St
- **M Finkel & Daughter** · 936 Pine St
- **Macy's** · 1300 Market St
- **Massage Arts Center of Philadelphia** · 519 S 4th St
- **Mitchell & Ness** · 1318 Chestnut St
- **Modern Eye** · 145 S 13th St
- **Old Navy** · 1001 Market St
- **Old Nelson Food Company** · 701 Chestnut St
- **Open House** · 107 S 13th St
- **PHAG** · 1225 Walnut St
- **R.E.Load Bags** · 301 N 11th St
- **Rustic Music** · 333 S 13th St
- **Sailor Jerry** · 116 S 13th St
- **SEPTA Transit Store** · 1234 Market St
- **Sound of Market Street** · 15 S 11th St
- **Spruce Street Video** · 252 S 12th St
- **Uhuru Furniture and Collectibles** · 1220 Spruce St
- **Wawa Food Market** · 912 Walnut St
- **Wawa Food Market** · 1038 Arch St

📼 Video Rental

- **Beaux Arts Video** · 1000 Spruce St
- **Spruce Street Video** · 252 S 12th St

Map 4 · **Old City / Society Hill**

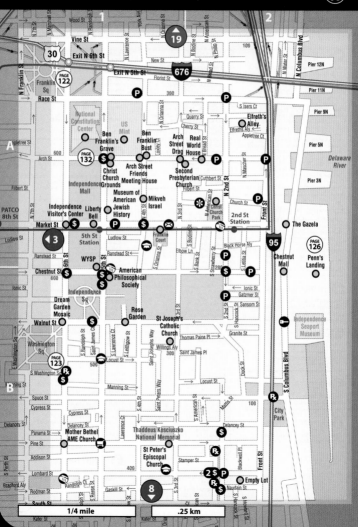

Old City is beautiful, steeped in history, and filled with dining and nightlife. This means that while there you'll need to avoid both fanny-pack-wearing tourists and tight-shirted club-goers from Jersey, but don't let that deter you. Christ Church Park is a quiet place to reflect, and dammit, you need to visit the Liberty Bell if you haven't already.

Banks

- **Beneficial Savings** · 530 Walnut St
- **Citizens** · Chestnut St & 2nd St
- **Commerce** · 200 Lombard St
- **Commerce (ATM)** · Independence Visitors Ctr · N 6th St & Market St
- **Firstrust** · 111 S Independence Mall E
- **PNC** · 400 Market St
- **PNC** · 602 Washington Sq S
- **PNC (ATM)** · Wawa · 518 S 2nd St
- **TD Bank** · S 5th St & Chestnut St
- **TD Bank (ATM)** · 513 S 2nd St
- **Wachovia** · 101 N Independence Mall E
- **Wachovia** · 340 S 2nd St
- **Wachovia** · 601 Chestnut St

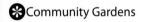 Car Rental

- **Avis** · 201 S Columbus Blvd

Cheesesteaks

- **Campo's Deli** · 214 Market St
- **Grande Olde Cheesesteak** · 21 S 5th St
- **Sonny's Famous Steaks** · 228 Market St

Community Gardens

Landmarks

- **American Philosophical Society** · 104 S 5th St
- **Arch Street Drag** · Arch St & N 3rd St
- **Arch Street Friends Meeting House** · 4th St & Arch St
- **Ben Franklin Bust** · N 4th St & Arch St
- **Chestnut Mall** · Chestnut St & Columbus Blvd
- **Christ Church Grounds** · 5th St & Arch St
- **Christ Church Park** · 2nd St & Market St
- **Dream Garden Mosaic** · 601-45 Walnut St
- **Elfreth's Alley** · b/w Front & 2nd Sts & Arch & Race Sts
- **Empty Lot** · b/w Front & 2nd Sts & South & Lombard Sts
- **Franklin Court** · Market St b/w S 3rd St & S 4th St
- **The Gazela** · Columbus Blvd & Market St

- **Independence Visitor's Center** · 6th St & Market St
- **Liberty Bell** · Market St b/w S 5th St & S 6th St
- **Mikveh Israel** · 44 N 4th St
- **Mother Bethel AME Church** · 6th St & Pine St
- **National Constitution Center** · 525 Arch St
- **National Museum of American Jewish History** · 101 S Independence Mall E
- **Penn's Landing Marina** · Penn's Landing & Columbus Blvd
- **Real World House** · 249-251 Arch St
- **Rose Garden** · Walnut St b/w S 4th St & S 5th St
- **Second Presbyterian Church** · 3rd St & Arch St
- **St Joseph's Catholic Church** · 321 Willings Aly
- **St Peter's Episcopal Church** · 313 Pine St
- **US Mint** · 151 N Independence Mall E
- **WYSP** · 101 S Independence Mall E

Parking

Pharmacies

- **Barclay Pharmacy** · 18 Spruce St
- **CVS** · 421 S 2nd St
- **Rite-Aid** · 522 S 2nd St

Post Offices

- **B Free Franklin** · 316 Market St

Schools

- **Mastery Charter High** · 35 S 4th St
- **St Mary's Interparochial** · S 5th St & Locust St
- **St Peters** · 319 Lombard St

Supermarkets

- **Super Fresh** · 309 S 5th St

Map 4 · **Old City / Society Hill**

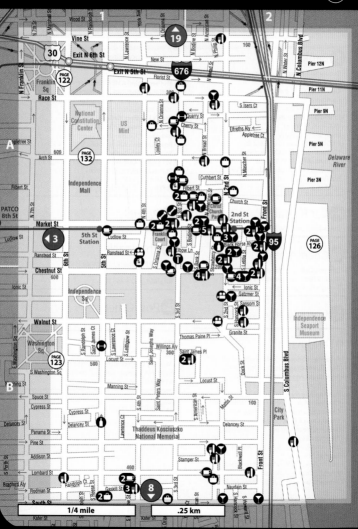

As long as you like your scenes loud and your booze pricey, you've got it all here. Home to perhaps more whipped-up-to-frothing bars/clubs per capita than any other area of the city, you can nibble hella good (and hella pricey) tapas at Amada, hit the make-your-own-bloody-Mary bar during brunch at National Mechanics, or devour a sundae from Franklin Fountain.

Coffee

- Bon Bon Artisan Gelato · 229 Market St
- Café Au Lait · 147 N 3rd St
- Café Ole · 147 N 3rd St
- Cosi · 325 Chestnut St
- Double Shots Espresso Bar · 211 Chestnut St
- Old City Coffee · 221 Church St
- Philadelphia Java Company · 518 S 4th St
- Starbucks · 57 N 3rd St
- Tuscany Cafe · 725 Walnut St

Copy Shops

- Goodway Copy Center · 49 S 4th St
- The UPS Store · 51 N 3rd St

Gyms

- Philadelphia Sports Club · 220 S 5th St
- Sweat · 45 N 3rd St

Hardware Stores

- Olde City Hardware · 41 S 3rd St

Liquor Stores

- State Liquor Store · 32 S 2nd St
- State Liquor Store · 326 S 5th St

Movie Theaters

- Ritz 5 · 214 Walnut St
- Ritz at the Bourse · 400 Ranstead St
- Ritz East · 125 S 2nd St

Nightlife

- 32 Degrees · 16 S 2nd St
- Beneluxx · 33 S 3rd St
- Bleu Martini · 24 S 2nd St
- Buffalo Billiards · 118 Chestnut St
- The Continental · 138 Market St
- Cuba Libre · 10 S 2nd St
- Dark Horse · 421 S 2nd St
- Downey's · 526 S Front St
- Eulogy Belgian Tavern · 136 Chestnut St
- Haru · 241 Chestnut St
- The Irish Pol · 45 S 3rd St
- Khyber Pass Pub · 56 S 2nd St
- LoungeOneTwoFive · 125 S 2nd St

- Mac's Tavern · 226 Market St
- National Mechanics Bar and Restaurant · 22 S 3rd St
- Paddy Whacks Pub · 150 South St
- Paradigm · 239 Chestnut St
- The Plough and the Stars · 123 Chestnut St
- Race Street Café · 208 Race St
- Red Sky · 224 Market St
- Rotten Ralph's · 201 Chestnut St
- Sassafras · 48 S 2nd St
- Society Hill Hotel Bar · 301 Chestnut St
- Sugar Mom's · 225 Church St
- Swanky Bubbles · 10 S Front St
- Tangerine · 232 Market St
- Triumph Brewing Company · 117 Chestnut St
- Woolly Mammoth · 430 South St

Pet Shops

- Bonejour Pet Supplies · 14 N 3rd St
- Doggie Style · 315 Market St

Restaurants

- Amada · 217 Chestnut st
- Anjou · 206-08 Market St
- Beneluxx · 33 S 3rd St
- Bistro 7 · 7 N 3rd St
- Bistro Romano · 120 Lombard St
- Bookbinder's · 125 Walnut St
- Campo's Deli · 214 Market St
- Chloe · 232 Arch St
- The Continental · 138 Market St
- Cuba Libre · 10 S 2nd St
- Dark Horse · 421 S 2nd St
- DiNardo's Famous Seafood · 312 Race St
- Dolce · 241 Chestnut St
- Eulogy Belgian Tavern · 136 Chestnut St
- European Republic · 213 Chestnut St
- Farmicia · 15 S 3rd St
- Fork · 306 Market St
- The Franklin Fountain · 116 Market St
- Gianfranco Pizza Rustica · 6 N 3rd St
- Karma · 114 Chestnut St
- Kisso Sushi Bar · 205 N 4th St
- Konak · 228 Vine St
- La Famiglia · 8 S Front St
- La Locanda del Ghiottone · 130 N 3rd St
- Margherita Pizzeria · 60 S 2nd St
- Marrakesh · 517 S Leithgow St
- Mexican Post · 104 Chestnut St
- Mizu Sushi Bar · 220 Market St
- Moshulu · 401 S Columbus Blvd

- Mrs. K's Koffee Shop · 325 Chestnut St
- National Mechanics Bar and Restaurant · 22 S 3rd St
- Old City Cheese Shop · 160 N 3rd St Race St
- Old City Coffee · 221 Church St
- Pagoda Noodle Café · 125 Sansom St
- Paradigm · 239 Chestnut St
- Patou · 312 Market St
- Philadelphia Java Co · 518 S 4th St
- Pizzicato · 248 Market St
- The Plough & the Stars · 123 Chestnut St
- Race Street Café · 208 Race St
- Restorante Panorama · 14 N Front St
- Sassafras · 48 S 2nd St
- Serrano · 20 S 2nd St
- Sonny's Famous Steaks · 228 Market St
- Spasso · 34 S Front St
- Swanky Bubbles · 10 S Front St
- Xochitl · 408 S 2nd St
- Zahav · 237 St James Pl

Shopping

- AKA Music · 27 N 2nd St
- Brave New Worlds Comics · 45 N 2nd St
- Cappelli Hobbies · 313 Market St
- Charlie's Jeans · 233 Market St
- Friedman Umbrellas · 217 Market St
- Gourmet of Olde City · 26 N 3rd St
- Matthew Izzo · 151 N 3rd St
- Nike Samsun · 324 South St
- Olde City Tattoo · 44 S 2nd St
- The Papery Of Philadelphia · 57 N 3rd St
- Pierre's Costumes · 211 N 3rd St
- Red Red Red Hair Salon · 222 Church St
- Sugarcube · 124 N 3rd St
- Tartes · 212 Arch St
- Topstitch Boutique · 54 N 3rd St
- Triune · 325 Cherry St
- Vagabond · 37 N 3rd St
- Viv Pickle · 21 N 3rd St
- Wawa Food Market · 518 S 2nd St
- Zeke's Fifth Street Deli Bakery · 318 S 5th St

Map 5 · Gray's Ferry

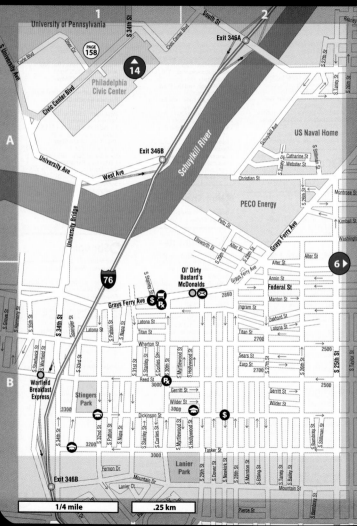

It's only now dawning on us—this area is sort of, in a way, close to Center City. While not an outward beauty, it has its own kind of tree-starved, industrially-ravaged gorgeousity. To get your cheap mob thrills, head to the the Warfield Breakfast Express, where La Costa Nostra member Joe Ciancaglini was almost rubbed out back in '93.

$ Banks

· **Bank of America** · 3021 Grays Ferry Ave
· **Conestoga Bank** · 1501 S Newkirk St

◎ Landmarks

· **Ol' Dirty Bastard's McDonalds** ·
S 29th St & Grays Ferry Ave
· **Warfield Breakfast Express** · Warfield St & Reed St

℞ Pharmacies

· **Pathmark** · 3021 Grays Ferry Ave ℗
· **Rite-Aid** · 3000 Reed St

✉ Post Offices

· **Schuylkill** · 2900 Grays Ferry Ave

🎓 Schools

· **Audenried Senior High** · 3301 Tasker St
· **James Alcorn** · 3200 Dickinson St
· **Our Lady of Angels** · 2917 Dickinson St

🛒 Supermarkets

· **Pathmark** · 3021 Grays Ferry Ave ℗

Map 5 · Gray's Ferry

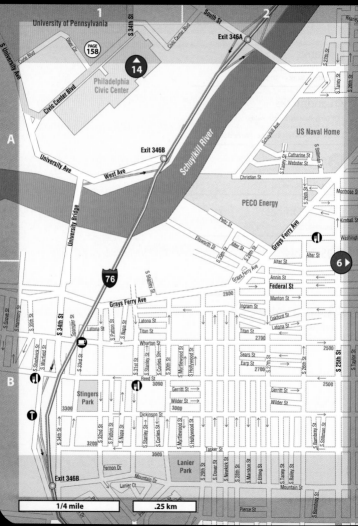

You shouldn't miss the infamous breakfast pizza at La Rosa, at least if you can stand to put that many carbs in your gullet at one time. For those carnivorous corned beef cravings, head straight to Bridgit's Deli. But the real gem here is Moe's Hot Dog House, providing both meat and veggie dogs smothered in all sorts of toppings.

Coffee
- **Dunkin' Donuts** · 3313 Wharton St

Hardware Stores
- **Diamond Tool** · 2900 Grays Ferry Ave

Restaurants
- **D'ambrosio's Bakery** · 1401 S 31st St
- **La Rosa's Café** · 1300 S Warfield St
- **Moe's Hot Dog House** · 2601 Washington Ave

Map 6 • **Graduate Hospital / Gray's Ferry**

Perhaps the very definition of an on-the-rise neighborhood, a few scant years ago the area was known more for urban decay than anything else. Since then, however, things have definitely turned around. West South Street has gotten much-needed new blood and new bars, and while being in a subway dead-zone doesn't really help, the area is well worth the walk.

Banks

- **Firstrust** · 1332 Point Breeze Ave
- **Sharon Savings (ATM)** · 1900 South St
- **United Bank of Philadelphia (ATM)** · 2000 Federal St

Cheesesteaks

- **Old Town** · 2301 Grays Ferry Ave

Community Gardens

Libraries

- **Queen Memorial Library** · 1201 S 23rd St

Pharmacies

- **Christian Street Pharmacy** · 1947 Christian St

Police

- **17th Police District** · 1201 S 20th St

Schools

- **Chester A Arthur** · 2000 Catharine St
- **Peirce Middle** · 2400 Christian St
- **School of Moorish Science Temp** · 2022 South St
- **Smith** · 1900 Wharton St
- **St Charles Borromeo** · 2019 Montrose St

Map 6 • **Graduate Hospital / Gray's Ferry**

Most of the action remains on South Street, including the influential Ten Stone and L2 bars. But don't be afraid to venture outward—La.Va Café has great coffee, and the Sidecar Bar is great for when you want, well, a sidecar. For crafters there's Loop and Spool, two stores with gorgeous materials and classes if you think you have two left thumbs.

Coffee

- **Beauty Shop Café** · 2001 Fitzwater St
- **La.Va Café** · 2100 South St

Hardware Stores

- **AS Hardware & Home Center** ·
  1229 Point Breeze Ave
- **Center City Home Center & Millwork** ·
  1931 Washington Ave
- **PAEK Hongki Home Center** ·
  1320 Point Breeze Ave
- **South Square Hardware** · 2235 Grays Ferry Ave

Liquor Stores

- **State Liquor Store** · 1446 Point Breeze Ave
- **State Liquor Store** · 2429 South St

Nightlife

- **Grace Tavern** · 2229 Grays Ferry Ave
- **L2** · 2201 South St
- **Ten Stone Bar & Restaurant** · 2063 South St

Restaurants

- **Ants Pants Cafe** · 2212 South St
- **Betty's Speakeasy** · 2241 Grays Ferry Ave
- **Divan Turkish Kitchen & Bar** · 918 S 22nd St
- **L2** · 2201 South St
- **My Thai** · 2200 South St
- **Phoebe's Bar-B-Q** · 2214 South St
- **Sidecar Bar & Grille** · 2201 Christian St
- **Ten Stone Bar & Restaurant** · 2063 South St

Shopping

- **Bicycle Therapy** · 2211 South St
- **Loop** · 1914 South St
- **Spool** · 1912 South St

Map 7 · **Southwark West**

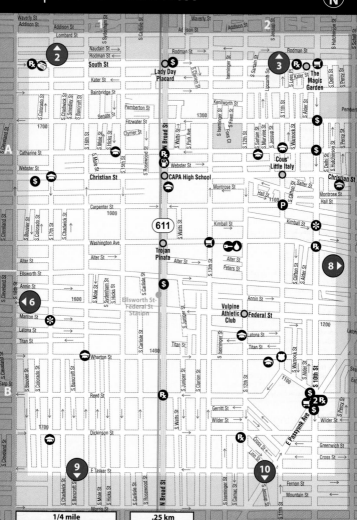

Looking for proof that South Philly changes radically from block-to-block? You've got it right here, buddy. From new condos to crumbling lots, from some of the best food in the city to dubious holes-in-the-wall (okay, sometimes they're the same thing); this is one of the most varied areas of the city.

💲 Banks

- **Citizens (ATM)** · 1400 E Passyunk Ave
- **Commerce (ATM)** · Universal Mini-Mart · 1744 Christian St
- **Conestoga Bank** · S 10th St & Catherine St
- **United Bank of Philadelphia (ATM)** · S Broad St & South St
- **United Savings** · 732 S 10th St
- **Wachovia** · 1165 S Broad St
- **Wachovia** · 1400 E Passyunk Ave

🚗 Car Rental

- **Enterprise** · 1236 Washington Ave

🚿 Car Washes

- **Washington Auto Shine** · 1208 Washington Ave

🧀 Cheesesteaks

- **Lazaro's** · 1743 South St

✳️ Community Gardens

⛽ Gas Stations

- **Sunoco** · 801 S Broad St

⭕ Landmarks

- **CAPA High** · 901 S Broad St
- **Cous' Little Italy** · 901 S 11th St
- **Lady Day Placard** · Broad St & South St
- **The Magic Garden** · 1022 South St
- **Trojan Pinata** · S Broad St
- **Vulpine Athletic Club** · 12th St & Federal St

🅿️ Parking

℞ Pharmacies

- **Acme** · 1400 E Passyunk Ave
- **Bertolino's Pharmacy** · 1500 S 12th St
- **Broad Street Family Pharmacy** · 1414 S Broad St
- **CVS** · 1001 Washington Ave
- **CVS** · 1051 South St
- **CVS** · 1405 S 10th St ⏰
- **Lombard Apothecary** · 1745 South St
- **Rite-Aid** · 810 S Broad St

👮 Police

- **3rd Police District** · 11th St & Wharton St
- **4th Police District** · 11th St & Wharton St

🎓 Schools

- **Academy at Palumbo** · 1122 Catharine St
- **Anuciation BVM** · 1150 Wharton St
- **Audenried Senior High** · S 11th St & Catharine St
- **Barratt Middle** · 1599 Wharton St
- **Childs** · 1541 S 17th St
- **Christopher Columbus Charter** · 916 Christian St
- **Creative and Performing Arts** · 901 S Broad St
- **Jackson** · 1213 S 12th St
- **Stanton** · 1700 Christian St
- **Universal Institute Charter** · 800 S 15th St

🛒 Supermarkets

- **Acme** · 1400 E Passyunk Ave
- **Save-A-Lot** · 1300 Washington Ave
- **Super Fresh** · 1001 South St

Map 7 • Southwark West

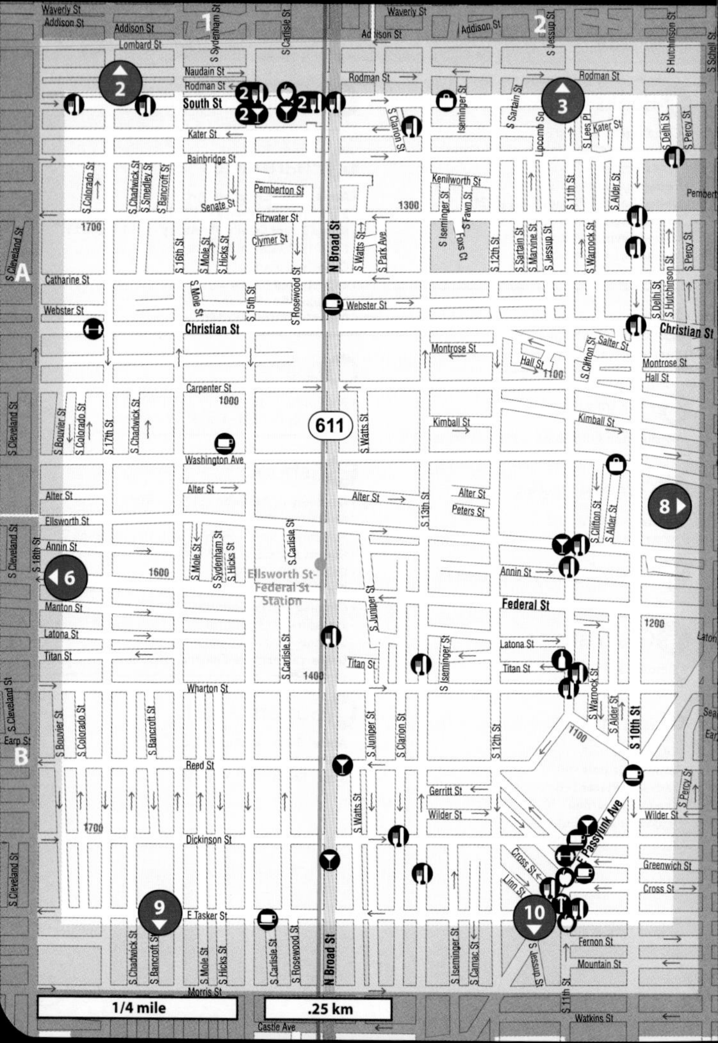

N

1   2

Waverly St
Addison St
Lombard St
Naudain St
Rodman St
South St
Kater St
Bainbridge St
Senate
Pemberton St
Fitzwater St
Clymer St
Catharine St
Webster St
Christian St
Carpenter St
Washington Ave
Alter St
Ellsworth St
Annin St
Manton St
Latona St
Titan St
Wharton St
Reed St
Dickinson St
E Tasker St
Morris St
Castle Ave
Watkins St

Waverly St
Addison St
Rodman St
Kater St
Kenilworth St
Christian St
Montrose St
Hall St
Kimball St
Peters St
Annin St
Federal St
Latona St
Titan St
Gerritt St
Wilder St
Cross St
Greenwich St
Cross St
Fernon St
Mountain St

S Sydenham St
S Carlisle St
N Broad St
S Watts St
S Park Ave
S Juniper St
S Clarion St
S 12th St
S Isminger St
S Camac St

S Colorado St
S Chadwick St
S Smedley St
S Bancroft St
S 16th St
S Mole St
S Hicks St
S 15th St
S Rosewood St
S Cleveland St
S Bouvier St

S Iseminger St
S Fawn St
S 11th St
S Sartain St
S Marvine St
S Jessup St
S Warnock St
S Clifton St
S Alder St
S Salter St
S Darien St
S Percy St
S Delhi St
S Hutchinson St

Christian St
Montrose St
Hall St 1100
Kimball St

Frankurt Ave
S 10th St
S 11th St

611

Ellsworth St–
Federal St
Station

1700
1600
1400
1300
1200
1100
1000

3   6   8 ▶   9 ▼   10 ▼

1/4 mile   .25 km

If you can't find food or fun you're asking for a whooping. And goodness gracious, that food! Head to P.O.P.E. for a frosty one, a delectable pastry at Isgro, and delicious BYOB dinner at August. And did we mention that the best dive bar on Earth is here? Long live Bob & Barbara's.

Coffee

- **B2** · 1500 E Passyunk Ave
- **Black n Brew** · 1523 E Passyunk Ave
- **Coffee Shop** · 1428 Tasker St
- **Dunkin' Donuts** · 1401 S 10th St
- **Dunkin' Donuts** · 1551 Washington Ave
- **Dunkin' Donuts** · 809 S Broad St

Farmers Markets

- **Fountain Farmers Market (Wed, 3 pm–7 pm through October)** · E Passyunk Ave & S 11th St
- **South Street West at the Jamaican Jerk Hut (Wed, 2 pm–6 pm)** · 1436 South St
- **Tasker & 11th (Wed, 3pm–7pm)** · Tasker St & S 11th St

Gyms

- **Sweat** · 1509 E Passyunk Ave
- **YMCA-Christian Street** · 1724 Christian St

Hardware Stores

- **1540 Hardware** · 1540 Passyunk Ave

Liquor Stores

- **State Liquor Store** · 1237 S 11th St

Nightlife

- **Bob & Barbara's Lounge** · 1509 South St
- **Devil's Den** · 1148 S 11th St
- **Dolphin Tavern** · 1539 S Broad St
- **Fiso Lounge** · 1437 South St
- **Pub on Passyunk East (P.O.P.E.)** · 1501 E Passyunk Ave
- **Triangle Tavern** · 1338 Reed St
- **Tritone** · 1508 South St

Restaurants

- **August** · 1247 S 13th St
- **Bitar's** · 947 Federal St
- **Carmen's Country Kitchen** · 1301 S 11th St
- **Chiarella's Ristorante** · 1600 S 11th St
- **Dante & Luigi's** · 762 S 10th St
- **Da Vinci Ristorante** · 1533 S 11th St
- **Devil's Den** · 1148 S 11th St
- **Fiso Lounge** · 1437 South St
- **Franco's & Luigi's** · 1549 S 13th St
- **Govinda's** · 1408 South St
- **Green Eggs Cafe** · 1306 Dickinson St
- **Isgro Pastries** · 1009 Christian St
- **Jamaican Jerk Hut** · 1436 South St
- **JNA Institute of Culinary Arts** · 1212 S Broad St
- **Lazzaro's Pizza House** · 1743 South St
- **Morning Glory Diner** · 735 S 10th St
- **Ms. Tootsie's** · 1314 South St
- **Nam Phuong** · 1100 Washington Ave
- **Pico de Gallo** · 1501 South St
- **Ricci Brothers** · 1165 S 11th St
- **Ron's Ribs** · 1627 South St
- **Tritone** · 1508 South St

Shopping

- **Anvil Iron Works** · 1022 Washington Ave
- **Harry's Occult Shop** · 1238 South St

The neighborhood has arrived: Anyone who bought in early is a lucky duck, and anyone who rents now is paying for their hesitancy. Home to everything from the delicious Italian Market to the suburbanite-fueled horror that is South Street, it's hard to believe that if you head south of Washington, the housing is actually affordable. Really, it's true.

$ Banks

- **PNC** · 801 Christian St
- **PNC (ATM)** · 701 E Passyunk Ave
- **PNC (ATM)** · Wawa · 847 S 2nd St
- **Sharon Savings** · 420 Bainbridge St
- **TD Bank** · 1100 S Columbus Blvd
- **TD Bank** · 135 South St

Car Washes

- **Southport Plaza Car Wash** · 1600 Columbus Blvd

Cheesesteaks

- **Cosmi's Deli** · 1501 S 8th St
- **Geno's Steaks** · 1219 S 9th St
- **Ishkabibbles Eatery** · 337 South St
- **Jim's Steaks** · 400 South St
- **Pat's King of Steaks** · 1237 E Passyunk Ave
- **Steaks on South** · 308 South St

Community Gardens

Landmarks

- **Emanuel Evangelical Lutheran Church** · 1001 S 4th St
- **Fabric Row** · S 4th St b/w Bainbridge St & Catharine St
- **Firefighter Statue** · Queen St b/w S Front St & S 2nd St
- **Fleisher Art Memorial** · 719 Catharine St
- **Gum Tree** · 3rd St & South St
- **Hovering Bodies** · 4th St & Catharine St
- **Italian Market** · S 9th St b/w Bainbridge St & Washington Ave
- **Jefferson Square Park/Sacks Rec Center** · Washington Ave b/w S 4th St & S 5th St
- **Lebanon Cemetary** · 9th St & Passyunk St
- **Mario Lanza Park** · Queen St b/w S 2nd St & S 3rd St
- **Mummers Museum** · 1100 S 2nd St
- **Pat's & Geno's Showdown** · S 9th St & E Passyunk Ave
- **Rizzo Ice Skating Rink** · 1101 S Front St
- **Sarcone's** · 758 S 9th St
- **Sherlock Holmes Mural** · S 2nd St b/w Christian St & Moyamensing St
- **Weccocoe Playground** · Catharine St b/w S 4th St & S 5th St

Libraries

- **Charles Santore Branch** · 932 S 7th St

P Parking

Pharmacies

- **Oaks Pharmacy Inc** · 1401 S 4th St
- **Rite-Aid** · 1443 S 7th St
- **Rite-Aid** · 704 E Passyunk Ave
- **Rite-Aid** · 801 S 9th St
- **Wal-Mart** · 1601 S Columbus Blvd
- **Washington Avenue Pharmacy** · 600 Washington Ave

Police

- **South Street Detail (3rd District)** · 905 South St

Post Offices

- **Penns Landing Postal Store** · 622 S 4th St
- **Southwark** · 925 Dickinson St

Schools

- **Kirkbride** · 1501 S 7th St
- **Meredith** · 725 S 5th St
- **Nebinger** · 601 Carpenter St
- **St Casimir** · 324 Wharton St
- **Sacred Heart of Jesus** · 1329 E Moyamensing Ave
- **Washington** · 1198 S 5th St

Supermarkets

- **Whole Foods** · 929 South St

Sabrina's poofs up pancakes with fruity oomph, and they've got killer omelets, too. Get your Schwinn on at Via Bicycle. At night, feast and quaff at one of the more in-the-know Philly treasures, the Royal Tavern. Or if it's date night, don't pass on local-food fav Supper.

Coffee

- **Alhambra Café** · 609 S 3rd St
- **Anthony's Italian Coffee** · 903 S 9th St
- **The Bean Café** · 615 South St
- **Benna's Café** · 1236 S 8th St
- **Cafe Fulya** · 727 S 2nd St
- **Chapterhouse Café & Gallery** · 620 S 9th St
- **Dairy Queen** · 514 South St
- **Dunkin' Donuts** · 1580 Columbus Blvd
- **Fitzwater Café** · 728 S 7th St
- **Gleaner's Café** · 917 S 9th St
- **Mr Joe's Café** · 1514 S 8th St
- **Philadelphia Java at the Gym** · 700 E Passyunk Ave
- **Red Hook Coffee and Tea** · 765 S 4th St
- **Starbucks** · 347 South St
- **Starbucks** · 600 S 9th St

Copy Shops

- **Staples** · 1300 S Columbus Blvd
- **The UPS Store** · 211 South St

Farmers Markets

- **South & Passyunk** (May–Nov; Tues, 2 pm–7 pm) · South St b/w S 5th St & E Passyunk Ave

Gyms

- **Curves** (women only) · 1100 S Columbus Blvd
- **Fitness Works Philadelphia** · 714 Reed St
- **Jacky's Gym** · 600 Washington Ave
- **Pennsport Athletic Club** · 325 Bainbridge St
- **Sweat** · 700 Passyunk Ave

Hardware Stores

- **Cohen & Co Hardware & Home Goods** · 615 E Passyunk Ave
- **Wilensky's Hardware & Locks** · 1113 E Passyunk Ave

Liquor Stores

- **State Liquor Store** · 724 South St

Movie Theaters

- **United Artists Riverview Stadium 17** · 1400 S Columbus Blvd

Nightlife

- **12 Steps Down** · 831 Christian St
- **Bridget Foy's** · 200 South St
- **Cheers to You** · 430 South St
- **Connie's Ric Rac** · 1132 S 9th St
- **The Dive** · 947 E Passyunk Ave
- **Fluid** · 613 S 4th St
- **For Pete's Sake** · 900 S Front St
- **Friendly Lounge** · 1039 S 8th St
- **Jon's Bar and Grille** · 300 South St
- **L'Etage** · 624 S 6th St
- **Laff House** · 221 South St
- **Lyon's Den** · 848 S 2nd St
- **Makoís** · 301 South St
- **New Wave Café** · 784 S 3rd St
- **O'Neal's** · 611 S 3rd St
- **Ray's Happy Birthday Bar** · 1200 E Passyunk Ave
- **Reef Restaurant and Lounge** · 605 S 3rd St
- **Royal Tavern** · 937 E Passyunk Ave
- **Saloon** · 750 S 7th St
- **Tattooed Mom** · 530 South St
- **Teri's** · 1126 S 9th St
- **Theatre of the Living Arts** · 334 South St
- **Vesuvio** · 736 S 8th St

Pet Shops

- **Accent on Animals** · 804 South St
- **Aquarium City Center** · 740 S 4th St
- **Chic Petique** · 616 S 3rd St

Restaurants

- **Anni Cent'** · 770 S 7th St
- **Beau Monde** · 624 S 6th St
- **Brauhaus Schmitz** · 718 South St
- **Bridget Foy's** · 200 South St
- **Café Huong Lan** · 1037 S 8th St
- **Café Nhuy** · 802 Christian St
- **Caffe Valentino** · 1245 S 3rd St
- **Cataboula** · 775 S Front St
- **Copabanana** · 344 South St
- **Cucina Forte** · 768 S 8th St
- **Dmitri's** · 795 S 3rd St
- **Famous 4th Street Deli** · 700 S 4th St
- **Fitzwater Café** · 728 S 7th St
- **Geno's Steaks** · 1219 S 9th St
- **Gnocchi** · 613 E Passyunk Ave
- **Golden Empress Garden** · 610 S 5th St
- **Hikaru** · 607 S 2nd St
- **Horizons** · 611 S 7th St
- **Hosteria Da Elio** · 615 S 3rd St
- **Ishkabibble's Eatery** · 337 South St
- **James** · 824 S 8th St
- **Jim's Steaks** · 400 South St
- **Johnny Rockets** · 443 South St
- **La Fourno Trattoria** · 636 South St
- **La Lupe** · 1201 S 9th St
- **Latest Dish** · 613 S 4th St
- **Lorenzo Pizza** · 900 Christian St
- **Lorenzo & Son Pizza** · 305 South St
- **Lovash** · 236 South St
- **Monsu** · 901 Christian St
- **Mustard Greens** · 622 S 2nd St

- **Napoli Pizzeria** · 944 E Passyunk Ave
- **New Wave Café** · 784 S 3rd St
- **Pat's King of Steaks** · 1237 E Passyunk Ave
- **Ralph's** · 760 S 9th St
- **Rita's** · 239 South St
- **The Royal Tavern** · 937 E Passyunk
- **Sabrina's Café** · 910 Christian St
- **Sarcone's Deli** · 734 S 9th St
- **Snockey's** · 1020 S 2nd St
- **South Street Diner** · 140 South St
- **Supper** · 926 South St
- **Taco Loco** · Jefferson Square Park
- **Tamarind** · 117 South St
- **Taqueria La Veracruzana** · 908 Washington Ave
- **Termini Brothers Bakery** · 1523 S 8th St
- **Trattoria Alla Costiera** · 769 E Passyunk Ave
- **The Ugly American** · 1100 S Front St
- **Vesuvio** · 736 S 8th St
- **Villa di Roma** · 936 S 9th St

Shopping

- **Adidas** · 436 South St
- **Anastacia's Antiques** · 617 Bainbridge St
- **Atomic City Comics** · 642 South St
- **Bella Boutique** · 527 S 4th St
- **Center City Pretzel Co** · 816 Washington Ave
- **Cohen Hardware** · 615 E Passyunk Ave
- **Crash Bang Boom** · 528 S 4th St
- **EB Games** · 505 South St
- **Essene** · 719 S 4th St
- **Fante's Kitchen Wares Shop** · 1006 S 9th St
- **Garland of Letters** · 527 South St
- **Goldstein's Boy's & Men's Wear** · 811 S 6th St
- **Hats in the Belfry** · S 3rd St & South St
- **Headhouse Books** · 619 S 2nd St
- **House of Moore** · 739 S 4th St
- **House of Tea** · 720 S 4th St
- **Kroungold's Better Furniture** · 710 S 5th St
- **Masquerade** · 1100 S Columbus Blvd
- **Maxie's Daughter** · 724 S 4th St
- **Mostly Books** · 529 Bainbridge St
- **Nocturnal Skateshop** · 610 S 3rd St
- **PAT (Philadelphia AIDS Thrift)** · 514 Bainbridge St
- **Pearl of Africa Gates of Zion** · 624 South St
- **Philadelphia Bar & Restaurant Supply** · 629 E Passyunk Ave
- **Philadelphia Eddie's Tattoo** · 621 S 4th St
- **Philadelphia Record Exchange** · 618 S 5th St
- **Repo Records** · 538 South St
- **Retrospect** · 534 South St
- **Rode'o Designs** · 721 S 4th St
- **South Street Antique Market** · 615 S 6th St
- **Triple Play Sporting Goods** · 827 S 9th St
- **Via Bicycle** · 606 S 9th St

Hey, want to see where Beanie Siegel claims he got shot? That's here. Things around this neighborhood are sort of friendly and the rents are super-cheap (with good reason), but parking at night is nigh impossible. Yeah, that's right. Nigh.

$ Banks

- **Bank of America** · 2300 W Oregon Ave
- **Bank of America** · 2330 W Oregon Ave
- **Conestoga Bank** · S 21st St & Passyunk Ave
- **PNC (ATM)** · Shoprite · 2301 Oregon Ave
- **Prudential Savings** · 1834 Oregon Ave
- **Wachovia** · 2300 Snyder Ave

Car Washes

- **Car's** · 1927 W Passyunk Ave
- **Classic Car Cleaners** · 1937 S 17th St

Cheesesteaks

- **Primo Hoagies** · 1528 W Ritner St

P Gas Stations

- **Citgo** · 2101 W Passyunk Ave
- **Getty** · 2101 W Oregon Ave
- **Independent** · 2700 S 15th St
- **Sunoco** · 1825 Oregon Ave
- **Sunoco** · 2101 S 17th St

Landmarks

- **Melrose Diner Parking Lot** · 1501 Snyder Ave

Libraries

- **Thomas F Donatucci Sr Branch** · 1935 Shunk St

Pharmacies

- **CVS** · 1901 W Oregon Ave ⊕
- **The Medicine Shoppe** · 1951 W Passyunk Ave
- **Rite-Aid** · 1500 W Moyamensing Ave
- **Rosica Pharmacy** ·2065 Snyder Ave
- **Walgreens** · 2310 W Oregon Ave ⊕

Post Offices

- **Point Breeze Postal Store** · 2437 S 23rd St

Schools

- **Delaplaine McDaniel** · 1901 S 23rd St
- **Girard** · 1800 Snyder Ave
- **Girard Academic Music Program** · 2136 W Ritner St
- **McDaniel** · 2100 Moore St
- **McDaniel Elementary** ·2230 Mifflin St
- **St Monica** · 1720 W Ritner St
- **St Thomas Aquinas** · 1800 Morris St
- **Trinity Christian** · 3200 South 18th St

 Supermarkets

- **Save-A-Lot** · 2120 S 23rd St

South Philadelphia Tap Room is the gem around here, serving up delicious food and good beer (after beer, after beer). Melrose Diner is your place for classic 24-hour eats. For ravioli and BYOB, L'Angolo will do the trick.

Coffee

- **Brew/Ultimo** · 1900 S 15th St
- **Dunkin' Donuts** · 2308 W Passyunk Ave
- **Dunkin' Donuts** · 2654 S 18th St
- **Caffe Italia** · 1424 Snyder Ave

Gyms

- **Bally Total Fitness** · 2500 S 24th St, 2nd Fl
- **Body World** · 1622 W Passyunk Ave
- **Curves (women only)** · 2115 Oregon Ave

Hardware Stores

- **Albert's Supply** · 1814 S 20th St
- **The Home Depot** · 2200 Oregon Ave
- **Ritner Hardware Store** · 1641 W Ritner St

Nightlife

- **Brew/Ultimo** · 1900 S 15th St
- **Di Nic's Tavern** · 1528 Snyder Ave
- **JR's Bar** · 2327 S Croskey St
- **South Philadelphia Tap Room** · 1509 Mifflin St

Restaurants

- **Barrel's** · 1725 Wolf St
- **L'Angolo** · 1415 Porter St
- **La Stanza** · 2001 Oregon Ave
- **Hardena Restaurant** · 1754 S Hicks St
- **Melrose Diner** · 1501 Snyder Ave ⏲
- **Plenty** · 1710 E Passyunk Ave
- **Royal Villa Café** · 1700 Jackson St
- **Tap Room** · 1509 Mifflin St

Shopping

- **Indonesia Store** · 1701 S Bancroft St
- **RKO Video & South Philly Comics** ·
  1621 Passyunk Ave

Map 10 • Moyamensing / East Passyunk   N

1/4 mile   .25 km

A busy (and somewhat congested) section of South Philly that features lots of residential living space stacked not-so-neatly on top of itself. South Broad takes on the appearance of a blocked artery during peak rush hours, and the curious parking regulations (leaving your car in the middle of the street, anyone?), wholly unique to the area, don't really help matters.

💲 Banks

- **Beneficial Savings** · 2037 S Broad St
- **Citizens** · 2001 S Broad St
- **Citizens (ATM)** · Walgreens · 2014 S Broad St
- **Commerce** · 2201 S Broad St
- **Conestoga Bank** · 1833 E Passyunk Ave
- **Conestoga Bank** · S Broad St & W Porter St
- **Philadelphia Federal Credit Union (ATM)** · St Agnes Medical Ctr · 1900 S Broad St
- **Prudential Savings** · 1722 S Broad St
- **Sovereign** · 2701 S 10th St
- **St Edmond's Federal Savings** · 1901 E Passyunk Ave
- **United Bank of Philadelphia (ATM)** · Rite Aid · 2017 S Broad St
- **United Savings** · Broad St & Passyunk Ave
- **Wachovia** · 1931 S Broad St
- **Wachovia** · 2039 S 10th St
- **Wachovia** · 2532 S 13th St

➕ Emergency Rooms

- **Methodist Hospital** · 2301 S Broad St ⊕

🅿 Gas Stations

- **Lukoil** · 2101 S 11th St

📖 Libraries

- **Fumo Family Branch** · 2437 S Broad St
- **South Philadelphia Branch** · 1700 S Broad St

℞ Pharmacies

- **Broad Street Apothecary** · 2426 S Broad St
- **Ninth Street Pharmacy** · 2400 S 9th St
- **Rite-Aid** · 2017 S Broad St ⊕
- **Walgreens** · 2014 S Broad St ⊕
- **Walgreens** · 2655 S 10th St
- **Zevin's Pharmacy** · 800 McKean St

✉ Post Offices

- **Castle Finance** · 1713 S Broad St

🏫 Schools

- **Breath of Life Christian Academy** · 1638 S 6th St
- **Edward Bok Voc-Tech** · 1901 S 9th St
- **Epiphany of Our Lord** · 1248 Jackson St
- **Fell** · 900 W Oregon Ave
- **Jenks** · 2501 S 13th St
- **Key** · 2230 S 8th St
- **Philadelphia Performing Arts** · 2600 S Broad St
- **South Philadelphia High** · 2101 S Broad St
- **Southwark** · 1835 S 9th St
- **St Maria Goretti High** · 1736 S 10th St
- **St Nicholas of Tolentine** · 913 Pierce St

Revamped Passyunk Avenue has something for everyone. Paradiso serves Italian in a sophisticated setting while down the street, Cantina buzzes with hipsters buzzed on margaritas. For a low-key evening, try a specialty pizza at Marra's or head to Lucky 13 for beer and meatball shots.

Coffee

- **Caffe Chicco** · 2532 S Broad St
- **Dunkin' Donuts** · 2025 S Broad St
- **Starbucks** · 2201 S Broad St

Gyms

- **Vitality Health & Wellness** · 2439 S Broad St

Hardware Stores

- **Albert Hardware** · 1609 S 7th St
- **Bruskin Hardware & Lock** · 2451 S 5th St
- **Jam's Hardware** · 2323 S 9th St

Nightlife

- **Cantina Los Cabalitos** · 1651 E Passyunk Ave
- **Le Virtu** · 1927 E Passyunuk Ave

Pet Shops

- **Doggie Style** · 1700 Passynuk Ave

Restaurants

- **10th Street Café** · 1000 Snyder Ave
- **Artisan Boulanger Patissier** · 1648 S 12th St
- **Bomb Bomb Bar-B-Que Grill** · 1026 Wolf St
- **Cantina Los Cabalitos** · 1651 E Passyunk Ave
- **Criniti Restaurant** · 2611 S Broad St
- **El Zarape** · 1648 S Passyuk Ave
- **Fond** · 1617 E Passyunk Ave
- **Izumi** · 1601 E Passyunk Ave
- **Le Virtu** · 1927 E Passynuk Ave
- **Mamma Maria** · 1637 E Passyunk Ave
- **Marra's** · 1734 E Passyunk Ave
- **Mazza Mediteranean Takeout** · 1100 Jackson St
- **Mr Martino's Trattoria** · 1646 E Passyunk Ave
- **Paradiso** · 1627 E Passyunk Ave
- **Pop's Water Ice** · 1337 W Oregon Ave
- **Scannicchio's** · 2500 S Broad St
- **Tre Scalini** · 1915 E Passyunk Ave

Shopping

- **Beautiful World Syndicate** · 1619 E Passyunk Ave
- **Fabulous Finds Boutique** · 1535 S Broad St
- **Interior Concepts Furniture** · 1701 E Passyunk Ave
- **Mia** · 1748 E Passyunk Ave
- **Mike's Bikes** · 1901 S 13th St
- **Nice Things Handmade** · 1731 E Passyunk Ave
- **St Jude Shop** · 1807 E Passyunk Ave
- **Shoe Barrel** · 1812 E Passyunk Ave

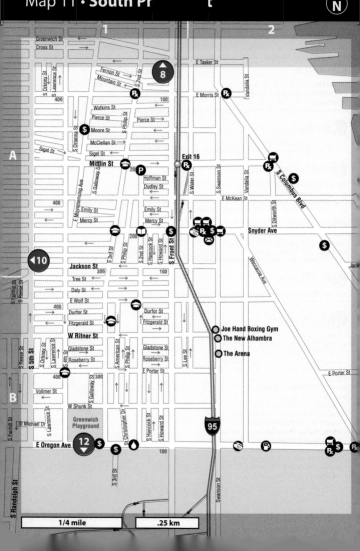

Map 11 • South Pr ... t

N

Greenwich St
Cross St

Fernon St
Mountain St

E Tasker St

8

Watkins St
Pierce St
Pierce St

E Morris St

Moore St

McClellan St

Sigel St

Sigel St

Mifflin St

Exit 16

Hoffman St
Dudley St

E McKean St

Emily St
Mercy St

Emily St
Mercy St

Snyder Ave

Jackson St

Tree St

Daly St

E Wolf St

Durfor St
Fitzgerald St

Durfor St
Fitzgerald St

W Ritner St

Gladstone St
Roseberry St

Gladstone St
Roseberry St

E Porter St

Joe Hand Boxing Gym
The New Alhambra
The Arena

Vollmer St

W Shunk St

Greenwich
Playground

E Oregon Ave

12

95

E Porter St

S Columbus Blvd

S Swanson St
S Water St
S Front St
S Howard St
S Hancock St
S 2nd St
S 3rd St
S Philip St
S Galloway St
S American St
S 4th St
S Lawrence St
S 5th St
S Reese St
S Fairhill St
St Michael Dr
S Randolph St

Vandalia St
Vandalia St
S Dilworth St

Wharton Ave

S Lee St

S Christopher Dr
S Hancock St
S Howard St
S 3rd St
Swanson St

1/4 mile   .25 km

For all intents and purposes, the area is connected to the stadiums, if for no other reason than its proximity to both 95 and to Columbus—the two main conduits to the sports complex. It is also land of the Mummers, with "Two Street" being their main thoroughfare.

$ Banks

- **Bank of America** · 1950 S Columbus Blvd
- **Bank of America (ATM)** · 330 Oregon Ave
- **Citizens** · 330 E Oregon Ave
- **PNC (ATM)** · Ikea · 2206 S Columbus Blvd
- **PNC (ATM)** · Shoprite · 29 Snyder Ave
- **Prudential Savings** · 238 A Moyamensing Ave
- **Wachovia** · 2710 S 3rd St

Car Washes

- **Ritz Car Wash & Detail Center** · 234 W Oregon Ave

Cheesesteaks

- **John's Roast Pork** · 14 E Snyder Ave
- **Tony Luke's** · 39 E Oregon Ave

Gas Stations

- **Exxon** · 80 E Oregon Ave

Landmarks

- **The Arena** · 7 W Ritner St
- **Joe Hand Boxing Gym** · 7 Ritner St
- **The New Alhambra** · 7 Ritner St

Libraries

- **Whitman Branch** · 200 Snyder Ave

Parking

Pharmacies

- **KMart** · 424 W Oregon Ave
- **Linsky Pharmacy** · 1701 S 2nd St
- **Pathmark** · 330 E Oregon Ave ♿
- **Rite-Aid** · 10 Snyder Ave
- **Super Fresh** · 1851 S Columbus Blvd
- **Target** · 1 Mifflin St
- **Wal-Mart** · 1675 S Columbus Blvd

Post Offices

- **Snyder Plaza Finance Station** · 58 Snyder Ave

Schools

- **Furness High** · 1900 S 3rd St
- **Our Lady of Mount Carmel** · 2329 S 3rd St
- **Sharswood** · 2300 S 2nd St
- **Taggart** · 400 W Porter St
- **Vare** · 1621 E Moyamensing Ave

Supermarkets

- **Pathmark** · 330 E Oregon Ave ♿
- **Save-A-Lot** · 48 Snyder Ave
- **ShopRite** · 29 Snyder Ave ♿
- **Super Fresh** · 1851 S Columbus Blvd

47

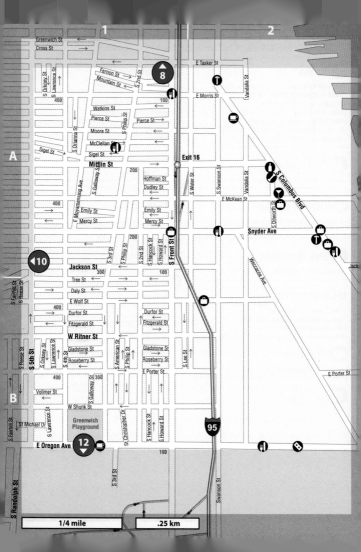

A sampling of South Philly in all its glory: lots of Italian joints, with a growing faction of Asian and Latino restaurants emerging. You also have a Tony Luke's for your hoagie-craving needs and pretty close proximity to the growing shopping region on South Columbus, especially attractive Ikea and Lowe's.

12

Ma

Coffee

- **Dunkin' Donuts** • 330 W Oregon Ave
- **Dunkin' Donuts** • 1850 S Columbus Blvd

Hardware Stores

- **The Home Depot** • 1651 S Columbus Blvd
- **Lowe's** • 2106 S Christopher Columbus Blvd

Liquor Stores

- **State Liquor Store** • 1940 S Columbus Blvd

Nightlife

- **Penn's Port Pub** • 1920 S Columbus Blvd

Pet Shops

- **Monster Pets** • 1946 S Columbus Blvd

Restaurants

- **Chic-Fil-A** • 2204 S Columbus Ave
- **Chuck E Cheese's** • 9 Snyder Ave
- **Gooey Looie's** • 231 McClellan St
- **Langostino** • 100 Morris St
- **Tony Luke's** • 39 E Oregon Ave

Shopping

- **Barry's Home Brew** • 101 Snyder Ave
- **Forman Mills** • 22 E Wolf St
- **Ikea** • 2206 S Columbus Blvd
- **Lowe's** • 2106 S Columbus Blvd
- **Schafer's Brakes & Mufflers** • 1924 S Columbus Blvd

Video Rental

- **Blockbuster** • 200 Oregon Ave

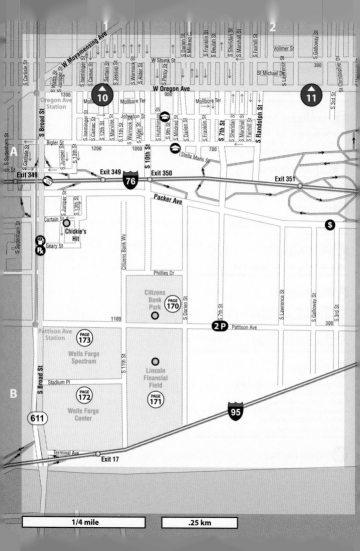

Oh to live in the shadow of the goalposts and foul poles! Of course, for this extreme proximity to Philly's fabled stadia, you must pay a heavy price in daily aggravation, from extreme noise pollution (lots of booing, which carries surprisingly far), to always-jammed streets and drunken louts peeing on your zinnias.

$ Banks

· **PNC** · 330 Packer Ave

Cheesesteaks

· **Talk of the Town** · 3020 S Broad St

Gas Stations

· **Citgo** · 3000 S Broad St

Landmarks

· **Chickie's Hit** · Curtain St & Juniper St
· **Citizens Bank Park** · 1 Citizens Bank Wy
· **Lincoln Financial Field** · 1020 Pattison Ave

Parking

Pharmacies

· **CVS** · 3300 S Broad St

Schools

· **Stella Maris** · 814 Bigler St
· **Thomas** · 927 Johnston St

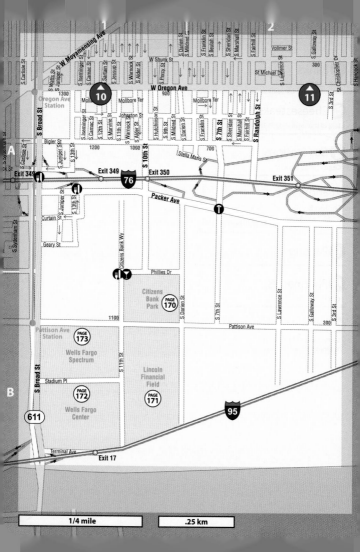

Pretty much everything revolves around the stadium complex here, from nightlife to dining and entertainment. If you want a nice restaurant either following the afternoon game or before the late game, stop into Medora's Mecca and be sure to try some of that fabulous tiramisu.

Hardware Stores

• **Right-Way** • 700 Packer Ave

Nightlife

• **McFadden's at Citizen's Bank Ball Park** •
  1 Citizens Bank Wy

Restaurants

• **McFadden's at Citizen's Bank Ball Park** •
  1 Citizens Bank Wy
• **Medora's Mecca** • 3101 S 13th St
• **Talk of the Town** • 3020 S Broad St

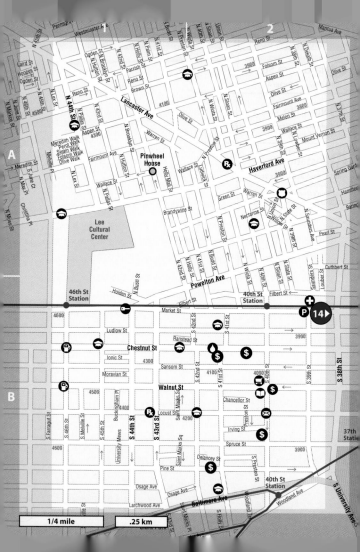

West Philly's giant, gorgeous victorian houses give this neighborhood a distinct feeling, and the tenants of the houses vary widely from squatting anarchists to African immigrants to college kids and more. Don't miss Clark Park just off the map here on 45th and Baltimore—it's a hub of community activity.

Banks

- **PNC (ATM)** • 200 S 40th St
- **PNC (ATM)** • Veterinary Hospital • 3900 Delancey St
- **PNC (ATM)** • Harrison College • 3910 Irving St
- **PNC (ATM)** • 4040 Chestnut St
- **United Bank of Philadelphia (ATM)** • 104 S 40th St

 Car Rental

- **Hertz** • 4422 Market St

Car Washes

- **High Tech Brushless** • 4131 Chestnut St

Emergency Rooms

- **Penn Presbyterian Medical Center** • 51 N 39th St ♿

Gas Stations

- **BP** • 4600 Chestnut St
- **Sunoco** • 4601 Walnut St

Landmarks

- **Pinwheel House** • 42nd St & Wallace St

Libraries

- **Walnut Street West** • 201 S 40th St

Parking

Pharmacies

- **Bell Apothecary** • 4014 Lancaster Ave
- **CVS** • 4314 Locust St

Police

- **16th Police District** • 3900 Lancaster Ave

Post Offices

- **University City** • 228 S 40th St

Schools

- **Belmont Charter** • 4030 Brown St
- **Christ Academy** • 4233 Chestnut St
- **Greater Love Christian Academy** • 437 N 40th St
- **Locke** • 4550 Haverford Ave
- **Martha Washington** • 766 N 44th St
- **Penn Assisted** • S 42nd St & Locust St
- **Robeson High** • 4125 Ludlow St
- **Spruce Hill Christian** • 4115 Baltimore Ave
- **West Philadelphia Catholic High** • 4501 Chestnut St

Supermarkets

- **The Fresh Grocer** • 4001 Walnut St

The West Philly melting pot is perhaps best demonstrated by the incredible variety in restaurants, from Ethiopian (Abyssinia) to Pakistani (Kabobeesh) to Thai (Thai Singha House) to fancy Mexican (Distrito). It's a little harder to find a good bar here, but you can always try Fiume or Local 44.

Coffee

- **Cafe Clave** • 4305 Locust St
- **The Green Line Cafe** • 4239 Baltimore Ave
- **The Green Line Cafe** • 4305 Locust St
- **Kaffa Crossing** • 4423 Chestnut St

Farmers Markets

- **Clark Park**
  (May–Dec; Thurs, 3 pm–7 pm, Sat 10 am–2 pm) •
  S 43rd St & Baltimore Ave

Hardware Stores

- **CI Presser** • 4224 Market St
- **Mike's Hardware** • 4118 Lancaster Ave
- **Monarch Hardware** • 4502 Walnut St

Liquor Stores

- **State Liquor Store** • 4049 Market St
- **University City Beverage** • 4300 Walnut St

Movie Theaters

- **The Bridge: Cinema de Lux** • S 40th St & Walnut St

Nightlife

- **Cavanaugh's** • 119 S 39th St
- **Fiume** • 229 S 45th St
- **Local 44** • 4333 Spruce St
- **The New Angle Lounge** • 3901 Lancaster Ave
- **Smokey Joe's** • 210 S 40th St
- **University Pinball** • 4008 Spruce St
- **Watutsi II** • 232 S 45th St

Pet Shops

- **Trade Winds** • 27 S 40th St

Restaurants

- **Abyssinia Ethiopian Restaurant** • 229 S 45th St
- **Allegro Pizza** • 3942 Spruce St
- **Colonial Pizza** • 400 S 43rd St
- **Distrito** • 3945 Chestnut St
- **Ethio Cafe & Carry Out** • 4400 Chestnut St
- **Evan's Varsity Pizza** • 4311 Locust St
- **The Greek Lady** • 222 S 40th St
- **Izzy and Zoe's** • 224 S 40th St
- **Lee's Hoagie House** • 4034 Walnut St
- **Kabobeesh** • 4201 Chestnut St
- **Kaffa Crossing** • 4423 Chestnut St
- **Kilmandjaro Restaurant** • 4317 Chestnut St
- **Koch's Deli** • 4309 Locust St
- **Local 44** • 4333 Spruce St
- **Marathan Grill and MarBar** • 200 S 40th St
- **Marigold Kitchen** • 501 S 45th St
- **Mexicali Café** • 110 S 40th St
- **Nan** • 4000 Chestnut St
- **Pattaya Grill** • 4006 Chestnut St
- **Philly Diner** • 3901 Walnut St
- **Pho & Cafe Saigon** • 4248 Spruce St
- **Rx** • 4443 Spruce St
- **Saad's Halal Place** • 4500 Walnut St
- **Tandoor India** • 106 S 40th St
- **Thai Singha House** • 3939 Chestnut St

Shopping

- **Donut Plus** • 4325 Chestnut St
- **Eak Chuong Grocery** • 4421 Chestnut St
- **International Foods and Spices** • 4203 Walnut St
- **The Last Word Bookshop** • 220 S 40th St
- **Makkah Market** • 4249 Walnut St
- **The Marvelous** • 208 S 40th St
- **Metropolitan Bakery** • 4013 Walnut St
- **The Natural Shoe Store Inc.** • 220 S 40th St
- **P&P Grocery** • 4307 Locust St
- **Pasqually's Pizza & Pasta** • 200 S 45th St
- **The Second Mile Center Thrift Stores** •
  214 S 45th St
- **Toviah Thrift Shop** • 4211 Chestnut St
- **Wawa Food Market** • 3744 Spruce St

1

2

Mantua Ave

16

I-76

Art Museum Dr

Aquarium Dr

Spring Garden S

Folsom St

Aspen St

Olive St

Fairmount Ave

Melon St

Melon St

Wallace St

Mount Vernon St

Brandywine St

N 33rd St

Spring Garden St

Spring Garden Rmp St

Exit 344

Kelly Dr

N 34th St

N Dekalb St

N Sheridan St

N 35th St

N Douglas St

N Naycen St

N Napa St

N 31st St

Exit 345

Exit 345

A

Haverford Ave

Hamilton St

Baring St

Pearl St

Powelton Ave

Spring Garden St

Pearl St

Race St

3300

Winter St

Summer St

Circa Center

Arch St

Exit

N Saunders St

N State St

N 38th St

N 37th St

N 36th St

Saunders St

Louber St

Cuthbert St

13

Lancaster Ave

Chestbucka St

Warren St

Cherry St

Arch St

Cuthbert St

34th St Station

30th St Station

184

John F Kennedy Blvd

30th St Station Bolt Bus

1

Filbert St

Market St

P

Face Fragment

Ludlow St

3900

S 34th St

33rd St Station

148

Drexel University

P 30th St Station Bathrooms

P **2** 30th St Station Post Office

Chestnut St

Sansom St

S 38th St

S 37th St

S McAlpin St

Moravian St

2

36th St Station

Moravian St

Walnut St

Chancellor St

3200

3100

Exit 345

Ben and His Bench

Locust Walk

Hill Square

2

Split Button

Self-Immolation Point

University of Pennsylvania

158

B

37th St Station

Spruce St

Hamilton Walk

+5

S 40th St

S 39th St

Biopond

S University Ave

Olnet Ext

Civic Center Blvd

Exit 346A

South St

Schuylkill River

S 30th St

Cypre

Delanc

Panam

Reaney St

Wavert

S 27th St

S Taney St

S 26th St

S Bamber St

Curie Blvd

Philadelphia Civic Center

Exit 346A

5

1/4 mile

.25 km

If UC seems a bit forced to you, you're not crazy—the neighborhood didn't even exist until the mid-1950s when it was created as a marketing ploy. Things can be tense between students and their neighbors thanks to "Penntrification," but mostly the area remains a small safe haven for collegians.

$ Banks

- **Citizens** • 134 S 34th St
- **Citizens** • 2929 Arch St
- **Citizens (ATM)** • Moravian Café • S 34th St & Walnut St
- **Commerce** • 3735 Walnut St
- **PNC** • 3535 Market St
- **PNC (ATM)** • Hill House • 3333 Walnut St
- **PNC (ATM)** • 3400 Spruce St
- **PNC (ATM)** • Houston Hall • 3417 Spruce St
- **PNC (ATM)** • Johnson Pavilion • 3600 Hamilton Wk
- **PNC (ATM)** • Upenn–Bookstore • 3600 Walnut St
- **PNC (ATM)** • Wawa • 3604 Chestnut St
- **PNC (ATM)** • Steinberg • 3620 Locust Wk
- **PNC (ATM)** • Grad Tower A • 3650 Locust St
- **PNC (ATM)** • McClelan Hall • 3700 Spruce St
- **PNC (ATM)** • Upenn Hospital • S 34th St & Spruce St
- **PNC (ATM)** • Wawa • S 38th St & Spruce St
- **Sovereign** • 3131 Market St
- **United Bank of Philadelphia** • 3750 Lancaster Ave
- **United Bank of Philadelphia (ATM)** • VA Medical Center • S University Ave & Woodland Ave

Car Rental

- **Avis** • 2951 Market St
- **Budget** • 30th St Train Station
- **Enterprise** • 15 S 36th St
- **Hertz** • 2951 Market St
- **National** • 30th St Train Station

Cheesesteaks

- **Abner's Cheesesteaks** • 3801 Chestnut St

+ Emergency Rooms

- **Hospital of the University of Pennsylvania** • 3400 Spruce St ⊕

⊙ Landmarks

- **30th St Station Bathrooms** • Market St & S 30th St
- **Ben and His Bench** • Locust Walk & S 37th St
- **Biopond** • 3740 Hamilton Wk
- **Bolt Bus** • 30th St & Market St
- **Face Fragment** • 35th St & Market St
- **Hill Square** • 34th St & Walnut St
- **Self-Immolation Point** • 34th St & Locust St
- **Split Button** • b/w 34th & 36th Sts & Locust & Spruce Sts

📖 Libraries

- **Charles L Durham Branch** • 3320 Haverford Ave

P Parking

℞ Pharmacies

- **Amber Pharmacy** • 3535 Market St
- **CVS** • Wawa • 3401 Walnut St

✉ Post Offices

- **30th Street Train Station** • 2955 Market St
- **Philadelphia Main Office** • 3000 Chestnut St

🎓 Schools

- **The Cittone Institute** • 3600 Market St
- **Drew** • 3724 Warren St
- **Drexel University** • 3141 Chestnut St
- **Maritime Academy Charter** • 3020 Market St
- **McMichael** • 3543 Fairmount Ave
- **Powel** • 301 N 36th St
- **University City High** • 3601 Filbert St
- **University of Pennsylvania** • 3451 Walnut St

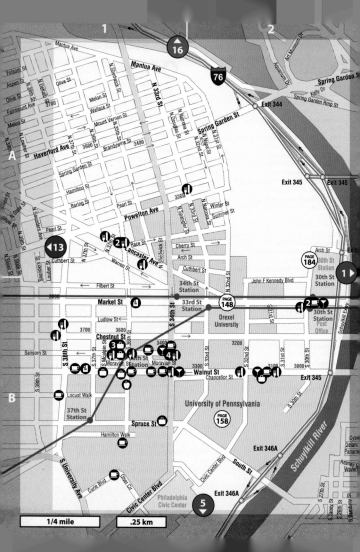

The University City District's main goal is to take everything Center City does and make a bastardized version of it. While this leaves a sour taste in our mouths, one can't forget that the area is full of excellent restaurants, bars, food carts, and theatres. Oh, and frat parties. Lite beer in the house!

☕ Coffee

- **Au Bon Pain** • 2951 Market St
- **Au Bon Pain** • 421 Curie Blvd
- **Avril 50** • 3406 Sansom St
- **Bucks County Coffee** • 3430 Sansom St
- **Cosi** • 140 S 36th St
- **Cosi** • 2955 Market St
- **Dunkin' Donuts** • 3437 Walnut St
- **Gia Pronto** • 3736 Spruce St
- **Starbucks** • 3401 Walnut St
- **Starbucks** • 3800 Locust Wk

🍴 Restaurants

- **Abner's of University City** • 3813 Chestnut St
- **Ed's/Rana** • 3513 Lancaster Ave
- **La Terrasse** • 3432 Sansom St
- **Laurent** • 305 N 33rd St
- **Lemon Grass Thai** • 3630 Lancaster Ave
- **Mad Mex** • 3401 Walnut St
- **New Deck Tavern** • 3408 Sansom St
- **Paris Cafe Creperie** • 3417 Spruce St
- **Penne** • 3600 Sansom St
- **Picnic** • 3131 Walnut St
- **Pod** • 3636 Sansom St
- **Powelton Pizza** • 3651 Lancaster Ave
- **Sitar India** • 60 S 38th St
- **Slainte** • 3000 Market St
- **White Dog Café** • 3420 Sansom St
- **Zocalo** • 3600 Lancaster Ave

📋 Copy Shops

- **Campus Shipping Center** • 3731 Walnut St
- **FedEx Office** • 3535 Market St

🛍 Shopping

- **American Apparel** • 3661 Walnut St
- **EMS** • 3401 Chesnut St
- **Philadelphia Runner** • 3621 Walnut St
- **Trophy Bikes** • 3131 Walnut St
- **Urban Outfitters** • 110 S 36th St
- **Wawa Food Market** • 3604 Chestnut St

Farmers Markets

- **University Square Farmers' Market**
  (Wed 10am–2 pm; May–Nov) •
  S 36th St b/w Walnut St & Sansom St

🍸 Nightlife

- **Biba Wine Bar** • 3131 Walnut St
- **Bridgewater's Pub** • 2951 Market St
- **Mad Mex** • 3401 Walnut St
- **Mikey's American Grill & Sports Bar** •
  3180 Chestnut St
- **New Deck Tavern** • 3408 Sansom St

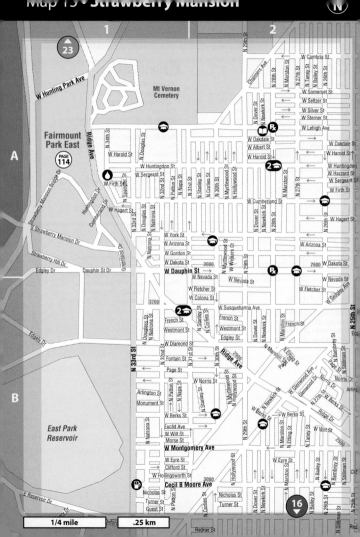

This gritty North Philly nabe hugs less-frequented portions of Fairmount Park from East Park Reservoir to spooky Mount Vernon Cemetery. Cecil B. Moore Avenue—named for famed Philadelphia Civil Rights activist—serves as main artery on the south. Save for few exceptions, dining is limited to take out and casual fare.

Car Washes

- **Clarence Soft Glove Car Wash** • 2533 N 34th St

Gas Stations

- **Getty** • 1701 N 33rd St
- **Sunoco** • N 33rd St & W York St

Libraries

- **Widener Branch** • 2808 W Lehigh Ave

Pharmacies

- **Rite-Aid** • 2801 W Dauphin St
- **Samuel J Robinson Pharmacy** • 2848 W Lehigh Ave

Schools

- **Blaine** • 3001 W Berks St
- **Church of God Victory Academy** • 2340 N 30th St
- **Dr Ethel Allen** • 3200 W Lehigh Ave
- **Fitzsimons Middle** • 2601 W Cumberland St
- **Gideon** • 2817 W Glenwood Ave
- **Hill** • 3133 Ridge Ave
- **John Barry** • 2601 N 28th St
- **Muhammads Islamic Academy** • 2600 Cecil B Moore Ave
- **Strawberry Mansion High** • 3133 Ridge Ave
- **Walton** • 2601 N 28th St
- **Wright** • 2700 W Dauphin St

Map 15 · **Strawberry Mansion**

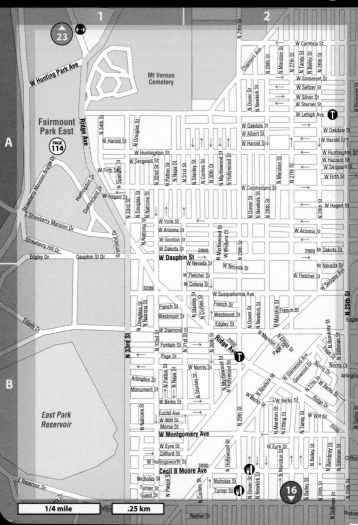

While much of Philadelphia is undergoing a real estate boom, some neighborhoods remain depressed. Such is this pocket of North Philly where dining options are largely limited to take out, but fish fans opt for Dominic's Fish Market for the best of what's around. Maybe you should buy now and cross your fingers. If Camden can go luxury loft...

Gyms

• **East Falls Fitness** • 3751 Ridge Ave

Hardware Stores

• **Bob's Hardware** • 2548 W Lehigh Ave
• **Ridge True Value Hardware** • 2915 Ridge Ave

Restaurants

• **Dominics Fish Market** • 2842 Cecil B Moore Ave
• **Yuri Deli** • 1618 N 29th St

Map 16 · **Brewerytown**

Named for the large number of breweries that once populated the area, the people in this neighborhood range from cold-cash professionals to college students to families trying to make ends meet. But be warned that when real-estate marketers refer to part of it as "up-and-coming," a lot of the area hasn't quite, er, come up yet.

Banks

- **United Bank of Philadelphia (ATM)** •
Health First Pharmacy • 2820 W Girard Ave

Landmarks

- **Art Museum Steps** •
26th & Benjamin Franklin Pkwy
- **Giant Slide** • 33rd St & Oxford St
- **Lloyd Hall** • Boathouse Row

Pharmacies

- **Ellis Pharmacy** • 2441 Brown St

Schools

- **Boone** • 1435 N 26th St
- **Kelley** • 1601 N 28th St
- **Morris** • 2600 W Thompson St

For music-lovers, the North Star Bar is one of the premier venues for off-beat tunes, indie rock, and occasional alt-comedy shows. Nearby Kelly Drive is a great place to skate, bike, run and meet/pick up similar-minded folk. Eat at Era for cheap Ethiopian and Butter's for solid soul food.

Coffee

- **Flying Saucer** • 2545 Brown St

Hardware Stores

- **Nagelberg Hardware** • 2721 W Girard Ave

Nightlife

- **North Star Bar** • 2639 Poplar St

Restaurants

- **Butter's Soul Food** • 2821 W Girard Ave
- **Era** • 2743 Poplar St
- **Granite Hill** • 2600 Benjamin Franklin Parkway
- **Trio** • 2624 Brown St
- **Water Works Restaurant and Lounge** •
  640 Water Works Dr

Map 17 · **Fairmount**

Map 17

Lots of families, students, and young couples are here, living in sin and duplexes. The area is close to both Fairmount Avenue and 676, which makes it convenient to many places (except public transit). On the positive side, Eastern State Penitentiary is one of the best attractions in Philly and has a rocking Halloween haunted house.

$ Banks

- **PNC (ATM)** · Wawa · 2101 Hamilton St
- **PNC (ATM)** · Girard College · 2101 S College Ave
- **Polonia** · 2133 Spring Garden St
- **Wachovia** · 2401 Pennsylvania Ave

Car Washes

- **Executive Auto Salon of Center City** ·
  N 22nd St & Benjamin Franklin Pkwy

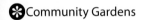 Community Gardens

Gas Stations

- **Amoco** · Ridge Ave & Girard Ave
- **BP** · 900 W College Ave
- **BP** · 1801 Ridge Ave
- **Gulf** · 2201 Spring Garden St
- **Sunoco** · 2300 Fairmount Ave

Landmarks

- **Eastern State Penitentiary** ·
  N 22nd St & Fairmount Ave
- **Rodin Museum** ·
  N 22nd St & Benjamin Franklin Pkwy
- **The Thinker** · N 22nd St & Benjamin Franklin Pkwy

P Parking

Pharmacies

- **CVS** · 2320 Fairmount Ave
- **Eckerd** · 2000 Hamilton St
- **Fairmount Pharmacy** · 1900 Green St
- **Henneberry Pharmacy** · 838 N 24th St
- **Philadelphian Pharmacy** · 2401 Pennsylvania Ave
- **Rite-Aid** · 1924 Fairmont Ave

Police

- **9th Police District** · 401 N 21st St

Post Offices

- **Fairmount** · 1939 Fairmount Ave
- **Fairmount Station** · 900 N 19th St

 Schools

- **Bache-Martin** · 2201 Brown St
- **Girard College** · 2101 S College Ave
- **Hope Christian Academy** · 2222 W Master St
- **John W Hallahan Catholic Girls** · 311 N 19th St
- **Philadelphia Mennonite High** · 860 N 24th St
- **St Francis Xavier** · Wallace St and N 24th St
- **Vaux Middle** · 2300 W Master St
- **Waring** · 1801 Green St

Supermarkets

- **Whole Foods** · 2001 Pennsylvania Ave

Map 17 · **Fairmount**

Mugshots is the hangout du jour, serving organic and fair-trade treats to students, couples, and young mamas with strollers. The Belgian Café, opened at the tail end of Philly's Belgian-spot boom, serves powerful beer and food that'll delight meat-eaters and vegans alike. For cheap, late-night munchies, Little Pete's has you covered. Rose Tattoo, while having a name that reminds us of an 80s mistake, is a long-time date-night favorite.

Coffee

- **Java's Brewin at City View Condominium** · 2001 Hamilton St
- **Mugshots** · 2100 Fairmount Ave
- **Starbucks** · 1945 Callowhill St

Copy Shops

- **FedEx Office** · 1816 Spring Garden St

Gyms

- **Curves (women only)** · 2333 Fairmount Ave
- **Life Sport Fitness Resource Center** · 2112 Fairmount Ave
- **Philadelphia Sports Club** · 2000 Hamilton St

Hardware Stores

- **Farimont Hardware** · 2011 Fairmount Ave

Liquor Stores

- **State Liquor Store** · 1935 Fairmount Ave
- **State Liquor Store** · 2511 W Girard Ave

Nightlife

- **The Bishop's Collar** · 2349 Fairmount Ave
- **Urban Saloon** · 2120 Fairmount Ave

Pet Shops

- **Fairmount Pet Shoppe** · 2024 Fairmount Ave
- **In the Doghouse** · 706 N 24th St

Restaurants

- **Angelino's Restaurant & Pizzeria** · 849 N 25th St
- **The Belgian Café** · 2047 Green St
- **The Bishop's Collar** · 2349 Fairmount Ave
- **Bridgid's** · 726 N 24th St
- **Doma** · 1822 Callowhill St
- **Figs** · 2501 Meredith St
- **Illuminare** · 2321 Fairmount Ave
- **Jack's Firehouse** · 2130 Fairmount Ave
- **Little Pete's** · 2401 Pennsylvania Ave
- **L'Oca Italian Bistro** · 2025 Fairmount Ave
- **London Grill** · 2301 Fairmount Ave
- **Rembrandt's** · 741 N 23rd St
- **Rose Tattoo Café** · 1847 Callowhill St
- **Rybread** · 2319 Fairmount Ave
- **Sabrina's Cafe** · 1804 Callowhill St
- **Tavern On Green** · 2047 Green St
- **Umai Umai** · 533 N 22nd St

Shopping

- **The Beehive** · 2323 Fairmount Ave
- **Bookhaven** · 2202 Fairmount Ave
- **JK Market** · 2001 Green St
- **Oliver's Antiques** · 2052 Fairmount Ave
- **Philly Flavors** · 2004 Fairmount Ave
- **Wawa Food Market** · 2040 Hamilton St

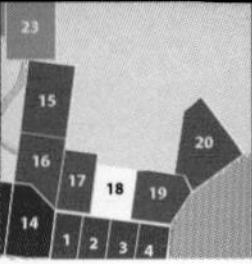

Essentials

By day this area is dominated by students of all kinds, but it gets pretty quiet after dark. Gentrification is just starting to make inroads, so the housing is still affordable, excluding the loft/studio condo spaces that dot the outskirts on either side. It's less friendly at night thanks to the abandoned Reading railroad tracks, so put away the map, yeah?

$ Banks

- **Citizens** · 1201 Spring Garden St
- **Citizens (ATM)** · 1500 Spring Garden St
- **Philadelphia Federal Credit Union (ATM)** · Wallace Building · 642 N Broad St
- **PNC** · 702 N Broad St
- **PNC (ATM)** · 1356 Girard Ave
- **PNC (ATM)** · Community College of Philadelphia · 1700 Spring Garden St
- **Wachovia (ATM)** · School District of Philadelphia Education Center · 440 N Broad St

Car Washes

- **Spring Garden Wash & Lube** · 1111 Spring Garden St

Community Gardens

Emergency Rooms

- **St Joseph's Hospital** · N 16th St & W Girard Ave ⊗

Landmarks

- **Divine Lorraine Hotel** · 699 N Broad St
- **Metropolitan Opera House** · Broad St & Fairmount Ave

P Parking

Rx Pharmacies

- **CVS** · 922 N Broad St
- **Rite-Aid** · 1201 W Girard Ave

Post Offices

- **Girard Avenue** · 905 N Broad St

Schools

- **Community College of Philadelphia** · 1700 Spring Garden St
- **Eastern University-Campolo School for Social Change** · 990 Spring Garden St
- **Franklin High** · 550 N Broad St
- **Franklin Learning Center** · 616 N 15th St
- **Masterman** · 1699 Spring Garden St
- **Math Civics and Sciences Charter** · 1326 Buttonwood St
- **People for People Charter** · 800 N Broad St
- **Philadelphia Academic** · 1421 W Girard Ave
- **Spring Garden** · 1130 Melon St
- **Spring Garden** · 685 N 12th St
- **St Joseph's Preparatory** · 1733 W Girard Ave
- **Stoddart-Fleisher Middle** · 540 N 13th St

Map 18

75

Map 18 · **Spring Garden / Francisville**

N

W Seybert St
W Thompson St
W Cabot St
W Stiles St
W Flora St
1500
W Flora St

W Girard Ave
Girard Ave Station

Harper St
Cambridge St
W George St

Edwin St
1100
Harmer St
Ogden St
Parrish St

A
Parrish St
Reno St

Ridge St
N Burns St
N Carlisle St
N Nodens St

Brown St
Swain St

Folsom St
Fairmount Ave Station

Fairmount Ave
W Potts St
Melon St
Melon St
Lemon St

Melon St
North St
Wallace St

17
Mount Vernon St
Green St

Brandywine St
Spring Garden St
Spring Garden St Station

Spring Garden St
1100

Buttonwood St
Community College of Philadelphia
Hamilton St

B
Callowhill St
Carlton St
Franklin Town Blvd
N 16th St
N 15th St
Wood St

2
Exit 3
Exit 3
Vine St
676

Winter St
Summer St
Summer St
Spring Gdn St

1/4 mile   .25 km

W Thompson St
Patrick Henry Pl
Valley Green Pl
Lafayette Pl
N Jessup St
Curtis Pl
W Stiles St
W Flora St
1390
1100
W Girard Ave
W Harper St
N 12th St
Cambridge St
Poplar St
Ogden St
Sartain Pl
Jessup Pl
Myrtle Pl
Parrish Dr
N Watts St
N Camac St
N Budd St
Reno Pl

George Pl
N 11th St
N Hutchinson St
Ogden St
N Percy St
N Percy St
N 10th St
N Darien St

Parrish Dr
Reno Pl
Brown St
Olive St

Fairmount Ave
1200
North St
N Warnock St
N Alder St
Melon St

Lemon St
Mount Vernon St
Clay St
Green St
Brandywine St
Spring Garden St
1100
Nectarine St
Buttonwood St
Hamilton St
Noble St
Shamokin St

Nectarine St
Hamilton St

Ridge St
N 12th St
N Percy St
N Hutchinson St
N Darien St

Wood St
Carlton St
Pearl St
Vine St

19

3
Exit Us Hwy 3

N Sartain St
N Marvine St
N 11th St
N Jessup St
N 10th St
N Alder St
Winters Ct
Spring St

Summer St
Florist St
Winter St
Providence Ct
Weylies Ct

There's a ton of quick and easy all around here, it's just that most of it is ONLY accessible by foot. There are food trucks galore, and random taco spots that will blow you away. Get a bangin' breakfast at Café Lift—the atmosphere is casual, the food is crazy decadent, and the space is rarely crowded.

Coffee

- **Dunkin' Donuts** · 1500 Spring Garden St
- **Dunkin' Donuts** · 839 N Broad St
- **Dunkin' Donuts** · 917 W Girard Ave
- **WB's Cafe** · 990 Spring Garden St

Copy Shops

- **Docucare Copy Service** · 900 N Broad St
- **US Copy Center** · 1541 Spring Garden St

Hardware Stores

- **Kessler's Paint & Hardware** · 1204 W Girard Ave

Nightlife

- **The Institute** · 549 N 12th St
- **J & J Trestle Inn** · 339 N 11th St

Restaurants

- **Café Lift** · 428 N 13th St
- **City View Pizza** · 1547 Spring Garden St
- **Jose's Tacos** · 469 N 10th St
- **Osteria** · 640 N Broad St
- **Prohibition Taproom** · 501 N 13th St
- **Sazon** · 941 Spring Garden St
- **Westy's Tavern & Restaurant** · 1440 Callowhill St

Shopping

- **Diving Bell Scuba Shop** · 681 N Broad St
- **Philadelphia Tire & Auto** · 545 N Broad St

Map 19 • **Northern Liberties**

Northern Liberties might be getting too hip for its own good—and it doesn't help when people call it "NoLibs." The post-hip yuppie types are moving in and rents are going up up up. Don't let that scare you, though—it's still a great 'hood.

Banks

- **PNC** · N 6th St & Spring Garden St
- **Third Federal** · 905 N 2nd St
- **Third Federal** · 136 W Girard Ave
- **Wachovia** · 2 W Girard Ave

Car Rental

- **Enterprise** · 510 N Front St
- **Rent-A-Wreck** · 959 N 8th St

Community Gardens

Gas Stations

- **Citgo** · 959 N 8th St

Landmarks

- **Edgar Allen Poe National Historic Site** · 532 N 7th St
- **Liberty Lands Park** · 3rd St & Poplar St
- **St John Neumann Shrine** · 1019 N 5th St

Libraries

- **Ramonita de Rodriguez Branch** · 600 W Girard Ave

Pharmacies

- **Get Well Pharmacy** · 708 W Girard Ave
- **Rite-Aid** · 339 Spring Garden St

Schools

- **Bodine High** · 1101 N 4th St
- **Kearny** · 601 Fairmount Ave
- **St Peter the Apostle** · 1009 N 5th St

Supermarkets

- **Palm Tree Market** · 717 N 2nd St
- **Spring Garden Market** · 400 Spring Garden St

N

1

2

E Jefferson St

N Lee St

E Girard Ave

Sharswood St

Harlan St

Master St

Marshall St

W Thompson St

W Stiles St

E Girard Ave

Cambridge St

Cambridge St

20

E Poplar St

Edward St

Girard

18

Parrish St

St John Neumann

W George St

W Wildey St

W Wildey St

Poliard St

Pollard St

95

E Allen St

Fairmount Ave

Green Ct

Reno St

W Laurel St

Cozzens Pl

E Poplar St

Olive St

Oldham

New Market St

Fairmount Ave

Wallace St

Green St

Rains Ct

Philip St

Spring Garden St

Edgar Allan Poe
National
Historic Site

600

Spring
Garden

Noble St

N Beach St

N Columbus Blvd

Front St

Delaware
River

Noble St

Willow St

B

Callowhill St

Exit 17 / I-95

Exit 17 / I-95

3

Vine St

Wood St

York St

4

Exit US
Hwy 30

Exit N 8th St

Exit N 5th St

30

New St

Florist St

N Columbus Blvd

N Water St

**PAGE
132**

Race St

Independence
National
Historic
Park

Quarry St

Cherry St

S Isers Ct

Elfreths Aly

Appletree

Benjamin Franklin Bridge

676

1/4 mile

.25 km

The New Jerseyites have Delaware Avenue, and the hipsters and down-to-earth beer lovers carve their nightlife niche in Northern Liberties (although those darn suburbanites are creeping in). The Standard Tap is still the OG for local beer on, well, tap; and Bar Ferdinand and Modo Mio are the best date-night spots.

☕ Coffee

- **Coffee House** · 113 W Girard Ave
- **Dunkin' Donuts** · 329 Spring Garden St
- **Higher Grounds** · 631 N 3rd St
- **One Shot Coffee** · 1040 N 2nd St
- **The Random Tea Room and Curiosity Shop** · 713 N 4th St

🏋 Gyms

- **City Fitness** · 200 Spring Garden St
- **The Training Station** · 1033 N 2nd St

🍾 Liquor Stores

- **The Foodery** · 837 N 2nd St
- **State Liquor Store** · 232 W Girard Ave

🍸 Nightlife

- **700 Club** · 700 N 2nd St
- **The Abbaye** · 637 N 3rd St
- **The Barbary** · 951 Frankford Ave
- **Bar Ferdinand** · 1030 N 2nd St
- **Club Ozz** · 1155 N Front St
- **Electric Factory** · 421 N 7th St
- **Finnigan's Wake** · 547 N 3rd St
- **The Fire** · 412 W Girard Ave
- **The Foodery** · 837 N 2nd St
- **Johnny Brenda's** · 1201 Frankford Ave
- **Liberties** · 705 N 2nd St
- **The Manhattan Room** · 15 W Girard Ave
- **McFadden's** · 461 N 3rd St
- **North 3rd** · 801 N 3rd St
- **Palmer Social Club** · 601 Spring Garden St
- **Shampoo** · 417 N 8th St
- **Standard Tap** · 901 N 2nd St

🐾 Pet Shops

- **Chic Petique** · 1040 N 2nd St

🍴 Restaurants

- **A Full Plate** · 1009 N Bodine St
- **The Abbaye** · 637 N 3rd St
- **Bar Ferdinand** · 1030 N 2nd St
- **Cafe Estelle** · 444 N 4th St
- **Darling's** · 1033 N 2nd St
- **El Camino Real** · 1040 N 2nd St
- **The Foodery** · 837 N 2nd St
- **Green Eggs Cafe** · 719 N 2nd St
- **Hikari** · 1040 N American St
- **Home Slice** · 1030 N American St
- **Honey's Sit 'n Eat** · 800 N 4th St
- **Il Cantuccio** · 701 N 3rd St
- **Johnny Brenda's** · 1201 Frankford Ave
- **Koo Zee Doo** · 614 N 2nd St
- **Las Cazuelas** · 426 Girard Ave
- **Liberties** · 705 N 2nd St
- **Modo Mio** · 161 W Girard Ave
- **North 3rd** · 801 N 3rd St
- **The New Acropolis** · 1200 Frankford Ave
- **Paesano's** · 152 W Girard Ave
- **Pura Vida** · 527 Fairmount Ave
- **PYT** · 1050 N Hancock St
- **Radicchio** · 314 York Ave
- **Rustica Pizza** · 903 N 2nd St
- **Silk City Diner** · 435 Spring Garden St
- **Soy Café** · 630 N 2nd St
- **Standard Tap** · 901 N 2nd St
- **Tiffin** · 710 W Girard Ave

🛍 Shopping

- **Almanac Market** · 900 N 4th St
- **Art Star Gallery** · 623 N 2nd St
- **Brown Betty Dessert Boutique** · 1030 N 2nd St
- **City Planter** · 814 N 4th St
- **Delicious Boutique** · 1040 N American St #901
- **Euphoria** · 1001 N 2nd St
- **The Foodery** · 837 N 2nd St
- **Hansuey Music & Gifts** · 244 N Girard Ave
- **Jerusalem** · 115 W Girard Ave
- **The Little Candy Shoppe** · 1030 N American St
- **Northern Liberties Mailbox Store** · 630 N 3rd St
- **Palm Tree Market** · 717 N 3rd St
- **Quince Fine Foods** · 209 W Girard Ave
- **Random Tea Room** · 713 N 4th St
- **Reverie** · 205 N 2nd Ave
- **Spring Garden Market** · 400 Spring Garden St
- **Tequila Sunrise Records** · 525 W Giard Ave
- **Trax Foods** · 1204 N Front St
- **Very Bad Horse** · 1050 N Hancock St

Map 20 • Fishtown / Port Richmond

Long a working-class, European-immigrant area, Fishtown and Port Richmond are brimming with neighborhood bars and pride. This area has recently received a shot in the arm from downtown refugees seeking affordable first buys. Even though housing prices are shooting up in response, it remains a relatively affordable area.

$ Banks

- **Beneficial Savings** • 2500 Aramingo Ave
- **Citizens** • 2497 Aramingo Ave
- **PNC (ATM)** • Wawa • 2535 Aramingo Ave

Car Washes

- **New City Car Wash & Detail Center** • 1868 Frankford Ave

Cheesesteaks

- **Slack's Hoagie Shack** • 2499 Aramingo Ave

Community Gardens

Gas Stations

- **Exxon** • 2330 Aramingo Ave
- **Sunoco** • 2750 Aramingo Ave
- **Sunoco** • 2685 Frankford Ave
- **Wawa** • 2535 Aramingo Ave

Landmark

- **Penn Treaty Park** • E Columbia Ave & Delaware Ave
- **Philadelphia Brewing Company** • 2439 Amber St
- **Pop's Playground** • 2572 Collins St

Libraries

- **Fishtown Community Branch** • 1217 E Montgomery Ave
- **Kensington Branch** • 104 W Dauphin St

Pharmacies

- **CVS** • 2400 Aramingo Ave ℗
- **Friendly Pharmacy** • 2258 N Front St
- **Rite-Aid** • 2545 Aramingo Ave
- **Save-A-Lot** • 2132 E Lehigh Ave

Police

- **26th Police District** • Girard Ave & Montgomery Ave

Post Offices

- **Kensington** • 1602 Frankford Ave

Schools

- **Alexander Adaire** • 1300 E Palmer St
- **Bethel Baptist Academy** • 2210 Susquehanna Ave
- **Douglas High** • 2700 E Huntingdon St
- **HA Brown** • 1946 E Sergeant St
- **Hackett** • 2161 E York St
- **Holy Name of Jesus** • 1429 E Berks St
- **Kensington Culinary Arts** • 2463 Emerald St
- **Kensington High** • 2051 E Cumberland St
- **Mariana Bracetti Academy Charter** • 2501 Kensington Ave
- **Penn Middle** • 600 E Thompson St
- **St Anne** • Cedar St & E Tucker St
- **St Laurentius** • 1612 East Berks St

Supermarkets

- **Thriftway** • 2497 Aramingo Ave
- **Save-A-Lot** • 2132 E Lehigh Ave

Map 20 · **Fishtown / Port Richmond**

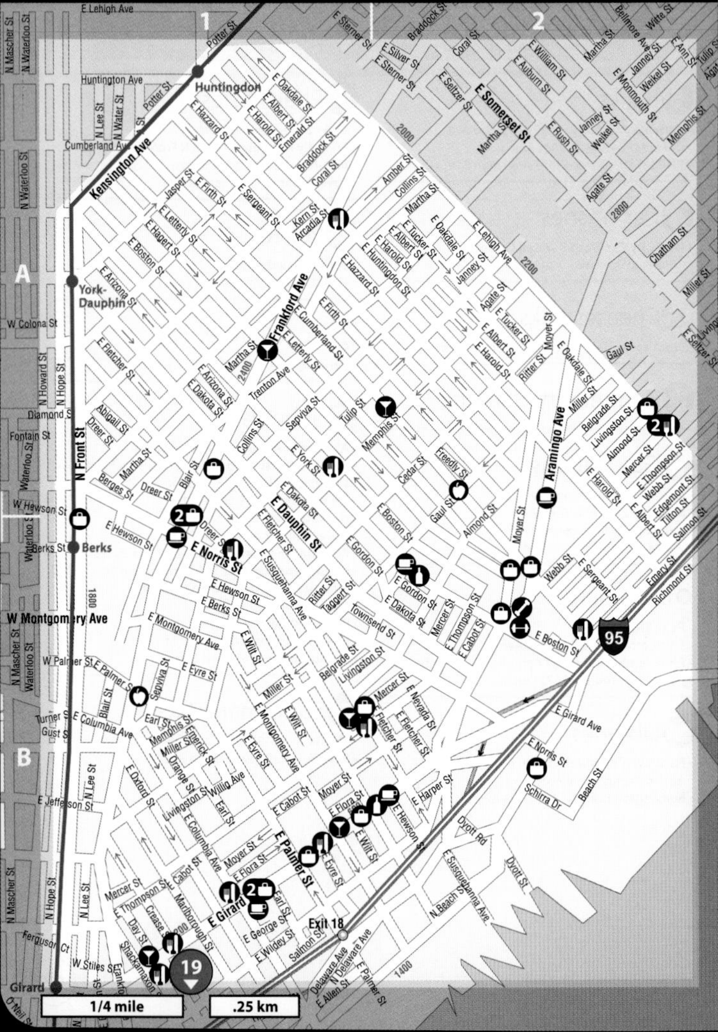

E Lehigh Ave

1

2

E Potter St

Huntington Ave

Huntingdon

E Oakdale St

E Somerset St

E Silver St

E Stephen St

E William St

E Auburn St

N Mascher St

N Waterloo St

N Lee St

N Water St

Palmer St

E Harold St

Emerald St

Braddock St

Coral St

Martha St

E Lehigh Ave

E Albert St

E Tucker St

Janney St

Cumberland Ave

Kensington Ave

E Firth St

Jasper St

E Letterly St

E Frith St

E Sergeant St

Kern St

Arcadia St

Collins St

Amber St

Martha St

E Dakota St

E Huntington St

Agate St

E Tucker St

E Albert St

2900

Chatham St

York-Dauphin

A

E Fletcher St

Memphis St

E Hazzard St

Frankford Ave

Tulip St

E Cumberland Ave

E Letterly St

Trenton Ave

2000

Sepviva St

E Albert St

E Harold St

Aramingo Ave

Gaul St

Ritner St

Moyer St

Oakdale St

Belgrade St

Livingston St

Almond St

Mercer St

E Thompson St

Edgemont St

Tilton St

E Harold St

Salmon St

Richmond St

W Colona St

N Howard St

N Hope St

W Hewson St

Diamond St

Fontain St

Waterloo St

N Front St

E Fletcher St

Abigail St

Orear St

Martha St

E Arizona St

E Dakota St

Collins St

Seviva St

Memphis St

E York St

Cedar St

Friendly St

Gaul St

Almond St

Webb St

E Sergeant St

Emory St

W Hewson St

Berks

E Hewson St

Orear St

Blair St

E Fletcher St

Thompson St

E Gordon St

Moyer St

E Cabot St

E Boston St

95

Berks St

2

E Norris St

E Boston St

B

W Montgomery Ave

N Mascher St

N Howard St

N Hope St

W Palmer St

Turner St

Gust St

E Columbia Ave

Earl St

Memphis St

E Berks St

E Hewson St

E Montgomery Ave

E Berks St

Willie St

Belgrade St

Miller St

E Montgomery Ave

Mercer St

Tulip St

Thompson St

E Dakota St

Townsend St

Livingston St

E Girard Ave

E Norris St

Schirra Dr

Beach St

W Jefferson St

E Jefferson St

N Mascher St

N Lee St

E Oxford St

Miller St

Crease St

E Columbia Ave

Willig Ave

E Cabot St

Moyer St

E Flora St

E Willi St

E Harper St

E Hewson St

Bean St

E Girard Ave

Gunner's Run

E Norris St

Dyott Rd

19

Mercer St

N Hope St

E Thompson St

Crease St

Manheim St

E Girard

W Stiles St

E George St

E Wildey St

E Palmer St

Eyre St

Salmon St

Exit 18

Delaware Ave

N Beach St

1400

Girard

Ferguson Ct

W Stiles St

1/4 mile

.25 km

Ida Mae's is a must for any self-respecting pancake lover. Tacconelli's serves up perfect pizza. Memphis Taproom has an incredible list of brews (and vegan eats). Caffeine up at Rocket Cat Cafe.

Coffee

- **Coffee House Too** • 2514 E York St
- **Dunkin' Donuts** • 717 E Girard Ave
- **Dunkin' Donuts** • 2530 Aramingo Ave
- **Milkcrate Cafe** • 400 E Girard Ave
- **Rocket Cat Cafe** • 2001 Frankford Ave

Farmers Markets

- **Greensgrow Market Stand (Jun–Nov; Thurs, 12 pm–7 pm; Fri 10 am–5 pm; Sat & Sun, 10 am–3 pm)** • 2501 E Cumberland St
- **Palmer Park (Jun to Oct; Thurs, 2 pm–6 pm)** • Frankford Ave & E Palmer St

Gyms

- **City Fitness** • 200 Spring Garden St
- **Planet Fitness** • 2641 E York St
- **The Training Station** • 1033 N 2nd St

Liquor Stores

- **Beer City** • 701 E Girard Ave
- **Philadelphia Beer Company** • 2525 E York St

Nightlife

- **Atlantis the Lost Bar** • 2442 Frankford Ave
- **Kraftwork** • 541 E Girard Ave
- **Les & Doreen's Happy Tap Kitchen** • 1301 E Susquehanna Ave
- **Memphis Taproom** • 2331 E Cumberland St
- **Murph's Bar** • 202 E Girard Ave

Pet Shops

- **Accent On Animals** • 2425 Aramingo Ave

Restaurants

- **Best Deli & Pizza** • 2616 E Lehigh Ave
- **Ekta** • 250 E Girard Ave
- **Father & Sons Pizza & Pasta** • 2500 Frankford Ave
- **Fathom Seafood House** • 200 E Girard Ave
- **Ida Mae's Bruncherie** • 2302 E Norris St
- **Jovan's Place** • 2327 E York St
- **Les & Doreen's Happy Tap Kitchen** • 1301 E Susquehanna Ave
- **Sketch** • 413 E Girard Ave
- **Stock's Bakery** • 2614 E Lehigh Ave
- **Sulimay's Restaurant** • 632 E Girard Ave
- **Tacconelli's Pizza** • 2604 E Somerset St

Shopping

- **Circle Thrift** • 2007 Frankford Ave
- **DiPinto Guitars** • 407 E Girard Ave
- **Dollar Plus Party Fair** • 2415 E Lehigh Ave
- **Jay's Pedal Power** • 512 E Girard Ave #12
- **Little Shop of Treasures** • 419 E Girard Ave
- **Scoops** • 812 E Thompson St
- **Stocks Bakery** • 2614 E Lehigh Ave
- **Thrift Fair** • 2403 Aramingo Ave
- **Thriftway** • 2497 Aramingo Ave

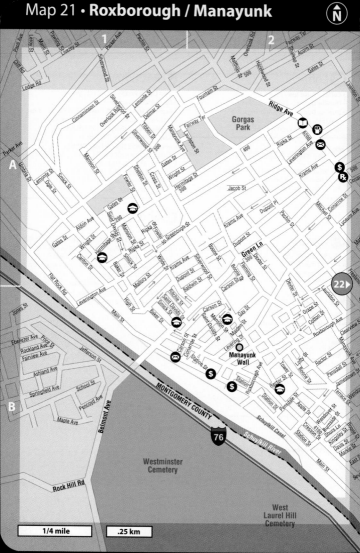

Referred to mostly—particularly by landlords—as just "Manayunk," this area is synonymous with Main Street—where young, post-collegiate pals and gals can be seen biking down the Tow Path, boozing in the evening hours, and spicing up their prep with a splotch of chintz. The nation's largest agricultural high school—W.B. Saul—is nearby on Henry Avenue.

$ Banks

- **Citizens (ATM)** • 4354 Main St
- **TD Banknorth** • 4312 Main St
- **Wachovia** • 6128 Ridge Ave

Gas Stations

- **Sunoco** • 6201 Ridge Ave

Landmarks

- **Manayunk** • Levering St

Libraries

- **Roxborough Branch** • 6245 Ridge Ave

Pharmacies

- **Morrison Pharmacy** • 6113 Ridge Ave

Post Offices

- **Manayunk** • 4431 Main St
- **Roxborough Postal Store** • 6184 Ridge Ave

Schools

- **Dobson** • 4667 Umbria St
- **Holy Family Parish Elementary** • 242 Hermitage St
- **St John the Baptist** • 119 Rector St
- **St Lucy** • 146 Green Ln
- **St Mary of Assumption** • 171 Conarroe St

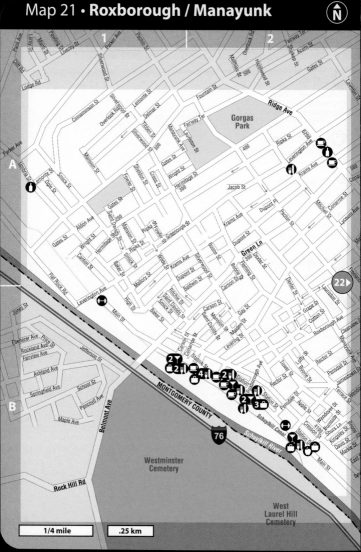

Map 21 • **Roxborough / Manayunk**

You'll either love everything or detest most of it. But either way, for the love of burritos, please visit Adobe, one of the city's best Mexican spots. Not into Mexican? Join the post-frat party downtown, or visit the array of toned-down furniture stores and maternity shops, which give big clues to who really lives here----nesting grown ups.

Coffee

- **Crossroads Coffee House** · 6156 Ridge Ave
- **Dunkin' Donuts** · 6191 Ridge Ave
- **La Colombe Torrefaction** · 4360 Main St
- **Mugshots** · 110 Cotton St

Farmers Markets

- **Manyunk (Wed–Sun; 8 am–7 pm)** · 4120 Main St
- **Roxborough (Jun–Oct; Fri, 2 pm–6 pm)** · Ridge Ave & Leverington Ave

Gyms

- **Curves (women only)** · 4590 Main St
- **Sweat** · 4151 Main St

Liquor Stores

- **Javies Beverages** · 4901 Umbria St
- **State Liquor Store** · 6174 Ridge Ave

Nightlife

- **Agiato** · 4359 Main St
- **Bayou Bar and Grill** · 4245 Main St
- **Bourbon Blue** · 2 Rector St
- **Castle Roxx Café** · 105 Shurs Ln
- **Flat Rock Saloon** · 4301 Main St
- **The Grape Room** · 105 Grape St
- **Kildare's** · 4417 Main St
- **Manyunk Brewery and Restaurant** · 4120 Main St
- **Pitchers Pub** · 4326 Main St

Restaurants

- **Adobe Cafe** · 4550 Mitchell St
- **Chabaa Thai Bistro** · 4371 Main St
- **Couch Tomato Café** · 102 Rector St
- **Dairyland** · 4409 Main St
- **Hikaru** · 4348 Main St
- **Il Tartufo** · 4341 Main St
- **Jake's** · 4365 Main St
- **Kildare's** · 4417 Main St
- **La Colombe Torrefaction** · 4360 Main St
- **Le Bus** · 4266 Main St
- **Manayunk Brewery & Restaurant** · 4120 Main St
- **Mom's Bake at Home Pizza** · 4452 Main St
- **Mugshots** · 110 Cotton St
- **Zesty's** · 4382 Main St

Shopping

- **Main St Music** · 4444 Main St
- **Pompanoosuc** · 4120 Main St
- **Pottery Barn** · 4230 Main St
- **Restoration Hardware** · 4130 Main St
- **VAMP Consignment** · 4231 Main St
- **Worn Yesterday** · 4235 Main St

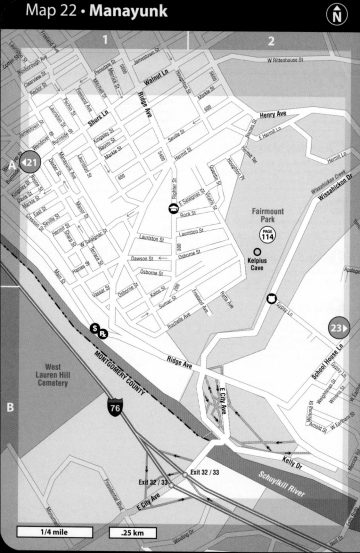

An ever-popular area to live for its simultaneous access to downtown and to nature, every third person here is wearing spandex and is on their way to the Wissahickon Trail. More residentially-oriented than upper Main Street, there's more room to breathe and less rent to pay.

$ Bank
• **Sovereign (ATM)** • 3780 Main St

○ Landmarks
• **Kelpius Cave** • Sumac St & Wissahickon Park

Ⓡ Pharmacies
• **CVS** • 3780 Main St

⬤ Police
• **92nd Police District** • Lincoln Dr & Gypsy Ln

⬢ Schools
• **Cook-Wissahickon** • 201 E Salaignac St

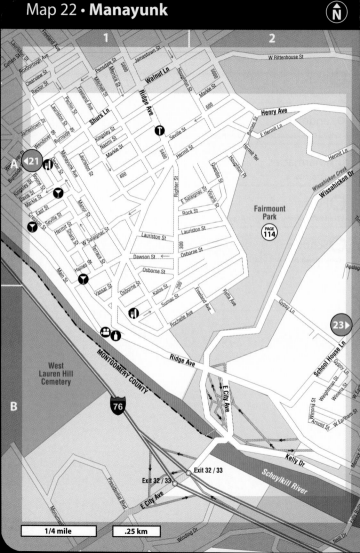

Sundries / Entertainment

While it's far easier to walk the couple blocks into our Map 21 than to look for stuff to do in old Map 22, if you must, there's the decidedly casual Dawson Street Pub, as well as pleasant movie-going at the United Artists Main Street 6. Or just stroll the hills and enjoy the views.

Hardware Stores
- **Stanley's Hardware** • 5555 Ridge Ave

Liquor Stores
- **State Liquor Store** • 3720 Main St

Movie Theaters
- **United Artists Main St 6** • 3720 Main St

Nightlife
- **Dawson Street Pub** • 100 Dawson St
- **Old Eagle Tavern** • 3938 Terrace St
- **Vaccarelli's East End Tavern** • 4001 Cresson St

Restaurants
- **Terrace Street Bistro** • 3989 Terrace St
- **Urban Cafe** • 5109 Rochelle Ave

Map 23 • **East Falls**

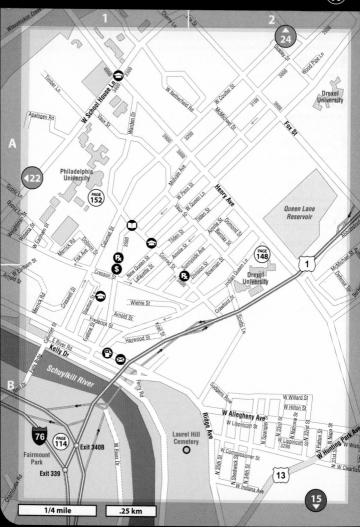

Close to Center City while preserving a country feeling, East Falls has been home to many famous Philadelphians. Grace Kelly lived here before that whole princess gig came up, for example. A short drive away from the main goings-on, the perks are proximity to River Drive for a run and owning your own delightful, ivy-covered chunk of yesteryear.

$ Banks

• **National Penn** • 3617 Midvale Ave

Gas Stations

• **Sunoco** • 4168 Ridge Ave

Landmarks

• **Laurel Hill Cemetery** • 3822 Ridge Ave

Libraries

• **Falls of Schuylkill Branch** • 3501 Midvale Ave

Pharmacies

• **Falls Pharmacy** • 3421 Conrad St
• **Rite-Aid** • 3601 Midvale Ave

Post Offices

• **East Falls** • 4130 Ridge Ave

Schools

• **Mifflin** • 3624 Conrad St
• **Philadelphia University** •
  School House Ln & Henry Ave
• **Randolph Career Academy** • 3101 Henry Ave
• **St Bridget Elementary** • 3636 Stanton St

Map 23 · **East Falls**

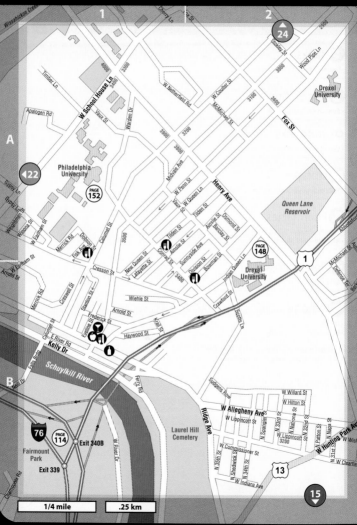

Not a hotspot by any means, nature lovers and families are more suited for the area. The number of restaurants remains small, though the food is generally good, and Falls Taproom is a good place to grab a beer. Laurel Hill Cemetery offers tours during the fall and quaint-yet-drunken parties at various points in the year.

Farmers Markets

· **East Falls (Jun–Oct; Fri, 3:30 pm–7 pm)** ·
  Midvale Ave & Ridge Ave

Liquor Stores

· **State Liquor Store** · 4177 Ridge Ave

Nightlife

· **Falls Taproom** · 3749 Midvale Ave

Restaurants

· **Brothers Old Style Deli** · 3492 Tilden St
· **Epicure Cafe** · 3401 Conrad St
· **Frank's Pizza** · 3600 Fisk Ave
· **Johnny Manana's** · 4201 Ridge Ave

Map 24 · **Germantown South**

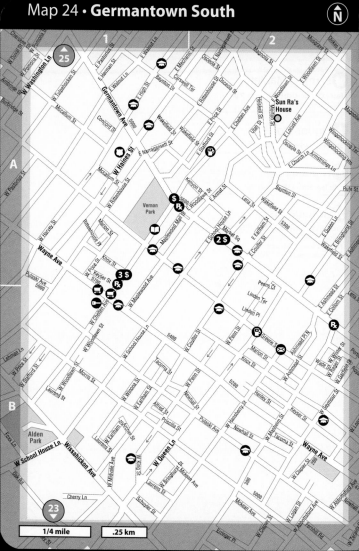

The area was drained in the early nineties by white flight, and ever since has been regrouping into what most of us would call a block-by-block neighborhood. But what gorgeous blocks they can be—full of history (check out Rittenhouse Town), bursting greenery, and some very cool people.

Banks

- **Bank of America (ATM)** • Pathmark • 176 W Chelten Ave
- **Citizens** • 5500 Germantown Ave
- **PNC** • 150 W Chelten Ave
- **PNC (ATM)** • Walgreens • 5627 Germantown Ave
- **United Bank of Philadelphia (ATM)** • Rite Aid • 160 W Chelten Ave
- **Wachovia** • 5458 Germantown Ave

Car Rental

- **Enterprise** • 217 W Chelten Ave

Gas Stations

- **Hess** • 102 E Chelten Ave
- **Sunoco** • 100 W Queen Ln

Landmarks

- **Sun Ra's House** • 5626 Morton St

Libraries

- **Joseph E Coleman Branch** • 68 W Chelten Ave

Pharmacies

- **Germantown Pharmacy** • 5100 Germantown Ave
- **Rite-Aid** • 164 W Chelten Ave
- **Walgreens** • 5627 Germantown Ave

Police

- **14th Police District** • 43 W Haines St

Post Offices

- **Germantown** • 5209 Greene St

Schools

- **Greene Street Friends** • 5511 Greene St
- **Eagle's Nest Christian Academy** • 501 W King St
- **Filter Academics Plus** • 140 W Seymour St
- **Fulton** • 60 E Haines St
- **Germantown Friends** • 31 W Coulter St
- **Germantown High** • 40 E High St
- **High Street Christian Academy** • 222 East High St
- **Hope Charter** • 100 W Coulter St
- **Imani Educational Circle Charter** • 5612 Greene St
- **Kelly** • 5116 Pulaski Ave
- **Pickett Middle** • 5700 Wayne Ave
- **St Barnabas Episcopal** • 5421 Germantown Ave
- **Wister** • 67 E Bringhurst St

Supermarkets

- **Pathmark** • 176 W Chelten Ave
- **Save-A-Lot** • 5753 Wayne Ave

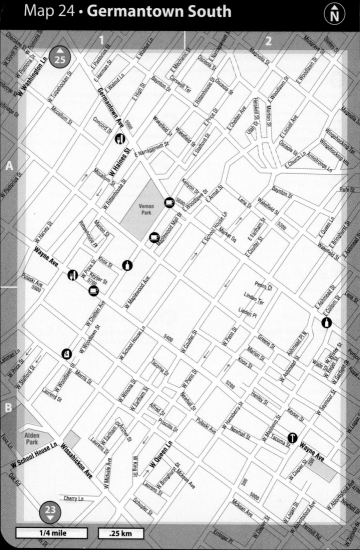

Map 24 · Germantown South

N

while not the eating empire that resides slightly further north, this section of Germantown can still boast of an eclectic mix of possibilities, from sublime (Dahlak's Ethiopian fare) to fascinating (K&J's Caribbean-flavored diner of Americana) and beyond (House of Jin's mix of Asian cooking and jazz).

Coffee

- **Dunkin' Donuts** • 5701 Germantown Ave
- **Dunkin' Donuts** • 5753 Wayne Ave
- **The Flower Café at Linda's** •
  48 W Maplewood Mall

Copy Shops

- **Cogan Blue Prints** • 326 W Chelten Ave

Hardware Stores

- **Kane & Brown Hardware** • 5011 Wayne Ave

Liquor Stores

- **State Liquor Store** • 135 W Chelten Ave
- **State Liquor Store** • 5113 Germantown Ave

Restaurants

- **Aprons** • 5946 Germantown Ave
- **Dahlak** • 5547 Germantown Ave
- **House of Jin** • 234-36 W Chelten Ave
- **K&J Caribbean and American Diner** •
  5603 Greene St
- **The Urban Cafe** • 5815 Wayne Ave

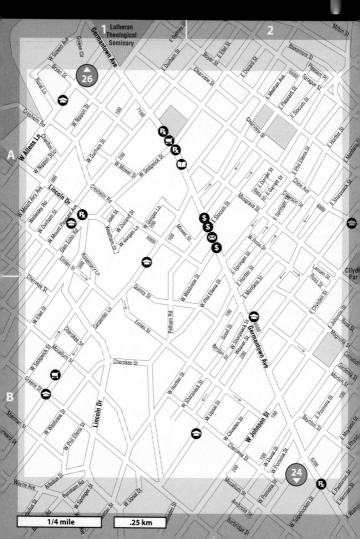

An urban miracle—roving properties rich in trees, ivy-grazed mansions with Obama signs in the windows, and it's minutes away from downtown. Lesbians and likeminded progressives build their grassy roots here—and don't forget to send your kids to Quaker school!

$ Banks

- **Philadelphia Federal Credit Union** ·
  6707 Germantown Ave
- **Sovereign** · 6740 Germantown Ave

Libraries

- **Lovett Branch** · 6945 Germantown Ave

Pharmacies

- **Acme** · 7010 Germantown Ave
- **Cooperman's Pharmacy** · 7060 Germantown Ave
- **CVS** · 7065 Lincoln Dr
- **Rite-Aid** · 6201 Germantown Ave

Post Offices

- **Mount Airy Postal Store** · 6711 Germantown Ave

Schools

- **Blair Christian Academy** · 220 W Upsal St
- **Cecilian Academy** · 144 Carpenter Ln
- **Emlen** · 6501 Chew Ave
- **Henry** · 601 Carpenter Ln
- **Houston** · 135 W Allens Ln
- **Project Learn** · 6525 Germantown Ave
- **Revival Hill Christian High** ·
  322 W Mt Pleasant Ave

Supermarkets

- **Acme** · 7010 Germantown Ave
- **Weaver's Way Co-op** · 559 Carpenter Ln

Map 25 · **Germantown North**

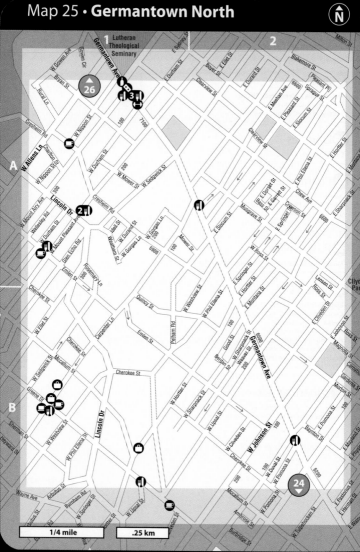

Weaver's Way Co-op is the place to see, be seen and work, and the other businesses nearby—the High Point Café and the excellent progressive bookstore, Big Blue Marble—make it the coziest nook in the area.

Coffee

- **High Point Cafe** · 7210 Cresheim Rd
- **High Point Cafe** · 602 Carpenter Ln
- **InFusion Coffee & Tea** · 7133 Germantown Ave
- **Point of Destination** · 6460 Greene St

Gyms

- **FitLife** · 7140 Germantown Ave

Liquor Stores

- **State Liquor Store** · 7204 Germantown Ave

Restaurants

- **Bacio** · 311 W Mt Pleasant Ave
- **Chef Ken's Café** · 7135 Germantown Ave
- **Earth Bread + Brewery** · 7136 Germantown Ave
- **Geechee Girl Riece Cafe** · 6825 Germantown Ave
- **Golden Crust Pizza** · 7155 Germantown Ave
- **High Point Café** · 602 Carpenter Ln
- **Lincoln Pizzeria** · 277 W Mt Pleasant Ave
- **Mi Puebla Restaurant** · 7157 Germantown Ave
- **Rib Crib** · 6333 Germantown Ave
- **Tiffin** · 7105 Emlen St
- **Toto's Pizzeria** · 6555 Greene St
- **Umbria** · 7131 Germantown Ave

Shopping

- **Big Blue Marble Bookstore** · 551 Carpenter Ln
- **Joa Mart** · 361 W Hortter St
- **Weaver's Way Co-op** · 559 Carpenter Ln

Video Rental

- **Video Library** · 7139 Germantown Ave

Map 26 • **Mt Airy**

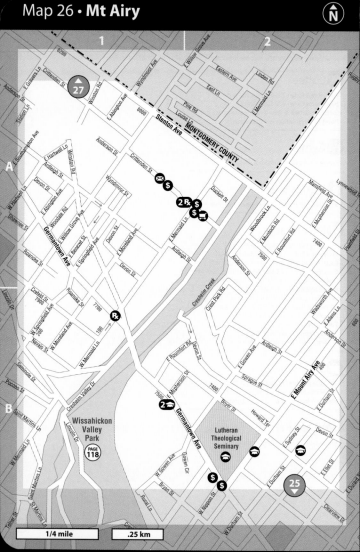

More of that roving greenery can be found here, giving way (resplendently) to choice shopping on Germantown Avenue. There is a large and welcoming gay/lesbian contingency, as well as traditional families and young couples. Not surprisingly, it's becoming more difficult to buy a house here, since nobody wants to sell.

$ Banks

- **Bank of America** • 7167 Germantown Ave
- **Citizens** • 7700 Crittenden St
- **PNC (ATM)** • Wawa • 7236 Germantown Ave
- **PNC (ATM)** • Super Fresh •
  E Mermaid Ln & Crittendon St
- **Wachovia** • 7782 Crittenden St

R Pharmacies

- **CVS** • 7700 Germantown Ave
- **Pathmark** • 7700 Crittenden St
- **Rite-Aid** • 7700 Crittenden St

Post Offices

- **Market Square** • 7782 Crittenden St

Schools

- **Holy Cross Parish** • 144 E Mount Airy Ave
- **Islamic Day School of Philadelphia** •
  222 E Durham St
- **Lutheran Theological Seminary** •
  7301 Germantown Ave
- **Parkway-Northwest** • 7500 Germantown Ave
- **The Waldorf School of Philadelphia** •
  7500 Germantown Ave

Supermarkets

- **Super Fresh** • Mermaid Ln & Crittendon

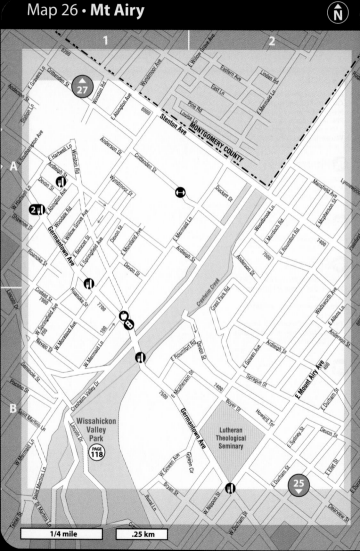

Map 26 · Mt Airy

In keeping with the eclectic nature of the population here, you can find all kinds of innovative and delicious cuisine, including CinCin's popular Chinese fare and North by Northwest's winning mix of soul food and jazz. But perhaps the area's most emblematic joint, Cafette, follows its bohemian roots with a varied menu and outdoor sculpture garden.

 Farmers Markets

- **Chestnut Hill Growers Market (Sat, 9:30 am–1:30 pm, through Oct)** • Winston Rd & Germantown Ave

Gyms

- **Curves (women only)** • 7733 Crittenden St

Restaurants

- **Bredenbeck's Bakery & Ice Cream Parlor** • 8126 Germantown Ave
- **Cafette** • 8136 Ardleigh St
- **CinCin** • 7838 Germantown Ave
- **North by Northwest** • 7165 Germantown Ave
- **Roller's Restaurant at Flying Fish** • 8142 Germantown Ave
- **Trolley Car Diner** • 7619 Germantown Ave

Video Rental

- **TLA Video** • 7630 Germantown Ave

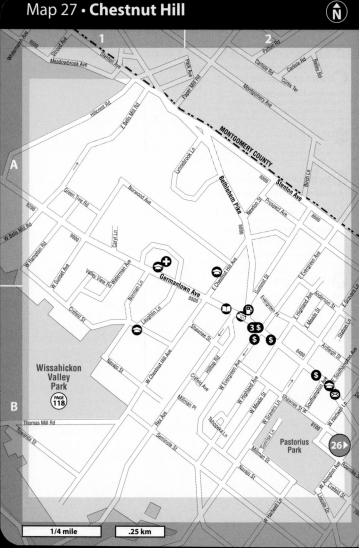

Map 27 · Chestnut Hill

N

1

2

Whitemarsh Ave 9500
Stroud Ave
Stenton Ave
Meadowbrook Ave
Patton Rd
Carlisle Rd
Carlisle Rd
Bailey Rd
Curtis Ter
Park Ave Rd
Paper Mill Rd
Montgomery Ave

Hillcrest Rd
E Bells Mill Rd
Lynnebrook Ln

MONTGOMERY COUNTY

A

Green Tree Rd
Norwood Ave
Bethlehem Pike
8800
Newton St
Prospect Ave
8600
Birch Ln
Stenton Ave

W Bells Mill Rd
9200
W Hampton Rd
9000
Caryl Ln
Valley View Rd
Waterman Rd
Norman Ln
W Sunset Ave
Crefeld St
Laughlin Ln
Germantown Ave
8900
E Chestnut Hill Ave
Summit St
Evergreen Pl
E Evergreen Ave
E Highland Ave
E Meade St
Anderson St
E Gravers Ln
Station Ln

Shawnee St
Hilltop Rd
W Chestnut Hill Ave
Navajo St
3 $
$
$
$
8400
Ardleigh St
W Southampton Ave

Wissahickon
Valley
Park
PAGE
118

B

Thomas Mill Rd
Towanda St
Rex Ave
Crefeld Ave
Millman Pl
Seminole St
Navajo St
Tohickon Ln
W Evergreen Ave
W Highland Ave
W Meade St
W Gravers Ln
Seminole Ln
Millman St
Shawnee St
W Southampton Ave
W Hartwell Ln

8100

Pastorius
Park
26

W Abington Ave
Crefeld Ln
Roanoke Ln
Lincoln Dr
W Hartwell Ln

| 1/4 mile | .25 km |

Our liberal baby boomers' most prized possession, the Hill is a cobblestone mix of New England-esque shopping (white, cute, and useless) with breaks along the way for some exceptional eats. The beautiful old houses with gardens that tumble onto the sidewalk will inspire you to get your stroll on.

$ Banks

· **Bank of America** · 8601 Germantown Ave
· **Citizens** · 8616 Germantown Ave
· **National Penn** · 9 W Evergreen Ave
· **PNC** · 8340 Germantown Ave
· **Sovereign** · 8623 Germantown Ave
· **Wachovia** · 8527 Germantown Ave

Cheesesteaks

· **McNally's Tavern** · 8634 Germantown Ave

+ Emergency Rooms

· **Chestnut Hill** · 8835 Germantown Ave ℗

Gas Stations

· **Sunoco** · 10 Bethlehem Pike St

Libraries

· **Chestnut Hill Branch** · 8711 Germantown Ave

Post Offices

· **Chestnut Hill** · 8227 Germantown Ave

Schools

· **The Crefeld School** · 8836 Crefeld St
· **Jenks** · 8301 Germantown Ave
· **Norwood-Fontbonne Academy** ·
  8891 Germantown Ave
· **Our Mother-Consolation** · 17 E Chestnut Hill Ave

Map 27 · Chestnut Hill

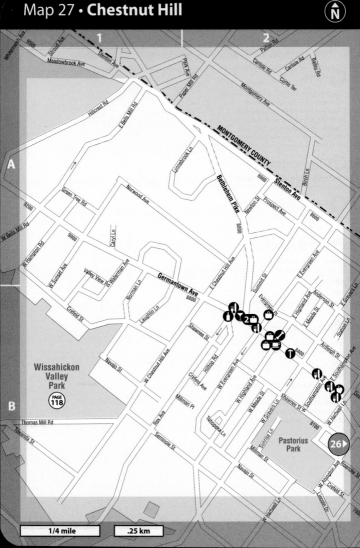

With quaint cobblestones and long-existing shops that sell re-imagined kitsch (or art gunk), it's New England without ever leaving Philly. The Chestnut Grill is a great place to grab outdoor seating when the weather's right. Hippie-goods favorite Mango, meanwhile, is a must, and there's a Metropolitan Bakery up here too, because seriously, where is their bread not in Philly?

Coffee

- **Chestnut Hill Coffee Co** · 8620 Germantown Ave
- **Starbucks** · 8515 Germantown Ave

Farmers Markets

- **Chestnut Hill Farmers Market (Thurs & Fri; 9 am–6 pm; Sat, 8 am–5 pm)** · 8229 Germantown Ave

Hardware Stores

- **Kilian Hardware** · 8450 Germantown Ave

Liquor Stores

- **State Liquor Store** · 8705 Germantown Ave

Nightlife

- **McNally's Tavern** · 8634 Germantown Ave

Pet Shops

- **Bone Appetit K9 Bakery** · 8505 Germantown Ave

Restaurants

- **Campbell's Place** · 8337 Germantown Ave
- **Chestnut Grill & Sidewalk Cafe** · 8229 Germantown Ave
- **Chestnut Hill Coffee Co** · 8620 Germantown Ave
- **Metropolitan Bakery** · 8607 Germantown Ave
- **Thai Kuu** · 35 Bethlehem Pike

Shopping

- **Cake** · 184 E Evergreen Ave
- **Chestnut Hill Cheese Shop** · 8509 Germantown Ave
- **Hideaway Music** · 8612 Germantown Ave
- **Kitchen Kapers** · 8530 Germantown Ave
- **Mango** · 8622 Germantown Ave

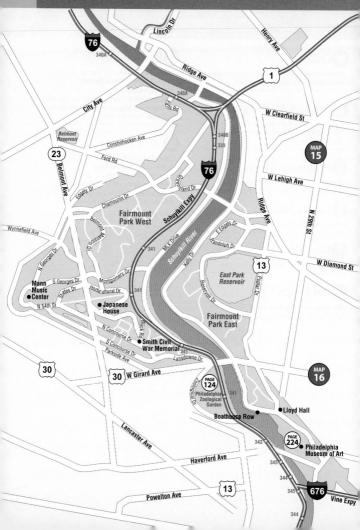

General Information

NFT Maps: 15 & 16
Address: 4231 N Concourse Dr
Philadelphia, PA 19131
Phone: 215-683-0200
Website: www.fairmountpark.org

Overview

Although all three major Philly parks (Fairmount Park, Wissahickon Valley Park, and Pennypack Creek Park) are part of the Fairmount Parks System, when we refer to "Fairmount Park" here, we mean only this particular section, not the entire sprawling Parks System. Okay? Okay.

Fairmount Park is where the sports fields are located. People usually go there to be active, whether it's playing in a softball league, jogging along Kelly Drive, or rowing on the Schuylkill. There's also a very popular free "disc golf" course near Strawberry Mansion. This park is not the place to go when you want to commune with nature, smoke an apple bong, or gulp home-stilled Kahlua. That said, the locals on the west side do throw some kickin' barbecues in summertime over at the Belmont Plateau.

Fairmount Park is also home to the Mann Center, the Philadelphia Museum of Art, the Japanese House, and the Smith Civil War Memorial (the place where the Statue of Liberty was supposed to end up).

The Drives

Kelly and MLK Drives make up what locals call "the Loop." (Until recently, MLK was known as West River Drive, and Kelly, somewhat less recently, as East River Drive. Locals sometimes go by the old names, so don't be confused by them.) The paved path that runs along these roads on the east and west banks of the Schuylkill River is 8.4 miles if you cross the river at the Falls Bridge and loop back to the beginning. The trail (happily separated from the curvy road, where idiots tend to drive way too fast) is Philly's somewhat misbegotten answer to South Beach: there are lots of expertly fit, hot-assed singles giving each other the long once-over as they pass (and sometimes barely avoiding smashing into each other) on bike, blades, or foot. On Saturdays and Sunday from April to October, most of MLK Drive is closed to cars between 8 am and 5 pm, giving walkers, cyclists, runners, skaters, and anyone else without an engine at their disposal open use of the road.

The Loop is also home to numerous runs, bike races, and regattas. If a few miles of open road are required for a race, you can bet at least some of it will occur here. It's also the host of charity walks like the annual AIDS Walk, the Walk for the Whisper (ovarian cancer), and Philadelphia Cares Day.

Boathouse Row

www.boathouserow.org
Just around the corner from the Art Museum, ten charming and colorful 19th-century Victorian structures comprise Boathouse Row, including the oldest rowing club in the country, Bachelor Barge Club, founded in 1853. It's definitely worth seeing the Row at night when the houses are lit like Whoville at Christmas. One of the best views, believe it or not, is from the Schuylkill Expressway— at least when you're stuck in traffic you'll have something nice to look at.

Lloyd Hall

1 Boathouse Row, Kelly Dr, 215-685-3936;
Hours vary by season
Open to the public, Lloyd Hall has a multi-purpose gym, lockers, and restrooms, making it a popular meeting place for those heading out on the Loop.

How to Get There—Driving

We can't tell you how to get to every spot in the park. It's over 1,000 acres with countless destinations. In general, if you want to get to the western section, take the MLK Drive. If you want to go to the eastern part, take Kelly Drive.

From I-95 to Fairmount Park East, take 676 W to the Ben Franklin Parkway exit. Make a left onto the parkway, then keep the Art Museum on your left, and you will end up on Kelly Drive. From I-95 to Fairmount Park West, do the same except once you're on the parkway, keep the Art Museum on your right (you have to go around Eakins Oval in front of the museum), and you'll end up on MLK Drive (unless you goof and end up on the Spring Garden Bridge or back on the Parkway heading towards the city).

From the west, take the Schuylkill (I-76) Eastbound For Fairmount Park East and get off at the exit for Lincoln Drive/Kelly Drive #340A. Stay in the left-hand lane to exit on Kelly Drive. For Fairmount Park West, take the Montgomery Avenue Exit #341. Go left at the bottom of the ramp, and you'll run into MLK Drive.

Parking

Parking depends entirely on where and when you visit the park. There are free parking lots scattered throughout, but on warm and sunny weekends, you'd better arrive early.

How to Get There—Mass Transit

Again, this really depends on where you want to go. Your best bet is to go to www.septa.com and click on the link for the "Plan My Trip" page. Addresses for most points in the Park can be found through the park's website.

General Information

Environmental Center Address: 8600A Verree Rd
  Philadelphia, PA 19115
Environmental Center Phone: 215-685-0470
Fairmount Park System Phone: 215-683-0200

Overview

Once used as hunting and fishing grounds by the Lenni-Lenape Indians, Pennypack Creek Park was established in 1905. Today, the 1,600 acres of woodlands, meadows, wetlands, and fields still provide a great habitat for wildlife: More than two hundred species of birds and a variety of native mammals, reptiles, and amphibians call Pennypack home (including the occasional rogue alligator). Located right in the middle of Philly's Northeast section, the park runs roughly from Huntingdon Pike all the way over to I-95 N. Hiking trails and biking trails (both off-road and paved) are filled with people walking their dogs and children.

A 65-acre stretch called Pennypack on the Delaware was added to the southern end of the park in 1998. New additions include a large recreational complex with soccer and softball fields, a paved path, fishing piers, picnic venues, and extraordinary views of the Delaware River.

Pennypack Environmental Center

8600 Verree Rd, 215-685-0470;
Surrounded by a bird sanctuary, the Pennypack Environmental Center on Verree Road is a massive historical and environmental information bank. In addition to the earthy animal displays, the center also has an Early America exhibit and a new 300-gallon aquarium. The resource library is open to the general public, but materials are not available for loan. The center is open weekdays from 9 am until 4 pm, and some weekends for special events.

Fox Chase Farm

8500 Pine Rd, 215-728-7900; www.foxchasefarm.org
Fox Chase Farm on Pine Road is the only remaining working farm in Philadelphia, and it doubles as a school campus. The farm is open to the general public only for special events and festivals, including the once-a-month Saturday Morning Open House. For a complete schedule of events, check the website or visit the Pennypack Environmental Center. Activities in the past have included tours of the farm and workshops in various crafts, wood working, ice cream churning, and flower pressing. Most of the activities cost $3 per person.

Friends of Pennypack Park

215-934-PARK; http://balford.com/fopp
While the budget for Pennypack Park has remained the same for the past two decades, many of the improvements to the park have been carried out by hundreds of local volunteers. The park is almost always crowded with the neighbors who have fallen in love with the park, and it's clear how much they care by the many trash cans, lack of garbage, and friendly passersby. The FOPP website has information about everything from the best place for wedding photos to why the dams have not been repaired to which musicians are playing during Pennypack Park's summer concert series.

How to Get There—Driving

The park is huge, and depending on where you want to go and what you want to see in the park, there are many entrances. From Center City Philadelphia, take I-95 N about five miles to the Bridge Street exit (Exit 27). Continue on Aramingo Avenue 0.3 miles to Harbison Avenue. Take Harbison for about two miles and turn right on East Roosevelt Avenue. Take East Roosevelt 1.7 miles to the park entrance. You can also take the Cottman and Rhawn Street exit off I-95, make a right on State Road, then a left on Rhawn Street take that for about 2 miles until the area turns green, then look for parking on side streets, or find the entrance on the left.

Parking

There is loads of free parking within the park, and on side streets around the park. Never fear because the PPA's evil clutch does not reach here, but police will ticket for normal violations.

How to Get There—Mass Transit

Many buses will take you close or into Pennypack Park, depending on which part of the park you're headed to. For the southeast side of the park, ride bus 10, 20, 14, or 77. To get to the northwest section and the Environmental Center, hop on the 67. For the northernmost tip of the park, take the 88.

By Regional Rail, take the R7 and get off at Holmesburg Junction at the southern end of the park. You can also take the R3 to Bethayres and walk a few minutes south to reach the northern end.

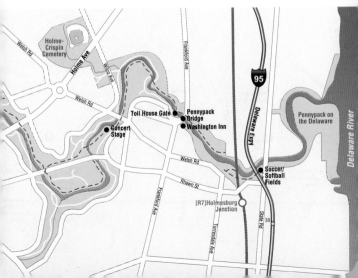

General Information

Environmental Center Address:
    300 Northwestern Ave
    Philadelphia, PA 19118
Environmental Center Phone:
    215-685-9285
Websites: www.fow.org
         www.fairmountpark.org

Overview

While Pennypack Park is deep trails and rolling hills, Wissahickon is huge cliffs and gorges where you can actually climb and feel challenged. Part of the massive Fairmount Parks System, the Wissahickon Valley consists of 1,800 acres of urban forest. While Fairmount Park East/West is known for its ball fields and recreational areas, just like Pennypack, the Wissahickon Valley offers Philadelphians the opportunity to really get back to nature.

The Park is also loaded with Wissahickon schist (that's a type of rock, for you non-geologists) and many varieties of trees, such as Lofty Hemlock, American White Elm, and Native Beech.

The valley is an ideal location for hiking, canoeing and kayaking, rock climbing, mountain biking, picnicking, ice skating, fishing, and horseback riding. (Permits are required to bicycle or ride horseback on all trails except Forbidden [Wissahickon] Drive.) The mountain bike trail is a 30-mile loop that swoops and drags over the terrain—many sections are fine for amateurs, but there are enough technical climbs and downhills to keep even experienced riders entertained.

Trail Highlights

Devil's Pool, once a spiritual area for the Lenape tribes, can be reached on foot from Valley Green by taking the footpath on the eastern bank and walking downstream to the mouth of Cresheim Creek. For a truly stunning view, take a walk to Lover's Leap. Enter the main footpath at the Ridge Avenue entrance and follow the west bank over to Hermit's Lane Bridge. You'll find yourself peering over a giant precipice to the gorge below. Legend has it the daughter of a mighty Indian chief and her lover plunged to their deaths in a desperate attempt to escape the woman's wily marital arrangement to an old chieftain.

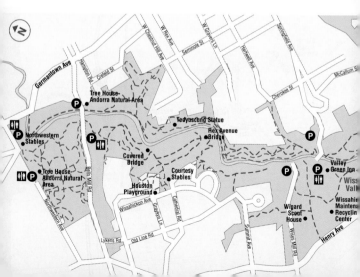

Maps of the Wissahickon trails (and other parts of the Fairmount Park system) can be printed for free on the Fairmount Park website, or you can purchase maps at the Wissahickon Park Environmental Center.

How to Get There—Driving

Park, big. Roads, many. In other words, it all depends on where you want to go. If you've never been to the Wissahickon Valley before, consider cruising up Lincoln Drive, which takes you right along part of the Wissahickon Creek. To get to Lincoln Drive from the Schuylkill/76, get off at Exit 340A Lincoln Drive/Kelly Drive. From the exit ramp, get in the middle lane and follow the signs for Lincoln Drive.

Henry Avenue is a good way to get to many points as well. From the Schuylkill/76, still get off at Exit 340A, but instead follow the signs for Ridge Avenue E (stay left, left, then left again). At the dead end, go right onto Ridge Avenue South Drive through three lights, then turn left on Midvale Avenue. Go through three lights again, and turn left on Henry Avenue. The Park runs along the right hand side of Henry Avenue.

Parking

It's not hard to find parking in the Wissahickon Valley Park. There are numerous locations throughout the park where parking is free.

How to Get There—Mass Transit

For the southern part of the park, take the R6 to Wissahickon Station or any of the buses that go through the Wissahickon Transit Center (1, 9, 27, 35, 38, 61, 65, 124, 125, R). The R-8 makes regular stops to the east of the park including Chelten Ave, Tulpehoken, Upsal, Carpenter Lane, Allen Lane, St Martins, Highland, and Chestnut Hill West. Using septa.com's "Plan My Trip" feature will help you find your way by public transportation.

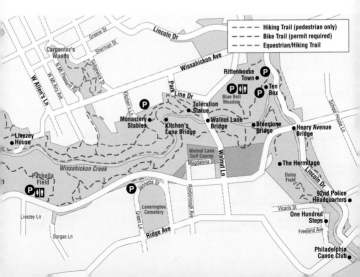

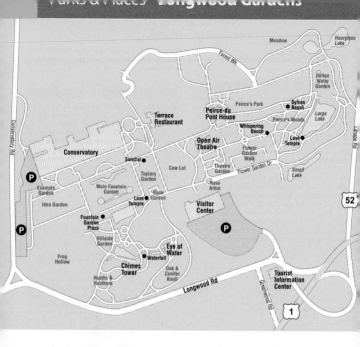

Meadow

Hourglass Lake

Forest Wk

Italian Water Garden

Terrace Restaurant

Peirce-du Pont House

Peirce's Park

Sylvan Bench

Whispering Bench

Peirce's Woods

Large Lake

Love Temple

Conservatory

Sundial

Open Air Theatre

Topiary Garden

Cow Lot

Theatre Garden

Flower Garden Walk

Flower Garden Dr

P

Example Garden

Main Fountain Garden

Rose Garden

Rose Arbor

Small Lake

Love Temple

52

Idea Garden

Visitor Center

P

Fountain Garden Plaza

Hillside Garden

Eye of Water

P

Frog Hollow

Waterfall

Chimes Tower

Oak & Conifer Knoll

Heaths & Heathers

Longwood Rd

Tourist Information Center

Greenwood Rd

1

Conservatory Rd

Lafrate Rd

Conservatory

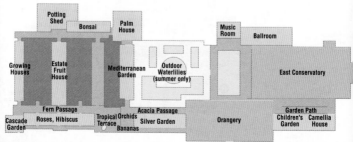

Potting Shed

Bonsai

Palm House

Music Room

Ballroom

Growing Houses

Estate Fruit House

Mediterranean Garden

Outdoor Waterlilies (summer only)

East Conservatory

Cascade Garden

Fern Passage

Roses, Hibiscus

Tropical Terrace

Bananas

Orchids

Silver Garden

Acacia Passage

Orangery

Garden Path

Children's Garden

Camellia House

General Information

Address:	1001 Longwood Rd
	Kennett Square, PA 19348
Phone:	610-388-1000
Website:	www.longwoodgardens.org
Hours:	Open daily from 9 am
	(closing time depends on season)
Admission:	Adults $18, Seniors (62+) $15,
	Students (5-22) $8, Children (under 4) free.
	Prices for performances vary.

Overview

If you're not into horticulture, you're probably not reading this. If you are, you'll be happy to learn that over 11,000 different types of plants grow at Longwood. We strongly urge you to look at their website, which includes dozens of pages dedicated to the gardens.

Although Longwood is sprawled over 1,050 acres, most visitors limit themselves to the impressive collection of forty outdoor gardens, indoor gardens, and heated greenhouses located within a 4-acre radius. Because of the wealth of wondrous plants, it's difficult to give all of them individual shout-outs, but we feel compelled to point out the breath-taking orchid display in the Conservatory. And the Bonsai exhibit. And the various banana trees. And the super-cool insect-catching plants display. And that's just the indoor plants. The fountains are also a huge draw year-round, with various water shows playing daily and special holiday presentations come Christmastime.

When you've had enough greenery, head inside the stately Du Pont House and check out the exhibits on the life of chemical magnate Pierre du Pont and those of his most prominent decendents. You can even listen to an audio clip of the "Du Pont Song", a rousing ditty that declares, in words a hundred years ahead of their time, "Du Pont is the man!" Indeed.

Eating

If you look in your wallet and exclaim, "There's just way too much money in here!" we recommend the Terrace Restaurant located next to the Conservatory. The cafeteria (in the same building) is a more reasonably priced dining option. If you enjoy a limited budget, you can always pack some food and eat it in the picnic area located outside of the gardens.

Pets

Service dogs are the only animals permitted at Longwood. There are no kennels or other pet-housing facilities, so no chance for Queenie to weigh anchor on the Italian Water Garden.

Annual Events

Every year Longwood features a variety of pretty spectacular events. We recommend checking the website for their current schedule, but here are some past celebrations that you can expect to see permutations of again:

Mid-January - Mid-March - Welcome Spring
Witness the early blooming stages of bulbs. Expect to see the classic daffodils and tulips as well as their more exotic relatives, like the blue poppy.

Mid-March - Early April - Easter Display
The conservatory is filled with over 1,000 lilies. Outside, bulbs tentatively press upward through the still thawing soil.

April & May - Acres of Spring
Outdoor color-fest with purple phlox, white foam flowers, and azaleas to die for.

June - September - Festival of Fountains
Visit the fountain gardens for concerts and water spectaculars, all while sitting surrounded by roses and water lilies. If you go to one event at Longwood all year, make it one of the "Fireworks & Fountains" evenings that are part of this festival. You haven't seen fireworks until you've seen rich people fireworks.

Mid-September - Early October – GardenFest
The garden railway takes visitors on a ride through the heritage trail, while experts point out autumn gourds and squash. The Gardens also host talks and demonstrations on the art of gardening.

October - Autumn's Colors
Indoor and outdoor gardens alike explode in shades of yellow, red, and gold. Local bands perform during the weekends.

November - Chrysanthemum Festival
See chrysanthemums in quantities and shapes that you've never seen before.

Late November - December – Christmas
400,000 tasteful decorative lights transform the gardens into a winter wonderland. Water and light shows set to music are staged in the Open-Air Theater.

How to Get There—Driving

From Philly and vicinity, take I-95 to Route 322 W (Exit 3A), to Route 1 S. Longwood is located just off Route 1 once you cross Route 52. Alternatively, take I-76 to I-476 S, to Route 1 S.

Parking

Free parking is available in the parking lot. On busy days, expect a short trek from your car to the visitor center. Accessible parking is located next to the visitor center but it fills up quickly; passenger drop-off at the visitor center is permitted.

How to Get There—Mass Transit

Become buddies with a car owner or join Philly Car Share. If your social skills suck or you don't have a license, take the R2 to Wilmington on SEPTA Regional Rail. From Center City to Wilmington, Delaware, you'll pay $6.25 one-way if you buy your ticket ahead of time, or $7 if you purchase it on the train. From there, you'll have to take a taxi or rent a car, since there is no regularly scheduled public transit to Longwood. Taxis run about $30 one-way. So, to recap: Septa = $12.50 round trip. Taxi = $60 round trip. Total = $71 + tip for cab driver. You make the call.

General Information

Websites: www.fairmountpark.org/squares.asp
www.ushistory.org/lovepark
www.clarkpark.info

Overview

When William Penn initially imagined the city of Philadelphia back in 1682, he pictured "a green country town" filled with lush trees and garden escapes. Penn envisaged multiple city squares that would provide a welcome retreat from the swirl of city activity—certainly an advanced method of city planning.

Each of the five city squares originally bore the names of their locations: Northeast, Northwest, Center, Southwest, and Southeast. Many decades later, in the nineteenth century, the parks were renamed after important historical figures. Aside from the five central squares, there are several other quaint neighborhood parks to wile away the time.

1. Logan Square

Logan Square, originally Northwest Square, was once the site of burial plots, pasturage, and public executions. In 1919, a French architect remodeled the square to include a large traffic circle with an area for gardens, monuments, and a memorial fountain. The fountain still serves as a memorial, but is most often used by hot children in the summertime as an impromptu public swimming area. Plenty of adult supervision is almost always at hand. If you happen to come by on the last day of school, you'll see a parade of girls from nearby Hallahan High School taking a traditional plunge, school uniforms and all.

2. Franklin Square

Just outside Old City's main drag, Franklin Square's once seedy green space was recently redone in honor of Ben Franklin's tercentenary. Now home to a carousel, miniature golf, playgrounds, and a restored fountain, it's the sort of place that's fun when it's not overrun with screaming children.

3. Penn Square

Center Square is the largest of the original five city parks. It was renamed Penn Square in tribute to William Penn, whose initial desire to see this land used for public buildings was overruled; instead, early Philadelphians used the space for residential properties. It wasn't until the late-19th century that the square became a location for new public buildings and the mammoth City Hall was built. The square has some of the most intriguing architecture in the city, including the imposing Penn statue, standing high over City Hall.

4. Rittenhouse Square

Southwest of Rittenhouse Square remains the most fashionable residential district in Philly, home to the equivalent of an affluent Victorian aristocracy. You can still see some of the mansions from that period, though most of the homes were turned into apartment buildings after 1913. Of all the squares, Rittenhouse Square is the most neighborly of the parks. Some of the city's best-loved sculptures reside here among the plants, annual flower markets, and outdoor art exhibits. Fancy bars and restaurants circle the area, keeping it chic and elite.

5. Washington Square

Washington Square, the Southeast Square, is known as the final resting place of more Revolutionary soldiers than anywhere else in the United States. It wasn't until 1825 that the city renamed the square and its uppity reputation began to grow. In the first half of the 20th century, this became the heart of Philly's publishing industry, and such popular publications as *The Saturday Evening Post* and *Ladies' Home Journal* were conceived here. Be sure to check out the Bicentennial Moon Tree. This sycamore was planted from a seed carried to the moon by the Apollo Space Mission. There is also a large public fountain in the center that serves as a great place for people and their pooches to chill out during summer months.

6. Fitler Square

Just a few blocks southwest of Rittenhouse Square and five blocks east of the Schuylkill River, Fitler Square is surrounded by a slew of expensive single-family dwellings and an array of fine restaurants, quaint shops, and small businesses. Named for Edwin H. Fitler, a well-regarded 19th-century mayor of Philadelphia, the square lays just a stone's throw from Philly's most commercial Center City shopping district. It plays host to a series of annual events like the Spring Fair, Easter Egg Hunt, and Christmas tree lighting. Woe betide you if you walk on the grass or let your dog do same; they are very pricklish about the lawn.

7. Love Park

This little enclave across from City Hall opened in the free-loving '60s. The park is famous for Robert Indiana's 20-foot tall LOVE sculpture, the symbol for the "City of Brotherly Love." For years, Love Park was a mecca for skateboarders, who came in droves to test their mettle against the park's ramps, stairs, and fountains. But the mayor has imposed a strict no-skating policy, forcing the young-uns to sneak around like ninjas in order to snag a few blissful runs.

8. Headhouse Square

This charming, cobblestone-lined street square in Old City is definitely worth strolling. Surrounded by cozy restaurants and picturesque parks, Headhouse Square also houses the nation's oldest firehouse. For fourteen consecutive weekends during the year, beginning at Memorial Day, check out the Creative Collective Craft and Fine Arts Fair. It's a great way to spend the weekend, meeting with local artists, browsing their wares, and sending the kids off to any one of the free art workshops for an afternoon of T-shirt painting or puppet-making. Most shows are on Saturdays and run from 10 am to 10 pm. There is also a popular Farmer's Market here that runs from 10 am to 2 pm on Saturdays and Sundays throughout the summer.

9. Clark Park

Initially established in 1895, Clark Park (43rd St & Chester Ave), adds to the West Philly scene by attracting artists and musicians who showcase their talents throughout the nine acres of greenery. The Clark Park Music and Arts Community play a huge role in facilitating an array of festivals in the park. The CPMAC and The Friends of Clark Park are two key organizations working to help maintain and promote the park. Check out the life-sized Charles Dickens statue, or take a look at the Friends of Clark Park website to check out upcoming events.

10. Penn Treaty Park

Penn Treaty Park is located at the site of where William Penn and the Lenape Indians signed a friendship agreement. Well, maybe. There are actually no hard historical documents confirming this fact—but don't tell that to the statue of Penn that presides over the park. Today Penn Treaty Park serves as a beautiful spot on the edge of the Delaware River to go fishing (but we don't recommend eating anything that you catch), fly kites, barbecue, and smoke weed (apparently).

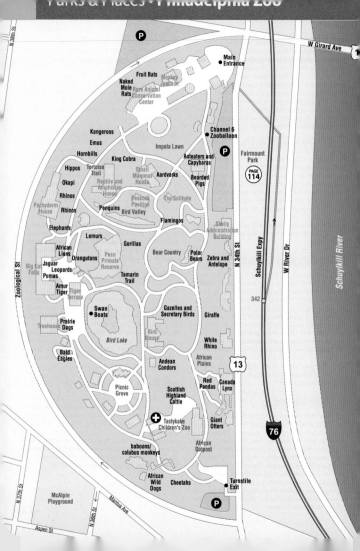

General Information

Address: 3400 West Girard Ave
                Philadelphia, PA 19104-1196
Phone: 215-243-1100
Website: www.philadelphiazoo.org
Hours: In-Season - Mar–Nov
                9:30 am–5 pm daily
                Off-Season - Dec–Feb
                9:30 am–4 pm daily
Admission: In-Season - Children (ages 2–11) $15,
                Adults $18
                Off-Season - $12.95

Overview

Opened in 1874, the Philadelphia Zoo is the oldest in the country. Drawing 1.1 million visitors per year, it's laid out over 42 acres and has 1,300 animals from six continents, a remarkable display of historic architecture, an impressive botanical collection of over 500 plant species, and superior research and veterinary facilities.

But kids today have become more jaded than their predecessors. These days, maybe because of television shows like Animal Planet and the Discovery Channel, it seems to take more than a moping hippo hiding in the corner of his cage to excite the kiddies. So, like zoos in most cities, the Philadelphia Zoo has been evolving with the times and placing greater emphasis on its amusement park facilities than on its animals.

In order to fit in these new rides, the play areas, and—but of course—the ubiquitous market places, the zoo has scaled down its number of actual animals. Fewer than ten years ago, the zoo had 1,800 animals; today, the zoo's collection is down to 1,300 and dropping fast. Ironically enough, the Philly Zoo, known as the setting of the first chimpanzee birth in the country (1928), no longer houses chimps.

Rides and Activities

The Zooballoon (open April through October), takes visitors 400 feet above the ground to see the giraffes and zebras oddly juxtaposed against the Philadelphia skyline. The quaint Amoroso PZ Express Victorian-era train is another fun attraction for the kids (and adults) who prefer the comfort of feeling ground beneath their feet. The crowds around Bird Valley waiting to ride the Swan Boat (open April through October) are bigger than the ones trying to catch a glimpse of the rhino. And the Camel Safari does come complete with your own spitting, smelly camel ride. Make sure to bring along some extra cash if you're planning on partaking in the fun, as all of these rides cost $2–$15 on top of the entrance fee.

How to Get There—Driving

From I-76, take Exit 342 to Girard Avenue. Follow signs to the Zoo.

From I-95, take exit 676 W to I-76 W. Get off at Exit 342 to Girard Avenue. Follow signs to the Zoo.

Parking

As you drive toward the zoo, turn right on Girard Avenue or continue straight to the 34th Street parking lot. The cost of parking is $12 (unless you're a member—then it's free).

How to Get There—Mass Transit

Ride SEPTA bus 15 to 34th Street and Girard Avenue. Bus 32 stops at 33rd Street and Girard Avenue. Bus 38 stops close by at 34th Street and Mantua Avenue. A $2 shuttle departs half hourly from the Museum of Art in summer.

Zoo Tours

All tours are lead by volunteer docents and are $5. For more information about Zoo Tours, or to make reservations (which are required), call 215-243-5317.

Thematic Tours:
• Conservation/Endangered
  Species Tour
• Adaptations
• Reptiles and Amphibians
• Up Close and Personal (Adults only)
• Bible

About the Zoo Tours:
• Art and Architecture
• Horticulture

Children's Tours
• The Five Senses Tour
• Adaptations

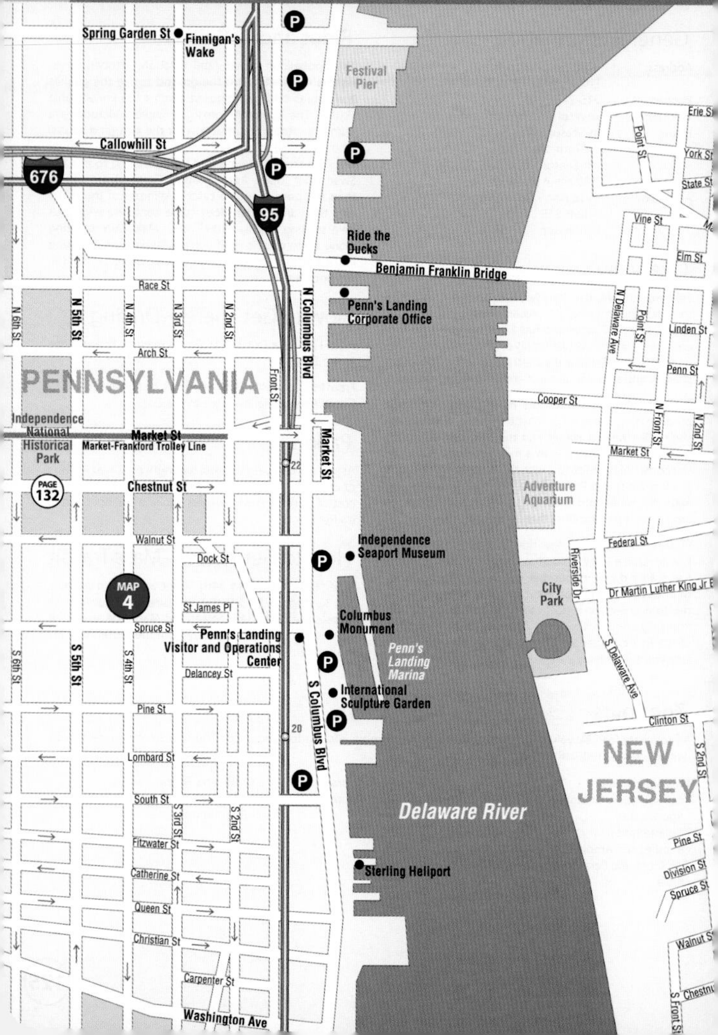

Spring Garden St
Finnigan's Wake

Festival Pier

Callowhill St

676

95

Ride the Ducks

Benjamin Franklin Bridge

Penn's Landing Corporate Office

Erie St

York St

State St

Vine St

Elm St

N Delaware Ave

Linden St

Penn St

Race St

Arch St

N 6th St
N 5th St
N 4th St
N 3rd St
N 2nd St
Front St

PENNSYLVANIA

Cooper St

N Front St
N 2nd St

Independence National Historical Park

Market St
Market-Frankford Trolley Line

Market St

22

Market St

PAGE 132

Chestnut St

Adventure Aquarium

S 6th St
S 5th St
S 4th St

Walnut St

Dock St

MAP 4

St James Pl

Independence Seaport Museum

Federal St

City Park

Riverside Dr

Dr Martin Luther King Jr B

Spruce St

Penn's Landing Visitor and Operations Center

Columbus Monument

Penn's Landing Marina

Delancey St

International Sculpture Garden

Pine St

20

Clinton St

S 3rd St
S 2nd St

S Delaware Ave

Lombard St

NEW JERSEY

South St

Delaware River

N 2nd St

Fitzwater St

Pine St

Catherine St

Sterling Heliport

Division St

Queen St

Spruce St

Christian St

Carpenter St

Walnut St

Washington Ave

S Chestnut St
S Front St

General Information

NFT Map: 4
Phone: 215-928-8801
Website: www.pennslandingcorp.com

Overview

Comprising 13 acres stretching from Spring Garden Street to Washington Avenue along the Delaware, Penn's Landing is gradually becoming more than just the port where all the Jersey kids get off the Camden ferry in order to snort glue and get their asses pierced on South Street. In spite of the improvements, it still houses the regrettable "Jersey Night Out" mix of huge, unbearably lame dance clubs and stripper bars, and many darkened sections of wharf and park where you can get into drunken throw-downs with like-minded barbarians.

Events

Despite all that, Penn's Landing does host many of Philly's biggest events and festivals each year. Many concerts take place at the Great Plaza (Columbus Blvd & Chestnut St), and others occur at the Festival Pier (Columbus Blvd & Spring Garden St), such as the Sippin' by the River Festival (www.sippinbytheriver. com) in September. Most recently, Philly's LGBT pride parade and festival culminated by the Marina, chock full of leather daddies, lesbian mothers, and everyone in between.

Blue Cross River Rink

Located on Columbus Boulevard and Market Street, the Blue Cross River Rink (www.riverrink.com) hosts ice skating for everyone November through February (you can even skate with Santa a couple of times in December). Entry costs $8 for everyone ($9 on Friday and Saturday nights), and skate rental is an additional $3.. The rink is open 6 pm–9 pm weeknights (and until 1 am Friday nights), 12:30 pm–1 am on Saturdays, and 12:30 pm–9 pm on Sundays. Check the website or call 215-925-RINK before you go though, because sometimes the rink is closed for private rentals.

Other Attractions

There's the Seaport Museum, which chronicles the history of Penn's Landing, one of American's oldest ports. There are also some fine restaurants which reside near the Marina. And the aforementioned lame-ass clubs are towards the north, past the BF Bridge. Otherwise, you'll find interesting park space

and absolutely filthy-rich yachts if you walk south towards South Street. If you want to get out on the water—notice we said on, not in, pollution being what it is—and you don't own one of those expensive yachts, you'll find everything from 12-minute ferry rides to paddle wheel riverboat dining departing from the banks of the Delaware. Just don't ride one of those damn duck boats. If you live in Philly and ride a duck boat, you deserve to get punched in the face.

How to Get There—Driving

From I-95, take Exit 20 (Washington Ave/Columbus Blvd). Make a left onto Columbus Boulevard and proceed north.

From the Walt Whitman Bridge, take I-95 N to Exit 20. Follow directions above.

From I-76, travel east to I-676 E until you hit I-95. Take I-95 S to Exit 20, and follow the above directions.

Parking

There are loads of parking options around Penn's Landing. Most charge $12–$15 per day:

Festival Pier
  Spring Garden & Columbus Blvd - 300 spaces.
Pier 24
  Columbus Blvd & Cavanaugh's River Deck - 120 spaces.
Vine St & Columbus Blvd
  (across from Dave & Buster's) - 280 spaces.
Columbus Blvd & Market St - 400 spaces.
Columbus Blvd & Walnut St - 220 spaces.
Lombard Cir & Columbus Blvd - 220 spaces.
South Street Pedestrian Bridge &
  Columbus Blvd - 400 spaces.

Ticketed concert parking at Festival Pier costs $20. Monthly parking permits are also available the last five days through the first five days of every month. They offer 24-hour parking for permit holders, and can be purchased at the Penn's Landing Operations/ Visitor Center at 301 S Columbus Boulevard for first-time buyers. There is also ample street parking in the surrounding area if you're willing to feed the meter every 2 hours.

How to Get There—Mass Transit

Take SEPTA bus 17 to Penn's Landing via 20th Street and Market Street, or bus 48 Tioga.

By subway, ride the Market-Frankford Line east, get off at 2nd Street, and walk south to Penn's Landing.

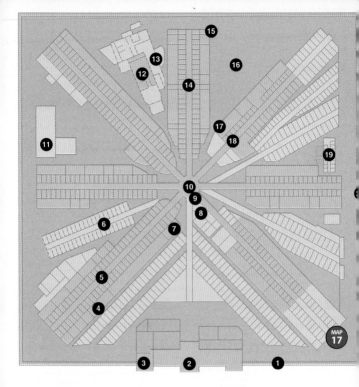

1. Facade
2. Front Tower
3. Administration Building Office
4. Synagogue
5. Cellblock 7
6. Cellblock 12
7. Al Capone's Cell
8. Chaplain's Office
9. Rotunda
10. Central Guard Tower
11. Chapel
12. Kitchen
13. Dining Hall
14. Cellblock 4
15. Exercise Yard
16. Baseball Diamond
17. Hospital
18. Outside the Operating Room
19. Death Row
20. Outside the Cellblocks

General Information

NFT Map: 17
Location: 22nd St & Fairmount Ave
Philadelphia, PA 19130
Phone: 215-236-3300
Website: www.easternstate.org
Hours: Open 7 days a week, year-round,
10 am–5 pm.
Admission: Adults $12, Seniors $10, Students $8,
Kids (7–12 years) $8
Children under the age of 7 not permitted

Overview

There's no use denying it: Eastern State Penitentiary is a genuinely interesting, albeit touristy, destination.

Built in 1829 in what is now the Fairmount section of Philadelphia, ESP was once the largest and most expensive building in America. People flocked from around the globe to marvel at the prison's architecture and penal system. The prison was closed in 1971 and promptly fell into disrepair.

The non-profit preservationist group, Eastern State Penitentiary Historic Site, was formed in 1994, and today organizes tours and educational programs in an effort to restore the crumbling prison. Recently, several archaeologists were hired to excavate around the building's exterior, and came up with some actual buried, er… treasure. The findings included pieces of discarded silverware, glass bottles and bottle caps, and remnants of homemade tools possibly used for (what probably proved futile) escape plans.

ESP's once-oppressive environment is also used today as an art gallery. Art installations, inspired by the prison's history and created specifically for the space, are featured throughout the complex, and many change with the seasons. Among the more permanent installations is a piece called *Ghost Cats*; the 39 cat sculptures scattered all around the grounds represent the colony of cats that ran wild in the penitentiary following its desertion in the '70s. Another work, entitled *The End of the Tunnel*, features a two-inch red steel pipe that snakes around the outside of the cell blocks and over the walls, symbolizing escape routes prisoners might have used.

During Halloween, the prison hosts a haunted house event called *Terror Behind The Walls*. Although it's ranked ninth in the country by *HauntWorld Magazine*, the truly creepy environment can be somewhat reduced by gaggles of teenagers talking on their cell phones behind you.

They also throw a big Bastille Day party every July. There's a playful reenactment of the Storming of the Bastille (influenced more by Monty Python than the French Revolution), followed by a French-themed street party. Tres Bien!

History

Eastern State Penitentiary was created by Quakers who believed that true penitence could come only from a life of solitude and reflection. To prohibit communication between inmates and guards, prisoners were required to wear masks anytime they left their cells. They received meals through small feed doors. Although the concept for Eastern State Penitentiary was based on ending ill treatment common in prisons of the day, the punishments exacted were far from pleasant. If inmates were caught trying to communicate with other prisoners, they would be denied meals or sentenced to solitary confinement for several days. If the infraction was more serious, an inmate might be chained to an outside wall in the winter months, stripped from the waist up, and doused with water until ice formed on his body. The "iron gag" was another form of punishment involving a five-inch piece of metal clamped onto a tongue. If captives exhibited resistance, the gag would be forced deeper into their mouth. At least one inmate died from the iron gag.

The prison is also famous for its inmates, some of whom have reached near-celebrity status. Over the years, ESP's quarters hosted the likes of gangster Al Capone and bank robber Willie Sutton.

How to Get There—Driving

From the north or west, take I-76 (Schuylkill Expressway) to Exit 344 (Old Exit 38)/I-676 (Vine Street Expressway). On I-676 take the fourth exit, Benjamin Franklin Parkway/23 Street, then take the first left onto 22nd Street. Pass the Philadelphia Museum of Art (on your left) and continue five blocks north, to Fairmount Avenue.

Coming from the south or east, take I-95 to Exit 22 (Old Exit 17) and follow I-676 W. Get off at the Art Museum/Benjamin Franklin Parkway exit. At the top of the ramp, turn right onto 22nd Street, pass the Philadelphia Museum of Art (on your left) and continue five blocks north to Fairmount Avenue.

Parking

While there is plenty of un-metered street parking in the area around the penitentiary, some streets have a two- or three-hour limit. If you're planning on taking your time touring the prison, there's a public lot next door which will cost between $3 and $10, depending on the length of your stay.

How to Get There—Mass Transit

Take the 7, 32, or 48 SEPTA bus to 22nd Street and Fairmount Avenue then walk east one block to the penitentiary. The 33 bus stops at 20th and Fairmount; walk west one block to the entrance. The 43 bus stops at 21st and Spring Garden Streets. Walk north to Fairmount Avenue, the next major street parallel to Spring Garden Street.

Big Bus (Stop #8) and Philadelphia Trolley Works (Stop #11) both stop right in front of the ESP, a sure sign that you're smack bang in the middle of the tourist route. Be sure to show your ticket stub from the tours and save $1 on admission to the prison. The Phlash trolley has an Eastern State Penitentiary stop at 22nd Street and Benjamin Franklin Parkway. Get off and walk four blocks north on 22nd Street to Fairmount Avenue.

Overview

To Philadelphians, Benjamin Franklin is more than just the picture on the $100 bill or the dude who flew a kite. Arriving here in 1723, he started, well, just about everything. He's responsible for our first fire company (Union Fire Company, 1736), our first insurance company (Philadelphia Contributionship, 1752), our first university (University of Pennsylvania, 1740), our first hospital (Pennsylvania Hospital, 1751), and our first library (Library Company, 1731). In addition, he was one of our first postmasters (appointed in 1737) and he ran one of our first newspapers, *The Pennsylvania Gazette*, in which he penned the very first political cartoon. Not to mention what he did for the country. (You remember that whole Declaration of Independence thing, right?)

He might have even gone a little overboard. But nobody's gone more overboard than us, especially since his 300th birthday in 2006 when we finally named what we all have a nasty, infectious, and idolatrous case of. We named our disease *Benergy*, and told everybody, drool-fanged, "We got it!"

Benergy, once named as such, provoked *Philadelphia Weekly* writer Steven Wells to lambaste our *Benefactor* for eight tight-fonted pages ("An avuncular saint, inventor and bootstrap capitalist—a PG-friendly, George-Bush-approved, sanitized, shrink-wrapped, deboned and prechewed establishment revolutionary for the whole family to enjoy.") all the while raising up quite rudely the revolutionary efforts of Thomas Paine, another Philadelphian, whose followers (i.e. traitors) claim had more to do with the Declaration of Independence than anybody, but who is largely back-f***ed by the rest of us because, well, he ain't Ben. Chill, Steven Wells. Don't get all *Bent* out of shape.

Panting and sighing, we've named just about everything we can after Ben—from our museums to our hoagie shops to our little babies. From almost any street corner in Philadelphia, you can spot something named after our man. Here are just a few choice examples—let's *Bengin*!

The Franklin Institute

222 N 20th St, 215-448-1200; www.fi.edu;
Daily 9:30 am–5 pm

It's virtually impossible to go to the Franklin Institute and not be overrun by children. That being said, it's still a good place for adults to go—if you're young at heart and you don't mind wading through school groups.

The Giant Heart, which recently celebrated its 50th birthday, is a legend. If you're a kid, the legendary thing to do would be to get lost and cry inside of it, or at least get injured during rough play near a ventricle. If you're an adult, it's the number one spot in the city to have existential thoughts and wonder what the hell that smell is (hint: it's the reek of thousands of dirty children all walking through an enclosed space).

The Franklin National Memorial, located in the rotunda and free of charge, is the only national memorial held in private hands. Not one penny of federal funds helped to create it or support its upkeep. Oh, and there's a massive 20+ foot, 100+ ton statue of ol' BF there. After the rotunda, the Franklin Institute would like your money, please. Exhibits change regularly, so every few months you can go back and see something new. Prices vary depending on the exhibit, but expect to pay at least $20 for adults. The awesome 79-foot IMAX dome screen movies cost $9 for everybody.

Franklin at Franklin's University (a.k.a. the University of Pennsylvania)

Penn likes to call itself Franklin's University because Ben founded the joint in 1749. Two buildings are named after the big man: Franklin Field and the Franklin Building (we're not counting the meaningless Franklin Building Annex). The Franklin Building, located at 3451 Walnut Street and used for office space, is among the ugliest buildings on the historic campus. Penn's own website has only this to say about it: "Economical and utilitarian office tower that misses most of the important lines of development of the 1960s campus."

When you think of Ben Franklin, athleticism is probably not the first thing that springs to mind. Nevertheless, Franklin Field, located on 33rd Street between South and Walnut Streets, is old (built in 1922), attractive, and has some historical cache: The first televised football game was played there in 1940; it used to be the home of the Eagles and the yearly Army-Navy football game; it's the country's oldest two-tiered stadium; and it seats 52,000 to boot. Those who saw M. Night Shyamalan's *Unbreakable* (2000) will recognize Franklin Field as the nameless sports stadium that David Dunn (Bruce Willis) worked at as a security guard.

In addition to buildings named after him, it's hard to walk around campus without tripping over a statue of Benjamin Franklin:

- In front of **College Hall** sits a well-known plaster statue of a seated Ben that once resided in front of the old Post Office (9th and Chestnut Streets) as a tribute to Franklin, the United States' first Postmaster General.

- Outside **Weightman Hall** is a statue of a youthful Benjamin as he might have looked when he arrived in Philadelphia: seventeen years old, standing with a staff in one hand and a small bundle in the other. The adorning inscription reads: "I have been the more particular in this description of my journey that you may compare such unlikely beginnings with the figure I have since made there."

- At **37th Street and Locust Walk** is a life-sized bronze of Franklin reading one of his own publications: *The Pennsylvania Gazette*.

- On the second floor alcove of **Stiteler Hall** is a middle-aged, six-foot Ben Franklin holding a scroll in his left hand and a three-cornered hat in his right. Originally displaced from the Odd Fellows Cemetery Company and stored in a crate at Franklin Field for more than twenty years, the figure now resides on campus.

Franklin Statues Everywhere

Around the rest of the city, you'll see Ben popping up everywhere. Catch him wearing a firefighter's helmet at the Fire Hall at **4th and Arch Streets**, or at the **City Hall courtyard** looking out above the east entrance. On **Chestnut Street near 23rd**, Ben is featured seated in a huge mural. In addition, there's an abstract, very shiny bust of his head on **17th and Vine** (you'll see it while driving on I-676), and check out the lightning bolt sculpture at the base of the—you guessed it—Ben Franklin Bridge at **5th and Vine Streets**.

Benjamin Franklin Bridge

When they consider their bridges, most Philadelphians think two thoughts, neither of which is pleasant: New Jersey and traffic. However, the BFB is a beauty. A pedestrian footpath (oddly only open on one side at a time and then for set hours) allows you to run, walk, or bike the expanse. The light show it displays at night is mesmerizing when you're getting loaded at Penn's Landing.

The BFB was designed by Paul Cret, who was also involved in designing the Ben Franklin Parkway. Finished in 1926, the bridge connects Center City Philadelphia to Camden and was originally called the Delaware River Port Authority Bridge. In 1956, it was dedicated to Ben Franklin and renamed in his honor. Like all bridges, keep in mind that it's always free to get to New Jersey (jail doesn't charge rent either), but they make you pay to come back.

Benjamin Franklin Parkway

The view of Ben Franklin Parkway was made famous in the 1976 movie classic, *Rocky*. In it, Rocky Balboa (Sylvester Stallone) runs to the top of the Art Museum stairs, turns around and raises his arms in victory. Before him is the view of the parkway. This magic moment is recreated endlessly by tourists and visitors, who request their loved ones to make digital cell phone movies of themselves striding up the steps and holding their arms aloft.

Us locals prefer to climb on the museum's statues at two in the morning and watch all of the lights on the parkway turn green in unison—then red. And if you don't happen to have a pool in your apartment building complex, the Swann Memorial Fountain on 19th and Parkway is the perfect spot for requisite summer night dips.

Next time you're there, we've got a trick for all of you grown-ups with a juvenile sense of humor. From the top of the museum's steps, look south to the statue of William Penn atop City Hall. From this perspective, you'll see what we jokingly call the "the Penn Endowment." Heh.

The Parkway was constructed from 1917 to 1926 with the main objective of getting people from the business district to Fairmount Park. The aforementioned Philadelphia Museum of Art, the Rodin Museum, the Franklin Institute, and the Central Free Library are all along the Franklin Parkway, which has become a popular place for parades and other events by day, and for homeless somnambulists at night.

Franklin Square

Finally refurbished for Ben's 300th, this somewhat oddly placed park houses a carousel, a fountain, green space, a playground, and what we can only assume was one of Mr. Franklin's favorite pastimes, miniature golf.

Franklin Court

316 Market St, 215-965-2305; Daily 9 am–5 pm
This is the spot where Franklin's house stood before it was razed in 1812. That's right: razed. Whoops, our bad. In its place now stands a "ghost structure" (essentially the outline of the house done up in steel support beams) built for the 1976 bicentennial. When digging around in the rubble beneath its construction, some other cool stuff turned up, including Franklin's privy pit.

B. Free Franklin Post Office & Museum

315 Market St, 215-592-1292; Mon–Sat, 9 am–5 pm,
closed New Years Day and Christmas Day
Franklin first accepted the role of postmaster of Philadelphia in 1737, mainly to ensure that his newspaper, *The Pennsylvania Gazette*, was distributed properly. As a royal official, Franklin had "franking privileges," and signed his letters B. Free Franklin. Since he was allowed to send letters for free, some think that Franklin was alluding to the fact that his letters were being mailed at no charge. Others believe that "B. Free" was Franklin's statement to the colonies. Since he apologized for and profited from slavery, it's doubtful this was his cry to free the slaves he sold.

The B. Free Franklin Post Office and Museum is an actual working post office. Geeky philatelists will be especially happy to get a letter or postcard from this office hand-stamped with a hand-stamp bearing Franklin's "B. Free Franklin" signature. Also of note is the fact that this post office is the only one in the country *not* to fly the US flag outside. Why? Because there was no US flag in 1775 when the post office first opened.

Franklin's Grave

After Franklin's death on April 17, 1790, Carl Van Doren wrote, "No other town burying its great man, ever buried more of itself than Philadelphia with Franklin." His grave is located in the Christ Church Cemetery at the southeast corner of 5th and Arch Streets. You can also pay a minimal fee to enter the cemetery during the day. Philadelphia tradition claims that throwing a penny onto Franklin's grave will bring good luck. The pennies are collected each night and promptly donated toward the creation of a *Benergy* clinic, where, hopefully, one day in the future, we can all get treated. And guess what we're going to name it.

Franklin Square
PAGE 122

Race St →

National Constitution Center

US Mint

Betsy Ross House

← Arch St

Benjamin Franklin's Grave

Independence Park Institute

Free Quaker Meeting House

Christ Church Burial Ground

Christ Church

7th St

6th St

5th St

4th St

3rd St

2nd St

P

P

MAP 4

Independence Visitor Center (Security Screening Facility)

Market St

Market Street Houses

Franklin Court

Declaration House

Liberty Bell Pavilion

Independence Mall

Independence Mall W

Independence Mall E

Liberty Bell Center

Chestnut St

Old City Hall

Second Bank of the US

New Hall Military Museum

Pemberton House

Congress Hall

Independence Hall

Philsophical Hall

Library Hall

Carpenters' Hall

First Bank of the US

Welco

Sansom St

Independence Square (Security Screening Required)

18th Century Garden

Todd House

Bishop White House

Philadelphia Exchange

City Taver

Dock St

Dock St

← Walnut St

Thomas Paine Pl

Washington Square

Tomb of the Unknown Soldier of the American Revolution

PAGE 123

Rose Garden

St Joseph's Church

Willings Aly

Locust St

Magnolia Garden

Independence National Historical Park

General Information

NFT Map: 4
Websites: www.nps.gov/inde
www.betsyrosshouse.org

Overview

Instead of the namby-pamby "Philadelphia: The Place That Loves You Back" slogan, perhaps the city should consider a new offering, "Philadelphia: Lots of Significant Stuff Happened Here 200 Years Ago." Tourists flock here because the city's history is so interconnected with the creation of the United States itself. Of course, jaded residents saunter right by these historic buildings where our forefathers determined the country's course with nary a glance. In fact, many of us avoid the Historical Park altogether until out of town guests force us to go downtown and see the Liberty Bell. Paris has the Eiffel Tower; we have the Liberty Bell. Hoo-rah.

INHP comprises "America's most historic square mile." Founded in 1956 on (of course) July 4th, INHP oversees eighteen landmark American institutions, but the most popular attraction by a landslide is the Liberty Bell.

We had to include the Betsy Ross House somewhere, and even though it is not part of INHP, it seems to fit in seamlessly (no sewing pun intended) with the INHP landmarks. And after all, the Betsy Ross House is Philadelphia's second-most visited tourist attraction after INHP.

We should mention, though, that we're pretty sure that's not actually her house. Yeah, her real house was demolished, and what we say is her house was the one next door. Whoops.

Admission

Inside the "security zone", access to all buildings is free and generally includes a tour guide and/or some sort of schpiel about the history of each building, including Independence Hall (plus its East and West Wings), Old City Hall, Congress Hall, and the Liberty Bell Pavilion. Outside of the security zone, the Declaration (Graff) House is also free, as is the Betsy Ross House (although their request for a "donation" feels suspiciously like a requirement). The one place you do have to pay for a ticket is the National Constitution Center.

Between March 1st and December 31st

There's a lot of stuff to see, but it can all be covered in one pretty full day. Hit the Independence Visitor Center at 6th and Market Streets first, so you can score a ticket for an Independence Hall tour. Your timed entry ticket could be anywhere from 45 minutes to three or four hours later, depending on how busy it is. Once you have your tour time secured, you can plan the rest of your day. In addition to all "the Man's" tours and sites, there's also a bunch of other tours that show other aspects of historic Philadelphia. One thing to note: the Declaration (Graff) House is only open

9 am–11 am, whereas everything else is open throughout the afternoon.

Audio Tour

The 74-minute, self guided AudioWalk & Tour narration is available for rent at the Independence Visitor Center. The tour visits twenty important historical sites and the CD (player included) has 64 narrated segments. The cost is $16 for one person, $17 for two people, $18 for three people, and $20 for four people.

Independence Visitor Center

NW corner of Market St & 6th St, 215-965-7676; www.independencevisitorcenter.com; 8:30 am–6 pm (extended in summer till 7 pm)
This is the spot where you pick up the free tickets for your Independence Hall tour time. The ticket window is towards the back of the building on the right. It's also got over-priced food and an over-priced gift shop; on the positive side, it does have a bathroom that might have a line.

Liberty Bell Center Museum

6th St b/w Market St & Chestnut St (security entrance on 5th St); www.nps.gov/inde/liberty-bell.html; 9 am–5 pm
This is it, the fulcrum of Philadelphia tourism. Used to be that you could touch it, but after some crazy took a hammer to it in 2001, they initiated the same "airport security" measure as everywhere else. A National Parks Department Ranger will give a little speech, allow a few brief moments for photography, and then shuffle you out towards Independence Hall.

Independence Hall

Chestnut St b/w 5th St & 6th St, 215-965-2305; www.nps.gov/inde/independence-hall-1.htm; 9 am–5 pm
The Independence Hall tour is where you line up and wait for your tour guide like a good school child. Tours run every fifteen minutes and last about half an hour. First stop is the East Wing of Independence Hall, where the ranger will tell you things about the hall and Philadelphia in general. The quality of your experience will depend entirely on the ranger you draw.

Independence Hall is split into two rooms: the Court Room and the Assembly Room. In the Court Room, you'll learn how a trial was held way back when. The good stuff is in the Assembly Room—that's where the Declaration of Independence and the U.S. Constitution were signed.

After you've covered Independence Hall proper, wander into the West Wing. The Declaration of Independence that was read out loud by Colonel John Nixon to the public for the first time on July 8, 1776 in the State House Yard (now Independence Square) resides here. You'll also find a second draft of the Articles of Confederation and Perpetual Union, a draft of the Constitution of the United States, and the inkstand that historians believe was used for the signing of the Declaration and the Constitution.

(133)

Congress Hall

6th & Chesnut Sts; www.nps.gov/inde/congress-hall.htm

A little bit further westward, you'll run into Congress Hall, which once housed the Senate and House of Representatives. Beyond that, it's special for another remarkable reason. During 1797, Philadelphia was the nation's capital (while Washington, DC, was being built), and on March 4th, George Washington transferred the power to run the country to John Adams, our second president. This was the first time in the modern age that power was transferred peaceably between two people who were not related.

Old City Hall

5th & Chestnut Sts; www.nps.gov/inde/old-city-hall.htm

To the east of Independence Hall is Old City Hall, which housed the city's government from 1791 to 1854 and was also the first Supreme Court of the United States. Upstairs was the Mayor's Office and Council Chambers and downstairs was the Mayor's Court, shared with the U.S. Supreme Court for nine years. You'll be struck by how small a space it is.

National Constitution Center

525 Arch St; www.constitutioncenter.org
Sunday–Friday 9:30–5, Thursday 9:30–8, Saturday 9:30–6
Tickets: $12 adults, $11 seniors 65+, $8 children 4–12, children under 4 and people with active military IDs free

All things Constitutional. You can see life-sized bronze statues of the signers, get your picture taken behind the presidential seal, and even complain to your congressional representative at the Participation Café. For $12, it's probably worth it. Currently there's massive landscaping in front of the Constitution center, and random storyteller areas in the surrounding region.

Betsy Ross House

239 Arch St, 215-686-1252; www.betsyrosshouse.org
Open 10 am–5 pm daily April–Oct; Closed Mondays Oct–Mar

Did Betsy Ross really make the first flag? We do know that her descendents claim that she made and helped design the first flag in 1776, although the flag we consider to be the Betsy Ross flag (with the 13 stars in a circle) did not appear until the 1790s. Whatever the case may be, this stop is a favorite of children, who don't know any better.

Declaration (Graff) House

7th St & Market St;
www.nps.gov/inde/declaration-house.htm
Open 9 am–11 am

This building, like many "historical" buildings in Philadelphia, was razed a long, long time ago. Then for the bicentennial, the city decided to rebuild it real quick in order to capitalize on some fat tourist dollars. Thomas Jefferson rented two rooms in this location from Jacob Graff, Jr. to escape the heat of the city.

City Tavern

138 S 2nd St at Walnut St; 215-413-1443;
www.citytavern.com; Opens at 11:30 am daily

Another building rebuilt for the bicentennial. The original burned down in 1834. While other reproductions (Betsy Ross House, Declaration [Graff] House, Franklin Court) are at best guesstimates, City Tavern is supposed to look for any low-carb meals here. Apparently 18th-century types required either bread or potatoes (usually both) with their giant slabs of meat. It isn't cheap, but you're dining in the same air space in which Washington, Jefferson, Adams, and Franklin once dined.

Parking

There's no lack of public parking near INHP—just be prepared to pay for it!

Central Parking Auto Park – 6th St b/w Market St & Arch St
Central Parking System – Market St b/w 8th St & 9th St
Parkway Parking - 8th St & Ranstead Street
Five Star Parking – 8th St & Chestnut St
Parking Plaza-Quaker City Auto – 8th St & Filbert St
HC Parking - 7th St & Cherry St
Bourse Parking – 4th St & Ranstead St

Whatever you do, do not try to park on the street unless you want to pick your vehicle up from one of the many impound lots. The PPA has this area on lockdown.

How to Get There—Mass Transit

The Market-Frankford line stops along Market Street at 8th, 5th, and 2nd Streets, with the 5th Street stop being the closest to the Independence Mall.

Many other trains stop at the 8th St/Market terminal, including the subway, trolley, and light rail. Take the Broad-Ridge Spur, Patco High Speed, or Septa bus routes 61 and 47 to the Market Street stop. Many, many other buses stop nearby; consult septa.com for all of the routes.

All Septa Regional Rail trains (R1-2-3-5-6-7-8) stop at the Market East Station, which is six blocks from INHP.

Then there's PHLASH. Nothing says, "Look at me, I'm a tourist!" like the big, purple PHLASH bus. But it is cheap and convenient, costing $2 per ride or $5 per day. The purple bus makes many stops along Market Street between Penn's Landing and City Hall, before cutting up Ben Franklin Parkway to the Philadelphia Museum of Art.

In addition to the food, there's also a large selection of random crap that the vendors will yell about. We don't know anywhere else where you can get a down winter jacket for $20.

Let us not forget Fante's at 1006 S 9th Street, one of the best kitchen stores in the country, not to mention, somewhat further south, the cheesesteak landmarks, Pat's and Geno's (Ninth St & Passyunk Ave). Beware where you pick to cheesesteak, purchasing from Geno's over Pat's carries with it an implied mentality. (Pick Pat's).

Then, if you're REALLY brave, there's the Italian Market Festival held in late May or early June; it features live music, activities, and mangoes on sticks. Check out www.9thstreetitalianmarketfestival.com for the program schedule. The same organization also provides Christmas cheer through December.

How to Get There— Driving

From points north or south of Philly, take I-95 to the PA-611 N/Broad Street exit (Exit 14) towards Pattison Avenue. Merge onto S Broad Street. Turn right onto E Passyunk Avenue, then right onto Wharton Street.

From the west, take the US-422 E to I-76 E. Get off at the I-676 E/US-30 E exit (Exit 38) and turn left towards Central PA. Merge onto the Vine Street Expressway and exit at Broad Street/Central PA. Turn right onto N 15th Street. Make a left onto S Penn Square, another right on S Broad Street, and a left onto Washington Avenue. At S 10th Street, turn right, then make a left onto Wharton Street.

Parking

There are four lots that charge by the hour (reasonable rates) and three municipal parking lots in nearby streets. There is also free Saturday parking lot between S Darien Street and S Mildred Street, one block above Christian Street. However beware, the PPA does have this area on lockdown.

How to Get There—Mass Transit

Take bus 23 and get off at Christian Street. Turn right and walk one block to the market. By subway, take the Broad Street line and get off at Ellsworth-Federal. Walk east to 9th Street and turn left. Walk six blocks north and you'll arrive at the market.

General Information

NFT Map:	8
Address:	700-1100 S 9th St
	Philadelphia, PA 19147
Phone:	215-334-6008
Website:	www.phillyitalianmarket.com
Hours:	Tue–Sat: 9 am–5 pm, Sun: 9 am–2 pm

Overview

If going to a supermarket and seeing a freezer filled with frozen chickens isn't a personal enough experience for you, you might consider the Market. You can wander around living, breathing chickens, and many, many fresh carcasses (vegans can find all kinds of great stuff there, but they'll have to learn to avert their eyes). Freshness is what the Italian Market is all about, from meat to produce to bread to homemade cheese and spices.

Located in the heart of South Philly's vibrant Italian community, the Italian Market (sometimes referred to as "9th Street") is the country's oldest daily outdoor market—one hundred years and counting. Whereas the Italian Market used to be just that— Italian—there is a huge South East Asian and Latino presence in this section of South Philly.

Arch St

Dienner's Bar-B-Q Chicken

Lancaster County Dairy

Old City Coffee

Blue Mountain Vineyards & Cellars

$

Beiler's Bakery

Dutch Eating Place

Golden Fish Market

Metropolitan Bakery

PA General Store

Market Operations

The Rib Stand

Hatville Deli
Glick's Salads

Fisher's Soft Pretzels and Ice Cream

Seating Area

Foster's Gourmet Cookware

Foster's Gourmet Kitchen

Rick's Philly Steaks

Hatville Deli

12th Street Cantina

Amazulu

Don't Forget Your Pet

Bee Natural

Kauffman's Lancaster County Produce

Tootsie's Salad Express

Cold Storage

Carmen's Famous Hoagies

Olympic Gyro

Natural Connection

Dutch Country Meats

Andro's Fine Prepared Foods

Market Office Upstairs

Golden Bowl

Kamal's Middle Eastern Specialties

Martin's Quality Meats & Sausages

John Yi Fish Market

DiNic's

Spataro's

Spice Terminal

Seating Area

The Shoe Doctor

Bassett's Ice Cream

The Flower Basket
Four Seasons Juice Bar

Shanghai Gourmet

Mezze

Seating Area

❶ Terralyn

Philbert

Seating Area

Flying Monkey Patisserie

Le Bus Bakery
Delilah's

Tea Leaf

Harry G Ochs & Son

Hershel's East Side Deli

The Original Turkey
Basic 4 Vegetarian

Tokyo Sushi Bar
Franks-A-Lot

Beer Garden

Seating Area

Pearl's Oyster Bar

Profi's Creperie
Sang Kee Peking Duck

Nanee's Kitchen

OK Lee's Produce

Terralyn
De' Village

Godshall's Poultry

Coastal Cave

Seating Area

Old City Coffee

Downtown Cheese

Cookbook Stall

Little Thai Market

Salumeria

Market Blooms and Garden

L Halterman Family Country Foods

Famous 4th St Cookie Co

Le Bus Bakery

Amy's Place

Chocolate by Mueller

Wan's Seafood

Giunta's Prime Shop

Iovine Brothers Produce

Market Information

$

Chocolate by Mueller

Termini Brothers Bakery

Down Home Diner

Down Home Diner

by george!

Iovine Brothers Produce

MAP 3

Miscellanea Libri

11th St

12th St

Filbert St

❶ Livengood's Produce (Sat only)

Groceries	Shops
Bars/Beverages	Parkings
Restaurants	Other

General Information

NFT Map: 3
Address: 12th St & Arch St
Phone: 215-922-2317
Website: www.readingterminalmarket.org
Hours: Mon–Sat: 8 am–6 pm, Sun 9 am–5 pm

Overview

A giant food market, with representative cuisine from all over the area (and then some), Reading offers everything from organic produce to Amish bakeries to fresh seafood.

From 1889 through 1985, the market lived in the train shed beneath the tracks of the station at 12th and Market streets. When the commuter-rail system was rerouted to bypass the station, the tracks were removed and the market remained. Today, many Philadelphians make Reading their lunch destination, while some venture into Amish breakfast territory, which is serving butter soup on a measly pancake (or, alternately, a pancake with the measles)... On our way home from work, we like to do our specialty grocery shopping here—selecting from locally grown fruit and vegetables and an excellent assortment of choice meat. Reading is, aside from the Italian Market, the best place to get cheese.

Reading is also the place for some choice people-watching. The contrast of function and dysfunction, tourists and locals, Midwestern conventioneers, cute babies, and the decrepit elderly is all so poetic. There's a sea-clogged piano near the 12th and Filbert Streets entrance, where seriously loony (and very sweet) old people stamp out arrhythmic Joplin, against the loud shouts just beyond them—"Shoeshine! Shoeshine!" Then there are the red plastic six-seater pull-trains full of adorable pre-schoolers, and the gawk-worthy DNA-similarity of all the Amish girls and boys. And now that Reading's been implanted with surprisingly never-faltering free wireless, there's really no reason not to sit here all day.

It's impossible to name all the varieties of chow involved, but here are some can't-misses: **Downtown Cheese**, **Little Thai Market**, **Old City Coffee**, the farmer's market on Saturday, **Nanee's Kitchen** (Indian cuisine), **Kamal's Middle Eastern Specialties** where they'll give you a shot of wheatgrass, **LeBus** for all bread needs (that's right, **Metropolitan** is way more expensive and "artisanal," it turns out, is a euphemism for "too hard"), **Dutch Eating Place**, **DiNic's**, and lovine **Brothers Produce** for all the fruit you can carry. For some of the best donuts and bakes goods on the planet, the friendly Amish folks at **Beiler's** will hook you up. Remember these two words: whoopie pie. Throw nutritional concerns aside and make a meal of a butter-dipped Amish soft pretzel and a scoop of ice cream from the legendary **Bassett's**. If you want to impress the snooty foodies who come to visit you (meaning, among others, anyone from NYC) take 'em here, load them up with a Vietnamese hoagie and a giant mint chocolate milkshake, then buy them a copper sauté pan. You'll learn 'em.

If you really want an insiders' view of the market you can take a Taste of Philly Tour with a local food expert. Learn about the vibrant history of the market, the story behind cheesesteaks, and lots more. Check out the events section on the website for more information.

How to Get There—Driving

From the Schuykill/76, take Exit 344/676 E. From 676, take the second exit, Broad Street. From the exit ramp, continue straight on Vine Street and follow the signs that say "PA Convention Center." Turn right onto 12th Street and proceed two blocks to Arch Street. Reading Terminal Market is on the southeast corner of Arch and Market. From I-95 S/N, take Exit 22/676 W. From 676 take the first exit, Broad Street. Turn right off of exit ramp onto 15th Street. Turn left onto Vine Street (second light) then right onto 12th St and proceed two blocks to Arch Street. Reading Terminal Market is on the southeast corner of Arch and Market.

Parking

"Free" parking is available to market shoppers (as long as you spend big at the market) on the 3rd, 5th, and 7th floors of the Parkway Garage, located across the street from the 12th Street market entrance on Filbert Street between 12th and 13th Streets. The only catch is that you have to be done shopping in two hours.

Parking at the 12th and Filbert St Garage is $2 provided you spend over $10 at any of Reading's many merchants, which given all the delicious possibilities shouldn't be too hard. Just remember to bring your ticket with you to market (and back again). If you park for longer than 2 hours, the regular garage rates apply so check the current rates as you enter (or call 215-922-2317). If you have patience and time to spare, there's a less complicated alternative—nearby metered parking.

How to Get There—Mass Transit

Take any of SEPTA's Regional Rail lines to the Market East Station and follow signs to the PA Convention Center and Reading Terminal Market.

From the Broad Street subway, get off at City Hall and walk east on Market Street. Turn left on 12th Street and walk one block until you hit RTM. From the Market/Frankford line, get off at 13th Street. Walk one block east to 12th Street and RTM is one block along 12th Street.

By trolley, get off at Juniper Station and walk two blocks east to 12th Street. Turn left onto 12th Street and walk one block to RTM.

There are loads of buses that pass close to the market. Routes 9, 17, 23, 33, 38, 44, 61 Express, and 121 all go by 12th and Market Streets.

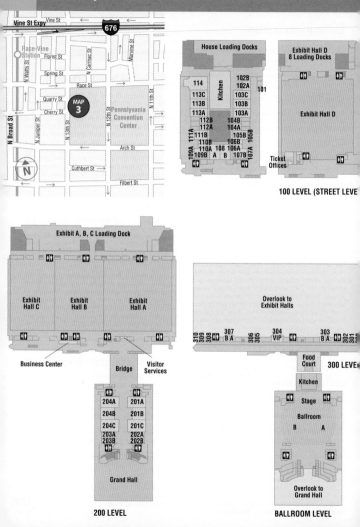

Pennsylvania Convention Center

100 LEVEL (STREET LEVEL)

Vine St Expy
676

Race-Vine Station

Florist St
Spring St
Race St
Quarry St
Cherry St
Arch St
Cuthbert St
Filbert St

N Broad St
N Juniper St
N 13th St
N 12th St
N Carmac St
Marvine St
N 11th St
N Watts St

MAP 3

Pennsylvania Convention Center

N

House Loading Docks

114
113C
113B
113A
112B
112A
111B
111A
110B
110A
109B A B
109A

Kitchen

102B
102A
103C
103B
103A
104A
104B
105B
105A
106B
106A
108 107B
107A 106B

101

Exhibit Hall D
8 Loading Docks

Exhibit Hall D

Ticket Offices

200 LEVEL

Exhibit A, B, C Loading Dock

Exhibit Hall C
Exhibit Hall B
Exhibit Hall A

Business Center
Bridge
Visitor Services

204A 201A
204B 201B
204C 201C
203A 202A
203B 202B

Grand Hall

300 LEVEL

Overlook to Exhibit Halls

310 309 308
307 B A
306 305
304 VIP
303 B A
302 301

Food Court

BALLROOM LEVEL

Kitchen
Stage
Ballroom
B A

Overlook to Grand Hall

Pennsylvania Convention Center

General Information

NFT Map: 3
Address: 1101 Arch St
             Philadelphia, PA 19107
Phone: 215-418-4700
Website: www.paconvention.com

Overview

Spanning six downtown city blocks and covering 1.3 million square-feet, the Pennsylvania Convention Center is gigantic; the second largest convention center in the Northeast, as a matter of fact. This would be wonderful indeed if conventioneers packed the place week after week but, because of union squabbles and poor city planning, such has not been the case. After years of bickering, the Convention Center is still not being used anywhere near its capacity, which, if you're of the inclination, can work as an apt metaphor for the bureaucracy of the city at large: the party is ready to roll up in the penthouse suite, but the guests aren't allowed to use the elevator to get there. And to top it all off, there's the city's latest cockamamie plan for expansion, which will wipe out valued art spaces in the factory buildings just beyond.

Unless you are attending an event, the Convention Center is not open to the public. Ergo, it's not really a hangout. It's more, with its aimless brick rest-stop chic, a fist fight on the eyes. If you happen to be there for business, however, you will be pleased to note it has state-of-the-art meeting facilities, high-speed Internet access with gigabit LAN connections, and many of the other flashy amenities true-blue bizzers crave.

For the rest of us, it's still worth checking out the calendar of events listed on the Convention Center's website. Cool exhibits and events come along every year, including such faves as the Philadelphia Auto Show (www.phillyautoshow.com), the Wizard Comic Convention, and—for God's sake, people!—the Philadelphia Flower Show (www.theflowershow.com), to which the entire city kowtows every March.

As for eating in the area goes, it's as much of a story about what to avoid as what to go to. Try as hard as possible to coax your friend into the Reading Terminal Market. It's chaotic, sure, but there's pretty much every cuisine you can think of, from fresh seafood to vegan cheesesteaks to Thai curries, and everyone can find something pleasing. We'd also recommend walking a couple of blocks to Chinatown, where there's cheap, amazing eats a-plenty.

How to Get There—Driving

From the Schuykill/76, take Exit 344/676 E. Once you're on 676 E, take the second exit, Broad Street. From the exit ramp, continue straight on Vine Street and follow all the huge signs that say "PA Convention Center." Turn right onto 12th Street and proceed two blocks to the Convention Center.

From I-95 S or N, take Exit 22/676 W. Once you're on 676 take the first exit, Broad Street. Turn right off of the exit ramp onto 15th Street. Turn left onto Vine Street (second light) then right onto 12th Street and proceed two blocks to the Convention Center.

Parking

There are 42 private lots located within a 7-block radius of the Convention Center. The only street parking in that area is at two-hour meters, with restrictions on Arch Street during rush hours (check the signs).

How to Get There—Mass Transit

All Regional Lines (R1, R2, R3, R5, R6, R7, and R8) connect directly to the Convention Center via the Market East Station. From Market East, follow signs inside the station for the Convention Center. There's no need to go outside to get to the Convention Center, which is perfect on cold or rainy days.

The Market-Frankford line stops at the Pennsylvania Convention Center/11th Street Station for easy access to the center. If you're taking the Broad Street line, make a free transfer at City Hall for the Market-Frankford line.

Trolley routes 10, 11, 13, 34, and 36 go to the Juniper Station. Walk one block north to Arch Street and then one block east (right) to 12th Street.

Bus routes 12, 17, 23, 33, 38, 44, 48, and 121 all stop at the Convention Center.

Essentials

One of Philadelphia's more overlooked limbs, the Northeast is barely noticed by locals who live in other neighborhoods. The only time they really pay attention to it is when there's another accident on Roosevelt Boulevard. As the oldest north- and south-running artery in the country, established over fifty years before I-95, the Boulevard is famous for having two of the most dangerous intersections in America.

Despite being treated as the least-favorite child by most Philadelphians, though, this area possesses just as much culture, shopping, nightlife, and restaurants as the rest of Philadelphia. Just on a more diffuse scale. Okay, it is true that when you hear about ill-behaved Philly spots Phanatics many of them are from one of the many neighborhoods in the Northeast, like Bustleton, Pennypack, and Torresdale in the far northeast and Foxchase, Frankford, Mayfair, and Oxford Circle in the near northeast.

Philly all around is a different kind of friendly, and the Northeast is a different kind of friendly again. With its own terms, food, and attitudes, the NE is too big and *special* to ignore.

⊙ Landmarks

- **The Boulevard** · Roosevelt Blvd
- **Burholme Park** · Cottman & Central Aves
- **Flyer's Skate Zone** · 10990 Decatur Rd
- **Knowlton Mansion** · 8001 Verree Rd
- **Nabisco Factory** · Comly Rd & Roosevelt Blvd
- **Northeast Philadelphia Airport (PNE)** · 9800 Ashton Rd
- **Pennypack Creek Park** · 8600 Verree Rd

Sundries

☕ Coffee

- **Quaker Diner** · 7241 Rising Sun Ave

🍸 Nightlife

- **Chickie and Pete's** · 11000 Roosevelt Blvd
- **Dave & Buster's** · 1995 Franklin Mills Cir, Franklin Mills Mall
- **The Grey Lodge** · 6235 Frankford Ave
- **Sweeney's Station Saloon** · 13639 Philmont Ave
- **Whiskey Tango Tavern** · 14000 Bustleton Ave

Restaurants

- **Benny the Bum's** · 9991 Bustleton Ave
- **Blue Ox Brauhaus** · 7980 Oxford Ave
- **Chink's Steaks** · 6030 Torresdale Ave
- **Dining Car** · 8826 Frankford Ave ⊗
- **Guido's Restaurant** · 3545 Welsh Rd
- **Joseph's Pizza** · 7947 Oxford Ave
- **Macaroni's Restaurant** · 9315 Old Bustleton Ave
- **Mayfair Diner** · 7353 Frankford Ave ⊗

- **Moe's Deli** · 7360 Frankford Ave
- **Moonstruck** · 7955 Oxford Ave
- **Nick's Roast Beef** · 2212 Cottman Ave
- **Nifty Fifty's** · 2491 Grant Ave
- **Santucci's Pizza** · 4010 Cottman Ave
- **Steve's Prince of Steaks** · 7200 Bustleton Ave
- **Sweet Lucy's Smokehouse** · 7500 State Road
- **Tiffany Diner** · 9010 Roosevelt Blvd ⊗

🛍 Shopping

- **Contempo Cuts** · 2857 Holme Ave
- **Dutch Country Farmers' Market** · 2031 Cottman Ave
- **Harry's Natural Food Store** · 1805 Cottman Ave
- **International Coins Unlimited** · 1825 Cottman Ave
- **Lipkin's Bakery** · 8013 Castor Ave
- **Roosevelt Mall** · 2311 Cottman Ave
- **St Jude Shop** · 6902 Castor Ave

Keansburg • Sandy Hook •
Twin Lights

35 · 36

109

18

34 · 18

33 · 102

195 · 100

88

Spring Lake

34

Sea Girt Lighthouse

70 · Point Pleasant

91

90

89

88

Atlantic Ocean

9

166

82

81

80

Seaside Heights

77

74

9

Island Beach State Park

69

Barnegat Lighthouse

67

63

72 · Long Beach Island

9 · Edwin B Forsyth National Wildlife Refuge

Asbury Park
Ocean Grove

Garden State Pkwy

General Information

Websites: www.virtualnjshore.com
www.shore-guide.com

Overview

Beginning in Sandy Hook in the north and extending down to Cape May in the south, the 127-mile Jersey Shore is a prime destination for weekenders and summer vacationers. People of all ages flock to the shore for its fishy-smelling waters and pebbly beaches. Some of these people may even have been known to you at one time.

There are many communities lining the shore, and each is known for its own distinct attractions, from sandy dunes and lighthouses to gambling and shopping (and a lot of other crap). Whatever their differences, all of the towns are known for their abundance of fresh seafood—by far the Shore's best asset. The Jersey Shore experience is an indispensable part of what it means to be a Philadelphian (and, no, not all memories involve fake IDs, ugly tattoos, and vomit—only most). If you're planning a trip to the shore, check out Virtual New Jersey Shore's calendar of events at www.virtualnjshore.com/events.html.

Towns/Cities

Asbury Park

While efforts are being made to restore this "seaside ghost town," Asbury Park has struggled with its growing decrepitude since the July 4, 1970 race riots. In its heyday, Asbury Park was one of the most prominent and thriving seaside resorts along the Jersey Shore. The Convention Hall, designed in the 1920s, hosted The Rolling Stones, Jefferson Airplane, The Doors, The Who, and, of course, Bruce Springsteen (who adopted Asbury as his hometown). At one point, Asbury Park drew over half a million visitors to its wide tree-lined streets, swanky hotels, lively restaurants, and packed boardwalks. The beach is still beautiful, but today there are more empty lots than tourists. That may change soon. Look beneath the grit and you'll find intrepid yuppies (try Brickwall and Bistro Olé), a large LGBT community (try Georgies Bar or The Empress), and rockers of all ages (try the legendary Stone Pony, Wonder Bar, or Asbury Lanes).

Atlantic City

www.atlanticcitynj.com

Visitors expecting a Vegas-like wonderland are in for a serious surprise. Sure, Atlantic City features the same gambling and topless dancers as does Sin City, but AC doesn't shield its guests from the more distressing side of the gambling world. The winos, the bums, and the broke grandmothers are inescapable. And while the surrounding population sinks deeper into its own morass, the casinos keep getting glitzier, with additions like the swanky billion-dollar Borgata, a new convention center, and a new upscale shopping area for all the Gucci you'll want to buy with your winnings. Right.

Harrah's remains the premiere casino venue, regularly playing host to the 2005 World Series of Poker. Donald Trump himself owns three glittering casinos here, and the Hilton provides a touch of old-school glam. Caesar's is one of the largest casinos in the city, while Bally's Wild Wild West Casino attracts a mixed clientele. When it comes to choosing a casino, you can't really go wrong—until you start dipping into Junior's college fund.

But gambling and strip joints aren't Atlantic City's only attractions. There is golf, sailing, fishing, shopping malls on boardwalks, and slums too! Plans for a new multi-billion-dollar state-of-the-art Convention Center and Grand Boulevard are currently in the works. Stay tuned.

Long Beach Island
www.longbeachisland.com

Perhaps the least-crowded and least-schlocky of all shore destinations, LBI is a family-oriented stretch of small and even smaller towns such as Beach Haven, Surf City, Loveladies, Harvey Cedars, and Barnegat. Each town has its own character (Harvey Cedars = $$$; Beach Haven = mellow) and one or two decent restaurants/attractions. However, without a boardwalk like Seaside Heights, LBI will fortunately never get hordes of teenage jerkbags cruising the main drag and puking in hotel rooms. Courses in sea kayaking, yoga, pottery, and photography are set against a panorama of waves, white sand, blue skies, and brilliant sunsets (thank you, New Jersey pollution!). Albert Music Hall (www.alberthall.org) hosts live country, folk, and bluegrass music year-round on Saturday nights. Broadway fans can take in their favorite song and dance routines at the Surflight Theatre (www.surflight.org).

Ocean City

Ocean City without the Boardwalk is like Paris without the Champs d' Elysées: so much of this Jersey Shore town's gestalt is fashioned down at the boardwalk. One of the last authentic walkways in the area, the Boardwalk is a mixture of classic and contemporary seaside attractions. The timeless 140-foot Ferris Wheel, the requisite rollercoaster, and the ubiquitous boardwalk bumper cars stand next to the newer mini-golf courses, water rides, and waterpark (Li'l Buc's Bay), where adults are admitted only with a child. It's easy to spend a packed day without leaving the ocean front, if you can subsist on a diet of soda and french fries. Boozehounds take note: this former Methodist retreat is still completely alcohol-free. Check out the Ocean City Ghost Tour, a candlelit walking tour which runs every evening between the end of May through October, where guides recount spooky tales of local folklore (www.ghosttour.com).

Cape May
www.capemay.com

Deemed worthy of historic preservation in 1976 by the National Register of Historic Places, Cape May is as distinguished as it gets at the Jersey Shore. Here you'll find the biggest collection of Victorian houses in the country; the elaborately built pastel-colored homes are on every block and run the gamut of Victorian sensibility from Mansard and Gothic style, to Colonial Revival, Queen Anne, and Italianate-influenced homes. The Mid-Atlantic Center for the Arts offers hourly walking tours explaining the history and significance of these mansions. If you'd rather trek solo, don't miss the Abbey Bed 'n Breakfast on the corner of Gurney Street and Columbia Avenue, and the 15 elaborately decorated period rooms at Emlen Physick Estate, located at 1048 Washington Street.

Point Pleasant
www.pointpleasantbeach.com

Point Pleasant offers up the archetypal beach experience: swimming, surfing, sun bathing, ice cream, Fun House, etc. The south end of the beach is public, but has no lifeguard on duty, while Bradshaw Beach at the north end requires an entry fee. The Sinatra House (on the corner of West Street and Boardwalk) heats things up at night with Old Blue Eyes' crooning out the window. There's no shortage of bars or dance clubs to choose from.

Sandy Hook

Think pristine white sandy beaches, old wooden boardwalks, surf fishing, historic lighthouses, bird observatories, salt marshes, and you've got a good picture of the NJ Shore. Sandy Hook is also known as home of the Ocean Institute— the oldest working lighthouse in America.

Seaside Heights

www.seasideheights.net

This is the spot for the surfing crowd. Seaside Heights touts itself as having "some of the top lifeguards anywhere," and its public beaches are open year-round. Beyond the waves and surf, the bustling boardwalk is another attraction. Local pubs and nightclubs line the vast stretch of wooden planks. All of them are bad. If you're older than 17 ½, this isn't the place for you.

Spring Lake

This 100-year-old, quiet family resort town is comprised of tranquil coastline, a non-commercial boardwalk, and sand dune beaches. The main street is full of quaint shops, gourmet restaurants, and cozy B&Bs. If you're looking for privacy, aim for a mid-week getaway, as the four beaches get crowded on the weekends. The area is known for great scuba diving (including an off-shore ship wreck to explore), and fresh- and salt-water fishing. If you're looking for high-energy activity, this may not be your spot, but it remains a romantic getaway for couples.

The Wildwoods

www.wildwoodsnj.com

Little-known fact: the collection of three resort communities that make up the Wildwoods— including Wildwood Crest, The City of North Wildwood, and the City of Wildwood—is known as the "Mecca of the Kiting World." Condé Nast Traveler Magazine also chose Wildwood as the "Best Sports Beach." Activities include golfing, shopping, deep-sea fishing, kayaking, biking, beach aerobics, water-parks, and a large beach Ultimate Frisbee tournament in the summer. Well-known fact: there are neon-drenched kitschy motels galore and a massively trashy honky-tonk boardwalk, complete with a blaring motorized tram to tote your fat vacationing ass from one end to the other. Kids can't get enough of the Morey Piers Amusement Park (www.moreyspiers.com), but adults definitely will.

Attractions

Barnegat Lighthouse

609-494-2016

Once upon a time, there were actually two lighthouses built in Barnegat. The first, standing at a puny 40 feet, was built in 1835 and crumbled shortly after. The second lighthouse, which soars nearly four times taller than its predecessor, at a majestic 165 feet, was built in 1859 and still stands to this day. Located at the north end of Long Beach Island, the Barnegat Lighthouse has become the symbol of the Jersey Shore. The red and white structure, retired in 1927, is affectionately referred to by the locals as "Old Barney." Barney is open for public viewing 9 am-4:30 pm during the winter and until 9:30 pm in the summer months.

Cape May Lighthouse

609-884-5404; Hours vary: Open daily April- November; $5 adults, $1 children; Free Parking

The 157-foot tall lighthouse is actually the third built in Cape May. The first (built in 1823) and the second (built in 1847) were both destroyed by erosion. The one that shines its beacon today, located in Cape May Point State Park's Lower Township, has been standing since 1859 and was built with bricks from the 1847 version. It's worth huffing and puffing up the 199 steps for spectacular panoramic vistas of the Cape May Peninsula. The lighthouse is currently managed by the Mid-Atlantic Center for the Arts (MAC). The non-profit group sponsors cultural and artistic events and offers daily guided tours (www. capemaymac.org).

Cape May Point State Park

609-884-2159; Open sunrise to sunset

Mockingbirds, warblers, and sparrows, oh my! Located just off the southern end of the Garden State Parkway, this 253-acre no-fee park is a haven for bird-lovers. Several trails lead to ponds, marshes, dunes, and forest habitats where all sorts of migratory birds can be spotted. Following one of the three main hiking trails, the Red Trail (0.5 mile), the Yellow Trail (1.5 miles), or the Blue Trail (2 miles), is the best way to explore the park. If you're looking to spice up your vacation with education, the park hosts nature clubs and programs for children.

Edwin B. Forsythe National Wildlife Refuge

b/w Brick Township & Brigantine

This refuge encompasses over 43,000 acres and has two divisions (Brigantine and Barnegat). Bird-watching, nature walks, great views of protected wetlands, and learning about migratory bird habitats are the main deal here. For more information, go to http://forsythe.fws.gov.

Island Beach State Park

This majestic barrier island is made up of 3,000 acres of preserved land and over ten miles of pure, untainted white sand. The park is filled with historic buildings, hiking and biking trails, naturalist programs, bathhouses, and pristine bird-watching spots. This natural wonder is a must-see for outdoor enthusiasts, and in complete contrast with the crazed, crowded Seaside Heights just up the road. Highly recommended.

Lucy the Elephant
9200 Atlantic Ave, Margate, NJ, 609-823-6473;
www.lucytheelephant.org,
Summer hours Mon-Sat 10 am-8 pm,
and Sun 10 am-5 pm
The legendary 65-foot wooden elephant, which stands mid-stride overlooking the sea, is one of the Shore's oddest intrigues. Built in 1881, Lucy's stout legs serve as a 350-step stairwell linking the bottom floor with the anterior rooms and howdah. She can be seen without binoculars from up to eight miles away. The 90-ton mammoth pachyderm was added to the National Registry of Historic Places in 1971 and now offers tours for groups of ten or more. Admission is $5 for adults and $3 for children under 12.

Rutgers University Marine Field Station/ Great Bay Boulevard
Great Bay Blvd, Tuckerton, NJ
A completely overlooked gem amidst a morass of mid-prole dreams, the drive out to Rutgers University's Marine Field Station along Great Bay Boulevard is absolutely incredible. Low wetlands, small wooden bridges, lots of wildlife, ruined canneries, amazing sunsets, and almost no people make this about as far an experience from Seaside Heights, Wildwood, or AC as you can get. You can find cheap-ass boat rentals along the Boulevard, so you can explore, go crabbing or fishing or swimming, or just be cool. The Field Station has tours occasionally, so for more information, go to: http://marine.rutgers.edu/cool/info/directions.html.

Sea Girt Lighthouse
Beach Blvd & Ocean Ave, 732-974-0514;
Open one Sunday/month
Sea Girt, once appropriately called "Wreck Pond," earned its menacing name because of the countless shipwrecks in the Manasquan River. With the construction of the lighthouse in 1896, which warned boats of the upcoming shoreline, "Wreck Pond" traded in its ill-omened moniker for the less threatening "Sea Girt." The lighthouse closed after the Second World War, 50 years after its opening, and has been preserved as a historic site. The site has

become a popular destination for elementary school fieldtrips, and public tours are given once a month on Sundays.

Twin Lights
732-872-1814; www.twin-lights.org; Memorial Day-Labor Day 9 am-4:30 pm daily, Rest of the year Wed-Sun 9 am-4:30pm
Towering 200 feet above sea level in Highlands, the two-towered Navesink Light station has been used as the shore's primary lighthouse since 1828. The lighthouse standing today was built in 1862, and has been open as a museum since it was acquired by the state in 1967. A climb to the top offers an unbeatable ocean-view panorama and the exhibition gallery offers historical background on the site.

Wildwood Boardwalk
16th Ave to Cresse Ave; Open daily Palm Sunday weekend through Columbus Day
Wildwood is filled with more rides than Disneyland, including the East Coast's tallest and fastest wooden coaster, the Great White. There are five amusement piers to visit with a cornucopia of carnival games, souvenir shops, and food stands (rumor has it that there are more pizza joints here per square foot than anywhere else in the world). If you're lucky at Skee-Ball, you may go home with a pair of fuzzy dice for your rearview. A tram line makes transportation between venues fast and easy. Dust off your poodle skirt for DooWop '50s Night, or mingle with the other car connoisseurs at Classic Car shows. Check out the *Cape May Times* newspaper for a calendar of events.

How to Get There—Driving

From Center City, cross the Franklin Bridge into New Jersey and follow signs to Cherry Hill (Route 38) and the beaches (stay to your left). Once on Route 38, get into the right hand lane and merge onto I-70. Take I-70 until you hit the I-72 Junction East and keep right around the circle. Follow I-72 for 26 miles and you'll end up at the Jersey Shore. If you leave on a weekday and it's not rush hour, you can make the journey in an hour and a half. At all other times, don't leave without your mix tapes, as you'll most likely be sitting in traffic.

From the northeast, go over the Tacony-Palmyra Bridge onto Route 73 S. Head to the I-70 intersection and drive east. At the I-72 Circle, take 72 E to Long Beach Island (about 26 miles). From the south, take Route 42 E to Route 35 N, which takes you to Route 70 E. Or take the 42 to the NJ Turnpike and get off at Exit 4 (Route 73 S). Follow the directions above.

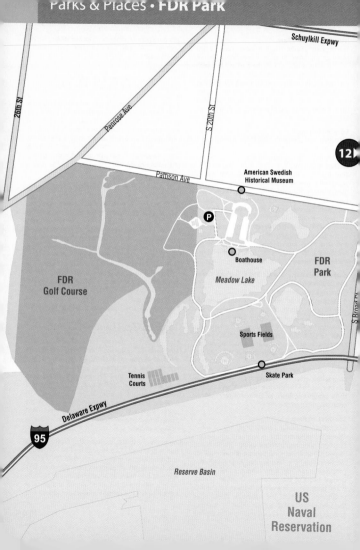

General Information

NFT Maps:	Adjacent to the west boundary of Map 12
Address:	2000 Pattison Ave Philadelphia, PA 19145
Phone:	n/a
Website:	www.fairmountpark.org/FdrPark.asp

Overview

Although thousands of fans pass through the south Philly stadiums each time there's a Phillies or Eagles game, the vast majority of them completely miss FDR Park, sitting there in plain view on the other side of Broad Street. The park offers baseball, softball, and rugby fields, tennis courts, and the infamous FDR Skate Park, which sits in the shadows directly under I-95 (more on that later). What was once a marsh is now home to the aforementioned fields and courts as well as ponds and creeks, the American Swedish Historical Museum, a gazebo and boathouse, and even a golf course, just west of the main park area.

American Swedish Historical Museum

This museum's library and various galleries are worth a visit if you're interested in Swedish history. The architecture of the building itself was intended to be a blend of Swedish and American styling; we don't know if it achieved that or not, but we will go so far as to say that it looks nice.

The Skate Park

The modern hallmark of FDR Park is the skate park. It started as a pathetic attempt by the city's part to mollify skaters barred from downtown Love Park, but has evolved into a mecca for skaters—and not just local ones. Mainly built by volunteers ("built by skaters, for skaters" is a phrase that comes up often), the shadowy collection of concrete includes installations known as the Bunker and the Minefield, among others; but regardless of the naming scheme, the park is not actually a battlefield unless BMX riders and skaters show up at the same time. Bikes are technically allowed in the park, but are generally unwelcome by the skaters, who say the bikes cause damage. Prepare to stand your ground if you show up with only two wheels.

As with many places in Philadelphia, the skate park is not for the faint of heart. It's not a terribly welcoming place in either attitude or architecture; the word "hardcore" comes to mind in describing the regulars, and this is *not* a beginner's skate park. If you're just starting out, look elsewhere. But if you're an intermediate skater looking for a challenging park in Philly, you won't do better than FDR.

How to Get There—Driving

The driving directions for FDR are essentially the same as the routes to get to the Sports Complex; you just want to end up on the west side of Broad Street instead of the east side. The most direct route is to take I-95 to Exit 17, go north on Broad Street, and make a left onto Pattison Avenue.

Parking

There's plenty of free parking inside the park.

How to Get There—Mass Transit

Take the Broad Street subway line south to the last stop-Pattison. When you come up out of the station, turn to face Broad Street. Cross Broad Street and walk to Pattison Avenue. You can enter the park just ahead on Pattison, on the left.

1. Neuropsychology Laboratories
2. Language and Communication Center
3. 3210 Cherry Street
4. Academic Building
5. 3201 Arch Street
6. Campus Security Office
7. Frederic O Hess Engineering Research Lab
8. Nesbitt Hall
9. Leonard Pearlstein Business Learning Center
10. Matheson Hall
11. Korman Center
12. Disque Hall
13. Bossone Research Enterprise Center
14. LeBow Engineering Center
15. Center for Automation Technology
16. Main Building
17. Randell Hall
18. Curtis Hall
19. Alumni Enginering Labs

Center City Campus
20. Myer Feinstein Polyclinic
21. Bobst Building
22. North Tower (Main Hospital Entrance)
23. South Tower
24. New College Building H
26. Franklin Office Center, 1427 Vine Street
27. Stiles Alumni Hall
28. Bellet Building
29. 221 N Broad Street
30. 219 N Broad Street
31. 207 N Broad Street

Center City Hahnemann Campus

Henry Ave/Queen Ln Campus

General Information

NFT Map: 2, 14, 23
Mailing Address: 3141 Chestnut St
Philadelphia, PA 19104
Phone: 215-895-2000
Website: www.drexel.edu

Overview

You could say that Drexel is experiencing a growth spurt. In the past decade, Drexel has amassed a medical school, a law school, and two new academic buildings with state-of-the-art technology. With change comes a bigger student body—the University is adding an additional underclassmen dorm building just to house everyone. Recently, Drexel made the US News & World Report's Top Schools In Pennsylvania list.

The actual campus is composed of three locations, though most classes are held at the University City Main Campus. Nursing and Health students hang out at the Center City Hahnemann Campus, and students at the Drexel University College of Medicine take their classes at the Queen Lane Medical Campus.

There are many extracurricular activities to keep students occupied, including 140 different student clubs. Athletic types should head over to the John A Daskalakis Athletic Center; an impressive facility housing a swimming pool and indoor basketball/volleyball and squash courts.

Part of Drexel's uniqueness stems from its location. Instead of being a closed campus, their buildings are scattered among the streets of Philly—which also contributes to the lack of community many students feel. Drexel students spend lots of time off-campus anyway thanks to Drexel Co-op, one of the nation's oldest and largest work-experience programs, allowing students up to 18 months of internships while still in school.

Tuition

Students choose between enrolling in a four- or five-year undergraduate degree program. The former will set you back around $39,700 a year, while the 5-year program costs about $32,300 a year (for tuition only—excluding fees, housing, and meal plans). Over 90% of students receive financial aid, and they actually encourage all students to apply regardless of whether they think they're eligible or not. As of yet, there are no financial aid incentives for students who can funnel beer through multiple orifices.

Sports

Calling all jocks! Drexel has 16 NCAA Division 1 teams to try out for, and they've been working on a major expansion of their athletic center. If you're not the ultra-competitive type, there are more casual activities, like the one-day bench-press or dart competitions. Various intramural sports also run year-round, such as beach volleyball and flag football. For the even less physically inclined, check out the Recreation Sports Office's fall term health and wellness program. Designed specifically to help you cope with the stress of those ruthless calculus assignments or how to manage those unyielding cheesesteak and Yuengling diets, the seminars are popular ways to help you survive your campus experience.

Culture on Campus

Like so many educational institutions, Drexel has its share of co-curricular and extra-curricular fun stuff. One particular favorite is the free Friday Night Movie Series that often showcases newly released flicks. Creative arts and progressive politics get equal time on DUTV's broadcasts, and the hipsters spinning at WKDU FM get a listen well beyond the campus. If theater sparks your interest, the Drexel Players put on one play per term, from musicals to dark comedies. And come early for the annual comedic performance, because tickets sell out early! (Past performers have included Lewis Black and Dane Cook.) Drexel has hosted cool theater companies for a full season in residence to great critical acclaim, so keep an eye out for future programs that bring pros to these stages. And due to the diverse student body, students can enjoy a cappella performances, impromptu cricket matches, and a Straight and Gay Alliance dance all in one weekend.

Departments

Log onto www.drexel.edu/contact for a more complete university directory.

Undergraduate Admissions 215-895-2400
Alumni Relations 888-DU-GRADS
Athletics 215-895-1999
Bursar, Office of Student Accounts 215-895-1445
Career Management: Steinbright
   Career Development (SCDC) 215-895-2185
Co-operative Education 215-895-2185
Computing Resources (IRT) 215-895-2698
Drexel Directory Assistance 215-895-2000
Facilities Management 215-895-1700
Financial Aid 215-895-2537
International Programs 215-895-1704
Institutional Advancement 215-895-2600
Library-Drexel University City
   Main Campus 215-895-1500
Library-Health Sciences Libraries 215-762-7631
President 215-895-2100
Provost 215-895-2200
Research Administration 215-895-5849
Sports 215-895-1999
Student Life- Drexel University City
   Main Campus 215-895-2506
Student Life- Center City
   Hahnemann Campus 215-762-1400
Student Resource Center (SRC) 215-895-2300
University Relations 215-895-1530

General Information

Address: 1900 W Olney Ave
           Philadelphia, PA 19141
Phone: 215-951-1000
Website: www.lasalle.edu

Overview

Founded in 1863 by the De La Salle Christian Brothers, La Salle University is a private Roman Catholic university located on a 100-acre campus not far from Center City. Between its School of Arts & Sciences, School of Nursing, and School of Business Administration, La Salle enrolls over 6,200 students a year in 61 different undergraduate and graduate degree programs. La Salle's ongoing dedication to its Roman Catholic roots is evident in its strong focus on community service and the existence of a theology and ministry graduate program.

Tuition

La Salle's 2011–2012 tuition was $34,840, and the basic room and board costs were $10,920. Just remember these figures do not include books, supplies, lab fees, sacramental ale, or personal expenses.

Sports

La Salle's student body is extremely athletic, with more than 500 of its undergraduates participating on one or more of the twenty-three NCAA Division I varsity athletic teams (not to mention the students playing intramural sports). Men's teams include baseball, basketball, crew, cross-country, golf, soccer, swimming, tennis, and indoor and outdoor track & field. Women's teams include basketball, crew, cross-country, field hockey, lacrosse, soccer, softball, swimming, tennis, volleyball, and indoor and outdoor track & field. The football team was dropped after a stellar 0-10 season. The Explorers basketball teams are also members of the Big Five; Philly's own annual basketball backyard rumble.

Culture on Campus

The La Salle University Art Museum (Lower level of Olney Hall, 1900 W Olney Ave, 215-951-1221) proudly touts itself as the only permanent collection of paintings, drawings, and sculpture from the West at any university museum in the Philadelphia region. The permanent collection focuses on European and American landscape, portraiture, still-life, and abstract paintings spanning the Middle Ages to modern times. Smaller collections include Old Master prints and drawings, illustrated rare bibles, ancient Greek terra cotta pottery, African tribal art, and Japanese prints from the 19th- and 20th-centuries. The museum is open Monday–Friday from 10 am to 4 pm and Sunday from 2 pm to 4 pm, with varying hours during the summer and holidays; call ahead before planning a visit. Access to the museum is free (though donations are encouraged). Group tours are offered by appointment.

Departments

Log onto www.lasalle.edu/contact for a more complete university directory.

Undergraduate Admissions 215-951-1500
Graduate Admissions 215-951-1100
Continuing Studies Admissions...... 215-951-1655

N

Wissahickon Creek

Wissahickon
Valley
Park

PAGE
118

Alumni
Field

Hughes
Gym

Physical Plant/
Carriage House

Haggar Hall
(Learning Center)

Fox St

Townhouses

Archer Hall

Wallenberg
Center

Downs
Hall

Athletic and
Recreation
Center

Art Center 1

Student
Center

Information
Technology

Kanbar
Campus
Center

Gutman
Library

Independence
Plaza

White
House

Architecture
& Design
Center

Nethe rfield Rd

Scholler
Hall

Roxboro
House

Henry Ave

Design
Center

Hayward Hall

Search
Hall

E Netherfield Rd

Fashion
Mechandising

White
Corners

W Netherfield Rd

Softball
Field

Timber Ln

Gibbs
Hall

Tuttleman
Center

Henry Ave

Apalogen Rd

W School House Ln

President's
House

Vaux St

Smith
House

Ronson Hall

MAP
23

Warden Dr

W Coulter St

Architecture/
Interior Design
Studios

Chapel

Weber
Design
Studios

Dining Hall
(Ravenhill)

Gypsy Ln

Ravenhill
Mansion

Mott
Hall

Partridge
Hall

Security

Fortress
Hall

Ravenhill
Athletic
Field

Powers St

General Information:

NFT Map: 23
Address: School House Ln & Henry Ave
Philadelphia, PA 19144
Phone: 215-951-2700
Website: www.philau.edu

Overview

Founded in 1884 and long known as the College of Textiles & Sciences (a.k.a. "Textiles"), Philadelphia University was finally granted university status by the state of Pennsylvania in 1999 and now operates six schools—Architecture, Business Administration, Design & Media, Liberal Arts, Science & Health, and Engineering & Textiles. The University offers more than forty undergraduate and graduate degree programs to its 3,200 full- and part-time students. The school is known for its interdisciplinary approach to higher education, combining a liberal arts base with professional training. The private university is located on a 100-acre campus about twenty minutes away from Center City, and is otherwise outside of the city's consciousness, despite its name.

Tuition

For the academic year, a full-time undergraduate's tuition and fees will total around $29,000 with an additional $10,000 for room and board. For more information about extra fees, alternative board plans, or financial aid packages, call 215-951-2940.

Sports

The Philadelphia University Rams compete at the Division II level in eleven sports: men's and women's basketball, cheerleading, cross country, rowing, soccer, and tennis, men's golf and baseball, and women's field hockey, lacrosse, softball, and volleyball. The men's soccer team is a tough competitor at the Division I level. Athletic scholarships are available to students in all varsity sports. Games are free and open to the public. For scores and game highlights, call the Rams Hotline on 215-951-2852.

Philadelphia University also offers club sports and intramural teams, open to all students, staff, and faculty, that allow participants to compete in athletic events on campus at a less rigorous level than that of the varsity sports teams.

Culture on Campus

The Design Center, located in the Goldie Paley House (4200 Henry Ave, 215-951-2860; www.philau.edu/designcenter), is one of Philadelphia's most under-rated exhibition spaces. The Hollywood rancher-style building holds over 200,000 artifacts related to textiles collected by the university over the past 125 years, from ecclesiastical attire and altar pieces to 19th-century haute-couture and a library of 19th- and 20th-century fabric. The center aims to explore the meaning of design in our everyday lives through ever-changing furniture and design exhibitions and remains a definite must-see for anyone with even a latent interest in fashion and design.

Departments

Log onto www.philau.edu/univphonenumbers.asp for a more complete university directory.

Undergraduate Admissions 215-951-2800
Graduate Admissions 215-951-2943
School of Liberal Arts............... 215-951-2600
School of Architecture 215-951-2896
School of Design & Media 215-951-2700
School of Business Administration 215-951-2810
School of Science & Health 215-951-2870
School of Engineering &
Textiles 215-951-2750

St Joseph's University

1. Lancaster Court
2. Merion Gardens
3. Wynnewood Hall
4. City Avenue Residence alls
5. Ashwood Hall
6. Overbrook Hall
7. Michael J Morris Quad
8. Alumni House
9. St Alphonsus House-Jesuit Residence
10. Tara Hall
11. Sourin Hall
12. LaFarge Hall
13. Quirk Hall
14. Power Plant
15. Simpson Hall-University Bookstore
16. Chapel of St Joseph
17. Wolfington Hall-Campus Ministry
18. Campion Hall
19. Science Center
20. Francis A Drexel Library
21. Bellermine Hall
22. Barblin/Lonergan Hall
23. Post Hall
24. Mandeville Hall
25. Barry Annex-Center for International Programs
26. Barry Hall
27. Flanigan Hall
28. ELS Language Center
29. Alumni Memorial Fieldhouse
30. AFROTC Program
31. Claver House-Honors Department
32. St Mary's Hall
33. McShain Hall/Haub Executive Center
34. St Albert's Annex
35. St Albert's Hall
36. Xavier Hall
37. Bronstein Hall-Office of Undergraduate Admissions
38. St Thomas Hall-Office of Financial Assistance
39. Jordan Hall
40. Boland Hall
41. Regis Annex
42. Regis Hall-President's Office
43. Loyola Center and Carriage House-Jesuit Residence
44. Hogan Hall
45. Sullivan Annex
46. Sullivan Hall
47. University Press-Merion
48. Human Resources-University Communications
49. University Press-Bala Cynwyd
50. Office of Development-5th Floor (off map, at 50th St & City Ave)

General Information

Address: 5600 City Ave
             Philadelphia, PA 19131
Phone: 610-660-1000
Website: www.sju.edu

Overview

Founded in 1851, St. Joseph's University is a Catholic college located on a 65-acre campus in western Philadelphia and Montgomery County. The 7,700 students (4,500 of them traditional undergraduates) are schooled in the Jesuit tradition with a strong liberal arts-focused curriculum that fosters rigorous and open-minded inquiry and maintains high academic standards.

St. Joe's also counts itself among the 142 schools in the country with a Phi Beta Kappa chapter and AACSB business school accreditation. With 75 undergraduate and 47 graduate programs to choose from, students have a variety of academic options.

But co-eds at St. Joe's aren't *all* work and no play. Following the men's basketball team's thrilling run to the Elite Eight in the NCAA tourney a few years back, the school seems to be suddenly garnering national attention. Romance seems to be in the air as well, as the long list of "Hawkmate" wedding announcements in the alumni newsletter and the ever-busy campus chapel can attest.

Tuition

Tuition for the 2011–2012 academic year was $36,480, and room and board was an additional $12,256. Of course, these prices exclude student fees, books, and getting the 'Benz waxed.

Sports

If you see a car with a bumper sticker that reads "Friends don't let friends go to Villanova," it's very likely headed here on game days. Even when St. Joe's isn't playing its crosstown rival, "The Hawk Will Never Die!" can be heard echoing from the Alumni Memorial Fieldhouse throughout the school year. In addtion to the championship men's and women's basketball squads, St. Joseph's fields teams in twenty varsity sports including cross-country, lacrosse, rowing, soccer, tennis, and track & field for men and women, men's baseball and golf, and women's softball and field hockey. The teams compete in Division I of the National Collegiate Athletic Association and belong to the Atlantic 10 as well as Philly's own Big Five. SJU athletics, however, extend much further than varsity competition. Hundreds of students participate in intramural and club sports; thousands, including alumni and friends of the university, make the Field-house and adjoining Student/Sports Recreation Center a thriving area on campus year-round. Visit www.sjuhawks.com for news and events on Hawks of all ages.

Culture on Campus

The University Gallery at Boland Hall (www.sju.edu/gallery/, 5600 City Ave, 610-660-1840) hosts eight art shows from September through May. The first five exhibitions feature professional artists who are mostly, but not exclusively, from the area. (Anyone may submit slides for consideration.) The sixth is the Senior Arts Thesis Exhibition that highlights the year-long projects of the senior art majors. Then there's a culminating Student Arts Festival that is an all-day celebration of art, music, and theater. Finally, the year closes with the Overbrook High School displaying their students' work. Open and free to the public throughout the school year (10 am–4 pm), the gallery is closed on weekends and during the summer months and holidays.

The Department of Fine & Performing Arts is also home to the Cap & Bells Dramatic Arts Society, the University Singers, and the Bluett Theatre. For specific event information call 610-660-1840 or visit www.sju.edu/fine_arts.

Departments

Log onto www.sju.edu/sju/contact.html for a university directory and links to division and department web pages.

Undergraduate Admissions 888-BE-A-HAWK
College of Arts & Sciences 610-660-1282
Haub School of Business 610-660-1645
University College
   (Continuing Education) 610-660-1267
Graduate Arts & Sciences............. 610-660-1289
Graduate Admissions 610-660-1101
Registrar's Office 610-660-1011

General Information

Address: 1801 N Broad St
             Philadelphia, PA 19122
Phone: 215-204-7000
Website: www.temple.edu

Overview

Every Philly native's safety school, Temple has risen in national standing and prominence to a point where graduating alumni (besides the Coz, who has always shown much love for the Owl) can feel very good about the quality of education they received. The school is pretty damn huge: more than 34,000 students in seventeen separate schools and colleges crowd its lecture halls. Education at Temple spans five regional campuses, including the flagship Main Campus, Health Sciences Campus, and Center City Campus in Philadelphia, as well as Temple University at Ambler and a suburban campus—Tyler School of Art—in Elkins Park. The university also has an education center in Harrisburg as well as international campuses in Tokyo, Japan, and Rome, Italy.

Tuition

For the 2011–2012 academic year, full-time undergraduate tuition and fees for Pennsylvania residents averaged $13,006, while out-of-state residents paid an average of $22,832 (although tuition sometimes varies depending on the school). Room and board for all undergraduate students averaged $8,275. Books, lab fees, and personal expenses are in addition to these prices. Graduate student tuition, fees, and expenses vary by department.

Sports

Perhaps it's better not to speak of the miserable football team, which lost its membership in the Big East and now participates in the Mid-Atlantic Conference. On the positive side, there are the hugely successful men's and women's basketball teams, who play their games in the sparkling Liacouras Center, a 10,200-seat multipurpose venue that also hosts a full range of concerts, dramatic presentations, and exhibitions. The Center is located less than two miles from City Hall. Public bus and subway transportation can take you directly to the center. If you're driving, parking is no problem—there's a connected parking garage as well as a number of well-lighted surface lots nearby. For more information call 215-204-2400 or visit www.liacourascenter.com.

Culture on Campus

The Boyer College of Music and Dance hosts the Temple University Concert Series—over 200 recitals, concerts, master classes, and lectures presented by faculty, students, and renowned guest artists. Classical music, jazz, and dance are just a taste of the series' fare. Call 215-204-8301 for info on specific events or visit www.temple.edu/boyer.

The Tyler School of Art features public programs in many forms that are offered at various campus locations, in the galleries, and in the community. Tyler Gallery (Elkins Park, 7725 Penrose Ave, 215-782-2776) in Tyler Hall holds exhibitions each year that exhibit works from emerging area artists as well as Tyler students.

Penrose Gallery (Elkins Park, 7725 Penrose Ave, 215-782-2776) in Penrose Hall has student-curated exhibitions (known as "Produce") as well as many other student retrospectives and installations. Other informal spaces within Penrose and Tyler Halls host many more student shows each year. On Main Campus the Architecture Department installs student works regularly throughout the school year in a flexible installation space in its building. Visit www.temple.edu/tyler for more information.

The Temple Theater Department, which runs out of the School of Communications and Theater, puts on three to four dramatic and comedic plays during each of the fall and spring semesters. Visit www.temple.edu/theater for ticket information and dates.

Departments

Visit https://directory.temple.edu/search/ for other university phone numbers and email addresses.

College of Health Professions 215-204-7543
Tyler School of Art 215-782-2828
Fox School of Business
   and Management 215-204-7676
School of Communications
   and Theater 215-204-8421
School of Dentistry. 215-707-2803
College of Education 215-204-8011
College of Engineering 215-204-7800
Beasley School of Law. 215-204-7861
College of Liberal Arts. 215-204-7743
School of Medicine. 215-707-7000
School of Pharmacy. 215-707-4990
College of Science and Technology 215-204-2888
School of Tourism
   and Hospitality Management 215-204-8701

University of Pennsylvania

1. 3216 Chancellor
2. Pafestra
3. Hutchinson Gym
4. Ringe Squash Courts
5. Rittenhouse Laboratories
6. Dunning Coaches' Center
7. Weightman Hall
8. Moore School Building
9. Skirkanich Hall
10. Levine Hall
11. Towne Building
12. Music Building
13. Music Annex
14. Morgan Building
15. Vegalos Labs of the IAST
16. Meyerson Hall
17. Fisher Fine Arts Library /Duhring Wing
18. Irvine Auditorium
19. Jaffe Building
20. Van Pelt Library
21. College Hall
22. Houston Hall
23. Dietrich Graduate Library
24. Sweeten Alumni House
25. Logan Hall
26. Williams Hall
27. Silverman Hall
28. Gittis Hall
29. Pepper Hall
30. Tanenbaum Hall
31. 3401 Walnut Street
32. La Terrasse
33. Franklin Building
34. 133 S 36th St
35. Penn Center for Rehabilitation & Care
36. Institute of Contemporary Art
37. Sansom Place West
38. Iron Gate Theater /Christian Association
39. Greenfield Intercultural Center
40. Newman Center
41. Addams Hall
42. 202 S 36th
43. The ARCH
44. Annenberg School
45. 3615/3619
46. Annenberg Center
47. Stiteler Hall
48. Graduate Education
49. Soloman Labs
50. Caster Building
51. Class of 1920 Commons
52. Clinical Research Building
53. Nursing Education Building
54. Biomedical Research Building
55. Stellar-Chance Laboratories
56. Blockley Hall
60. John Morgan Building
61. Anatomy-Chemistry Building

62. Richards Laboratories/Goddard Labs
63. Leidy Laboratories/Kaplan Wing/ Mudd Laboratory
64. Lynch Laboratory
65. Rosenthal Building
66. Mabel Pew Myrin Pavlion
67. Cupp Pavilion
68. Wright/Saunders Building
69. Scheie Eye Institute
70. Heart Institute/Mutch Building
71. Medical Science Research Laboratory
72. 3910 Building
76. Kelly Writers House
77. Fels Institute of Government

Wharton Business School
47. Colonial Penn Center/ Locust House
52. McNeil Building
53. Lauder Fischer Hall
73. Huntsman Hall
74. Steinberg Conference Center
75. Vance Hall

MAP 14

University of Pennsylvania

General Information

NFT Map: 14
Address: 3451 Walnut St
Philadelphia, PA 19104
Phone: 215-898-5000
Website: www.upenn.edu

Overview

Ladies and gentlemen, this is Pennsylvania's Ivy League school, and don't forget it. One of the oldest universities in the country and the first to institute a modern liberal arts curriculum, the University of Pennsylvania was established in 1749 by founding father Benjamin Franklin.

Today, with nearly 10,000 undergraduate students and 10,000 grad students enrolled in its schools, UPenn consistently ranks among the top ten universities in the annual *U.S. News & World Report* survey. The Wharton School is considered one of the country's top three business schools, and Penn's other graduate programs all rank among the top ten in their fields.

The urban campus spans a substantial 269 acres of West Philadelphia, and includes buildings by notable architects such as Frank Furness, Louis Kahn, Robert Venturi, and Denise Scott Brown. Locals once razzed UPenn students for sticking close to the campus walls, but there's no doubt that recent 'Penntrification' has changed once-decaying University City for the better. If only we could have Fresh Grocer and White Dog without the Gap and Anne Taylor. Well, you can't win them all.

Tuition

Ahem. In the 2011-2012 academic year, an undergraduate student's tuition and fees totaled $42,098, with an additional $8,450 for room and board. These figures do not include books, supplies, lab fees, furriers, therapists, polo attire, or other personal expenses. While the high tuition rate and abundance of business types has earned Penn a reputation as a 'rich kids' school," in fact, about fifty-five percent of the undergraduate student body receives some form of financial aid from the university.

Sports

All twenty-eight of Penn's sports teams, nicknamed "the Quakers," compete in the NCAA Division I Ivy League conference. Men's Division I teams include baseball, basketball, fencing, football, golf, lacrosse, rowing, soccer, squash, swimming, tennis, track/cross-country, and wrestling. Women's Division I teams include basketball, fencing, field hockey, gymnastics, lacrosse, rowing, soccer, softball, squash, swimming, tennis, track/cross-country, and volleyball. All intercollegiate athletic events are free and open to the public, with the exception of football and basketball games, wrestling matches, and the famous Penn Relays, which all charge admission. Tickets to these events can be purchased at the Penn Athletic Ticket Office at 215-898-6151. Box office hours are Monday through Friday, 10 am-3 pm. You can check out the full roster of all Penn sports events at www.pennathletics.com.

Culture on Campus

The Annenberg Center is a nationally renowned non-profit multi-disciplinary performance venue that offers 170 music, theater, and dance performances every year through the program *Penn Presents*. The Annenberg Center serves as a resource not only for the immediate university community, but for the entire Delaware Valley region. Check out www.pennpresents.org for more details.

The Institute of Contemporary Art (118 S 36th St) exhibits the work of established and emerging contemporary visual artists. Entrance to the exhibition space is free for everyone. It wasn't always this way, so we suggest visiting before they change their minds and want your cash again. For more information, visit www.icaphila.org or call 215-898-5911.

The University of Pennsylvania Museum of Archeology and Anthropology (3260 South St, 215-898-4000) has earned international acclaim as a leading resource for anthropologists and archeologists. The permanent collection includes Egyptian, Greek, Roman, Etruscan, Buddhist, Chinese, African, Native American, and Ancient Israeli art galleries. For information on visiting exhibitions, or to take a look at art galleries online, visit www.museum.upenn.edu.

Departments

Log onto www.upenn.edu/directories for a university directory and links to division and department web pages.

Undergraduate Admissions 215-898-7507
Annenberg School for Communication 215-898-7041
Arts and Sciences, Graduate Division 215-898-5720
Law School 215-898-7400
School of Dental Medicine 215-898-8942
School of Design 215-898-3425
School of Engineering .215-898-7246
School of Medicine 215-662-4000
School of Nursing 215-898-8281
School of Social Work .215-898-5511
School of Veterinary Medicine 215-898-5434
Wharton MBA Program 215-898-6183
Wharton Undergraduate Division 215-898-7608

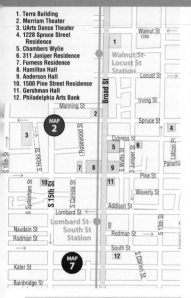

1. Terra Building
2. Merriam Theater
3. UArts Dance Theater
4. 1228 Spruce Street Residence
5. Chambers Wylie
6. 311 Juniper Residence
7. Furness Residence
8. Hamilton Hall
9. Anderson Hall
10. 1500 Pine Street Residence
11. Gershman Hall
12. Philadelphia Arts Bank

Tuition

In the 2010–2011 academic year, full-time undergraduate tuition was $33,500, with an additional $8,100 for room and board. For more information about extra fees, alternative board plans, or financial aid packages, call 215-717-6170.

Sports

Unfortunately, UArts students don't have the luxury of sports teams or even a school gym, though discounted rates are available for those who feel the need exercise more than just their paintbrush.

Culture on Campus

Where to begin. The plethora of Arts students showing off their latest work or performing in university-wide shows, most often in Philadelphia Arts Bank or at the UArts dance theater are difficult to miss. The University also owns the nearby Merriam Theater, home to traveling Broadway shows and local theater productions.

In addition, The Philadelphia Museum of Art, the Rodin Museum, the Institute for Contemporary Art, and dozens of other galleries and museums are free to UArts students, encouraging all to embrace their inner starving artist.

General Information:

NFT Map: 2, 7
Address: 320 S Broad St.
             Philadelphia, PA 19102
Phone: 800-616-ARTS
Website: www.uarts.edu

Departments

Log onto www.uarts.edu/about/contact.html for a university directory and links to division and department web pages.

Admissions 215-717-6030
Division of Liberal Arts 215-717-6260
Continuing Studies. 215-717-6095
Pre-College Programs 215-717-6430

Overview

Evolved from the Philadelphia College of Art (1876) and the Philadelphia College of Performing Arts (1870), University of the Arts draws hopeful actors, artists, writers, and unlabeled creative types from all over the country. Established in 1987 with the union of PCA and PCPA, UArts became the largest educational institution of its kind in the country, focusing on Art and Design, Performing Arts, Liberal Arts, and the newly established Media and Communication school. The school also has graduate and pre-college programs for budding and established artists.

General Information

The Bicycle Network (City):
    www.phila.gov/streets/Bike_Network.html
Bicycle Club of Philadelphia:
    www.phillybikeclub.org
Neighborhood Bike Works:
    www.neighborhoodbikeworks.org

Commuting

As part of its "Bicycle Network Plan," the city is currently completing a series of street-safe routes for commuting on two wheels. One hopes that the plan is implemented sooner rather than later; because of Philly's many narrow one-way streets, bikers and drivers are often at odds with one another, and you can imagine who normally wins these little tête-à-têtes. The automobile set treats bikers commuting to and from work with an air of hostility, especially during rush hour. As a result, bikers need to be defensively on Philly's streets.

City bikers have more to worry about than just drivers' road rage—the streets themselves are not always biker-friendly. Metal grooves in the roads are the last remnants of Center City's old trolley system. Today, instead of guiding trolleys through the city, the grooves have a nasty tendency to cause bicycle crashes if they're hit at the wrong angle or when they're wet. And let's not forget about all those historic cobblestones...

Our best advice it to be wary of irate drivers, avoid the trolley rails at all costs, and, whatever you do, wear a helmet! A detailed map of Philadelphia's commuter bike routes can be found on the City's website at www.phila.gov/streets/pdfs/PHILABIK.pdf. Check it out and plan your route before you go whizzing around town.

Recreational Riding

If inhaling exhaust fumes and dodging traffic is not your speed, venture towards Philly's more natural settings. Some of the best off-street stretches of pavement run through, or close to, the city's parks. Kelly Drive meanders through picnic areas and fishing holes along the east side of the Schuylkill River. West River Drive runs along the opposite side of the river, zipping past the zoo, the Mann Music Center, and Memorial Hall. If you feel like testing your fitness level, try Forbidden Drive; this spectacular eight-mile loop circles Wissahickon Valley Park. For off-road bikers, the

granddaddy is definitely the wild and woolly Wissahickon loop; the 30-mile trail offers sufficient challenge for even experienced riders. Pennypack Creek Park also offers a diverse array of dirt and paved trails near the Delaware River in the Northeast.

Bikes on Mass Transit

Bikes are allowed on SEPTA subway lines and regional rail, though only at specific times. All SEPTA busses (except trackless trolley routes 59, 66, and 75) now accommodate bikes.

On the Broad Street, Market-Frankford, and Route 100 Lines, passengers may board their wheels on weekdays before 6 am, between 9 am and 3 pm, and after 6 pm. Bikes can be taken on board at all times on weekends and the following holidays: Memorial Day, Independence Day, Labor Day, Thanksgiving, Christmas, and New Year's Day. On Regional Rail, there is a limit of two bikes per carriage during off-peak hours. Up to five bikes are allowed at any time during weekends and major holidays. Bikes are not permitted during peak hours.

Independent/ Underground Bicycling:

Philly has a long history of underground bicycle culture, where young daredevils on track bikes (read: no gears or brakes) race through the city at breakneck speeds.

The city also operates with an extensive bicycle courier system. At any hour of the day, you'll catch young girls and guys swerving around traffic, balancing brighter messenger bags brimming with packages on their backs. This is because the more packages they deliver per day, the more cash they bring in.

By law, the couriers must obey traffic laws and are not allowed to ride on the sidewalk, but for these bikers some rules were made to be broken. On their breaks, many bike messengers congregate at the entrance to Clark Park, playing chess or wolfing down hoagies before pedaling off to their next destination. If nothing else, it makes for great people-watching.

To let off steam, couriers can participate in sponsored bike races. There are also events for non-couriers, including Critical Mass, a loosely-organized bike ride through the city, which gets a group of riders together one day every month to raise awareness about using bicycles as transportation, as opposed to, say, gas-guzzling SUVs.

Yoga

	Address	Phone	Website	Map
Balance Studios	108 S Bonsall St	215-636-9661	www.balancestudios.net	1
Philly Power Yoga	2016 Walnut St	215-636-9642	www.phillypoweryoga.com	1
Bikram Yoga of Philadelphia	1520 Sansom St	215-977-9642	www.bikramphiladelphia.com	2
Dhyana Yoga	1737 Chestnut St	215-496-0770	www.dhyana-yoga.com	2
The Sporting Club at The Bellevue	220 S Broad St	215-985-9876	www.sportingclubbellevue.com	2
Toni Zuper Alternative Healing	1616 Walnut St	215-732-6242	www.tonizuper.com	2
Yoga Sutra	1401 Walnut St	215-640-0909	http://yogasutraphilly.com	2
Yoga Child	903 South St	215-238-0989	www.yogachild.net	8
Power Yoga Works	3527 Lancaster Ave	215-243-9642	www.poweryogaworks.com	13
BKS Iyengar Yoga Studio	2200 Benjamin Franklin Pkwy	215-568-1961	www.philayoga.com	14
Wake Up Yoga	2329 Parrish St	215-235-1228	www.wakeupyoga.com	17
Angler Movement Arts Center	1550 E Montgomery Ave	215-922-0866	www.anglermovementartscenter.com	20
Yoga On Main	4363 Main St	215-482-7877	www.yogaonmain.com	21
Spa Elysium	55 Bethlehem Pike	215-247-2008	www.spaelysium.com	27

Golf

Over the last few years, the majority of Philly's public courses have been taken over by Meadowbrook Golf, and the results have been mostly positive—by and large, the fairways and greens are vastly improved. In terms of accolades, Cobbs Creek, probably the best known of Philly's courses, was rated "6th Best Public Course" in 2000 by *Golf Week*. If you fear your game is not yet up to speed, try the Karakung Course at Cobbs Creek; it's a little cheaper and much more forgiving than the regular Olde Course. Walnut Lane, tucked neatly into Wissahickon Park, is also a very nice run for your money—watch out for the occasional out-of-control mountain biker from the abutting Wissahickon Trail wiping out on the greens. Check out www.golfphilly.com for more information about Meadowbrook courses.

Golf Courses	Address	Phone	Rates	Par
Cobbs Creek Olde Golf Course	7400 Lansdowne Ave	215-877-8707	Regular: $33-$48; twilight: $23-$38	Par-72, 18 holes
Franklin D Roosevelt Golf Club	1954 Pattison Ave	215-462-8997	Regular: $28-43; twilight: $23-$33	Par-69, 18 holes
John F Byrne Golf Club	9550 Leon St	215-632-8666	Regular: $28-$43; twilight: $18-$33	Par-67, 18 holes
Juniata Golf Club	1363 E Cayuga St	215-743-4060	Regular: $20-$35; twilight: $15-$30	Par-66, 18 holes
Karakung Golf Course at CobbCreek	7400 Landsdowne Ave	215-877-8707	Regular: $23-$33; twilight: $18-$28	Par-72, 18 holes
Phila Quartet Golf Club	1075 Southampton Rd	215-676-3939	$35 for associate membership fee; after Par-3, 9 holes that, $15-$17 a day.	
Walnut Lane Golf Club	700 Walnut Ln	215-482-3370	Regular: $24-$40; twilight: $12-$35	Par-62, 18 holes

Bowling

Bowling in Philadelphia is no longer limited to those who can stand the stereotypically dark and smoky alleys, although you can still hit up the no-frills BYOB **Thunderbird Lanes (5830 Castor Ave)**; it's by far the most established and popular for purists of the Philadelphia bowling scene. The best new alley is **South Philly's Pep Bowl (Map 7)**, and if you start a league or host a party there, it's BYOB. If you want your booze built-in, North Bowl in **Northern Liberties (Map 19)** oozes with neo-retro charm, plus it can fill all of your photo booth and arcade machine needs.

Center City's **Lucky Strike (Map 2)** can be kind of a jerk parade (there's a dress code…for bowling), and the high prices reflect that.

Numerous smaller alleys are scattered throughout the city; there are too many to list, but a quick web search will give you plenty of options if the big bad boys of bowling don't interest you. (Plus a lot of the websites have coupons.) Regardless, whether you want to bowl in ripped jeans with a cigarette tucked behind your ear or hobnob with big spenders sporting Banana Republic garb downtown, you don't have to drive to Jersey to do it

All rates are per person/per game, including shoes and tax.

Bowling Alleys	Address	Phone	Rates day/eve	Map
Lucky Strikes	1336 Chestnut St	215-665-9501	Day $4.95/game; Evening $5.95/game; Weekend Evening $6.95/game. $3.95 for shoes.	3
North Bowl	909 N 2nd St	215-238-2695	Mon–Fri 5–7 pm, $3.95/game. Mon–Thurs after 7 pm, $4.95/game. After 9 pm and weekends, $5.95/game. $3 for shoes.	19
Hi Spot Lanes	3857 Pechin St	215-483-2120	$3.75/game.	21
AMF Boulevard Lanes	8011 Roosevelt Blvd	215-332-9200	Day $2/game, Evening $3.75/game. $4.28 for shoes.	n/a
Brunswick Adams Lanes	649 Foulkrod St	215-533-1221	Day $2.50–$4.34/game. $2 for shoes.	n/a
Brunswick Erie Lanes	1300 E Erie Ave	215-535-3500	Day $3.09/game, Evening $4.09/game. $2.49 for shoes.	n/a
Center Lanes	7550 City Line Ave	215-878-5050	Day $3.25/game, Evening $3.75/game. $2.50 for adults, $2 for children, for shoes.	n/a
Pep Bowl	1200 S Broad St	215-952-BOWL	$3.50 per game, $3 for shoes.	n/a
Sproul Lanes	745 W Sproul Rd, Springfield	610-544-4524	Weekdays 9 am–5 pm, $3.65/game. All other times, $4.70/game. $3.40 for shoes.	n/a
Thunderbird Lanes	3081 Holme Ave	215-464-7171	Day $3.50/game, Evening $4.50/game. $2.95 for shoes.	n/a
Thunderbird Lanes	5830 Castor Ave	215-743-2521	Day $3/game. $2.95 for shoes. They hold nightly specials. Call for details.	n/a
V& S Elmwood Lanes	7235 Elmwood Ave	215-365-1626	Day $2.75/game, evenings and weekends, $3.50/game. $1.50 for shoes.	n/a

Looking for a hobby to replace your increasingly frightening American Idol habit? There are plenty of clubs and organizations you can join to get yourself off the couch.

General Tips

Start with a club or league, but keep your eyes and ears open for related groups and events. If you join the Bicycle Coalition (www.bicyclecoalition.org) and are particularly interested in racing, chances are you'll eventually run into a member who can tell you more about the area's racing-focused clubs than you'd get from a web search. Word of mouth is still one of the best ways to find out about new groups and leagues in the city.

Cycling

Philadelphia is a great cycling city, and there are plenty of groups around who love to take advantage of it. Start with the Bicycle Club of Philadelphia (www. phillybikeclub.org); they offer rides for cyclists of all skill levels, and membership will get you discounts at many of the local bike shops. The Bicycle Coalition of Greater Philadelphia puts a lot of emphasis on advocacy and bike education and less on scheduled rides and events, but offers tons of great information on their website and recently began offering an Urban Cycling Course.

Running

If you sit on one of the benches along the Schuylkill River Banks every morning for a few days, you'll see familiar faces running by. But rather than springing up from your bench and running alongside the regulars hoping for an invitation to join them, why not just join one of the local clubs?

The Frontrunners (www.frontrunnersphila.org) have been "running since 1983," and have regularly scheduled walks and runs. The Fairmount Running Club (www.runfairmount.org) also offers many group runs throughout the week, and no membership fees. For those interested in racing, check out the Wissahickon Wanderers (www.wanderersrunningclub.org) running club for competitive, but friendly, fun.

Sailing

The Bachelors Barge Club (www.bachelorsbargeclub. org), established in 1853, is the oldest rowing club in the country and still going strong. The Philadelphia Sailing Club (www.webcom.com/psc/), based in Bala Cynwyd, is better suited for casual sailors and welcomes all skill levels.

Skating

The Landskaters (www.landskaters.org) pretty much rule the inline club scene. They offer events for all difficulty levels, including recreational skates aimed at entry-level city skaters.

Ultimate

The Philadelphia Area Disc Alliance (PADA) (www. pada.org) has the lock-down on local Ultimate leagues. The group's leagues are especially popular during the summer, but they do offer leagues during each of the four seasons, moving indoors for the winter. There are also club teams, tournaments, and PADA YO!, the organization's youth outreach program. If you're interested in disc-related events, start with these guys.

Benjamin Franklin Hwy

422

Valley Forge National
Historical Park

76

Pennsylvania Tpke

30

476

Northeastern Ext Pennsylvania Tpke

476

309

Pennsylvania Tpke

276

309

Ridge Ave

Wissahickon
River Gorge

PAGE
118

Schuylkill Expy

611

611

76

1

Broad St

1

95

Vine Expy   Ross Brdg

676

Ridley Creek
State Park

Middletown Rd   Bradyville Rd

1   Tyler
Aboretum

76

Franklin Brdg

John Heinz National
Wildlife Refuge at Tinicum

Lindbergh Blvd

Industrial Expy

76

95

Delaware River

295

130   Crown Point Rd

New Jersey Tpke

55

Overview

Greater Philadelphia offers plenty of potential refuge to those growing weary of buildings and asphalt. Fortunately, many of Philly's best parks are nearby and the tranquility and peace of mind that can be achieved on a hike makes a life lived in gridlock all the more bearable.

Relevant Books:

Hikes Around Philadelphia, by Boyd & Linda Newman
50 Hikes in Eastern Pennsylvania, by Carolyn Hoffman

John Heinz National Wildlife Refuge at Tinicum

http://heinz.fws.gov, 8601 Lindbergh Blrd, 215-365-3118

This 145-acre refuge just north of the Philadelphia Airport provides homes for birds (over 280 different types) and other animals, including rare endangered species such as the red-bellied turtle and southern leopard frog. Hikers and cyclists can enjoy more than ten miles of trails within the refuge, which is open from sunrise until sunset year-round. And for visual irony, you simply can't beat the view of nearby power converters and petroleum refineries over the tops of the trees.

From I-76 E, stay in the left lane and follow signs for Route 291 W/I-95 S/Airport. At the light, turn right onto Route 291 W. Follow signs to I-95 S. Traveling on I-95 S, take the Route 291/Airport Exit 10. Take the right fork, exiting for Route 291/Lester. At the first light, turn right onto Bartram Avenue. At the second light, turn left onto 84th Street, then at the second light, turn left onto Lindbergh Boulevard. SEPTA's route 37 and 108 buses both stop at 84th Street and Lindbergh Boulevard. Regional Rail stops at Eastwick Station, several blocks southeast of the refuge's main entrance at 86th Street and Lindbergh Boulevard.

Ridley Creek State Park

Located 16 miles outside Philadelphia, Ridley Creek State Park has an easy five-mile paved loop that accommodates wheelchairs and baby strollers. Four hiking trails (red, white, blue, yellow) through wooded terrain can be mixed and matched to form hikes of varying lengths and difficulty. The park can be reached from Gradyville Road—about 2.5 miles west of Newton Square—which can be found off either PA-352 or PA-252. Both these roads intersect Gradyville Road. You can also get there directly from PA-3 west of Newton Square.

Valley Forge National Historical Park

The 3,600-acre Valley Forge Park is a well-maintained tribute to the Revolutionary War. The main trail is a paved five-mile loop that reaches most of the major historical attractions in the park, and is good for hikers, cyclists, and rollerbladers. Trails intended solely for hiking and horseback include the Valley Creek Trail, Horse-Shoe Trail, and Schuylkill River Trail. Walnut Hill, an area seldom visited by tourists, also provides excellent hiking.

From Philadelphia, take the Schuylkill/76 W to Exit 327, the last exit before the tollbooth. Turn right at the first traffic light, then right onto N Gulph Road. Go north on N Gulph Road for 1.5 miles and turn left at the traffic light at the top of hill into the park entrance. If you're relying on public transportation, take SEPTA bus route 125 to the Valley Forge Visitor Center.

Wilderness Trail at Tyler Arboretum

Adjacent to Ridley Creek State Park, the Wilderness Trail is an 8.5-mile hike through the 260-hectare Tyler Arboretum. The arboretum also contains a few shorter routes—the Dogwood and Pinetum Trails—as well as unblazed trails and old roads. Spring is the best time to visit, when blooming wildflowers overtake the landscape. The $9 for adults and $5 for children (three and older) entrance fee charged by this private not-for-profit association contributes to the park's upkeep. The Tyler Arboretum is located off PA-352 about four miles north of Media. Or you can take PA-3 to PA-352 and travel south for 5.1 miles. Turn east onto Forge Road, then right onto Painter Road to reach the parking lot (www.tylerarboretum.org).

Wissahickon River Gorge

In the northernmost part of Wissahickon Park lies the steep-sided, six-mile-long Wissahickon River Gorge, referred to by locals as simply Valley Green. Forbidden Drive (the name applies to cars only), which runs mostly on the west side of the Wissahickon, is an old carriage road along the river. "Traffic" is heavy here, as many joggers, dog walkers, bicyclists, horseback riders, and anglers enjoy the trail. The eastern side of the gorge is steeper and has more rugged trails for serious hikers. Once you find Wissahickon Gorge (not the easiest place to get to by car), park in one of the three parking lots: Valley Green Inn, Kitchen's Lane, and Bell's Mill Road. Try to arrive early in the day as the lots fill quickly. The following SEPTA buses stop at the trailhead: 1, 9, 27, 35, 38, 61, 65, 124, 125, and the R6 Regional Rail line.

Rowing

The banks of Philadelphia's Schuylkill River (a.k.a. the "hidden river") possess a long and illustrious sporting history, one that many Philly residents take surprisingly seriously. Since the mid-19th century, rowers have been racing the waters along Boathouse Row. Today, this span of river is the practice course for top rowing talent in the United States—boat clubs along the Schuylkill count among their members Olympic gold medalists and World Championship winners. At the 2008 Beijing Olympic Games, the US Men's crew team included five Philadelphia-area rowers.

If the lure of Philadelphia's rowing history doesn't draw your interest, the scenery sure will. There are more than a dozen boat houses to view on Kelly Drive along the sublime Boathouse Row, all visible from I-76.

Boat Houses	Address	Phone
Bachelors Barge Club	#6 Boathouse Row, Kelly Dr	215-769-9335
College Boat Club of UPenn	#11 Boathouse Row, Kelly Dr	215-978-8918
Crescent Boat Club	#5 Boathouse Row, Kelly Dr	215-978-9816
Fairmount Rowing Association	#2 & #3 Boathouse Row, Kelly Dr	215-769-9693
Penn Athletic Club Rowing Association	#12 Boathouse Row, Kelly Dr	215-978-9458
Philadelphia Girls' Rowing Club	#14 Boathouse Row, Kelly Dr	215-978-8824
Undine Barge Club	#13 Boathouse Row, Kelly Dr	215-765-9244
University Barge Club	#7 & #8 Boathouse Row, Kelly Dr	215-232-2293
Vesper Boat Club	#9 & #10 Boathouse Row, Kelly Dr	215-769-9615

Marinas

If boating or sailing is more your speed, the Delaware River is the perfect playground. The Philadelphia Marine Center offers 338 deep-water slips with summer rates that run between $500 for personal watercraft and $5,800 for 70' craft. Winter slips are $44 per foot, $1,000 minimum. If you just want to dock your boat for a few days, the daily rate is $2.75 per foot, with a $60 minimum.

Penn's Landing Marina is another option for boat-docking but they have far fewer slips and you need to reserve one in February for the summer months. Rates depend upon the size of the boat. Up to 45 feet is $1.75 per foot, while 46-80 feet is $2.25. Penn's Landing Marina is also where you'll board river services such as the Riverboat Queen and the Spirit of Philadelphia.

The Piers Marina offers boat slips year-round for $75 per foot in the summer, and and a little less than half that in the winter. Boats can be stored year-round while full-time security staff watch out for your property.

Marinas	Address	Phone	Website	Map
Philadelphia Marine Center	Pier 12 N, Christopher Columbus Blvd & Franklin Bridge	215-931-1000	www.philamarinecenter.com	4
Penn's Landing Marina	S Columbus Blvd & Dock St	215-928-8801	www.pennslandingcorp.com	16
Piers Marina	Pier 3, 31 N Columbus Blvd b/w Market St & Race St	215-351-4101	www.thepiersmarina.com	16

Skating

Lengthy winters and cold temperatures make ice skating an ideal activity for denizens of the city. In fact, Philly is recognized for launching the first skating club in North America back in 1849—The Skater's Club of the City and County of Philadelphia. There are many beautiful outdoor settings in which to strap on your blades, including parts of the Schuylkill and Delaware Rivers and areas within the lush Fairmount and Pennypack Parks.

For a more controlled environment, check out the Blue Cross River Rink at Festival Pier (www.riverrink.com). It opens from late November to early March and costs $8–$9 to skate and an additional $3 for skate rental. On particularly frigid mid-winter days, indoor ice rinks are infinitely more appealing—try the Rink at Old York Road (www.oyrsc.org).

In the warmer months, inline skating is a fun way to exercise, sightsee, or commute. Skating on all bike paths throughout the city is permitted, providing miles of traffic-free skating surfaces. On rainy days or in cold weather, hit one of Philly's indoor rinks, which also run intramural roller hockey leagues. In evenings be sure to call ahead, local rinks are popular spots for private parties and all-out roller derby brawls alike.

Ice Skating Rinks	Address	Phone	Rates	Map
Class of 1923 Ice Rink	3130 Walnut St	215-898-1923	$5–$7, $3 rental	10
Blue Cross River Rink	Columbus Blvd & Spring Garden St	215-925-7465	$8–$9, $3 rental	19
Laura Sims Skatehouse	Cobbs Creek Pkwy & Walnut St	215-685-1996	$4, $2 rental	N/A
Rink at Old York Road	8116 Church Rd	215-635-0331	$7, $2 rental	N/A
Rizzo Ice Rink	1101 S Front St	215-685-1593	$4, $2 rental	11
Simons Ice Rink	Walnut Lane & Woolston St	215-685-3550	$4, $2 rental	N/A
Wissahickon Ice Skating Rink	550 W Willow Grove Ave	215-247-1907	$9, $3 rental	N/A

Roller Skating Rinks	Address	Phone	Rates	Map
Carman Roller Skating Rink	3226 Germantown Ave	215-223-2200	$7, free rental	N/A
Elmwood Roller Skating Rink	2406 S 71st St	215-492-8543	$6 weekends, $1 rental	N/A
Franklin Mills Mall	1455 Franklin Mills Cir	215-612-1168	$14/2-hours, no rental	N/A
Palace Roller Skating Center	11586 Roosevelt Blvd	215-698-8000	$3–6, $2–3 rental	N/A
JAMZ Roller Skating	7017 Roosevelt Blvd	215-335-3400	$4–$7, $3 rental	N/A

Billiards

Despite Philly's richly-deserved rep as an old-school, blue-collar city, there is a decided dearth of the kind of venerated pool halls that Fast Eddie Felson prefers. This is especially true in Center City, though the welcome addition of **Buffalo Billiards (Map 16)** on Chestnut and Front at least gives stick men a place to rack 'em at an hourly rate. **Dave & Busters (Map 19)** is fine, as long as you don't mind wading through a sea of screaming, hopped up kids playing Super Mega Assault IV and spilling nacho cheez all over your shoes. Pool at **Tattooed Mom's (Map 4)** is fun (and the beer is cheap), but there's only one table, so expect to wait. At least you can play erotic photo hunt.

Billiard Halls	Address	Phone	Fee	Map
Buffalo Billiards	118 Chestnut St	215-574-7665	$6–$10/hr	4
Tattooed Mom	530 South St	215-238-9880	$1/game	8
Vuong Viet Pool Hall	2464 Kensington Ave	215-423-8380	$1/game	18
Dave & Buster's	325 N Columbus Blvd	214-413-1951	$8–14/hr	19

The best thing about the city's 86 municipal pools is that they are all free The worst thing about them is that they are often closed for repairs or due to budget issues, frequently have no lifeguards, and aren't located in the Center City area. It's surprising our government provides pools in the first place—a freak leftover from before the days of privatization pollution—so it's not surprising it ain't perfect. Open daily during the summer from 11 am until 7 pm, the pools are much more relaxing during off-peak times. When school is out for the summer, expect thousands of children to flock to the water like some kind of crazed, freely urinating animal migration.Swimming in Center City requires a bit of renegade work, if not large sums of cash. **The Lombard Swim Club** (2040 Lombard St, 215-735-4144) is most desirable—and desired, with a multi-year wait list. And after you've graciously waited your turn, get ready to pay $950 per adult and $600 per child for a year. Some cheaper private options include the **Columbia North YMCA** (1400 N Broad St; $112 joining fee and $720 membership dues per family) and the **Roxborough YMCA** (7201 Ridge Ave; $149 joining fee and $954 membership dues per family, with a 25% discount for families with incomes below $70,000). While out in Blue Bell, Mount Airy families favor **Beachcomber Swim Club** (652 Dekalb Pk, 610-272-2870) for its huge grounds, several pools, tennis, mini-golf, classes, and community vibe. Mount Airy-ites can be found here all summer long,

perched perpetually on picnic blankets. Beachcomber is a co-op, which makes it slightly less expensive, but to join you have to buy in for over $500 and family membership dues average around $500.

Now for us brokies. There's **Swann Fountain in Lombard Square**—lean your bike against a bench anytime after midnight and dip right in—you won't be alone. There's also the most pressing option—that is, a big, salty wave. Shoot down the Atlantic City Expressway and run off the boardwalk, where they don't bother with beach tags, into one. And as far as the city's offering of water pits go, the **Marion Anderson Recreation Center (Map 1)** is actually awesome, and at 740 S 17th St it's convenient for those of us living downtown. Of course, the hotels that have pools are pretty easy to sneak into as well. Just act like you belong. If someone questions you, tell Mr. Snootypants you left your key-card in the deep end and you'll dive right in and get it.

The Philadelphia Department of Recreation (PDR) conducts aquatic programs at indoor pool locations throughout the city. The programs, many of which are free of charge, are conducted by certified Water Safety Instructors and Lifeguards. Classes include swimming lessons, team swimming, and life guard instruction.

* indicates indoor pool

Municipal Pools

Name	Address	Phone	Rates	Map
Lombard Swim Club	2040 Lombard St	215-735-4144	$950/yr	1
Marian Anderson	744 S 17th St	215-685-6594		1
Ford	631 Snyder Ave	215-685-1897		2
Swann Fountain in Lombard Square	Logan Circle (After midnight–swim illegally in public fountain)			2
Stinger	S 32nd St & Dickinson St	215-685-1882		5
Chew Recreation Center	1833 Ellsworth	215-685-6596		6
O'Connor	2600 South St	215-685-6593		6
Ridgway	S 13th St & Carpenter St	215-683-1887		7
Herron	250 Reed St	215-685-1884		8
Sacks	S 4th St & Washington Ave	215-685-1889		8
39th & Olive	39th St & Olive St	215-685-7686		9
Lee	4400 Haverford Ave	215-685-7656		9
Murphy	S 4th St & W Shunk St	215-685-1874		11
Columbia North YMCA	1400 Broad St	215-235-6440	$53/mo./ $100 joiner fee	12
12th & Cambria	29 N 11th St	215-685-9780		14
*University City	37th St & Filbert St	215-685-9099		14
Francisville	1737 Francis St	215-685-2762		15
Mander	N 33rd St & W Diamond St	215-685-3894		15
East Poplar	N 9th St & Parrish St	215-685-1786		18
Northern Liberties	321 Fairmount Ave	215-686-1785		19
Fishtown	E Montgomery Ave & E Girard Ave	215-685-9885		20
Venice Island	Schuylkill Canal & Cotton St	215-685-2598		21
Hillside	201 Fountain St	215-685-2595		22
*Pickett Pool	Wayne Ave & W Chelten Ave	215-685-2230		23
Shuler	3000 Clearfield St	215-685-9750		23
Pleasant Playground	6750 Boyer St	215-685-2230		24
Ferko Sprayground	E Cayuga St & J St	215-683-3663		n/a

* indicates indoor pool

Sports · **Swimming**

Municipal Pools

Municipal Pools	Address	Phone	Map
48th & Woodland Sprayground	48th St & Woodland Ave	215-685-2692	n/a
American Legion	Torresdale Ave & Devereaux St	215-685-8733	n/a
Amos	16th St & Berks St	215-685-2708	n/a
Baker	5431 Lansdowne Ave	215-685-0261	n/a
Barry	18th St & Bigler St	215-685-1886	n/a
Belfield	21st St & Chew Ave	215-685-2220	n/a
Bridesburg	Richmond St & Ash St	215-685-1247	n/a
Cecil B Moore	22nd St & Huntingdon St	215-685-9755	n/a
Christy Recreation Center	56th St & Christian St	215-685-1997	n/a
Cobbs Creek	280 Cobbs Creek Pkwy	215-685-1983	n/a
Cohocksink	Cedar St & E Cambria St	215-685-9884	n/a
Cruz	6th St & Master St	215-685-2759	n/a
Feltonville	Ella St & Wyoming Ave	215-685-9150	n/a
Fox Chase	Rockwell Ave & Ridgeway St	215-685-0575	n/a
Francis Myers Recreation Center	58th St & Kingsessing Ave	215-685-2698	n/a
Gathers	25th St & Diamond St	215-685-2710	n/a
Houseman	Summerdale Ave & Godfrey Ave	215-685-1240	n/a
Hunting Park	1101 W Hunting Park Ave	215-685-9153	n/a
Jacobs	4500 Linden Ave	215-685-8748	n/a
James Finnegan	S 70th St & Grovers Ave	215-685-4191	n/a
Jardel	Cottman Ave & Pennway St	215-685-0596	n/a
Junod	Mechanicsville Rd & Dunks Ferry Rd	215-685-9396	n/a
Kelly Pool	4231 N Concourse Dr	215-685-0174	n/a
Kendrick	Ridge Ave & Pensdale St	215-685-2584	n/a
Kingsessing	49th St & Kingsessing Ave	215-685-2695	n/a
Lackman	Chesworth Rd & Bartlett St	215-685-0370	n/a
Lawncrest	Rising Sun Ave & Comly St	215-685-0597	n/a
*Lincoln	Rowland Ave & Shelmire Ave	215-685-8751	n/a
Lonnie Young	E Chelten Ave & Ardleigh St	215-685-2236	n/a
*Marcus Foster	1601 W Hunting Park Ave	215-685-9154	n/a
Max Myers	Oakland St & Magee Ave	215-685-1242	n/a
McVeigh	D St & Ontario St	215-685-9896	n/a
ML King	22nd St & Cecil B Moore Ave	215-685-2733	n/a
Monkiewicz	Richmond St & E Allegheny Ave	215-685-9894	n/a
Morris Estate	16th St & Chelten Ave	215-685-2891	n/a
Penrose	12th St & Susquehanna Ave	215-685-2711	n/a
Piccoli	Castor St & Cayuga St	215-685-1249	n/a
*Rhodes Pool	29th St & Clearfield St	217-227-4907	n/a
Samuel	Gaul St & Tioga St	215-685-1245	n/a
*Sayre-Morris	59th St & Spruce St	215-685-1993	n/a
Schmidt	N Howard St & W Ontario St	215-685-9895	n/a
Shepard	57th St & Haverford Ave	215-685-1991	n/a
Simpson	Arrot St & Large St	215-685-1223	n/a
Smith Sprayground	2100 S 24th St	215-683-3663	n/a
Vogt	Cottage St & Unruh Ave	215-685-8752	n/a
Waterloo	2502 N Howard St	215-685-9891	n/a
Waterview Recreation Center	5826 McMahon St	215-685-2229	n/a

* indicates indoor pool

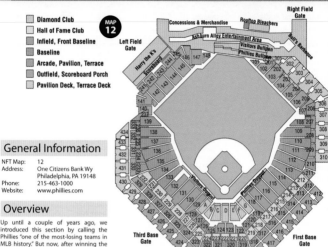

General Information

NFT Map: 12
Address: One Citizens Bank Wy
            Philadelphia, PA 19148
Phone: 215-463-1000
Website: www.phillies.com

Overview

Up until a couple of years ago, we introduced this section by calling the Phillies "one of the most-losing teams in MLB history." But now, after winning the World Series in 2008, we're pleased that's not the case. Citizens Bank Park opened in 2004. Replacing the reprehensible Veterans Stadium, the venue is an impressive collection of sporting and entertainment facilities including restaurants, stores, interactive baseball, a fine art collection, and even an engagement center. Not that we don't appreciate it, but it feels bit like the city took someone's horrifically ugly sister and draped her in Vera Wang. Still, Phillies fans have to like the new ballpark: unlike the cavernous and malodorous Vet, it has a moderate seating capacity (43,500) and maintains a real grass and dirt playing field. Grab a plastic cup of locally-brewed Yards, sit back, and get ready to boo...

How to Get There—Driving

The Stadium is conveniently located next to I-95. From the north, take I-95 S to Broad Street/Exit 17 and follow signs into the park. From the south, take I-95 N to Exit 17, turn right and follow signs to the lot. The Schuylkill Expressway (I-76) will also get you there via the Sports Complex Exit #349 or the Packer Avenue Exit #350.

Parking

Affordable parking is available for $12 per car or $24 per bus in the Sports Complex—if you've got a group of four or more and an operating vehicle, it's cheaper to split parking costs than it is to have everyone pay for a round-trip SEPTA fare. Regular cash lots for Phillies games can be found in the Wachovia Center, in the lots located near Packer Avenue and Pattison Avenue. While early birds can snatch up Linc Parking right next to the ballpark, late-comers are relegated to the cramped lots west of 11th Street. Handicapped parking is available for $12 in all Preferred Lots with a valid placard. But no matter where you park, be prepared to spend anywhere from fifteen minutes to an hour getting out of the complex after the game ends.

How to Get There—Mass Transit

Take the SEPTA Broad Street subway line southbound and get off at the last stop—Pattison Avenue. SEPTA Broad Street trains depart from Pattison Avenue immediately after the game ends, with Night Owl Bus service taking over after the trains stop running. Bus route C also stops at Broad Street.

How to Get Tickets

Ticket prices for Phillies games range from $17 to $65; don't worry if you're not pulling in the big bucks, because even the cheap seats at this park offer a good view of the game. For season and group sales, call 215-463-5000. (Hint: try the "six-pack" deal: you get to pick one game from a list of the toughest-ticket series-i.e. the Yankees or whoever won the World Series the previous year and five more from the entire season schedule.) For individual game sales, call 215-463-1000. The ticket office is located at the First Base Gate Entrance on Pattison Avenue. For home games, ticket windows also operate at Citizens Bank Way and on Phillies Drive. Tickets can also be purchased on the website.

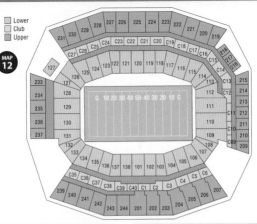

General Information

NFT Map:	12
Address:	11th St & Pattison Ave
	Philadelphia, PA 19148
Phone:	215-339-6700
Website:	www.lincolnfinancialfield.com
Eagles Phone:	215-463-2500
Eagles Website:	www.philadelphiaeagles.com
Ticketmaster Phone:	215-336-2000
Ticketmaster Website:	www.ticketmaster.com

Overview

Fondly referred to as "The Link," this 68,532-seat sports complex is home to the fightin' Philadelphia Eagles. On game days, tailgate parties are varied and plentiful and often begin before 9 am. It is not advisable to attend a game dressed in enemy garb, but if you must, take ear plugs and a crash helmet. As a study in odd pairings, the Link is also home to the lowly Temple University Owls. The Link also plays host to a variety of other sporting and cultural events throughout the year, but the main attraction are those green and silver birds.

How to Get There—Driving

While I-95 is the most direct route, taking Broad Street is a good alternative when traffic is heavy, which it undoubtedly will be if you're heading to a Link event. From the north, take I-95 S to Broad St/Exit 17 and follow signs to stadium parking. From the south, take I-95 N past the airport and Navy Yard, to Broad Street/Exit 17 (formally exit 14). Follow signs to parking.

Parking

Unless you have a parking pass or two club seats to the game you're attending, the closest cash parking is across the street at the Wachovia Center. Additional spots can be found further south in the Triple 7 Lot (b/w Pattison Ave & 7th St). If all else fails, check out the Naval Hospital parking lot. Prices for public lots vary from event to event. Check www.lincolnfinancialfield.com for the most current rates.

How to Get There—Mass Transit

Take the SEPTA Broad Street subway to Pattison Avenue. Once above ground, cross the street, keep your head up, and merge into the stream of event-goers. Broad Street trains are scheduled to depart from Pattison Avenue shortly after events finish. If a game runs past midnight, the reliable shuttle buses on Broad Street replace the closed subway lines. The Route C bus also stops at Broad Street. If you're debating whether to drive or take the subway, you need your head examined.

How to Get Tickets

General events tickets are available through Ticketmaster. To book Eagles tickets, call 215-463-2500. For club seats and group tickets of ten or more, call 888-332-CLUB. Box office hours are Monday to Friday, 9 am to 5 pm at Headhouse (the pre-game/post game plaza inside Lincoln Financial Field). On event days, tickets are available at the remote ticket booth located at the 11th Street side of the main Lincoln Financial Field parking lot.

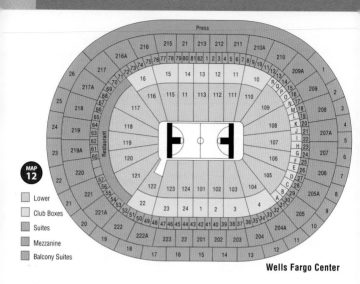

Wells Fargo Center

- Lower
- Club Boxes
- Suites
- Mezzanine
- Balcony Suites

MAP 12

General Information

NFT Map:	12
Address:	3601 S Broad St
	Philadelphia, PA 19148
Phone:	215-336-3600
Websites:	www.wellsfargocenterphilly.com
Flyers:	www.philadelphiaflyers.com
Sixers:	www.sixers.com
Soul:	www.philadelphiasoul.com
Wings:	www.wingslax.com

Overview

First off, don't get too accustomed to the name. In a few short years, these arenas have been named Spectrum II, Corestates Center, First Union Center, Wachovia Complex, and its present incarnation, Wells Fargo Center. Lord help us if the Wells Fargo Center ever gets bought out by Summer's Eve (inevitably: the Douche Center).

The Wells Fargo Center is home to the NBA 76ers, NHL Flyers, Indoor Football Soul, and Indoor Lacrosse Wings. The venue attracts over four million visitors each year, many of whom end up leaving drunk and dissatisfied. (Here's hoping some of that magic that worked for the Phillies in 2008 can rub off on some of the other &*#*%$# teams.)

The Spectrum was built in 1967. In 1974, the Flyers won their first Stanley Cup on the glistening rink, and in 1976 Elvis Presley shook his hips onstage for the last time in Philadelphia. Until 2009, the Spectrum was the place to go for circus shows, traveling kiddy shows, and for the concerts of pop stars slightly less famous than Madonna or the current American Idol. It was a classic Philly old-school arena that we miss. It closed for good on Halloween night 2009 with a concert by Pearl Jam.

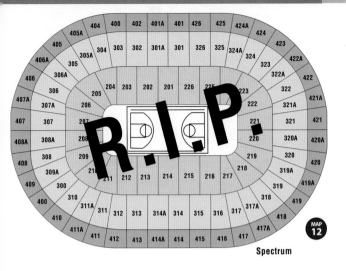

Spectrum

The somewhat fancy Wells Fargo Center, meanwhile, offers supreme spectator facilities for sporting events and concerts. With five levels and a seating capacity of 21,000, it's a prime venue for large-scale events. Check out the "in-arena" microbrewery for a pint or six (just be sure to have your credit card relatively free of debt beforehand) before the show.

How to Get There—Driving

Though directions to the Wells Fargo Center are simple, the major problem is traffic. From I-95 N/S, take the Broad Street exit and the complex is on the right.

Parking

Eight brightly lit lots with 6,100 spaces are available. You can reserve parking in advance through Ticketmaster or take your chances when you arrive. Patrons with disabilities can park in lots C and D. Rates vary from event to event. Call 215-336-3600 to get the rate for your event.

How to Get There—Mass Transit

Take the Broad Street subway to the last southbound stop—Pattison Avenue. Broad Street trains are scheduled to depart from Pattison Avenue shortly after events finish. If a game runs past midnight, the reliable shuttle buses on Broad Street replace the closed subway lines. The Route C bus also stops at Broad Street. Again, if you have the opportunity to avoid the snarling traffic by going the subway route, you would be wise to do so.

How to Get Tickets

All sports tickets can be obtained from the team's websites. Tickets for special events can be purchased at Ticketmaster. Tickets from the box office are available by calling 216-336-3600 or on location at the Broad Street side of Wachovia Center. Office hours are Monday to Friday 9 am-6 pm and Saturdays 10 am–4:30 pm and Sunday (event day only) 10 am–4 pm.

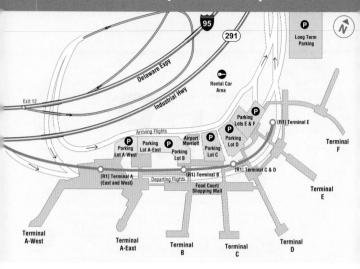

General Information

Address:	8000 Essington Ave Philadelphia, PA 19153
Phone:	215-937-6937
Websites:	www.phl.org
Flight/Gate Information:	800-PHL-GATE
Airport Police:	215-937-6918
Ground Transportation Hotline:	215-937-6958
Lost & Found:	215-937-6888
SEPTA (bus and rail):	215-580-7800

Overview

One of the first airports to feature such amenities as on-screen flight info and rocking chairs lining the waiting areas, Philadelphians can now gloat over one of the swankiest airports in the country. Passengers can fly to over 15 destinations in Europe and countless tropical islands to cure the winter blues. Domestic flights are still dominated by US Air and Southwest, whose fierce competition has proven beneficial for both parties.

Philly International has also added many new amenities, like the city's only Swatch store, local-cuisine restaurants, a Philly Museum Art Store, and Lamberti's Cucina. Ain't capitalism grand? And the lauded 'street pricing' ensures buyers won't pay out the nose for a last-ditch cheesesteak. Just keep in mind, butt-heads, PHL has a 100% smoke-free environment policy.

How to Get There—Driving

Believe it or not, getting to the airport from Center City, the PA/NJ Turnpikes, or Delaware is easiest on I-95. Conveniently situated next to the PHL, this busy interstate is your best option, depending on the part of the city from which you are leaving. From CC, simply take I-95 S to the airport exit.

The other option, when leaving from Center City, is I-76 E (Schuylkill Expressway) to the airport exit. During rush hour, bumper-to-bumper, snail-paced traffic is the norm, so I-76 is not the best route if you're in a hurry. From the Pennsylvania Turnpike, take 476 S to 95. Take 95 N to the airport exit. From the NJ turnpike, take Exit 3 to the Walt Whitman Bridge and be wary of the tricky toll plaza; stay to your far right to merge onto 95 S and keep your eyes peeled for the Philadelphia Airport exit.

How to Get There—Mass Transit

If you're not carrying a lot of luggage, mass transit is the best option. From Center City, take the R1 Regional Rail line, which stops at all terminals except F. The R1 makes many stops along its route to Warminster Station in the northwest, including 30th Street Station, Suburban Station, and Market East Station. The trains operate between 4:25 am and 11:25 pm, and depart every thirty minutes. For the most up-to-date schedules, call 215-580-7800 or visit www.septa.org. One-way fare is $8.75 ($10 if you buy your ticket on the train).

Navigating the buses is a little more challenging. Buses 37 and 108 have airport routes, though both are indirect and somewhat "scenic" rides. Bus 37 makes stops at Terminals B (arrivals) and E (arrivals and departures), whereas Bus 108 stops only at Terminal B (arrivals). The bus rides are both lengthy and tiresome—save yourself some pre-flight anxiety and stick with a taxi or the R1.

How to Get There—Really

A drop-off or pick-up buddy is a very handy resource at PHL. If that's not an option, the 24-hour taxi service is a convenient means of fleeing the hordes of travelers. Taxis charge a flat-rate of $28.50 if you're heading into or out of Center City. Flat rate hikes aren't the only way taxi drivers are gouging money out of their passengers, though. Drivers also charge $1 for each additional passenger beyond the first, not including kids under 12, for flat rate trips between the airport and Center City.

If you've a-hankerin' for some pamperin', door-to-door limousine services are also available. Limousines are an easy and luxurious way to travel, especially during peak hours or if you're with a larger group. A few mainstay services are Dave's Best Limo (215-288-1000), which is more "big-red van" than "long-stretch limo," or PHL Taxi (215-232-2000).

Parking

PHL has made way for over 6,000 brand new parking spaces in recent years. Though it's now much easier to secure a spot, the daily parking rates can be expensive, depending on where you park. If you're fortunate enough to find a space in one of the terminal garages, parking costs $20 per day. The partial rates here are $3 per 30 minutes, with prices climbing $2 for every additional half hour. The more costly ground level, short-term parking is available at every baggage claim except Terminal F. Hourly rates here are the same as the garage parking, but daily rates are $38. If you're going to be gone for more than a few hours, drive up to the garages.

If you're leaving for more than a couple of days, economy parking in the remote lot past Terminal F is the best bet. Parking costs $11 per day and blue and white shuttle buses ferry passengers to and from the airport around the clock.

An even more economical parking option, especially for longer stays, is private park-and-shuttle. There are many companies to choose from, including Pacifico Airport Valet (215-492-0990), located at the Airport AutoMall. Pacifico drives you to and from the airport in your own car, so you don't have to climb into the back of some packed shuttle bus—at the reasonable cost of $9 per day. Another reputable service that uses your own car to chauffer you around is Winner Airport Valet Parking (800-978-4848)and they charge $10.99 a day plus tax. If you're not in a rush and don't mind stopping at other travelers' terminals call Colonial Airport Parking (610-521-6900), located just two miles south of PHL, for a shuttle service with rates as low as $9.00 for 24 hours.

Car Rentals

	Phone
Alamo:	800-327-9633
Avis:	800-331-1212
Budget:	800-527-0700
Dollar:	800-800-4000
Enterprise:	800-RENTACAR
Hertz:	800-654-3131
National:	800-227-7368

Hotel

	Address	Phone
Airport Marriot	Airport Arrivals	215-492-9000
Embassy Suites	9000 Bartram Ave	215-365-4500
Extended Stay America	9000 Tinicum Blvd	215-492-6766
Extended Stay Studio Plus	8880 Bartram Ave	215-365-4360
Hampton Inn Philadelphia	8600 Bartram Ave	215-966-1300
Hilton Philadelphia Airport	4509 Island Ave	215-365-4150
Holiday Inn Stadium	10th St & Packer Ave	215-755-9500
Marriott Courtyard	8900 Bartram Ave	215-365-2200
Renaissance	500 Stevens Dr	610-521-5900
Residence Inn	4630 Island Ave	215-492-1611
Sheraton Suites	4101B Island Ave	215-365-6600

Airline	Terminal	Airline	Terminal
Air Canada	D	Lufthansa Airlines	A-West
Air France	A-East	Midwest Airlines	A-East
Air Jamaica	A-East	Northwest Airlines	E
AirTran Airways	D	Southwest Airlines	E
America West Airlines	B/C	United Airlines/United Express	D
American Airlines/American Eagle	A-East	US Airways International	A-West
ATA (American Trans Air)	D	US Airways	B/C
British Airways	A-West	US Airways Express	F
Charters	A-East	USA 3000	A-East
Continental/Continental Express	D		
Delta Air Lines/Delta Connection	A-East		
Frontier Airlines	A-East		

General Information

E-ZPass Information: 800-333-TOLL
E-ZPass Website: www.ezpass.com
DMV Phone: 800-932-4600
DMV Website: www.dmv.state.pa.us
Radio Traffic Updates: 1060 KYW
(every 10 minutes on the 2's)
Real-Time Traffic: www.traffic.com/Philadelphia-Traffic/Philadelphia-Traffic-Reports.html

Delaware River Crossings

Only you can answer why you want to go to New Jersey in the first place. But if you have to go, you're taking a bridge, which means you're sitting in bridge traffic. The Walt Whitman starts close to South Philly, the Ben Franklin takes you from Center City, and the Betsy Ross services most of the Northeast. None of the bridges charge you to go to New Jersey, but they all make you pay $4 to get back. E-ZPass is accepted on all three bridges but, unfortunately, there's no discount.

The I-676 or Vine Street feeds you onto the Ben Franklin, which goes to Camden. The Walt Whitman goes to Camden as well—take 10th Street down to Packer Avenue to get onto the Walt Whitman unless it's 2 am and then I-95 may be (no guarantees) your best option. As for the Betsy Ross (destination: Pennsauken), you're pretty much stuck taking I-95, although you could go from Aramingo to Castor to Richmond. As always, keep in mind that the second you cross over to Jersey, our maps are virtually useless—that's right, we're dropping you map-less in Camden. Get directions beforehand from Mapquest or someone who really knows the area. Otherwise, you're on your own—which sounds ominous because, well, it's ominous alright.

Philadelphia's Highways

Highways seem like a good idea until they turn into parking lots; which happens all too often. If you're planning on driving during the evening or on the weekend, check to see if there's a game at one of the stadiums, and devise plans accordingly, i.e. don't go. If you must, do your best to avoid I-95. Unfortunately, there's no good way to get north and south except on I-95, unless you want to go through the city. You can avoid the Schuylkill (I-76) from Center City westward by taking Kelly Drive or, better still, West River Drive. Kelly and West River have very few lights, and the scenery is nice to boot. On a weekend day and especially at night, if you're trying to get in or out of the city, sometimes what's best is to do what seems counterintuitive—ignore I-76 altogether and go straight up Broad St. If you hit on a good timing with the lights, you can go through uninterrupted, and it's pretty exhilarating. We should probably quickly mention I-676: it's the little bit of road that connects I-76 to I-95. 'Nuff said.

Driving in Center City

Avoid Broad Street going south and take Juniper, a tiny street between Broad and 13th—it's small and not many people know about it. It has mostly stop signs instead of stop lights, which generally gets you through more quickly. Also, you have the luxury of turning left anytime you like, something you can't do on Broad from City Hall to Pine. We recommend going out to 22nd to go north. If you want to stay on the east side of Center City, take 13th. If you're going east or west, head south a little to do it (take Spruce or Pine Streets), or head north and take Arch Street. If your ultimate destination is West Philly, keep in mind that the bridges are located at Walnut, Chestnut, and Market Streets—there's one at South Street too, but it's currently under construction until, gulp, probably 2011. For the love of God, don't ever drive up Walnut unless you absolutely have no choice. You will inevitably regret every second of the ride.

A word on traffic flow—for whatever reason, it's not in our character to switch lanes. Maybe we're freaked out by the narrow streets, or we're just so f***ing diffident. So if you're stuck behind a line of cars that don't want to move and there's a whole car's width of space next to you to maneuver down, don't think you're wrong to do it—everybody else is wrong. It can't be explained, we're just like that—and it drives the rest of you crazy!

Driving in Northwest Philadelphia

Take Kelly Drive or West River Drive to East Falls then get on Lincoln Drive to go to Mount Airy or Chestnut

Hill. If you're heading to Roxborough, Henry Avenue is a much better road to take than Ridge—get off Kelly and head up Midvale Avenue to get to Henry Avenue. Unfortunately for Manayunk, Main Street is pretty much *the* street. The good news is that you can completely avoid the Schuylkill to get to Northwest Philly except on some weekends that force the simultaneous closing of West River (closed to automobiles on Saturday and Sunday from April 1 to October 31) and Kelly Drive for regattas (damn boat races). Luckily, boat racing isn't popular enough that this will inconvenience you more than a handful of times each year. Then there are always those people who run or bike for charities that close Kelly Drive, too.

Selfish bastards.

Driving in South Philly

Believe it or not, Broad Street is not the worst route to South Philly. Stay in the middle lane to avoid frequently stopping buses and/or trash trucks. If you actually stick to the speed limit, you'll find that the lights are timed and you can pretty much drive straight through. If you want to avoid Broad Street, try 13th Street going north or 12th Street going south. Buses don't run those roads, however, double parking is a recreational activity in South Philly, and you're likely to spend more time trying to navigate the parking lot than you would toughing it out on Broad. Avoid Fitzwater until Mayor Nutter cleans that mess up.

Driving in West Philadelphia

The lights are timed on Walnut Street (which goes west) and Chestnut Street (which goes east). It's rare that going the speed limit is in your best interest, but, in this case, grit your teeth and stick to about 23 mph. Spruce Street is always a disaster, for reasons unknown, and should be avoided at all costs. If you want to go north and south, you're pretty screwed. 38th Street has four lanes and runs in both directions starting at Lancaster to the north, ultimately becoming University Avenue and feeding into I-76 to the south.

PENNDOT & Exam Centers

To take a driving test and complete the exam, you're going to need to visit one of the following PENNDOT locations. There are other offices in Philadelphia that deal with non-road-testing requirements such as renewals, learner's permits, and photo IDs—visit the Pennsylvania DMV website at www.dmv.state.pa.us and enter your zip code and the service you require to find the PENNDOT location nearest you. Or call 800-932-4600 for customer service.

Columbus • 1530 S Columbus Blvd
Island Avenue • 2320 Island Ave
Lawndale • Oxford Levick Shopping Center,
919 - B Levick St
West Oak Lane • 7121 Ogontz Ave

DMV Registration

Registering with the DMV is easy: Open up your phone book and look for "Licence Services" or "Auto Tags" and you'll find a list of places that will help you register your vehicle with the DMV.

General Information

Address:	125 S 9th St Suite 1000
	Philadelphia, PA 19107
Phone:	215-730-0988
24-hour Phone:	215-730-0988
Toll-free	
Reservation Line:	215-730-0988
Website:	www.phillycarshare.org
Hours:	Mon–Fri: 9 am–5 pm (cars can be reserved and accessed 24 hours a day, 7 days a week with on-call staff in the event of an emergency)

Overview

PhillyCarShare, the first program of its kind in a major US city, is an environmentally-concerned non-profit organization that makes cars available to members on an as-needed basis. Think of it as time-share car rental that gives you access to a car without the hassle, expense, and responsibility of ownership. PhillyCarShare members, charged a low hourly fee, don't pay for insurance, gas (each vehicle has its own gas card), maintenance, or cleaning and they never have to worry about finding a parking spot since pods are reserved for PhillyCarShare throughout the city.

Philadelphia has also seen a recent influx of Zipcars. If you still have a Zipcar account from another city, it might be a good option, but Zipcar doesn't have as many car locations here as PhillyCarShare does.

Reserving and Using Cars

You can reserve cars by telephone or online, months or minutes before you plan to pick it up. You can almost always get a car on the spur of the moment, but you probably want to reserve your car at least a day in advance, especially if you want it on a weekend. Reserving cars for holidays is ultra-competitive—be prepared to drag your ass across the city for a car if you don't make reservations a month in advance. Once you've reserved a car, pick it up at your requested location, open it with your special electronic key, drive away, and do your thing. An on-board computer tracks your time and mileage and cars must be returned to the location from whence they came. If you're looking to take weekend trip somewhere exotic, like the Jersey Shore, PhillyCarShare is probably cheaper than getting a rental car plus insurance. So if you're too good for public transportation or your friends are done carting you around because you've been stingy with gas money in the past, check out PhillyCarShare for options.

Most cars in the fleet are hybrid gas-electric Toyota Prius sedans, but some bigger hatchbacks with roof racks are available, as are pick-up trucks. CarShare has also added a Mini Cooper, VW Beetle convertible, BMWs, and the super cartoony, yet efficient, Smart Car.

Becoming a Member

To be eligible for membership, you must be at least 18 years old, have a driving record that is less than atrocious, and possess a driver's license that is at least two years old and legal in the state of Pennsylvania. The organization encourages you to join on the website, where you'll find an online application form. Allow seven to ten days for their driving and credit check.

Once approved, PhillyCarShare sends you an orientation packet including your key fob that will allow you access to the reserved cars. Once you're a member, you're able to attend some PhillyCarShare social functions, where if you convince your buddies to sign up for the service, your account will be credited $50.

Costs

Philadelphia Plan:	$15/month fee, hourly rates starting at $4.45, and a mileage fee of $0.25/mile.
Keystone Plan:	$35 annual fee, hourly rates starting at $7.50, and 185 miles included in each trip.

Rules

As a courtesy to the next driver, cars must be left with at least a quarter tank of gas. Pets are allowed in cars only if they are placed in an enclosed carrier. Smoking is also not allowed in the shared cars, for the same obvious reasons. The most important thing to remember about sharing a car is that it must be returned on time. If you use a vehicle without having made a reservation, you will be charged $50 the first time, and $100 for each subsequent offense.

Car Pick-Up Locations

Cars can be picked up at over 125 different pod locations. Check the website to find the closest one near you.

General Information

Philadelphia Parking Authority
Phone: 215-683-9812
Website: www.philapark.org

Meters

The Philadelphia Parking Authority is so brutal and ruthless that they've been given their own reality TV show, Parking Wars. Be sure to get back to your car before the meter runs out; they will ticket you the moment it does.

The city has finally switched over to electronic meters that accept credit cards. The green boxes that line the street aren't necessarily intuitive, but they're what we've got. Pay your price, print your ticket, and place it on your dashboard. If a meter is missing or broken, parking is still allowed for the maximum time limit on the posted sign. Vehicles can still receive "Over Time Limit" tickets in spots with broken or missing meters. At night, look for parking spaces in front of loading zones that only have time limits during the day.

Residential Parking Permits

Residential parking permits cost $35 per vehicle for the first year and $20 for annual renewal. Visitor permits are available for $15 for up to fifteen days. Permits can only be used on blocks posted for permit parking, and only within the district for which they are registered. To qualify for a parking permit, a vehicle must possess Pennsylvania license plates and be registered to a home address in Philadelphia. You will also need to provide a proof of residence (and the promise of giving up your first-born child) to apply. To request an application for a residential parking permit, call 215-683-9730.

General Parking Violations

- Vehicles can be ticketed or towed (by the request of the property owner) for blocking a driveway even when there are no signs indicating "No Parking."
- Many streets in Philadelphia are narrow, making it difficult for buses to navigate their way through the city. Vehicles can be ticketed if they are observed blocking the progress of any mass transit vehicle.
- Parking over the line of a marked crosswalk will earn you a $76 ticket in Center City.
- Throughout the city, it is illegal to park within fifteen feet of either side of a fire hydrant or within twenty feet of a curb—this ain't New York. Sometimes there will be a sign indicating the end of the legal parking area and sometimes there won't. Even in the case of the latter, you will get a ticket, so walk those twenty paces before leaving your car.

- Parking in a street-cleaning zone during street-cleaning times will result in a $31 ticket. Street cleanings are usually on the first and third Wednesdays and Fridays, or Tuesdays and Thursdays, of every month. Read the signs!
- School zone violations are enforced 7:30 am-3:30 pm on school days.
- Handicapped, Disabled Veteran, and People with Disabilities vehicles are granted an additional hour of parking time after the meter expires.

Vehicle Towing and Impoundment

Lost your car? Find out if it's been towed by calling 215-561-3636. Even if your car has been towed by a private towing company, it will be reported to the Philadelphia Parking Authority, and they can tell you where your vehicle has been taken.

To get your car back after it's been towed, you must pay all outstanding parking tickets and present a valid driver's license, registration, and insurance for your car. Vehicles not claimed within twenty-one days are sold at public auction.

Payment Locations

Parking Violations Branch
Address: 913 Filbert St
              Philadelphia, PA 19107
Phone: 215-561-3636
Hours: Mon–Fri: 8 am–8 pm
              Sat: 9 am–1 pm

Parking Authority Impoundment Lot
Address: 2501 Weccacoe St
              Philadelphia, PA 19148
Phone: 215-683-9550
Hours: Mon–Thurs: 8 am–9 pm
              Fri: 8 am–3 am
              Sat: 9 am–3 am
              Sun: 4 pm–3 am

Tow Pounds

- 4200 Wissahickon Ave, 215-683-9518
- 334-375 E Price St, 215-683-9521
- 4701 Bath St, 215-683-9510
- 6801 Essington Ave, 215-683-9880

Hours for all tow pounds:
Mon–Fri: 8 am–8 pm
Sat: 8 am–5 pm
Sun: 4 pm–8 pm

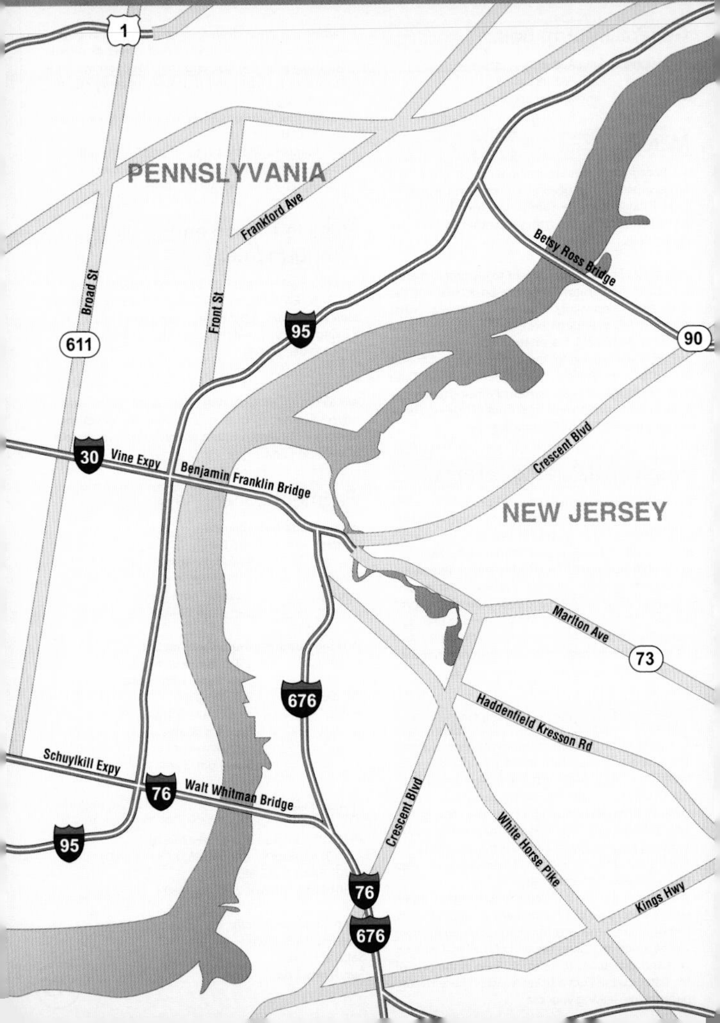

Transit · **Bridges**

PENNSLYVANIA

Frankford Ave

Betsy Ross Bridge

Broad St

Front St

611

95

90

30 Vine Expy

Benjamin Franklin Bridge

Crescent Blvd

NEW JERSEY

Marlton Ave

73

676

Haddonfield Kresson Rd

Schuylkill Expy

76 Walt Whitman Bridge

Crescent Blvd

White Horse Pike

95

76

676

Kings Hwy

Overview

The Benjamin Franklin Bridge (Philly's answer to the Golden Gate) is an essential component to any view of the cityscape. Drive westbound over the bridge at night from Camden, New Jersey into Philadelphia's Old City and you'll get the most breathtaking sight of Philadelphia's skyline, defined by the bright red PSFS sign (once the largest neon sign in the world).

Driving eastbound on I-676, you'll see the lighted blue BF Bridge looming large on your left, the skyline rising to your right, and you will feel overwhelmed by the technological achievements of mankind. The passing commuter PATCO trains trigger a computerized lighting system in each of the bridge's cables, making it look like an ethereal dancing figure floating above the dark water. Those of the athletic persuasion can bicycle, walk, or jog on the pedestrian walkway from 6 am to 7 pm daily to experience the longest stretch of traffic-less-ness in the city.

Built in 1926, the Ben Franklin Bridge was the largest suspension bridge in the world for three years (today it ranks a less impressive 54th place). The bridge spans the Delaware River, connecting Philadelphia and Camden, a city famous for being home to poet Walt Whitman (in his later life) and Campbell's Soup.

The Walt Whitman Bridge, meanwhile, is the Ben Franklin's Bridge's younger, uglier sibling. Opened in 1957 in order to relieve congestion on the Ben Franklin Bridge, the Walt Whitman carries with it no artistic pretense, serving a wholly utilitarian purpose.

The Walt Whitman Bridge is the best way to bypass Center City, connecting the Schuylkill Expressway (I-76) and the Delaware Expressway (I-95), as well as the North-South Freeway (I-76, I-676, and NJ 42) and US 30. Although the bridge is too far south to be included in any panoramic shots of the city, and is too unattractive for anyone to be sorry about that fact. The 27th longest suspension bridge in the world, the Walt Whitman Bridge spans 6.2 miles total.

The Betsy Ross Bridge, which connects the Bridesburg section of Philadelphia to Pennsauken, New Jersey, carries the distinction of being the first bridge in the country named after a woman. Plans for the Betsy Ross Bridge began almost 20 years before the cantilever bridge opened to traffic in 1976, when officials at the Delaware River Port Authority decided it was past time to replace the Tacony-Palmyra Bridge, whose low suspension level made it an obstacle for passing ships.

The Betsy Ross follows in the footsteps of the Walt Whitman, whose function outshines its art— 45,000 cars cross the Delaware on the back of the Betsy Ross Bridge everyday, making it a valuable asset to both Philadelphia and New Jersey. But the structure looks like it was fashioned out of steel remnants picked out of the scrap yard. This might be intetional, though, given that it leads to Pennsylvania. (You'll see what we mean when you get there.)

	Toll/E-ZPass	# of lanes	Pedestrians/bicyclists?	# of vehicles/day (in thousands)	Original cost (in millions)	Engineer	Main span/length	Operated by	Opened to traffic
Benjamin Franklin Bridge	4.00/4.00 (westbound only)	7	yes	100	37.1	Ralph Modjeski	1,750'	Delaware River PA	07/01/26
Betsy Ross Bridge	4.00/4.00 (westbound only)	6	no	45	103		729'	Delaware River PA	04/30/76
Walt Whitman Bridge	4.00/4.00 (westbound only)	7	no	100	90	Othmar Ammann	2,000'	Delaware River PA	05/16/57

Websites

- Ben Franklin Bridge: www.phillyroads.com/crossings/benjamin-franklin
- Betsy Ross Bridge: www.phillyroads.com/crossings/betsy-ross
- Delaware River Port Authority: www.drpa.org
- E-ZPass: www.e-zpassnj.com; www.paturnpike.com
- Traffic, weather, general   www.traffic.com/Philadelphia-Traffic/Philadelphia-Traffic-Reports.html
  transit information:
- Walt Whitman Bridge: www.phillyroads.com/crossings/walt-whitman

SEPTA

Phone: 215-580-7800
Website: www.septa.org

Overview

The SEPTA bus system is the best public transportation the city has to offer. The massive transportation network, with its nearly 170 intercity and suburban bus transit routes, will likely get you everywhere you need to go, if not in style. For the most part, the bus routes revolve around Philadelphia and the surrounding area's main hubs. For transit to major employment centers, entertainment and sporting complexes, shopping centers, and other popular professional and recreational facilities, SEPTA is a decent choice. While the majority of buses operate between the hours of 5 am and 1 am, there are over 20 buses, known as "Owl Buses," that run 24 hours a day on the major transit routes. You just have to keep Philly bus etiquette in mind: if possible, talk loudly about your preferred method of birth control on your cell phone; never give your seat up to anyone, for any reason; and always have a bag of take-out from which you can eat as you burn through your cell minutes.

Fares & Passes

Single Ride:	$1.55 each
	(packs of 2, 5, or 10),
	purchased on board:
	$2 cash
One Day Convenience Pass:	$7
Weekly TransPass:	$22
Monthly TransPass:	$83
A Cross County Monthly Pass:	$103

All passes and tokens can be purchased online. Exact change is required when paying cash. Like in most large metropolitan cities, having payment ready helps alleviate stressed searches for change and angry glares from impatient bus riders. Simply deposit the cash fare or token into the farebox, or place the transit pass through the electronic reader on top of the farebox. Be aware that some suburban routes and some city routes have additional zone charges of 50 cents.

Services

The major SEPTA terminals, where the most facilities and transfer options are available, are the Frankford Transportation Center, Olney Terminal, Wissahickon Transfer Center, 69th Street Terminal, and Norristown Transportation Center. These are also main stops on many of the bus routes. Individual route schedules are available on SEPTA's website, or can be picked up at the aforementioned terminals or other SEPTA locations including Market East Station and Suburban Station. For bike enthusiasts, front-mounted racks that accommodate two bikes are available on most routes.

Greyhound & Peter Pan

Greyhound Phone:	800- 231-2222
Greyhound Website:	www.greyhound.com
Greyhound Terminal:	1001 Filbert St
	Philadelphia, PA 19107
	215-931-4075
Philadelphia Sigler Travel:	5608 N Broad St
	Philadelphia, PA 19141
	215-924-1330
Peter Pan Phone:	800-343-9999
Peter Pan Website:	www.peterpanbus.com

Overview

Greyhound and Peter Pan are Philadelphia's main intercity bus services. Both are headquartered at the Greyhound terminal on Filbert Street, mere blocks from Market East Station. The Greyhound terminal and ticketing offices are open 24 hours a day. Greyhound also runs limited bus service out of Philadelphia Sigler Travel between 7:30 am and 9 pm.

Fares & Passes

Fares are comparable between the two bus companies, and booking at least seven days in advance can sometimes halve your fare. Sample fares and tickets are available on either company's website or at the terminal ticketing office. Make sure you check both websites before purchasing a ticket—sometimes they have sales like $12 one-way to NYC and $15 to Boston. A variety of student and senior discount fares are also available.

Services

Greyhound services 3,600 locations in North America and Mexico, while Peter Pan travels only to select locations in New Jersey, Connecticut, Massachusetts, Pennsylvania, New York, and New Hampshire. If you're in the mood for some high-falutin' dice-rollin' and chip-throwing, Greyhound runs a direct Philadelphia-Atlantic City Casinos line (800-231-2222). The bus leaves from both Philadelphia Greyhound locations and drops you off at the casino of your choice between 8:30 am and 11 pm daily. One of the stops in South Philly is Broad and Snyder. This is a great option if you are looking for a day in Atlantic City because you get money back! For instance on a Sunday you will pay $18.00 for the Greyhound to Bally's and once you get to Bally's Casino, you can get $15 back—that's a three-dollar trip to AC.

PHLASH Downtown Loop

Website: www.phillyphlash.com

Overview

The flamboyant purple trolley skittering up and down the tracks is not strictly for tourists. Though it does hit many of the city's prime attractions, such as the Philadelphia Museum of Art and Liberty Bell, and runs between major downtown hotels, the PHLASH is a quick and easy connection for locals and visitors alike.

For the affordable price of $2 per ride, the PHLASH hits 20 choice intersections and offers timely service every 12 minutes. Tickets can be purchased on the trolley, at the Independence Visitor Center (6th and Market Streets), or at the Riverlink Ferry at Penn's Landing. You can also make connections to all SEPTA and PATCO rail lines via the PHLASH. The convenient hop-on, hop-off service runs from May to September, between 10 am and 6 pm.

Fares & Passes

The PHLASH costs $2 per ride, $5 per day, or $10 per day for a family of four. Seniors ride free at all times except between 4:30 pm and 5:30 pm.

Services

The PHLASH makes stops near Market East Station and Suburban Station, as well as the PATCO Station at 8th and Market Streets. When driving into Center City, it's a good idea to park in the AutoPark at Independence Mall (5th and Market Streets), the AutoPark at Old City (2nd and Sansom Streets), or the AutoPark at the Gallery (10th and Filbert Streets). Show your PHLASH ticket here for discounted parking rates.

Chinatown Buses

New Century Travel: 55 N 11th St, Philadelphia, PA 19107
215-627-2666
www.2000coach.com

Today's Bus: 1041 Race St, Philadelphia, PA 19107
212- 351-9167
www.todaysbus.com

Overview

Craving some dim sum New York City-style? Or have a hankering to visit that big White House? Hop on any number of buses running directly from Philly's Chinatown to NYC's or Washington, DC's Chinatowns and, in less than three hours, you'll be gorging on pork dumplings and fried taro cakes to your heart's content. Even if 88 East Broadway in NYC isn't your main destination, passengers are conveniently dropped within walking distance of multiple New York City subway lines, the closest of which is the East Broadway F train stop.

Fares & Passes

New Century Travel currently offers both Philadelphia-New York City bus route and a Philadelphia-Washington DC express service. The first bus departs Philly for New York from 55 N 11th Street at 6:30 am and the last bus leaves at 11 pm. Tickets are $20 roundtrip and can be bought online (bring photo ID), at the bus station, or on the bus. Transfers can be made to Boston-bound buses in New York City. From Philly to the nation's capital, a round trip will cost you $28. Reservations are recommended and seat selection is made on a first-come, first-served basis so they suggest getting there with at least 30 minutes to spare.

Today's Bus provides another low-cost service between Philadelphia, New York City, Washington, DC, Richmond, and Atlanta. The buses depart every hour on the hour, between

7 am and 11 pm. Passengers are allowed two bags each (including a carry on) and bikes are permitted onboard. A $20 roundtrip ticket to and from New York or $28 round trip to DC can be purchased online at www.todaysbus.com or when boarding the bus, depending on availability.

New Jersey Transit Buses

Phone: 800-772-2222
Website: www.NJtransit.com

Overview

New Jersey Transit offers an extensive network of 17 bus services running intrastate routes. It is an excellent travel option, offering subsidized prices for students, families, children, and frequent riders.

Fares & Passes

Monthly passes can be purchased at various New Jersey bus terminals, or at the Greyhound Bus terminal at 1001 Filbert Street. Depending on zones traveled, fares vary between $1.45 (Zone 1) and $18.25 (Zone 21). On many of the bus routes, exact coin or dollar fare is required. Monthly passes or ten-fare packages are also available. Check the website for more details.

Discount Buses

Bolt Bus: 30th St between Market & Chestnut
1-877-BOLTBUS
www.boltbus.com

Megabus: JFK Boulevard and 30th St,
Market St between 6th & 7th
877-462-634
www.megabus.com

Overview

These relatively new discount carriers make multiple daily trips to and from New York City. Both offer free Wi-Fi on board, and Bolt Bus has outlets, just in case your phone or laptop's battery life is "the suck." If you think that makes Bolt the clear winner, hold on—if you don't need to stay ultra-connected, most Megabuses are double-decker, making for an especially freaky-fun situation traveling in one of the tunnels to/from Manhattan. The Megabus also has two pick-up/drop-off spots—30th Street and Independence Mall—where the Bolt Bus just runs from 30th Street.

Fares & Passes

Both busses offer $1 tickets (plus a 50 cent service charge) if you sign up early enough. You probably won't sign up early enough. In general, if you buy a week in advance, expect to pay between $5 and $11 for a Megabus ticket and $8 and $13 for a Bolt Bus ticket. If you travel from the cheesesteak to the apple regularly, consider signing up for the Bolt Rewards program—there's no cost, and after eight rides, you'll get a free ticket.

30th Street Station

NFT Map:	14
Address:	30th St & Market St
	Philadelphia, PA 19104
Phone:	215-249-3196
Website:	www.30thstreetstation.com
Amtrak:	215-349-2153
SEPTA:	215-580-7800
NJ Transit:	800-772-2222

Overview

Architecturally, it's a marvel. The 76-year-old, eight-story concrete framed building boasts a remarkable interior laden with marble statues and skyscraper-high ceilings.

30th Street Station is a hub for SEPTA, Amtrak, and NJ Transit, accommodating 25,000 commuters each day. Amtrak's intercity trains and NJ Transit's Atlantic City line run through the station's lower level, while SEPTA Regional Rail trains serve the upper level.

Ticket Windows

Tickets for NJ Transit, Amtrak, and SEPTA are sold at the main hall ticket windows, which are accessible through the 30th Street or Market Street entrances. Amtrak's ticket window is open from 5:15 am – 9:35 pm Monday through Friday, and 6:10 am–9:35 pm on weekends. You can also purchase tickets for the NJ Transit trains at the Amtrak ticket counter, as well as at some machines. Though the station is open 24 hours a day, if you are passing through during less-active hours (10 pm–5 am), the station assumes a more ominous aura because the shops are closed and the main clientele becomes folks escaping the elements.

Parking

Finding a spot at 30th Street Station is rarely a problem. There are many parking garages, though prices are far from wallet-friendly. Parking in the new garage or underground lot (both accessible on 30th Street) costs a whopping $15 for two hours. Pricing on Arch Street's surface lot and the 29th and 30th Street surface lots are slightly more affordable. Rates are listed at $1.50 for every 20 minutes. Valet service is available at an expectedly high price of $5 per half hour. For quick pick-ups and drop-offs, the meters are the best bet; scattered around 30th, Market, and Arch Streets, meters cost 25 cents for every 7.5 minutes and $2 per hour. Unreserved monthly garage parking is available for $200 a month. Unfortunately, "unreserved" often means "unlikely availability"—there is a lengthy waiting list for these in-demand spots. For all parking inquiries, call 215-382-3567.

Services

Most of the shops and restaurants maintain 7 am-8 pm business hours, though a select few stay open 24 hours. Among the many fast food joints and newsstands riddling the station there is a post office, a flower stand, Wachovia bank, National Car Rental (215-387-9087), Budget Rent A Car (215-222-4262), and some delectable eateries such as Delilah's Southern Cuisine (try their scrumptious fried chicken and strawberry lemonade) and and Bridgewater's Pub has surprisingly amazing beer and food. Ostrich burger? Yes please!

Transit Connections

All SEPTA Regional Rail lines, the Market-Frankford line, and Trolley routes 10, 11, 13, 34, and 36 stop at 30th Street Station. Due to a recent rise in crime and loitering, the underground passageway to the Frankford line is closed; now when transferring between the stations, you must walk above ground for about a block. The NJ Transit's Atlantic City line runs from 30th Street Station to Atlantic City, while SEPTA's R7 heads to Trenton and connects to the NJ Transit. If you're feeling weary from train travel, switch it up with a bus ride (Bus 30) from 30th Street Station to the 69th Street Terminal.

Suburban Station

NFT Map:	2
Address:	N 16th St & JFK Blvd
	Philadelphia, PA 19019
Phone:	215-580-6501

Overview

The fabulously ornate Suburban Station was once the shining star of Philadelphia's rail stations. That is, before the ultra-magnificent 30th Street Station came along and snatched the spotlight from its elder counterpart. Its proximity to City Hall, Love Park, and the shops at Liberty Place still make it a popular commuter station.

Built in the 1920s, with the aim of revamping Philadelphia's transportation system, the exterior of Suburban Station still stands as a glowing example of Art Deco architecture, with its gray limestone and elaborate gold and bronze gilded light fixtures. The top of Suburban Station houses an enormous 22-story office structure that spans an entire city block. From the exterior, the station is easily identifiable by the giant clothespin statue outside.

The bleak 1970s interior is disappointing in comparison to the grandiosity of its exterior. During rush hours, the station comes to life with the movement of corporate commuters and the sounds of street magicians, but when Friday evening arrives, the building becomes an empty cavern of closed stores and fast food joints.

Ticket Window
SEPTA's ticket office is on the underground's first level. The hours are Monday through Friday, 6 am-9 pm, and Saturday and Sunday, 8 am-6 pm. Service desks, public telephones, ATMs, and an abundant number of homeless folks are also available on this floor.

Parking
Unfortunately, SEPTA provides no parking at Suburban Station, though there is metered street parking in the vicinity for pick-ups and drop-offs. Honestly there is NO parking.

Services
During peak hours, the usual snack bars, fast food joints, and even a couple of sushi shops are open. There is little choice in terms of sundries on the weekends—you'll be lucky to find anything open other than Dunkin' Donuts.

Transit Connections
Dismal weekend atmosphere aside, Suburban Station is truly a connection haven. The Regional Rail lines, the Market-Frankford line, the Broad Street line, and several Trolleys all zip through this major hub. All connections are made via walkways running from Suburban Station to City Hall Station. Buses 17, 27, 31, 32, 33, 38, 44, 121, 124, 125, and C all arrive at City Hall. Bus 30 travels both east and westbound from 30th Street Station to the 69th Street Terminal, making a stop at Suburban Station. The PHLASH also has a pickup spot at 16th Street and Benjamin Franklin Parkway.

Market East Station

NFT Map:	3
Address:	12th St & Filbert St
	Philadelphia, PA 19107
Phone:	215-580-7800

Overview
Though Market East Station has little to offer visually, its location is convenient to many popular destinations including City Hall, Chinatown, Independence National Historic Park, Reading Terminal Market, and the Pennsylvania Convention Center. The station services SEPTA Regional Rail and the Market-Frankford line.

Originally labeled "the handsomest terminal passenger station of its time" after its completion in 1893, the old Reading Railroad Terminal is now the entrance to Pennsylvania's Convention Center. Also located at Market East Station is The Gallery, the first enclosed shopping mall in the US.

Ticket Window
It's best to enter the station on 12th or Filbert Streets, steering clear of The Gallery. Ticket office is open 6 am–10 pm, 8 am–9pm on Sat, 8 am–8pm on Sun.

Parking
SEPTA provides no parking, but there are some alternative parking options: two parking garages at The Gallery are nearby, as well as one at Reading Terminal Market. Metered street parking is available, however traffic in this section is among the WORST in the city, as is the parking.

Services
The range of food options at Market East Station, The Gallery, and the Reading Terminal Market is endless. Think delis overflowing with fresh produce, cafés brewing freshly roasted coffee, cheesesteak vendors simmering marinated meats, famous Italian bakeries offering fresh-baked bread—even the most picky palates will be pleased. The Gallery's stores compare to every other USA enclosed shopping mall.

Public Transportation
Beyond Regional Rail and the Market-Frankford line, buses 17, 27, 31, 32, 33, 38, 44, 121, 124, 125, and C stop at City Hall, not far from Market East. If you're looking to hit up some tourist attractions, hop on the purple PHLASH bus. With stops at 12th and Market Streets, it's convenient and cheap. The PATCO from New Jersey also stops nearby, dropping passengers off at the 8th Street Station, just blocks from Market East Station.

General Information

Phone:	215-580-7800
Website:	www.septa.org
System Map:	NFT Foldout

Overview

Philly's SEPTA subway system is relatively small. It only has two lines—the Broad Street Line and the Market-Frankford Line (known to locals as the "Frankford El"). The lines are efficiently integrated into the overall SEPTA system and provide a valuable link in Philly's transit network. The subway system manages a remarkably efficient routing and connecting schedule—a noteworthy distinction from its Regional Rail cousin.

The subway is a popular transit option for commuters traveling to venues where parking is difficult, such as the Wachovia Complex, Citizens Bank Park, or Market East Station.

It's also an efficient way to connect between regional and local rail services. It is, without question, a great alternative to the endless traffic-jams congesting the city's roadways.

Fares & Passes

A one-way subway ticket costs $2 cash or $1.55 token (available in packs of 2, 5, and 10). If you're going to be traveling around for the day, pick up a One Day Convenience Pass for $7. If you're a devoted subway user, the TransPass is a good investment ($22 per week and $83 per month). This card offers unlimited travel on all city transit routes, not just the subway.

The Market-Frankford Line

"You can't get to heaven on the Frankford El, because the Frankford El goes straight to Frankford"
-American Dream (1970)

The Frankford Elevated Line (a.k.a. the "Blue Line") carries many Northeast commuters between the Frankford Transportation Center and the 69th Street Terminal between 5 am and midnight. Anytime after midnight, a reliable bus service replaces the Market-Frankford course, making similar stops along the route. Free transfers are available at 15th and Market Streets (City Hall) to all connecting Broad Street Line buses, which pass every 15 minutes during the morning hours.

In addition to regular trains, the Market-Frankford line is served by A and B trains during peak hours from Monday to Friday, 7:00 am-8:30 am and 3:45 pm-5:15 pm. A and B signs are displayed on the side and front of trains, so make sure you get on a train that's stopping at your destination.

Broad Street Line

Also known as the "Orange Line," the BSL is actually divided into two parts—Broad Street proper, which runs 10.1 miles, and the Broad Ridge Spur, which extends 1.9 miles. The former runs mostly underground, from the Fern Rock Transportation Center down to Pattison Avenue (near the sports and entertainment complex). Broad Ridge Spur is an eastern extension line from Fairmount down to 8th/Market (Chinatown).

Seven days a week, local trains operate every few minutes from 5:02 am to 12:30 am. A bus service takes over at night, running every 15 minutes and making a connection to all Market-Frankford Line buses at City Hall.

Between 5:50 am and 6:32 pm, express trains make stops every seven minutes (during peak hours) and every 15 minutes (non-peak hours) at Fern Rock, Olney, Girard, Spring Garden, Race-Vine, City Hall, and Walnut-Locust. The Ridge Spur service starts its weekday southbound service at 5:25 am and its northbound service at 5:45 am. On weekends, the first train travels south at 6:15 am and heads north at 6:38 am. Bikes are allowed onboard only during non-peak hours—before 6 am (for the early-birds), from 9 am to 3 pm, of after the 6 pm rush.

The Broad Street Line is absolutely your best option for attending sporting events. The local train will get you there from City Hall in 11 minutes, and you won't have to deal with the hassle of parking. Sports Express trains make stops at Fern Rock, Olney, Erie, Girard, Race-Vine, City Hall, and Walnut-Locust en route to Pattison Station. After events, there are northbound trains standing by to provide local and express service back to City Hall and Fern Rock. The line is also a great choice if you wish to travel along the Academy of the Arts, because crossing Broad Street, especially in rush hour, is akin to taking your life in your hands.

Parking

Parking during the week costs $1 at most stations and $2 at the Frankford Transportation Center, Fern Rock, and the 69th Street Terminal. There is free parking on weekends in the daily lots, while overnight and permit parking is only available at stations that also operate as Regional Rail stations. Don't forget that the parking fare boxes at SEPTA only accept change.

General Information

Phone: 215-580-7800
Website: www.septa.org
Lost & Found: 215-580-7800
Parking Information: 215-580-3400
System Map: NFT Foldout

Overview

The streets of Philadelphia are covered in trolley tracks; some of them are in current use, but many of them are no longer in operation. You'll find yourself cursing the unused portions of rail as your car twists and bumps over the tracks like a 19th-century wagon (and God help you if you are on a bike or skateboard when you hit one), but their ubiquitous remains remind us of the city's past.

At the height of service in 1911, nearly 4,000 streetcars traveled more than 86 routes. After major financial difficulties, including multiple bankruptcies and debts with other transportation companies, SEPTA finally took control of the trolley service in 1968. Today, only a few select routes continue trolley service, also known as "Subway Surface Routes." To remind riders of the days of yore, in 2004, SEPTA began running its refurbished old-fashioned trolley cars on Route 15, which travels Girard Ave.

Route 10 runs from 13th Street Station to Overbrook in West Philadelphia, while Routes 11, 13, 34, and 36 travel to points in southwest Philadelphia and Delaware County. Trolleys make stops at Suburban Station and 30th Street Station, where transfers to Amtrak, Regional Rail, and other subway lines are available. Routes 100 and 101 connect at the 69th Street Terminal and run to points south in Delaware County. Light rail Route 100 also runs northwest out to Norristown in Montgomery County.

Trolley hours vary depending on the line, but most begin service around 5 am and run until just after 1 am. Bikes are permitted on trolleys and light rail lines only during non-peak hours (before 6 am, 9 am-3 pm, and after 6 pm, and anytime on weekends).

Fares & Passes

Trolley fare costs $2 cash or $1.55 with a token. Convenient multi-token packs are available in groups of 2, 5, or 10. Be aware that on Routes 100, 101, and 102 there is an additional charge of 50 cents for crossing suburban zones. A One Day Convenience Pass costs $7.

Like on the subways, the TransPass and TrailPass are good options for unlimited and cost-effective travel on a weekly or monthly basis. Tickets for seniors, students, and the disabled are also sold at reduced prices. Up to two children may ride free with any fare-paying adult, as long as they are less than 42 inches tall.

Parking

Finally, a place to park for free! Parking lots are available at many stations on Route 101 and 100. Visit www.septa.org for detailed listings. Most stations charge a meager $1 (in quarters!) for parking, except the 69th Street Terminal, Frankford Transportation Center, and Fern Rock which all charge $2.

General Information

Phone: 215-580-7800
Website: www.septa.com
System Map: NFT Foldout

Overview

After coming to terms with the expected rail delays and hassles (including the infamous strike season), you'll find SEPTA's Regional to be an effective, comfortable, and popular means of transportation. The eight-line service extends to the outer corners of Pennsylvania, carrying passengers to the airport and as far as Trenton, Doylestown, and Thorndale. Regional Rail also connects to Amtrak and NJ Transit services, making a trip to Washington DC, Chicago, Boston, and New York City very easy.

All SEPTA trains stop at Suburban Station, Market East Station, and 30th Street Station, and it's free to commute from one to another. All three stations connect to the Market-Frankford Line. A Broad Street Line connection can be made at Suburban Station, and Amtrak train service is available at 30th Street Station. Trolleys connect at Suburban Station and 30th Street Station.

Fares & Passes

Every Regional Rail station has a zone number, which is based on its distance from Center City. Tickets cost between $3.50 and $9 one-way. Regular riders can save some cash by purchasing 10 Trip Tickets. It's also cheaper to travel some zones off-peak. Keep in mind there is a varying surcharge for tickets bought on a train, regardless of whether or not the ticket office is open at the station where you boarded.

Zone	Peak	Off-Peak	10 Trip Tickets
1	$4.00	$3.50	$35.50
2	$4.50	$3.50	$42.50
3	$5.50	$4.75	$50.00
4	$6.25	$4.75	$58.00
5	$6.25	$4.75	$58.00
6	$8.75	$8.75	$77.50

All fares are one way, based on advance-purchase prices. Tickets purchased on trains are between 50 cents and $1 more.

In addition to single-fare rides, fare options such as TransPass, TrailPass, Cross County Pass, and Intermediate Two Zone passes are also available for purchase on SEPTA's website and at various locations throughout the city.

TransPass is a deal that offers unlimited travel on all city transit routes and the first zone of suburban transit routes. The pass costs $22 per week and $83 per month.

TrailPass is valid for travel on Regional Rail to destinations within the zone indicated on the pass. Depending on the zones you plan to traverse, pass prices vary between $91 (Zone 1) and $191 (anywhere) per month ($22.50–$50.50 per week).

The **Cross County Pass** offers unlimited travel in three zones or more operating outside Center City, including all suburban bus routes, Routes 100, 101, 102, and Regional Rail. Passes cost $103 per month.

The **Intermediate Two Zone** pass is valid on Regional Rail for travel through one or two zones outside Philadelphia. The past costs $75 per month (single trips are $3).

Regional Rail also offers discounts for persons with disabilities, seniors, students, some college students, families, and groups. Check www.septa.com for a detailed listing discounts and ticket purchase locations.

Bikes on SEPTA Regional Rail

There is a limit of two bikes per carriage during off-peak hours, and five bikes per carriage during weekends and major holidays. Bikes are never permitted during peak hours, unless they fold and can be stored out of the way.

Parking

Park-and-Ride is another cheap and efficient way to get into the city. Parking at most stations costs $1 while the Frankford Transportation Center, Fern Rock, and the 69th Street Terminal each charge $2. Be sure to take lots of loose change with you—the slot boxes only take quarters. Most SEPTA stations have numbered parking spaces next to the platform, but spots fill up quickly, so you should plan to arrive early or arrange for a drop-off buddy for the more bustling hubs like Jenkintown. Parking at smaller stations and connecting to your desired line is another option for avoiding parking congestion.

Overnight parking is also available at many stations *except* Ardmore, Bryn Mawr, Downingtown, Doylestown, Elkins Park, Haverford, Overbrook, Swarthmore, and Villanova. You need to reserve your overnight parking slot at least one day in advance and rates vary depending on location. For more information call 215-580-3400 24 hours-a-day.

General Information

Phone:	800-USA-RAIL (872-7245)
Website:	www.amtrak.com
30th Street Station (PHL):	30th St & Market St
North Philadelphia (PHN):	2900 N Broad St (& Glenwood Ave)
System Map:	NFT Foldout

Overview

Two stations provide Amtrak service in Philly. 30th Street Station (PHL) is the main Amtrak station, located in the heart of Philadelphia. This massive Art Deco architectural gem is on the National Register of Historic Places and serves as a hub for both Amtrak and SEPTA. To the north is the aptly named North Philadelphia (PHN) station. It's a decrepit stop with such limited service that you're better off catching a train at the 30th Street Station. If you're a Harrison Ford fan, you might experience a little déjà vu at 30th Street Station: it was here that Peter Weir shot the beginning of his film *Witness*.

Acela Express

Traveling at speeds of up to 150 mph, the Acela line serves major cities along the northeastern seaboard. Philadelphia and New York City are two major stops along the Boston to Washington DC route, with several smaller stops in between. Both the Metro-liner and the Regional trains run similar routes with more stops and at a slightly slower pace, but a significantly lower ticket price. Roundtrip tickets from Philadelphia to NYC on the Acela line start around $97 for a one-way ticket, but on holidays and at peak travel times, the fare rises dramatically. It's far from cheap, but if you want the quickest, least-hassle method of getting to New York, Acela is your best bet. Except, of course, when there are unexplained two hour delays.

If you're traveling to Boston, plan on paying somewhere near $200 for a one-way fare. And if you haven't maxed out your credit cards on Amtrak fares, you can head down to DC and back for a little more than $200.

Regional

The choice mode of travel for those who can afford the $54+ ticket, travelers heading from Philly to New York or Washington can reach their destination in 90 minutes for both cities. Ticket buying is generally simple on Amtrak's website or electronic kiosks (this way you can skip those painfully long lines at the station ticket booths). For longer trips, there are trains which run to destinations across the country. But comparing ticket price, travel time, and general aggravation with sleeping on the train, which can get rickety at times, other alternatives are suggested.

Baggage Check & Pet Policies

Each passenger can check up to three pieces of baggage thirty minutes before departure. You're allowed to check up to three more pieces for a $10 fee but, at that point, you'd be wiser renting a U-Haul truck. You can also take two items on board with you. Electronic equipment and plastic or paper bags cannot be checked. All pets are prohibited on Amtrak trains, except for service animals.

How to Get There—Driving

The 30th Street Station is conveniently located off of I-76. Take Exit 345 and follow the signs for the station. The North Philadelphia Station can be reached from US-13.

Parking

There are five parking lots at the 30th Street Station. Two short-term lots charge $25 per 24 hours. Two long-term lots charge $20 per 24 hours. One valet lot is available for $35 per 24 hours.

How to Get There—Mass Transit

SEPTA commuter trains offer frequent service between 30th Street and Center City Philadelphia (Penn Center/Suburban Station and Market Street Station). You can ride free on these trains to and from Center City with your Amtrak ticket stub. Visit www.septa.com for more information.

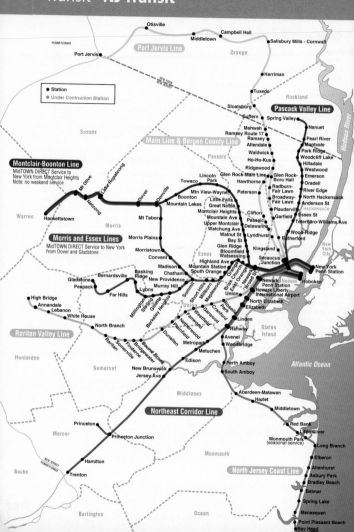

General Information

Address:	1 Penn Plz E Newark, NJ 07105
Phone:	973-491-7000 (out of state) 800-772-2222 (in state)
Website:	www.njtransit.com

Overview

New Jersey Transit's buses, rail, and light rail services, while less luxurious than Amtrak trains, provide a far more affordable means of transportation between Philadelphia, Jersey cities, Newark International Airport, and Manhattan. Combined NJ Transit and SEPTA trains can get you to New York for less than half of what it costs to travel Amtrak. Just hop on SEPTA's R7 train from Philadelphia's 30th Street Station to Trenton, NJ, then ride NJ Transit's Northeast Corridor line to New York.

Because of the low-cost fares and reliable schedules, travel during weekends and peak hours gets rather crowded—you might even find yourself standing all the way to New York on a holiday weekend. NJ Transit also provides service between Philadelphia and Atlantic City for $8 or less (and the ride takes less than an hour and a half). Just remember to buy your ticket before you get on the train, otherwise you'll be paying a five dollar surcharge (and you don't need to be wasting those five bucks before you even set foot in the casinos). The AC station is conveniently located just blocks from the boardwalk.

With fourteen bus terminals located in and around New Jersey, NJ Transit buses can take you across the river from Philadelphia to Camden, Six Flags Amusement Park, Trenton, or even to Bruce Springsteen's hometown, Asbury Park. Philadelphia's NJ Transit Bus Terminal is located at the Greyhound Bus Terminal, 1001 Filbert Street.

Fares & Passes

Bus passes must be purchased at an NJ Transit bus terminal—otherwise passengers are required to provide the driver with exact change in coins or $1 bills. Frequent riders can purchase ten trip tickets and monthly passes for reduced rates. Single-ride bus fares cost between $1.45 and $18.25, depending on the length of your trip.

Purchasing monthly passes for either the bus or train saves daily commuters about thirty percent of regular ticket costs. Monthly passes are valid for an unlimited number of trips between designated stations during the month for which they are purchased. Weekly passes, also valid for unlimited trips between designated stations, save about fifteen percent of the cost of regular tickets. Check out the Quik-Tik option on the NJ Transit website to purchase passes online.

BusinessPass, offered through employers, can save commuters even more money on monthly rail and bus passes by deducting a portion of the cost from pre-tax salaries. These monthly passes are mailed directly to the work site. **PatronPass** gives businesses an opportunity to buy one-way tickets in bulk for either the bus or train in advance.

NJ Transit also offers special Family SuperSaver Fares, Student Monthly Passes, Children's Fares, and Senior Citizens packages. For more information on fare options, check out www.njtransit.com. You can also view schedules and fares online at www.njtransit.com, or can pick up a hard copy of schedules at any station.

Parking

Some train and bus stations provide free daily parking. Parking at other stations requires a permit. For parking information for each station, visit www.njtransit.com.

Baggage & Pets

Small pets are permitted on trains, but must be transported in carry-on travel cases. Service animals are always allowed to ride. On buses, each passenger is allowed to store two pieces of "conventional sized" luggage in the under-seat storage area.

Bikes Onboard

Many—but not all—NJ Transit buses carry bike racks attached to the front of the bus. The "Bike Aboard" program allows passengers to carry their bikes on NJ Transit trains for no extra charge. Most train and bus stations also offer parking facilities for up to 1,600 bicycles.

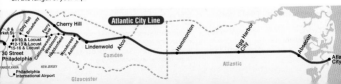

January

Mummer's Parade	Broad St	Men in dresses, drunk off their asses. www.mummers.org
MLK Jr Day of Service	Various locations	Day of action and celebration. www.campusphilly.org/mlkday

February

Philly Auto Show	Convention Center	More than 700 vehicles on show. www.phillyautoshow.com
Mardi Gras	South St	We just do the drinking part. www.southstreet.com
Chinese New Year	Chinatown	Day of the firecracker. www.phillychinatown.com
African American History Month	Various locations	City-wide events celebrate African American history. www.aampmuseum.org

March

Philly Flower Show	Convention Center	Biggest annual flower show in the country. www.theflowershow.com
St Patrick's Day Parade	City parade route	All the green beer you can stomach.

April

Cherry Blossom Festival	Various Center City locations	Japanese culture festival doused in pink.
Maya Weekend	UPenn	Mayan enthusiasts with a hankering for scholarly workshops cruise this annual event.
Penn Relays	UPenn	High-profile track meet. www.thepennrelays.com
Philadelphia Cinefest	Various locations	Fast-growing international cinema orgy. www.phillycinefest.com
Philly Antiques Show	UPenn Hospital	Proceeds go to the hospital. www.philaantiques.com

May

Broad Street Run	Broad St	10-mile road race in early May. www.broadstreetrun.com
Police & Fire Memorial	Franklin Square Park	Honors fallen police officers and firefighters. www.phila.gov
Dad Vail Regatta	Schuylkill River	Largest collegiate rowing race in the country. www.dadvail.org
Italian Market Festival	9th St Italian Market	South Philly's 'old man' event of the year.
Philly Book Festival	Free Library of Philly	A serious series of author events mixed in with music and fun for the kids—Lyle the Crocodile is alive and well! www.philadelphiabookfestival.org
Rittenhouse Row Spring Festival	Rittenhouse Square	Indoor/outdoor street fair. www.rittenhouserow.org
Race for the Cure	Fairmount Park	5K road race to support breast cancer cure. www.komen.org
Jam on the River	Penn's Landing	Musicfest to kick off the summer. www.jamontheriver.com
Mount Airy Day	Various locations	Performances, flea market, and games to celebrate the community. www.mtairyday.org

June

FirstGlance Film Festival	Various locations	Bi-coastal indie film fest. www.firstglancefilms.com
Philly Pride Festival	Broad & Pine Sts	LGBT pride extravaganza. www.phillypride.org
Pro Cycling Championship	Ben Franklin Pkwy	Commerce Bank-sponsored bike race. www.procyclingtour.com
Bloomsday	Rosenbach Library	Reading of Joyce's *Ulysses* on the day it supposedly took place (June 16th). www.rosenbach.org

First Person Arts Festival	Various locations	Literary, film, and performance events focusing on memoir and documentary genres. www.firstpersonarts.org
Manayunk Arts Festival	Main St in Manayunk	An impressive craft orgy. www.manayunk.com
Philadelphia Gay and Lesbian Theatre Festival	Various Locations	It's finally picking up some steam! www.philagaylesbiantheatrefest.org

July

Independence Day Ceremony	Independence Hall	Stars 'n stripes forever. www.americasbirthday.com
QFest	Various locations	A huge selection of gay and lesbian films, and lots of fun after each screening. www.phillyfests.com/piglff
Independence Day Regatta	Kelly Dr	Held since 1880—hope that your coxswain taught you well. www.boathouserow.org

August

| Unity Day | Ben Franklin Pkwy | Celebration of Brotherly Love. www.wdasfm.com |
| Philly Folk Festival | Various locations | Props for not spelling "folk" with a "ph." www.folkfest.org |

September

Center City Restaurant Week	Center City	Tons of restaurants offer fixed-price menus. www.centercityphila.org
Philadelphia Live Arts Festival and Philly Fringe	Various locations	Indie theater, dance, and art performances. www.pafringe.com
Puerto Rican Festival Parade	City parade route	Puerto Rican pride celebration. www.elconcilio.net

October

Dragon Boat Races	Schuylkill River	Over 100 teams and eight lanes of action. www.philadragonboatfestival.com
Terror Behind the Walls	Eastern State Penitentiary	Jail transforms into a haunted house. http://easternstate.org
OutFest	Various locations	Coming-out block party. www.phillypride.org
Columbus Day Parade	S Broad St	Name says it all. www.phila.gov
Pulaski Day Parade	City parade route	Polish heritage celebration. www.polishamericancenter.org
215 Festival	Free Library	Showcase of established and emerging writers/musicians. www.215festival.com
Revolutionary Germantown Festival	Rittenhouse Town	Reenactments of battles and other fun for the kids. www.rittenhousetown.org

November

| Philadelphia Marathon | City-wide | 26.2 grueling miles. www.philadelphiamarathon.com |
| Thanksgiving Day Parade | Ben Franklin Pkwy | Turkey Day family fun. http://abclocal.go.com/wpvi |

December

| City Hall Tree Lighting Festival | City Hall | The usual fanfare beginning Dec 1. |
| New Year's Eve | Penn's Landing | Fireworks over the Delaware River. www.pennslandingcorp.com |

Useful Phone Numbers

Emergencies: 911
General Information: 411
Philadelphia Police Headquarters: 215-686-1776
City Hall: 215-686-3410
Comcast: 888-633-4266
Fire Department: 215-686-1300
Parking Authority: 215-683-9812
Public Defender: 215-568-3190
Tourism Information: 800-537-7676
Free Library of Philadelphia: 215-685-6221
Block Party Permits: 215-686-5560
Bucks County Board of Elections: 215-348-6154
Philadelphia Board of Elections: 215-686-3469

Essential Philadelphia Movies

The Philadelphia Story (1940)
1776 (1972)
Rocky (1976)
Blow Out (1981)
Taps (1981)
Tattoo (1981)
Trading Places (1983)
Birdy (1984)
Witness (1985)
Mannequin (1987)
Philadelphia (1993)
Twelve Monkeys (1995)
Fallen (1998)
The Sixth Sense (1999)
Unbreakable (2000)
Invincible (2006)
Rocky Balboa (2006)
Baby Mama (2008)
Law Abiding Citizen (2009)

Websites

www.citypaper.net · Online version of Philly's free weekly newspaper that tells you what to do, where to live, and more.
www.digitalcity.com/philadelphia · AOL's local city guide, with lots of upcoming events coverage and better-than-most dining and club guides.
www.nba.com/sixers · Official website of Philly's favorite basketball team.
www.notfortourists.com · The ultimate website for everything you ever need to know about anything.
www.phawker.com · Source for under-the-radar Philadelphia news and culture commentary
www.phila.gov · The city's official home on the web.
http://philadelphia.about.com · Tons of information on the city, from walking tours to civic issues to recommended restaurants and more.
www.philadelphiaeagles.com · Official website of Philly's favorite football team.
http://philadelphia.phillies.mlb.com · Official website of Philly's favorite baseball team.
www.philadelphiaflyers.com · This site only matters if there actually is an NHL next year, of course.
www.philadelphiaweekly.com · Online version of Philly's free weekly newspaper that tells you what to do, where to live, and more.
www.philebrity.com · Prolific gossip and local politics blog: most of it's true."
www.philly.com · Local news, sports, jobs, cars, homes, etc.
www.philly1.com · Local news briefs and links to indie Philly-based publications.
www.phillychinatown.com · "We bring Asian market to you"
www.phillyist.com · All Philly, all the time.
www.phillyskyline.com · The skinny on new buildings, urban landscape crises and neighborhoods uncovered via blog and photography
www.uwishunu.com · Blogging for more tourists.

Essential Philadelphia Books

A House on Fire: The Rise and Fall of Philadelphia Soul (2004) by John A. Jackon
Benjamin Franklin: An American Life (2003) by Walter Isaacson
Common Sense (1776) by Thomas Paine
Diary of Independence Hall (1948) by Harold Donaldson Eberlein & Cortland Van Dyke Hubbard.
Shining Cycles of Love (1959) by Anna Coggins Dart.
The Papers of Benjamin Franklin, by Benjamin Franklin – more than 30 volumes edited and published by Yale University Press.
The Neal Pollack Anthology of American Literature (2002) by Neal Pollack

We're Number One!!!

America's first brick house: Penn House, 1682
America's first public school: Fourth & Chestnut Streets, 1698
America's first public fire engine: 1719
America's first botanical gardens: On the banks of the Schuylkill, 1728
America's first public library: Free Library of Philadelphia, 1731
America's first hospital: Philadelphia Hospital, 1732
America's first university: University of Pennsylvania, 1749
America's first anti-slavery society: 1774
America's first flag: Made in Philly by Betsy Ross, 1777
America's first Congressional meeting: Congress Hall, 1789
America's first law school: University of Pennsylvania Law School, 1790
America's first bank: Bank of North America, 1780
America's first bank robbery: $162, 821, August 31, 1798
America's first capital: Take that, Washington, 1790-1800
America's first lager: John Wagner brought lager yeast from his native Bavaria and brewed the nation's first lager beer, 1840.
America's first International Modernist skyscraper: We beat the Depression! Philadelphia Savings Fund Society Building at 12th and Market Streets, 1932.

Philadelphia Timeline—*a timeline of significant events in Philly history (by no means complete)*

1681: King Charles II grants charter of Pennsylvania.
1702: William Penn grants charter for city of Philadelphia.
1704: First Presbyterian Church erected.
1723: Benjamin Franklin arrives in Philadelphia.
1731: First Baptist Church erected.
1732: Independence Hall construction finished. Becomes home of the Liberty Bell.
1749: Ben Franklin founds the country's first university, University of Pennsylvania.
1752: Liberty Bell cracks.
1775: First Continental Congress elects Franklin as Postmaster General of colonies.
1776: Signing of the Declaration of Independence.
1777: British invade Philadelphia.
1778: American army spends cold winter in Valley Forge.
1784: Peace with England ratified by Congress.
1790: Ben Franklin dies in Philadelphia.
1803: Northern Liberties incorporated into city of Philadelphia.
1813: Spring Garden district incorporated into city of Philadelphia.
1829: Eastern State Penitentiary opened.
1829: *The Philadelphia Inquirer* founded.
1857: Academy of Music opens.
1865: City mourns Lincoln's assassination, celebrates defeat of Lee's army.
1866: Coldest night in history (18 degrees below zero); Schuylkill and Delaware freeze.
1872: Friends Meeting House (17th & Girard Sts) opened for public worship.
1874: Famous autopsy of first Siamese twins Chang and Eng completed at College of Physicians and Surgeons.
1875: South Street Bridge opened to pedestrians, 194 buildings erected throughout city.
1876: First train departs from Philadelphia to New York City.
1877: Philadelphia Museum of Art opens Memorial Hall.
1881: First African Americans join police force.
1883: Founding of the National League Team, the Phillies.
1885: City businesses closed for funeral of Ulysses S. Grant.
1889: Labor Day instituted as legal holiday in Pennsylvania.
1915: Phillies make it to the World Series with manager Pat Moran.
1922: Construction begins on the Benjamin Franklin Bridge (then the Delaware River Bridge).
1926: Benjamin Franklin Bridge opens for traffic.
1942: Phillies set club record of losing streak with 111 games.
1957: Walt Whitman Bridge opened for traffic.

1963: Philadelphia purchases Syracuse's NBA team, which becomes the 76ers.
1972: The Sixers post a 9-73 record, still the worst in NBA history.
1981: The Eagles make it to the Super Bowl. And lose to the Raiders.
1985: Infamous MOVE bombing kills 11 and burns 61 houses to the ground.
1991: Old City institutes the tradition of "First Fridays," an art community open house on the first Friday of every month.
1992: Ed Rendell begins first term as mayor of Philadelphia.
1994: Tom Ridge elected Governor of Pennsylvania.
1996: Larry Brown named coach of the 76ers.
1997: Debut of the Philadelphia Fringe Festival.
1998: Wachovia Center opens as new home of the 76ers and the Flyers.
1999: Sixers make it to the playoffs.
2000: John Street takes office as Mayor of Philadelphia.
2000: Republican National Convention held in Philadelphia.
2001: Sixers lose in the NBA finals in five games.
2002: Kimmel Center opens to rave reviews.
2003: Former mayor Ed Rendell becomes Governor of Pennsylvania.
2003: "Ride the Ducks" debuts and annoys all Philadelphians.
2003: With the purchase of "Striped Bass," Stephen Starr reaches ownership of ten restaurants in Philadelphia.
2003: Eagles open their new playing venue, Lincoln Financial Field.
2004: Eagles lose NFC Championship Game—third year in a row.
2004: Citizens Bank Park, new home of the Phillies, opens.
2004: Mayor John Street announces plans for city to become first major wireless Internet city in the country.
2005: Eagles redeem themselves (almost), making it to the Super Bowl.
2006: We celebrate Benergy!
2007: We elect Michael Nutter to be our next mayor.
2007: Comcast Center's giant phallus completes its erection, now the tallest building in the skyline.
2008: Philly rated America's "least attractive" and "most sedentary" city and then reveled in its First Annual Beer Week.
2008: Phils win the World Series, finally breaking the William Penn curse.
2009: Philadelphia Spectrum closes forever.

Media

Nothing to see here! Move right along! No, those aren't a bunch of aimless ex-journalists tossed on their butts after mass lay-offs at the *Inquirer* and *Daily News*. No, Philadelphia media isn't in a state of chaos and disrepair, driving up *New York Times*' sales and down the vibrancy of real, local reportage! Oh wait, that's pretty much the case. Owner Brian Tierney keeps the *Inquirer*'s wings clipped, leaving our two alt weeklies, *City Paper* and *Philadelphia Weekly*, to offer some surprisingly hard-driven reportage—read Kia Gregory in the *Philly Weekly*—paired, of course, with arts coverage, sex ads, and increasingly obsolete classifieds. *The Jewish Exponent* wants to bomb Iran and democrats. *Philadelphia Gay News* has ticked off the community more than once, and *Philadelphia Magazine* services the Main Line. For the real story, always rely on the hard-nosed yet compassionate Marty Moss-Coane on NPR. And Terry, we love you—keep on subtly confronting bigots in between Will Ferrell interviews.

Television

3 KYW (CBS) www.kyw.com		
6 WPVI (ABC)		abclocal.go.com/wpvi
10	WCAU (NBC)	nbc10.com/index.html
12	WHYY (PBS)	www.whyy.org
17	WPHL (WB)	wb17.trb.com
29	WTXF (FOX)	www.fox29.com
35	WYBE	www.wybe.org
51	WTVE	www.wtve.com
57	WPSG (UPN)	www.upn57.com
61	WPPX (PAX)	www.ionline.tv

AM Stations

560	WFIL	Religious
610	WIP	Sports
860	WWDB	Business News
900	WURD	News
950	WPEN	Sports
990	WNTP	Conservative Talk Radio
1060	KYW	All News
1210	WPHT	Talk
1260	WNAR	Drama/Nostalgia
1480	WDAS	Gospel
1540	WNWR	Ethnic
1600	WEXP	College/Sports

FM Stations

88.1	WPEB	Student Radio
88.5	WXPN	Public/Adult Alternative
90.1	WRTI	Public/Classical/Jazz
90.7	WKPS	Student
90.9	WHYY	Public Radio/News/Talk/ NPR Affiliate
91.7	WKDU	Drexel University
92.5	WXTU	Country
93.3	WMMR	Rock
94.1	WYSP	Rock
95.7	WBEN	Hot Adult Contemporary
96.5	WPTP	'80s Rock
98.1	WOGL	Oldies
98.9	WUSL	Hip Hop
101.1	WBEB	Adult Contemporary
102.1	WIOQ	Top 40
102.9	WMGK	Classic Rock
103.3	WPRB	Princeton University
104.5	WSNI	Oldies
105.3	WDAS	Urban Contemporary
106.1	WJJZ	Smooth Jazz

Print Media

Al Dia	211 N 13th St, Ste 704	215-569-4666	Latino daily.
Daily News	400 N Broad St	215-854-2000	Daily tabloid.
Daily Pennsylvanian	4015 Walnut St	215-898-6585	UPenn independent news.
Jewish Exponent	2100 Arch St	215-832-0700	Jewish weekly.
The Hawk	5600 City Avenue	610-660-1000	St. Joseph's University Weekly.
Northeast News Gleaner	9999 Gantry Road	215-969-5100	Oldest weekly newspaper in city.
Philadelphia Metro	30 S. 15th St.	215-717-2600	National daily.
Penn Gazette	3910 Chestnut St, 3rd fl	215-898-5555	UPenn alumni magazine.
Philadelphia Business Journal	400 Market St, Ste 1200	215-238-1450	Daily business report.
Philadelphia City Paper	123 Chestnut St, 3rd fl	215-735-8444	Weekly arts & entertainment.
Philadelphia Gay News	505 S 4th St	215-625-8501	Weekly news.
Philadelphia Inquirer	400 N Broad St	215-854-2000	Daily broadsheet.
Philadelphia Magazine	1818 Market St, 36th fl	215-564-7700	City mag with "Best Of" list.
Philadelphia New Observer	1520 Locust St, Ste 501	215-545-7500	Weekly African American.
Philadelphia Style	141 League St	215-468-6670	Monthly fashion/culture mag.
Philadelphia Tribune	520 S 16th St	215-893-4050	Weekly African American news.
Philadelphia Weekly	1500 Sansom St, 3rd Floor	215-563-7400	Weekly alternative.
Temple Times	302 University Services Bldg	215-204-8963 1601 N Broad St	Daily Temple University news.
The Triangle	3010 MacAlister Hall	215-895-2585 33rd & Chestnut Sts.	Weekly Drexel University news.

Libraries

Show us a Philadelphia without budget problems, and we'll show you library locations that are always open. As it is, though, City Hall struggles to keep the city chugging forward, and many of the Free Library's 54 neighborhood locations have limited hours, or, worse, stand to be closed.

The **main branch** of the library at 19th and Vine Streets (**Map 2**) is always there for you, though, and hosts a great reading series that features writers of all levels of fame, including comedians and political figures. Some of the events cost money to attend ($14; $7 students), but many are free. For a schedule, go to www.library.phila.gov.

In addition to the main branch, there are 55 smaller branches focusing on their specific communities—and with their own events. Visit www.library.phila.gov/calendar for all events listings.

If you can't make it to the actual library, you can take advantage of Philly's call or email a librarian. There's always a librarian standing by to guide you to the information and resources you need. They even have an online chat function know. Hooray, hooray for the library! http://libwww.library.phila.gov/faq/aska.cfm

Library	Address	Phone	Map
Central Library	1901 Vine St	215-686-5322	2
Charles L Durham Branch	3320 Haverford Ave	215-685-7436	14
Charles Santore Branch	932 S 7th St	215-686-1766	8
Chestnut Hill Branch	8711 Germantown Ave	215-248-0977	27
Falls of Schuylkill Branch	3501 Midvale Ave	215-685-2093	23
Fishtown Community Branch	1217 E Montgomery Ave	215-685-9990	20
Fumo Family Branch	2437 S Broad St	215-685-1758	10
Independence Branch	18 S 7th St	215-685-1633	3
Joseph E Coleman Branch	68 W Chelten Ave	215-685-2150	24
Kensington Branch	104 W Dauphin St	215-685-9996	20
Library for Blind and Physically Handicapped	919 Walnut St	215-683-3213	3
Lovett Branch	6945 Germantown Ave	215-685-2095	25
Philadelphia City Institute	1905 Locust St	215-685-6621	2
Queen Memorial Library	1201 S 23rd St	215-685-1899	6
Ramonita de Rodriguez Branch	600 W Girard Ave	215-686-1768	19
Roxborough Branch	6245 Ridge Ave	215-685-2550	21
South Philadelphia Branch	1700 S Broad St	215-685-1866	10
Thomas F Donatucci Sr Branch	1935 Shunk St	215-685-1755	9
Walnut Street West	201 S 40th St	215-685-7671	13
Whitman Branch	200 Snyder Ave	215-685-1754	11
Widener Branch	2808 W Lehigh Ave	215-685-9799	15

7

8

14

2

5

35

15

39

25

92

24

19

22

16

23

26

18

9

6

17

3

12

4

77

1

NEW JERSEY

Delaware River

Cobbs Creek

Northwestern Ave.

Stenton Ave.

Ivy Hill Rd.

Cheltenham Ave.

Cottman

Rhawn St.

Roosevelt Blvd.

Henry Ave.

Wayne St.

Wister St.

Roosevelt Blvd.

Broad St.

G St.

Frankford Cr.

City Ave.

Lehigh Ave.

Allegheny Ave.

Front St.

Lehigh Ave.

Montgomery Ave.

Poplar St.

52nd St.

Market St.

10th St.

Baltimore St.

49th St.

Broad St.

Lombard

Moore St.

Tasker St.

Police Stations

	Address	Phone	Map
12th Police District	6448 Woodland Ave	215-686-3120	n/a
14th Police District	43 W Haines St	215-686-3140	24
15th Police District	2831 Levick St	215-686-3150	n/a
16th Police District	3900 Lancaster Ave	215-686-3160	13
17th Police District	1201 S 20th St	215-686-3170	6
18th Police District	5510 Pine St	215-686-3180	n/a
19th Police District	61st St & Thompson St	215-686-3190	n/a
1st Police District	S 24th St & Wolf St	215-686-3010	n/a
22nd Police District	17th St & Montgomery Ave	215-686-3220	n/a
24th Police District	3901 Whitaker Ave	215-686-3240	n/a
25th Police District	3901 Whitaker Ave	215-686-3250	n/a
26th Police District	Girard Ave & Montgomery Ave	215-686-3260	20
2nd Police District	2831 Levick St	215-686-3020	n/a
35th Police District	N Broad St & W Champlost Ave	215-686-3350	n/a
39th Police District	N 22nd & W Hunting Park Ave	215-686-3390	n/a
3rd Police District	11th St & Wharton St	215-686-3030	7
4th Police District	11th St & Wharton St	215-686-3040	7
5th Police District	Ridge Ave & Cinnaminson St	215-686-3050	n/a
6th Police District	235 N 11th St	215-686-3060	3
7th Police District	Bustleton Ave & Bowler St	215-686-3070	n/a
8th Police District	Academy Rd & Red Lion Rd	215-686-3080	n/a
92nd Police District	Lincoln Dr & Gypsy Ln	215-686-7292	22
9th Police District	401 N 21st St	215-686-3090	17
Center City District	660 Chestnut St	215-440-5551	3
South Street Detail (3rd District)	905 South St	215-922-6706	8

Important Phone Numbers

Life-Threatening Emergencies:	911	Domestic Violence Hotline:	866-723-3014
Non-Emergency Police Service:	215-686-1776	Missing Persons Unit:	215-685-3257
Wanted Persons:	888-683-9268	Special Victims Unit:	215-685-3251
Rape Victims Hotline:	215-985-3333	Noise Complaints (NET):	215-686-5819
		Complaints (Internal Affairs):	215-685-5056

Crime Statistics

	2002	2003	2004	2005	2006
Murder	288	348	330	377	406
Rape	1,035	1,004	1,001	1,024	960
Robbery	8,869	9,617	9,757	10,069	10,971
Aggravated Assault	9,865	9,651	9,814	10,139	10,546
Burglary	11,244	10,656	10,536	10,960	11,542
Theft	38,789	37,864	37,808	38,039	39,413
Motor Vehicle Theft	13,302	13,934	12,587	11,420	11,655

Emergency Rooms

	Address	Phone	Map
Albert Einstein Medical Center	5501 Old York Rd	215-456-7890	n/a
Aria Health-Frankford Campus	4900 Frankford Ave	215-831-2000	n/a
Chestnut Hill	8835 Germantown Ave	215-248-8200	27
Germantown Community Health Services	1 Penn Blvd	215-951-8000	n/a
Hahnemann University Hospital	Broad St & Vine St	215-762-7000	2
Hospital of the University of Pennsylvania	3400 Spruce St	215-662-4000	14
Jeanes Hospital	7600 Central Ave	215-728-2000	n/a
Jefferson University Hospital	111 S 11th St	215-955-6000	3
Methodist Hospital	2301 S Broad St	215-952-9000	10
Nazareth Hospital	2601 Holme Ave	215-335-6000	n/a
Pennsylvania Hospital	800 Spruce St	215-829-3000	3
Penn Presbyterian Medical Center	51 N 39th St	215-662-8000	13
St Joseph's Hospital	N 16th St & W Girard Ave	215-787-9000	18
Wills Eyes	840 Walnut St	215-928-3000	3

Other Hospitals

	Address	Phone	Map
Belmont Center for Comprehensive Treatment	4200 Monument Rd	215-877-2000	n/a
The Children's Hospital of Philadelphia	34th St & Civic Ctr Blvd	215-590-1000	14
Fox Chase Cancer Center	333 Cottman Ave	215-728-6900	n/a
Magee Rehabilitation Hospital	1513 Race St	800-96-MAGEE	2
Mercy Philadelphia Hospital	501 S 54th St	215-748-9000	n/a
Penn Medicine at Rittenhouse	1800 Lombard St	215-893-5000	2
Temple University Hospital	3401 Broad St	215-707-2000	12

Part of the appeal of hanging out with kids is rediscovering the fun and frivolity of childhood. We've created a list of great stores, restaurants, and activities that you should enjoy as much as the little 'uns.

Shopping Essentials

Philadelphia is not often touted as one of the fashion capitals of the world. But with the help of these stores, your kids can be as adorably clothed and accessorized as their counterparts in London, Paris, New York, and Milan.

- **babyGap** · 160 North Gulph Rd, King of Prussia · 610-265-0620 · Timeless baby fashions at moderate prices.
- **Big Blue Marble Books** · 551 Carpenter Ln · 215-844-1870 · Progressive and multi-cultural titles for lefties in the making.
- **Book Corner: Books for Kids & Teens** · 1940 Pine St · 215-790-1727 · Tiny shop with a great selection and friendly staff.
- **Born Yesterday** · 1901 Walnut St · 215-568-6556. · Up-scale kiddie clothes.
- **Burberry** · 1705 Walnut St · 215-557-7400 · The famous raincoats and plaids in miniature.
- **Children's Boutique** · 1702 Walnut St · 215-732-2661 · First floor stocked with European kids' clothes and shoes, second floor devoted to toys.
- **Daffy's** · 1700 Chestnut St · 215-963-9996 · Discounted designer kids' clothes.
- **Gymboree** · 326 Mall Blvd, King of Prussia · 610-992-0470 · Clothing store and play center chain geared at children under the age of seven.
- **Happily Ever After** · 1010 Pine St · 215-627-5790 · Old-school toy store.
- **IKEA** · 2206 S Columbus Blvd · 215-551-4532 · Great deals on kids' furniture and accessories. And kids love playing in the showroom.
- **Karl's—Baby & Teenage Furniture & Clothing** · 724 Chestnut St · 215-627-2514 · The name says it all.
- **Little Beth Boutique** · 1540 Packer Ave · 215-468-2229 · Best christening gowns in the city.
- **Mimi Maternity** · 1615 Walnut St · 215-567-1425 · Maternity wear.
- **O' Doodles** · 8335 Germantown Ave · 215-247-7405 · High-quality toys and beautiful children's books.

- **SimplyCottage** · 367 W Lancaster Ave, Haverford · 610-642-2905 · Unique hand-made baby goods, from linens to bookcases, to wall hangings.
- **Supercuts** · 209 South St · 215-922-2970 · Cheap cuts for kids. No appointment necessary.
- **Toys "R" Us** · 2703 S 3rd St · 215-334-4600 · Toy superstore.
- **Worn Yesterday of Manayunk** · 4235 Main St · 215-482-3316 · Consignment shop for maternity wear, kids, and baby outfits—the place to go if you want your kid to look like one of Angie's, and at one third the cost.

Outdoor Activities

Kids cooped up are like fish out of water. Here are some outdoor activities they'll love.

- **Amish Village** · Rte 896, 717-687-8511 · Guided tours through Amish country and great souvenirs.
- **Dutch Wonderland** · 2249 Lincoln Highway E, Lancaster, 886-FUN-atDW · A lower key Disney-like experience that's really quite charming.
- **Fairmount Park** · Fairmount Ave, 215-683-0200 · Historic houses, boathouse row, running and biking paths, picnic grounds.
- **Longwood Gardens** · Rte 1, Kennett Square, 610-388-1000 · Horticultural display garden that hosts all kinds of activities for kids.
- **Lower Perkiomen Valley Park** · Oaks exit, Rte 422, Oaks, 610-666-5371 · Bike trails along the Schuylkill River, playground equipment along the way.
- **Philadelphia Zoo** · 3400 W Girard Ave 215-243-1100 · Oldest zoo in the country with a primate exhibit to write home about. Check out the Zooballoon!
- **Sesame Place** · 100 Sesame Rd, Langhorne · 215-752-7070) Sesame Street-based amusement park.

Websites

www.gocitykids.com
www.philly.parentzone.com
www.go.com/familyfun

Rainy Day Alternatives

Nothing can really beat baking or watching movies on a rainy day. But if you're motivated to leave the house, these popular destinations never come up short:

- **Academy of Natural Sciences** • 1900 Ben Franklin Pkwy, 215-299-1000 • Four floors of activities and exhibits about the world's most fascinating species and their habitats.
- **American Historical Theatre** • 2008 Mt Vernon St, 215-232-2690 • Educational, historical theater for kids and school groups.
- **Arden Children's Theater** • 40 N 2nd St, 215-922-1122 • Resident professional children's theater.
- **Dave & Buster's** • 325 N Columbus Blvd, 215-413-1951 • Arcade games, pinball machines, laser tag, batting cage (and word on the street is that Allen Iverson hangs out here).
- **The Franklin Institute** • 222 N 20th St, 215-448-1200 • Science museum that takes learning to a new level of fun (seriously).
- **Headhouse Books** • 619 S 2nd St, 215-923-9525 • Children's story hours, Chess Club 4 Kids, and art history lessons.
- **Independence Seaport Museum** • 211 S Columbus Blvd, 215-413-8655 • All things Davy Jones, plus ongoing exhibits of other nautical phenomena.
- **Insectarium** • 8046 Frankford Ave, 215-335-9500 • All-bug museum.
- **Mütter Museum** • 19 S 22nd St, 215-563-3737 • For the future doctors of the world.
- **North Bowl** • 909 N 2nd St, 215-238-BOWL • Kid friendly before 9 p.m.
- **Philadelphia Children's Theatre** • 2030 Sansom St, 215-528-2600 • Professional theater for the young 'uns.
- **Philadelphia Doll Museum** • 2253 N Broad St, 212-787-0220 • Diverse dolls from around the world, character dolls, talking action figures, and vintage barbies.
- **Philadelphia Museum of Art** • 26th St & Franklin Pkwy, 215-763-8100 • Art classes for kids aged 3–12.
- **Please Touch Museum** • 4231 Avenue of the Republic, 215-963-0667 • You're supposed to touch everything. That's the point. Fake supermarkets, science rooms, barnyards, and more.

Kid-Friendly Restaurants

They love kids and kids love them:

- **DiNardo's Famous Crabs** • 312 Race St, 215-925-5115 • Tasty crabs. Bibs are given to everyone, so the kids won't stand out as the messy ones.
- **Fiesta Pizza** • 8339 Germantown Ave, 215-247-4141 • Caters to kids—gives you crowns and fries while you wait for the 'za.
- **Hard Rock Café** • 1113 Market St, 215-238-1000 • Average food tastes better when you're staring at a signed Elvis EP. No matter how tacky you might find it, the fact of the matter is that kids really like this place.
- **Johnny Rockets** • 443 South St, 215-829-9222 • '50s-style chain diner with standard jukebox and kids' menu.
- **Keating's Grill** • 201 N Columbus Blvd, 215-928-1234 • Okay, it's a hotel restaurant, but it has a nice view.
- **More Than Just Ice Cream** • 1119 Locust St, 215-574-0586 • Ice cream in one room, vegetarian delights in the other.
- **Nifty Fifty's** • 2491 Grant Ave, 215-676-1950 • '50s-style diner.
- **Maron Chocolates and Scoop de Ville** • 1734 Chestnut St, 215-988-9992 • Part candy shop and part ice cream you can take to the park. How can you go wrong?
- **Spaghetti Warehouse** • 1026 Spring Garden St, 215-787-0784 • A primo spot for birthday parties.

The site of some of the earliest gay rights protests in the 1960s, Philadelphia has long been a gay-friendly town. The city cultivates this image, coining the slogan "Get your history straight, and your nightlife gay" to draw LGBT tourists. The Gayborhood, stretching roughly from Walnut to Pine Streets between 11th and 13th streets, is now official! Gay marriage, it's not, but the city, since this past year, now hangs rainbow flags in the area, and even gay-ed up the street signs. It's a conglomeration of plenty of gay-owned businesses and residents, as well as the 12th Street Gym (where gay bodybuilders of Philadelphia unite). Sisters is the only full-time lesbian bar; Thursday night is the most popular evening, by far, and they serve a wonderful brunch on Sunday morning.

Health Centers and Support Organizations

- **ACT UP Philadelphia**, www.critpath.org/actup
  Political advocacy group by and for people living with HIV/AIDS.
- **Attic Youth Center**, 255 S 16th St,
  215-545-4331; www.atticyouthcenter.org
  The largest GLBT youth center in Philadelphia, the Attic provides a safe social space for queer youth, as well as counseling and psychological services for young adults between the ages of 12-23.
- **Bi-Unity Social Group**, www.biunity.org
  Social group for people who identify as bisexual.
- **City of Brotherly Love Softball League**,
  215-GO-CBLSL; www.cblsl.org
  Openly gay softball league with men's and women's divisions.
- **Critical Path AIDS Project**,www.critpath.org
  Part of Philadelphia Fight, offers treatment, referrals, advocacy information, and more to HIV-positive individuals. Their website is a resource in itself.
- **Equality Advocates Pennsylvania** ,
  1211 Chestnut St, Ste 605,
  215-731-1447; www.equalitypa.org
  Advocating equality for the LGBT community in PA.
- **Fairmount Park Women's Softball League,**
  215-508-3922
  Fairmount Park Women's Softball League has been part of the women's sports community in Philadelphia for over 25 years.
- **Frontrunners Philadelphia,**
  www.frontrunnersphila.org
  Gay and lesbian running club.
- **Gay and Lesbian Lawyers of Philadelphia**,
  215-627-9090; www.galloplaw.org
  Call if you need a referral for a lawyer.
- **Lavender Visions,**
  www.lavendervisions.com/married.html.
  Programs for lesbian and bisexual women, with excellent resources for married women who are coming out or seeking individual or group counseling.
- **Mazzoni Center**, 1201 Chestnut St, 3rd Fl,
  215-563-0652; www.mazzonicenter.org
  Free and anonymous HIV testing and counseling.

- **PA Gay and Lesbian Alliance for Political Action**,
  610-863-0227, http://eqfed.org/pagala/home.html
  The group meets on the second Tuesday of each month at the William Way Center.·
  PFLAG Philadelphia,
  P.O. Box 15711, Philadelphia, PA 19103
  215-572-1833; www.pflagphila.org
  Parents, Families and Friends of Lesbians and Gays.
- **Philadelphia Family Pride**,
  www.phillyfamilypride.org
  Social events for gay and lesbian parents and their children.
- **Philadelphia Fight**, 1233 Locust St, 5thFloor
  215-985-4448, www.fight.org
  AIDS service organization focusing on research and education.
- **Philadelphia FINS**,
  267-971-7932, www.philadelphia-fins.org
  Philadelphia's LGBT Masters Swim Team.
- **Philadelphia Lesbian and Gay Task Force**,
  215-772-2000
  Works on political issues and has a hotline for violence directed at gays and lesbians. Makes use of volunteers.
- **The Safeguards Project**,
  260 S Broad St 10th Floor, 215-985-6873
  Non-profit community health organization promoting a healthy lifestyle for gay men and the LBGT community through workshops, HIV testing, community programs, and health information.
  www.safeguards.org
- **Sisterspace**, 215-546-4890; www.sisterspace.org
  Organizes social events for women, a volleyball league, and a women of color forum.
- **William Way Lesbian, Gay, Bisexual Transgender (GLBT) Community Center**,
  1315 Spruce St, 215-732-2220; www.waygay.org
  Home to a number of community groups and host of many regular events.
- **Women in Transition Hotline**,
  215-751-1111, www.womenintransitioninc.org
  Support for lesbians in abusive relationships.

Bookstores

- **Giovanni's Room**, 345 S 12th St, 215-923-2960; www.giovannisroom.com—One of the oldest gay bookstores in the country, this little nook offers a wide selection of gay, lesbian, and feminist texts and films. Women's book discussion group meets at 7:00 pm on the first Sunday of each month.

Publications and Media

- **Philadelphia Gay News**
  www.edgephiladelphia.com.
  Celebrating over 30 years in the gay press.
- **WXPN 88.5**—www.xpn.org.
  Hosts two programs targeted to gays and lesbians: "Amazon Country" and "Q'zine."

Annual Events

- **Blue Ball**—A circuit party weekend fundraiser held in collaboration with Equality Forum; www.blueballphilly.com.
- **Equality Forum**—Formerly PrideFest America, the GLBT conference and festival takes place every April. 215-732-FEST; www.equalityforum.com.
- **LGBT Pride Parade & Festival**—Held in June each year. 215-875-9288; www.phillypride.org.
- **Philadelphia Gay & Lesbian Theater Festival**—Held in June each year. 215-922-1122, www.philagaylesbiantheaterfest.org.
- **QFest**—Held every July, it's the biggest gay film festival on the East Coast. www.phillyfests.com/piglff.
- **QPenn**—Penn's annual Pride Week takes place every March; www.qpenn.org

Venues—Gay

- **12th Air Command** · 254 S 12th St · 215-545-8088 · www.12thair.com
- **Bike Stop** · 206 S Quince St · 215-627-1662 · www.thebikestop.com
- **Bump** · 1234 Locust St · 215-732-1800
- **Glam** · 52 S 2nd St · 267-671-0840 · www.glamphilly.com
- **Key West** · 207 S Juniper St · 215-545-1578
- **Pure Nightclub** · 1221 St James Pl · 215-735-5772 · www.purephilly.com
- **Shampoo** (Fridays) · Willow between 7&8th Sts · 215-922-7500 · www.shampooonline.com
- **Uncle's** · 1220 Locust St · 215-546-6660
- **Westbury** · 261 S 13th St · 215-546-5170
- **Woody's** · 202 S 13th St · 215-545-1893 · www.woodysbar.com

Venues—Lesbian

- **Pure Party Girl** (1st Sat) · 1221 St James St · 215-735-5772 · www.ladies2000.com
- **Sisters** · 1320 Chancellor St · 215-735-0735 · www.sistersnightclub.com

Venues—Mixed

- **Elevate** (4th Sat) · 207 S Juniper St · 215-545-1578 · www.elevatephilly.com
- **Tavern on Camac** · 243 S Camac St · 215-545-0900 · www.taverconcamac.com
- **Sal's on 12th** · 200 S 12th St · 215-731-9930

Websites

- **Gay and Lesbian Yellow Pages**—www.glyp.com
- **Greater Philadelphia Tourism Bureau**—www.gophila.com/gay.
  Information about GLBT events, culture, and community in Philly.
- **Out in Philadelphia**—www.outinphiladelphia.com.
  Community website with gay and lesbian news, personals, listings, travel information, and health advice.
- **Philadelphia Gay Singles**—http://philadelphiagaysingles.com.
  Online meeting place for Philly's gay and lesbians.
- **Philly Gayborhood**—http://phillygayborhood.com.
  All purpose community site with events calendar and listings.
- **QueerConnections**—http://groups.yahoo.com/group/queerconnections/
  Queer Connections (QC) is a social group for women in their twenties who are queer (lesbian, bisexual, gay, or transgendered), women who are questioning their sexuality, and friends of queers (who are straight but not narrow).
- **William Way Community Center**—www.waygay.org.
  Website with information on a number of community groups and gay & lesbian events.
- **Craigslist**—philadelphia.craigslist.org.
  General community site (for straights, gays, and everyone else) that includes local "women seeking women" and "men seeking men" personal pages.

Hotels

Philly doesn't have a lot of hotel culture, the way in other cities the locals crowd around the bars and lobbies and actually hang out. But there are a couple truly wonderful exceptions, such as the **Sofitel Hotel (Map 2)** and the **Society Hill Hotel (Map 4)**. At the Sofitel, the bar area is not too uptight (but very cool) and it has the smell of famous people having just left the room for a moment (they'll be right back)—and the lemon drop martinis are rock solid. The **Society Hill Hotel** is an elegant reminder of that breed of small, smoky hotels, in the Hitchcockian era, where people met for drinks and showed a little leg. Other than those two, we recommend Philly hotels for the rooms upstairs.

The **Doubletree Hotel (Map 2)** makes for an efficient if over-air-conditioned stay, and, located right on Broad St, it's situated to be a reasonable midpoint for everything downtown. The **Sheraton Society Hill Hotel (Map 4)**, while managing to be creaky and stuffy at the same time, has one of the best pools, and is convenient to all of Old City. The **Rittenhouse Hotel (Map 2)** is whoppingly overpriced—although we admit, it's totally supreme—and it seems to have pointed its nose, which is full of golden snot, away from the idea of special rates. The recently remodeled **Ritz Carlton (Map 2)** is still a classic, and the rooms have breathtaking views of the city. Right up against City Hall, you'll be able to examine just how well they did clean it, now that they're sort of done.

The **Omni Hotel at Independence Park (Map 4)**, close to the Ritz Theatres, is our top pick for anybody looking to swoop in for a film festival. The **Alexander Inn (Map 3)**, located in the Gayborhood, is convenient to Woody's and, well, men. The **Sofitel (Map 2)** is romance, and the **Loews (Map 3)** is retro-funky. The **Holiday Inn (Map 4)** is good for kids (they eat free, haven't you heard?), and for people planning on hardcore tourism, since it's near the old brick stuff—and the duck boat does its land dock close by. The **Thomas Bond House (Map 4)** is good if you want to get yourself gooped on by history, and you might want to pack your bonnet so you don't look like a total misfit.

There's also a whole jumble of old, elegant, if not totally hip, hotels that Philadelphia, being so old and elegant, and not so hip, can't help having plenty of—the **Westin (Map 2)** and the **Latham (Map 2)** are some better examples. The **Four Seasons (Map 2)** is a bit of a given, but, unless you want to get married, or are over 65, it's skip-able—although the restaurant is a different story. Another option, which is growing, is to look on **Craigslist.org** under "Sublets and Temporary." More and more, people with swanky studios right on Rittenhouse Square are giving it up for a couple nights in order to cash in—and they inevitably charge less than, say, the **Rittenhouse Hotel (Map 2)**.

Check out, let's presume, is at noon.

Map 2 · Rittenhouse / Logan Circle

		Phone	Price
Courtyard Philadelphia Downtown	21 N Juniper St	215-496-3200	165
Crowne Plaza	1800 Market St	215-561-7500	145
Doubletree Hotel	237 S Broad St	215-893-1600	150
Embassy Suites	1776 Benjamin Franklin Pkwy	215-561-1776	170
Four Seasons Hotel	1 Logan Sq	215-963-1500	400
Hyatt at the Bellevue	200 Broad St	215-893-1234	190
La Reserve	1804 Pine St	215-735-1137	125
Latham Hotel	135 S 17th St	215-563-7474	139
Radisson Plaza Warwick Hotel	1701 Locust St	215-735-6000	125
Residence Inn Philadelphia Center City	1 E Penn Sq	215-557-0005	169
Rittenhouse 1715	1715 Rittenhouse Sq	215-546-6500	239
The Rittenhouse Hotel	210 W Rittenhouse Sq	215-546-9000	285
The Ritz-Carlton Philadelphia	10 Ave of the Arts	215-523-8000	219
Sheraton Philadelphia City Center Hotel	N 17th St & Race St	215-448-2000	150
Sofitel Philadelphia	120 S 17th St	215-569-8300	175
Windsor Suites	1700 Benjamin Franklin Pkwy	215-981-5678	160
The Westin Philadelphia	99 S 17th St	215-563-1600	219

Map 3 · Center City East

		Phone	Price
Alexander Inn	Spruce St & 12th St	215-923-3535	99
Antique Row Bed & Breakfast	341 S 12th St	215-592-7802	65
Clinton St B&B	1024 Clinton St	215-802-1334	139
Hampton Inn	1301 Race St	215-665-9100	179
Hilton Garden Inn	1100 Arch St	215-923-0100	160
Holiday Inn Express	1305 Walnut St	215-735-9300	144
Loews Philadelphia Hotel	1200 Market St	215-627-1200	150
Morris House Hotel	225 S 8th St	215-922-2446	150
Parker Spruce Hotel	261 S 13th St	215-735-2300	45
Philadelphia Marriott Downtown	1201 Market St	215-625-2900	200
Trade Winds Bed & Breakfast	943 Lombard St	215-592-8644	88
Travelodge	1227 Race St	215-564-2888	112

Map 4 · Old City / Society Hill

		Phone	Price
Best Western Independence Park Hotel	235 Chestnut St	215-922-4443	225
Thomas Bond House	129 S 2nd St	215-923-8523	105
Comfort Inn Downtown/Historic Area	100 N Columbus Blvd	215-627-7900	130
Holiday Inn	400 Arch St	215-923-8660	170
Hyatt Regency	201 S Columbus Blvd	215-928-1234	160
Madame Saito Bed & Breakfast	124 Lombard St	215-922-2512	80
Omni Hotel at Independence Park	401 Chestnut St	215-925-0000	230
Penn's View Hotel	14 N Front St	215-922-7600	180
Sheraton Society Hill	1 Dock St	215-238-6000	189

Map 12 · Stadiums

		Phone	Price
Holiday Inn	900 Packer Ave	215-755-9500	120

Map 13 · West Philly

		Phone	Price
Spruce Hill Manor	331 S 46th St	215-472-2213	123

Map 14 · University City

		Phone	Price
Cornerstone Bed & Breakfast	3300 Baring St	215-387-6065	140
Hilton Inn at Penn	3600 Sansom St	215-222-0200	175
Spruce Hill Manor	3709 Baring St	215-472-2213	145
Sheraton University City Hotel	3549 Chestnut St	215-387-8000	169

Map 17 · Fairmount

		Phone	Price
Best Western City Center Hotel	501 N 22nd St	215-568-8300	125

Map 18 · Spring Garden / Francisville

		Phone	Price
Carlyle Hotel	1425 Poplar St	215-978-9934	50

Map 26 · Mt Airy

		Phone	Price
Anam Cara Bed & Breakfast	52 Wooddale Ave	215-242-4327	118

Map 27 · Chestnut Hill

		Phone	Price
Chestnut Hill Hotel	8229 Germantown Ave	215-242-5905	129
Silverstone Bed & Breakfast	8840 Stenton Ave	215-242-3333	95

Philly is essentially a city of landmarks, some obvious, some a little more esoteric. Some of the city's historic moneymakers are located in the recently refurbished **Mall of Independence (Map 4)**, which houses the **Liberty Bell (Map 4)**, the recently-opened **National Constitution Center (Map 4)**, and **Independence Hall (Map 4)**, where the Declaration of Independence was first signed. They are all well worth seeing, if only so you can direct friends and family members when they visit.

Whilst in Old City, you can also check out **Christ Church (Map 4)** (founded in 1695), which has a lovely garden, free-of-charge to muse in, and **Franklin Court (Map 4)**, which has a museum o' Ben and frame replica of his original house (what happens when the city doesn't have enough insight to keep the thing up). At **Franklin Fountain (Map 4)**, which dates to early twentieth century, you can stuff your face with phosphate.

With a great view of the city, the **William Penn Statue (Map 2)** sits high atop **City Hall (Map 2)**; from some angles he looks more excited to see you than in others (see page 131).

South Philly's dueling **Pat's** and **Geno's Steaks (Map 8)** are both legends, although Geno's might go down in history for its balls-out racism rather than for its meat (Google "Geno", "cheesesteak", and "racism" to relive the

fracas.). The bustling dirty gem that is the **Italian Market (Map 8)** has great cheese and greater personality, while **Reading Terminal Market (Map 3)** buzzes with old-timey commerce (and don't forget the Amish!).

In the artistic realm, the oft-endowed **Philadelphia Museum of Art (Map 17)** has an extensive permanent collection. The steps alone hold great fame, and are a top stop for midnight romance on the cheap. Nearby is the free **Rodin Museum (Map 17)**, where you can do your best to emulate *The Thinker*, ironically requiring no thought. If you have children in tow and want to reward them for trekking through art museums, they'll love the **Franklin Institute (Map 1)**, which has both an IMAX theater and planetarium—and the Giant Heart inside is a landmark all on its own.

Isaiah Zagar's mosaic murals are, literally, plastered all over the city, and most notably make up the **Magic Garden (Map 8)** on South St. Glistening with the chunk of yesteryear's ceramics, this garden *is* magic—if you only believe. Drop some money into the trashcan, believers, just beyond the gate, to help preserve this masterpiece.

Armchair athletes should check out the brand spanking new **Lincoln Financial Field (Map 12)** and **Citizens Bank Park (Map 12)** offering high-end amenities for fans of the Eagles and Phillies.

Map 1 · Center City West

23rd Street Armory	22 S 23rd St	Gorgeous building hosting events like antique fairs and roller derby. Cool.
First Unitarian Church	2125 Chestnut St · 215-563-3980	Frequent indie rock shows in the basement. Seriously.
Fitler Square	21st St b/w Locust & South Sts	Quakers are why Philly is so green, so pay respects.
The Franklin Institute	222 N 20th St · 215-448-1200	IMAX, Planetarium, and lots of kiddie-fare.
The Giant Heart at the Franklin Institute	222 N 20th St · 215-448-1200	Walk though the museum's freaky giant heart, around since 1954.
Schurylkill River Banks	2500 Spruce St	Running, biking, roller blading, hanging (out).

Map 2 · Rittenhouse / Logan Circle

Academy of Music	Broad St & Locust St · 215-893-1940	Scorsese shot the opening to *The Age of Innocence* here.
Allow Me Statue	1412 Chestnut St	Biz-dude holding umbrella is always creepy.
City Hall	Market St & 15th St	Perhaps the best-looking building in the city; it's the largest municipal building in the world.
Clothespin Sculpture	15th St & Market St	Obviously, a take on the ills of modern society. Or something.
The Comcast Center	1701 Arch St	Tallest green building in the nation.
Domino Sculpture	1401 John F Kennedy Blvd	Stand under a giant domino for a great photo op.
Friends Center	15th St & Cherry St	Check out the helicopters landing and taking off.
Grip the Raven	1901 Vine St · 215-567-7710	Inspiration to Poe and Dickens, at the Free Library.
Harriet's Nervous System	15th St & Vine St	Medical college entrance still displays her—since 1888.
Love Park	N 15th St & JFK Blvd · 215-636-1666	The skater mecca of the world, if only it were legal.
Market at Comcast Center	1701 Kennedy Blvd	Food court for office slaves.
Mary Dyer Statue	15th St & Cherry St	Hanged Quaker martyr makes for moving piece.
The Masonic Temple	1 N Broad St · 215-988-1900	Giant staircases and oak appointments.
Packard Building	15th St & Chestnut St	Shyamalanadingdong turned it into a train station for *Unbreakable*. Meh.
Philadelphia Art Alliance	251 S 18th St	Great exhibits and events. Black glasses required.
Rittenhouse Fountain	b/w 18th & 19th and Locust & Walnut Sts	The perfect wade-to-your-pant-cuffs pool to take the edge off the summer.
St Mark's Church	1625 Locust St · 215-735-1416	Scenes from *Fallen* were shot here. Too bad no one saw the movie.
Swann Fountain	Logan Cir	Summertime, kids swim for free.
Wachovia Building	Broad St & Sansom St	Parts of *Trading Places* were shot here. Wowee.
William Penn Statue	City Hall, Broad St & Market St · 215-686-6263	We will never dress him in Flyers' gear again.

Map 3 · Center City East

Antique Row	Pine St b/w S 12th St & S 9th St	Furniture, books, knick-knacks of all kinds.
Barbara's Florist Statue	1300 Walnut St	Watch him deteriorate through the seasons.

Camac Street	200 S Camac St	And they say the streets of Philly aren't paved in woodblocks...
Center for Architecture	1218 Arch St	Great exhibits and events. Black glasses required.
Kahn Park	Pine St & S 11th St	Named for revered Philly architect.
Midtown Village	b/w Spruce St & Market St	Where all the tchotchkes is.
Mikveh Israel Cemetary	Spruce St b/w S 8th St & S 9th St	Oldest Jewish cemetery in Philly, 1738.
Morris Animal Refuge	1242 Lombard St	Children giggle more here.
Paul Green School of Rock	1320 Race St · 215-988-9338	10-year-olds playing Zeppelin, AC/DC. Rock out!
Pennsylvania Hospital	800 Spruce St · 215-829-3000	Since 1751, the Nation's oldest. How cute.
Reading Terminal Market	12th St & Arch St · 215-922-2317	More Amish food than you can shake a stick at.
Space Tree	Walnut St & S 6th St	Sycamore grown from a seed from space.
Wanamaker Building	13th St & Market St · 215-241-9000	The Macy's moniker now hangs in the Wanamaker Building—also home of *Mannequin* (1 and 2!)
Washington Square Park	Walnut St b/w S 6th St & S 7th St	Tomb of the Unknown Soldier of the Revolution.
Woman in Window Statue	Chestnut St & S 7th St	Eerie woman-in-white always peers out sadly.

Map 4 · Old City / Society Hill

American Philosophical Society	104 S 5th St · 215-440-3400	Kant figure out Schopenhauer? That's off the Hook.
Arch Street Drag	Arch St & N 3rd St	Transformed into old-world Cinci for *Beloved*.
Arch Street Friends Meeting House	4th & Arch Sts	Fifty plus years in the making, the thing still beats and makes kids cry.
Ben Franklin Bust	N 4th St & Arch St	Made from 1,000 keys donated by local school kids. No joke.
Chestnut Mall	Chestnut St & Columbus Blvd	Exploring the well-lived life of William Penn.
Christ Church Grounds	5th St & Arch St	Where BF is buried—amongst other notables.
Christ Church Park	2nd St & Market St · 215-922-1695	Dogs, squirrels, and OC workers on lunch breaks.
Dream Garden mosaic	601-45 Walnut St	Maxfield Parrish's creation dominates the lobby.
Elfreth's Alley	b/w Front & 2nd Sts and Arch & Race Sts	The oldest residential street in the US, baby.
Empty Lot	b/w Front & 2nd Sts and South & Lombard Sts	It could be the biggest real-estate waste in the city.
Franklin Court	Market St b/w S 3rd St & S 4th St · 215-965-2305	Museum and "ghost" sculpture of Franklin's digs.
The Gazela	Columbus Blvd & Market St	Many-masted boat is more than a century old.
Independence Visitor's Center	6th St & Market St · 215-965-7676	Home of the first gay rights protests in 1965! Also signing of Constitution, et al.
Liberty Bell	Market St b/w S 5th St & S 6th St · 215-965-2305	The only reason anyone ever visits us.
Mikveh Israel	44 N 4th St · 215-922-5446	Oldest Jewish congregation with an impressive set of scrolls.
Mother Bethel AME Church	6th St & Pine St	Enclosed section of truly creepy-looking grave markers.
National Constitution Center	525 Arch St · 215-409-6600	A Presidential wonderland.
Penn's Landing Marina	Penn's Landing & Columbus Blvd	Gaze at the $30 million yachts and feel crappy about yourself.
Real World House	249-251 Arch St	The very house those brats used to flop in when they weren't getting wasted.
Rose Garden	Walnut St b/w S 4th St & S 5th St	A serene bit of civic space too rarely used.
Second Presbyterian Church	3rd St & Arch St	Sections of the burial grounds reserved for Africans.
St Joseph's Catholic Church	321 Willings Aly · 215-923-1733	Stunning stained glass a testament to old-world can-do.
St Peter's Episcopal Church	313 Pine St · 215-925-5968	Est. 1761, so you know it's gotta be good.
US Mint	151 N Independence Mall E · 215-408-0112	It's surprisingly easy to stand outside and look suspicious.
WYSP	101 S Independence Mall E · 215-625-9460	Crappy rock station often gives out schwag here.

Map 5 · Gray's Ferry

Ol' Dirty Bastard's McDonalds	S 29th St & Grays Ferry Ave	The site of ODB's last arrest (in 2002) before his death (in 2004).
Warfield Breakfast Express	Warfield St & Reed St	Failed mob hit on Joey Ciancaglini caught on tape.

Map 7 · Southwark West

The Arena	7 W Ritner St	Mixed-use arena occasionally hosts crazy awesome wrestling.
CAPA High	901 S Broad St · 215-952-2462	Where the Roots first met up and started rollin'.
Cous' Little Italy	901 S 11th St	Angelo Bruno, ancient Don, eats his last meal here before getting whacked.
Lady Day Placard	Broad St & South St	Billie was born in Philly, remember.
The Magic Garden	1022 South St	Isaiah Zagar's masterpiece in progress.
Trojan Pinata	S Broad St	Do not trust the pinata.

Vulpine Athletic Club	12th St & Federal St	Where James "Jimmy Brooms" Diadorrio met his ugly demise.

Map 8 • Bella Vista / Queen Village

Emanuel Evangelical Lutheran Church	1001 S 4th St • 215-336-1444	Saving Philly souls since 1868.
Fabric Row	S 4th St b/w Bainbridge St & Catharine St	From prom dresses to curtain rods.
Firefighter Statue	Queen St b/w S Front St & S 2nd St	Don't miss the weird-looking Dalmatian at his feet.
Fleischer Art Memorial	719 Catharine St • 215-922-3456	Art classes, exhibits, galleries on the DL.
Hovering Bodies	4th St & Catharine St	School kids' body molds now disintegrated into horror movie.
Italian Market	S 9th St b/w Bainbridge St & Washington Ave	You kiddin' me? Cheese, meat, bread, pasta.
Jefferson Square Park/ Sacks Rec Center	Washington Ave b/w S 4th St & S 5th St	Hoops, soccer and a pool to take a plunge afterward.
Lebanon Cemetary	9th St & Passyunk St	Early African burial ground, but the bodies have been moved.
Mario Lanza Park	Queen St b/w S 2nd St & S 3rd St	Great doggie run and film series.
Mummers Museum	1100 S 2nd St • 215-336-3050	Philly's answer to Mardi Gras krewes.
Pat's & Geno's Showdown	S 9th St & E Passyunk Ave	Stand in the crosswalk and watch humanity degrade itself by the second.
Rizzo Ice Skating Rink	1101 S Front St • 215-685-1593	Proud home of the Rink Rats.
Sarcone's	758 S 9th St • 215-922-0445	Get your bread on and don't pass up the pizza.
Sherlock Holmes Mural	S 2nd St b/w Christian St & Moyamensing St	Hidden maze of characters and images abound.
Weccocoe Playground	Catharine St b/w S 4th St & S 5th St	Best public tennis court in CC.

Map 9 • Point Breeze / West Passyunk

Melrose Diner Parking Lot	1501 Snyder Ave • 215-467-6644	Site of brutal mob hit of Frank Baldino.

Map 11 • South Philly East

The New Alhambra	7 Ritner St • 215-755-0611	Live fights of all types: boxing, muay thai, martial arts, etc.
Joe Hand Boxing Gym	7 Ritner St •215-271-4263	Kids train beside future Golden Glove Olympic champs.

Map 12 • Stadiums

Chickie's Hit	Curtain St & Juniper St	Frank Narducci shot 10 times after a court date.
Citizens Bank Park	1 Citizens Bank Wy • 215-563-6000	World phucking series!
Lincoln Financial Field	1020 Pattison Ave • 215-463-2500	Where the Iggles call home.

Map 13 • West Philly

Pinwheel House	42nd St & Wallace St	A folk-art explosion of pinwheels and whirligigs.
Slought Foundation	4017 Walnut St	Not-for-profit cultural organization with public programs in contemporary art.

Map 14 • University City

30th St Station Bathrooms	Market St & S 30th St • 215-349-3196	Re-create Witness and pretend you're a little Amish child.
Ben and His Bench	Locust Walk & S 37th St	Cuddle up with Ben F. and read the newspaper.
Biopond	3740 Hamilton Wk	A quiet lunch spot replete with benches and fishpond.
Bolt Bus	30th St & Market St	30th Street Bolt Bus Sation. The best and cheapest way to travel!
Face Fragment	35th St & Market St	Half a face with Roman nose, no eyes.
Hill Square	34th St & Walnut St	Great view of the city, and a series of benches upon which to recline.
Self-Immolation Point	34th St & Locust St	Where artist/activist Kathy Chang burned herself to death.
Split Button	b/w 34th & 36th Sts & Locust & Spruce Sts	Oldenburg's giant broken button a keeper.

Map 16 • Brewerytown

Art Museum Steps	26th & Benjamin Franklin Pkwy	Recreate Rocky's infamous romp like all the other jackasses.

General Information · **Landmarks**

| Giant Slide | 33rd St & Oxford St · 215-765-4325 | Smith Playground's single greatest attraction. |
| Lloyd Hall | Boathouse Row | Scullers and skaters share the space. |

Map 17 · Fairmount

Eastern State Penitentiary	N 22nd St & Fairmount Ave · 215-236-5111	Take a tour, buy a t-shirt. Get the daylights scared out of you.
Rodin Museum	N 22nd St & Benjamin Franklin Pkwy · 215-763-8100	Get your Thinker on.
The Thinker	N 22nd St & Benjamin Franklin Pkwy · 215-568-6020	We know, we know. A cliché. But it's still cool.

Map 18 · Spring Garden / Francisville

| Divine Lorraine Hotel | 699 N Broad St | Onetime divine guesthouse, ravaged by time. |
| Metropolitan Opera House | Broad St & Fairmount Ave | Former opera house used in fine *12 Monkeys* film. |

Map 19 · Northern Liberties

Edgar Allen Poe National Historic Site	532 N 7th St	Is it creepy to think he penned "The Black Cat" when you see the real chimney in his real basement? Yes it is.
Liberty Lands Park	3rd St & Poplar St	Recently reclaimed from junkies and winos.
St John Neumann Shrine	1019 N 5th St · 215-627-3080	Shrine of canonized Philly Bishop.

Map 20 · Fishtown / Port Richmond

Penn Treaty Park	E Columbia Ave & Delaware Ave	It's said William Penn made a treaty of friendship with the Lenape Indians in 1683 under a giant elm tree here.
Philadephia Brewing Company	2439 Amber S	Building dates back to the Weisbrod & Hess Oriental Brewing Company in 1885.
Pop's Playground	2572 Collins St	Abandoned playground soon to be a skate park (hopefully).

Map 21 · Roxborough / Manayunk

| Manayunk Wall | Levering Street | Philadelphia International Championship bicycle races race here. How 'bout that. |

Map 22 · Manayunk

| Kelpius Cave | Sumac St & Wissahickon Park | Historic monk retreat now used for secret bong shelter. |

Map 23 · East Falls

| Laurel Hill Cemetery | 3822 Ridge Ave · 215-228-8200 | Ancient, Victorian-style, and oddly beautiful. |

Map 24 · Germantown South

| Sun Ra's House | 5626 Morton St | Where the Arkestra for this jazz genius lived and played, Marshall Allen continues in the same vein.. |

Northeast Philly

The Boulevard	Roosevelt Blvd	Named after Teddy; it's a bustling bevy of shopping, eating, and sight-seeing stop-offs.
Burlhome Park	Cottman & Central Aves · 215-636-1666	Run, jog, or walk through this Northeast beauty.
Flyer's Skate Zone	10990 Decatur Rd · 215-618-0050	Book private parties and skate where the Philadelphia Flyers practice.
Knowlton Mansion	8001 Verree Rd	Designed in 1879; now hosts private events and weddings amidst breathtaking Victorian design.
Nabisco Factory	Comly Rd & Roosevelt Ave	Smell the unmistakable scent of Nilla Wafers from miles away.
Northeast Philadelphia Airport (PNE)	8000 Essington Ave · 215-677-5592	Pennsylvania's third-busiest airport.
Pennypack Creek Park	8600 Verree Rd	The park covers 1,334 acres in Northeast Philadelphia along Pennypack Creek—cool!

19038
19150
19118
27
26
19119
19138
19126
19111
1915
19128
25
19141
19120
19149
19144
19127
24
19004
22
19129
19140
19124
23
19131
19132
19133
19134
19137
15
19121
19122
20
19125
51
16
19139
17
19130
18
19123
19
13
19104
14
19103
19107
19106
1
2
3
4
19143
19102
5
19146
6
19147
8
19142
9
10
11
19145
19148
19153
12

Delaware River

NEW JERSEY

Branch	Address	Zip	Map
30th Street Train Station	2955 Market St	19104	14
B Free Franklin	316 Market St	19106	4
Castle Finance	1713 S Broad St	19148	10
Chestnut Hill	8227 Germantown Ave	19118	27
Continental	615 Chestnut St	19106	3
East Falls	4130 Ridge Ave	19129	23
Fairmount Finance Station	1939 Fairmount Ave	19130	17
Fairmount	900 N 19th St	19130	17
Germantown	5209 Greene St	19144	24
Girard Avenue	905 N Broad St	19123	18
John Wanamaker	1234 Market St	19107	3
Kensington	1602 Frankford Ave	19125	20
Land Title Bldg	100 S Broad St	19110	2
Manayunk	4431 Main St	19127	21
Market Square	7782 Crittenden St	19118	26
Middle City	2037 Chestnut St	19103	1
Mount Airy	6711 Germantown Ave	19119	25
Penn Center	1500 John F Kennedy Blvd	19102	2
Penns Landing Postal Store	622 S 4th St	19147	8
Philadelphia Main Office	3000 Chestnut St	19104	14
Point Breeze Postal Store	2437 S 23rd St	19145	9
Roxborough Postal Store	6184 Ridge Ave	19128	21
Schuylkill	2900 Grays Ferry Ave	19146	5
Snyder Plaza Finance Station	58 Snyder Ave	19148	11
Southwark	925 Dickinson St	19147	8
University City	228 S 40th St	19104	13
William Penn Annex	900 Market St	19107	3

General Information • FedEx

All times shown are for last pick-up

Map 1 • Center City West

FedEx Kinko's	2001 Market St	8 pm
Self-Service	2133 Arch St	7:15 pm
Self-Service	2000 Market St	7 pm
Self-Service	2001 Market St	7 pm
Self-Service	2037 Chestnut St	7 pm
Self-Service	222 N 20th St	7 pm
Self-Service	2400 Market St	7 pm
Self-Service	100 N 20th St	6 pm

Map 2 • Rittenhouse / Logan Circle

FedEx Kinko's	121 S Broad St	8 pm
FedEx Kinko's	1500 Market St	8 pm
Self-Service	1801 Market St	7:15 pm
Self-Service	1818 Market St	7:15 pm
FedEx Kinko's	216 S 16th St	7 pm
Self-Service	100 S Broad St	7 pm
Self-Service	1500 JFK Blvd	7 pm
Self-Service	1528 Walnut St	7 pm
Self-Service	1600 JFK Blvd	7 pm
Self-Service	1600 Market St	7 pm
Self-Service	1601 Market St	7 pm
Self-Service	1608 Walnut St	7 pm
Self-Service	1616 Walnut St	7 pm
Self-Service	1617 John F Kennedy Blvd	7 pm
Self-Service	1628 JFK Blvd	7 pm
Self-Service	1635 Market St	7 pm
Self-Service	1650 Arch St	7 pm
Self-Service	1650 Market St	7 pm
Self-Service	1700 Market St	7 pm
Self-Service	1717 Arch St	7 pm
Self-Service	1735 Market St	7 pm
Self-Service	1760 Market St	7 pm
Self-Service	1801 Walnut St	7 pm
Self-Service	1815 JFK Blvd	7 pm
Self-Service	1835 Market St	7 pm
Self-Service	1845 Walnut St	7 pm
Self-Service	200 S Broad St	7 pm
Self-Service	216 S 15th St	7 pm
Self-Service	216 S 16th St	7 pm
Self-Service	245 N 15th St	7 pm
Self-Service	260 E Broad St	7 pm
Self-Service	30 S 17th St	7 pm
Self-Service	222 N 17th St	6:30 pm
Self-Service	100 E Penn Sq	6 pm
Self-Service	1800 JFK Blvd	6 pm
Self-Service	2 Franklin Town Blvd	6 pm
Self-Service	230 N Broad St	6 pm
Self-Service	1500 Chestnut St	5:15 pm
Self-Service	1429 Walnut St	5 pm
Self-Service	1505 Race St	4 pm

Map 3 • Center City East

FedEx Kinko's	1201 Market St	7:05 pm
Self-Service	1015 Chestnut St	7 pm
Self-Service	1201 Market St	7 pm
Self-Service	1234 Market St	7 pm
Self-Service	20 N 8th St	7 pm
Self-Service	211 S 9th St	7 pm
Self-Service	615 Chestnut St	7 pm
Self-Service	700 Arch St	7 pm
Self-Service	701 Market St	7 pm
Self-Service	701 Market St	7 pm
Self-Service	714 Market St	7 pm
Self-Service	834 Chestnut St	7 pm
Self-Service	900 Market St	7 pm
Self-Service	925 Chestnut St	7 pm
Self-Service	1100 Walnut St	6 pm
Self-Service	718 Arch St	6 pm

Map 4 • Old City / Society Hill

Self-Service	21 S 5th St	7:15 pm
Self-Service	190 N Independence Mall E	7 pm
Self-Service	399 Market St	7 pm
Self-Service	510 Walnut St	7 pm
Self-Service	600 Market St	7 pm
Self-Service	605 Walnut St	7 pm
Self-Service	600 Chestnut St	6:30 pm
Self-Service	1 New Market Sq	6 pm
Self-Service	200 Chestnut St	5 pm
Self-Service	600 Arch St	5 pm
Self-Service	601 Market St	5 pm
Marathon	9 N 3rd St	3:30 pm

Map 5 • Gray's Ferry

FedEx Kinko's	3600 Grays Ferry Ave	8 pm

Map 8 • Bella Vista / Queen Village /

Self-Service	629 S 4th St	6:30 pm
South Street Mailbox Plus	808 South St	6 pm
Society Hill Mail Parcel	614 S 8th St	4:30 pm

Map 10 • Moyamensing / East Passyunk

Self-Service	1713 S Broad St	6 pm

Map 12 • Stadiums

Self-Service	3301 S Galloway St	6 pm
Self-Service	900 Packer Ave	6 pm

Map 13 • West Philly

Self-Service	228 S 40th St	7 pm
Self-Service	3900 Delancey St	7 pm
Self-Service	3900 Woodland Ave	7 pm
Self-Service	3930 Chestnut St	7 pm
Campus Copy Center	3907 Walnut St	5 pm

Map 14 • University City

FedEx Kinko's	3535 Market St	7 pm
Self-Service	125 S 31st St	7 pm
Self-Service	2955 Market St	7 pm
Self-Service	2970 Market St	7 pm
Self-Service	3001 Market St	7 pm
Self-Service	3340 Walnut St	7 pm
Self-Service	3400 Civic Center Blvd	7 pm
Self-Service	3400 Spruce St	7 pm
Self-Service	3535 Market St	7 pm
Self-Service	3535 Market St	7 pm
Self-Service	3600 Spruce St	7 pm
Self-Service	3620 Locust Wk	7 pm
Self-Service	3624 Market St	7 pm
Self-Service	3730 Walnut St	7 pm
Self-Service	415 Curie Blvd	7 pm
Self-Service	418 Service Dr	7 pm
Self-Service	420 Guardian Dr	7 pm
Self-Service	421 Curie Blvd	7 pm
Self-Service	133 S 36th St	6:30 pm
Self-Service	3149 Chestnut St	6:30 pm
Campus Copy Center	3731 Walnut St	5 pm

Map 17 • Fairmount

FedEx Kinko's	1816 Spring Garden St	7:05 pm
Self-Service	1816 Spring Garden St	7 pm
Self-Service Storage	2000 Hamilton St	6 pm
Self-Service Storage	2000 Hamilton St	6 pm
Self-Service	3 Benjamin Franklin Pkwy	6 pm

Map 18 • Spring Garden / Francisville

Self-Service	1500 Spring Garden St	7 pm
Self-Service	400 N Broad St	7 pm
Self-Service	400 N Broad St	7 pm
Self-Service	440 N Broad St	7 pm
Self-Service	1600 Callowhill St	4:30 pm

Map 19 • Northern Liberties

Federal Express	820 Spring Garden St	8 pm
Self-Service	300 Spring Garden St	7 pm
Self-Service	300 Spring Garden St	7 pm

Map 20 • Fishtown / Port Richmond

Self-Service	1341 N Delaware Ave	7 pm

Map 21 • Roxborough / Manayunk

Self-Service	10 Shurs Ln	7 pm
Self-Service	161 Leverington Ave	6:30 pm
Self-Service	6180 Ridge Ave	6:30 pm

Map 22 • Lower Manayunk

Self-Service	3901 Main St	6:30 pm
Self-Service	5511 Ridge Ave	6:30 pm

Map 24 • Germantown South

Self-Service	2900 W Queen Ln	6:30 pm

Map 26 • Mt Airy

Self-Service	7782 Crittenden St	5 pm

Map 27 • Chestnut Hill

Self-Service	9 W Highland Ave # 23	6:30 pm
Self-Service	8227 Germantown Ave	5 pm

Dog Runs

Websites:
www.philadelphiapawsandclaws.com
www.dogfriendly.com
www.phillyfido.net
www.dogloverscompanion.com
www.animalalliancepa.org

Overview

Despite the scarcity of dog runs and dog parks, Philly still REALLY loves its dogs. But the shortage of dog-designated areas may stem from the fact that the city is really one mammoth dog run. Dogs are welcome in many restaurants, cafés, hotels, parks, and most boutiques and clothing stores. The most fascinating place to watch dogs play is in Rittenhouse Square's fountain, a popular unleashing spot—dogs love to take a dip, and, yes, we love to watch. Pooch events include the Paws for the Cause Cancer Walk (www.fccc.edu): you can get some exercise for your pooch while you make money for a good cause.

Most dog runs prohibit aggressive dogs, and do not separate the small dogs from the larger dogs, making it a veritable doggie free-for-all. It goes without saying that you need to supervise your dog(s) at all times and pick up after them.

Dog Runs	Address	Comments
Ben Franklin Parkway	Ben Franklin Pkwy & 19th St	Beautiful downtown setting.
Carpenter Woods	Wissahickon & Mt Pleasant Aves	Woody paths, doggy swimming holes.
Chester Avenue Dog Club	48th St & Chester St	$15/year membership.
Dog Park	48th St & Chester St	Constantly in jeopardy due to UPenn expansion.
Eastern State Dog Pen	Brown St & Corinthian St	Designated fenced-in areas.
Horse & Carriage Rides	Market St & 5th St	Well-behaved dogs are welcome aboard the carriages.
Manayunk Towpath and Canal	Main St b/w Green Ln & Lock St	Two-mile path along the canal.
Mario Lanza Park	Queen St & 2nd St	Nice neighborhood vibe.
Pennypack Park	Algon Ave & Bustleton Ave	1,600 acres for leashed dogs only.
Rittenhouse Square Park	Walnut St & 18th St	Leashed dogs only.
Schuylkill River Dog Run	25th St & Spruce St	Benches for you, fences for them.
Seger Dog Park	11th St & Lombard St	Open 6 am-10 pm, daily.
SPOAC Dog Run	Passyunk St & Dickinson St	South Philly dogs unite.
Washington Square Park	Walnut St & 6th St	Leashed dogs only. (Yeah, right.)

Wireless Philadelphia was kind of a bust (although you can still hop on the network at certain points in the city). If you want to be sure you'll get a signal, though, check out one of these spots:

WiFi

	Address	Phone	Map
Café Loftus Downtown	136 S 15th St	215-988-9486	2
Cosi	1700 Market St	215-569-2833	2
Cosi	1720 Walnut St	215-735-2004	2
Cosi	235 S 15th St	215-893-9696	2
Hausbrandt	207 S 15th St	215-735-2242	2
Starbucks	1500 Market St	215-561-3699	2
Starbucks	1528 Walnut St	215-732-0708	2
Starbucks	1600 Arch St	215-564-6455	2
Starbucks	1801 Market St	215-569-4223	2
Starbucks	1900 Market St	215-564-2840	2
Starbucks	200 S Broad St	215-772-3148	2
Starbucks	254 S 15th St	215-545-6519	2
Starbucks	337 S Broad St	215-546-2810	2
Cosi	1128 Walnut St	215-413-1608	3
Joe's Coffee Bar	1101 Walnut St	215-592-7384	3
Last Drop Coffee House	1300 Pine St	215-893-9262	3
Old City Coffee	1136 Arch St	215-592-1897	3
Starbucks	1201 Market St	215-925-1580	3
Starbucks	200 W Washington Sq	215-627-2945	3
Village Coffee House	1112 Locust St	215-923-1992	3
Café Au Lait	147 N 3rd St	215-627-2140	4
Cosi	215 Lombard St	215-925-4910	4
Cosi	325 Chestnut St	215-399-0214	4
Old City Coffee	221 Church St	215-629-9292	4
Philadelphia Java Co	518 S 4th St	215-928-1811	4
Starbucks	57 N 3rd St	215-922-3890	4
LA.va Café	2100 South St	215-545-1508	6
Jouvay Java	1512 South St	215-545-0667	7
Chapterhouse Café & Gallery	620 S 9th St	215-238-2626	8
Philadelphia Java Co.	518 S 4th St	215-928-1811	8
Starbucks	347 South St	215-627-4060	8
Starbucks	600 S 9th St	215-923-2389	8
Kaffa Crossing	2201 S Broad St	215-468-0535	10
The Other Green Line	4423 Chestnut St	215-386-0504	13
Cosi	4305 Locust St	215-222-0799	13
Cosi	140 S 36th St	215-222-4545	14
Starbucks	2955 Market St	215-222-0758	14
The Coffee House	1945 Callowhill St	215-557-8060	17
Ground Floor Coffee & Tea House	113 W Girard Ave	215-426-5889	19
Higher Grounds	209 Poplar St	215-627-1420	19
Latte Lounge	631 N 3rd St	215-922-3745	19
Canvas Coffee Company	816 N 4th St	215-629-9808	19
The Coffee House	400 E Girard Ave	215-425-0524	20
Crossroads Coffee	113 W Girard Ave	215-426-5889	20
Well Grounded A Comfortable Coffee	6156 Ridge Ave	215-487-1923	21
Infusion Coffee & Tea	3720 Midvale Ave	215-843-8444	23
Starbucks	7133 Germantown Ave	215-248-1718	25
	8515 Germantown Ave	215-242-3860	27

Internet

	Address	Phone	Map
FedEx Kinko's	2001 Market St	215-561-5170	1
FedEx Kinko's	121 S Broad St	215-546-4710	2
FedEx Kinko's	216 S 16th St	215-732-2033	2
FedEx Kinko's	1201 Market St	215-923-2520	3
FedEx Kinko's	3923 Walnut St	215-386-5679	13
FedEx Kinko's	1816 Spring Garden St	215-567-2679	17

Self-Storage

	Address	Phone	Map
Walnut Bridge Parking & Storage	200 S 24th St	215-751-2727	1
Society Hill Self Storage	1100 Catharine St	215-925-0206	7
U-Haul	1015 S 12th St, #25	215-336-8080	7
Pier 40 Self-Storage	841 S Columbus Blvd	215-271-9010	8
Devon Self-Storage	12 E Oregon Ave	215-253-3232	11
Self Service Storage Of Philadelphia	2000 Hamilton St	215-268-6603	15
U-Haul	314 N 13th St	215-627-4100	18
Liberties Self Storage	1 Brown St	215-922-1800	19
Public Storage	456 N Delaware Ave	215-574-1098	19
U-Haul	501 Callowhill St	215-574-1098	19
Sergeant Storage	2541 Gaul St	215-739-9226	20
Manayunk Self Storage	116 Fountain St	215-508-9800	21
Mr Storage	5026 Ridge Ave	215-209-3715	22
Simply Self Storage	335 E Price St	215-844-1000	24
Safeguard Self Storage	6224 Germantown Ave	215-825-8539	25

Van & Truck Rental

		Phone	Map
Penske	1216 Washington Ave	215-271-6340	7
U-Haul	1015 S 12th St	215-336-8080	7
Budget	Pier 40 Self Storage, 841 S Columbus Blvd	215-462-2055	8
U-Haul	O&A Rentals, 7 W Ritner St	215-334-7630	11
U-Haul	Terries Getty, 1701 N 33rd St	215-769-7430	15
U-Haul	314 N 13th St	215-627-4100	18
Budget	Wolfsons, 959 N 8th St	215-922-2120	19
U-Haul	U Store It, 501 Callowhill St	215-574-1098	19
Budget	Simply Self Storage, 335 E Price St	215-849-1340	24

Pharmacies

		Phone	Map
Rite-Aid	2301 Walnut St	215-636-9634	1
CVS	1826 Chestnut St	215-972-0909	1
Pathmark	3021 Grays Ferry Ave	215-551-7284	5

Prescription counter closes at 9 pm.

		Phone	Map
CVS	1405 S 10th St	215-465-2130	7
CVS	1901 W Oregon Ave	215-551-8265	9
Walgreens	2310 W Oregon Ave	215-468-2478	9
Rite-Aid	2017 S Broad St	215-467-0850	10
Walgreens	2014 S Broad St	215-551-3818	10
Pathmark	330 E Oregon Ave	215-462-3450	11

Prescription counter closes at 9 pm.

		Phone	Map
CVS	2400 Aramingo Ave	215-291-8315	20

Copy Shops

		Phone	Map
FedEx Kinko's	2001 Market St	215-561-5170	1
IKON Document Services	1760 Market St	215-557-7070	2
FedEx Kinko's	1201 Market St	215-923-2520	3

Gyms

		Phone	Map
Pennsport Athletic Club	325 Bainbridge St	215-627-4900	8

Restaurants

		Phone	Map
Midtown IV	2013 Chestnut St	215-567-3142	1
Little Pete's	219 S 17th St	215-545-5508	2
Geno's Steaks	1219 S 9th St	215-389-0659	8
Pat's King of Steaks	1237 E Passyunk Ave	215-468-1546	8
South St Diner	140 South St	215-627-5258	8
Melrose Diner	1501 Snyder Ave	215-467-6644	9
Philly Diner	3901 Walnut St	215-382-3400	13
Dining Car	8826 Frankford Ave	215-338-5113	NE
Mayfair Diner	7353 Frankford Ave	215-624-4455	NE
Tiffany Diner	9010 Roosevelt Blvd	215-677-3916	NE

Supermarkets

		Phone	Map
Pathmark	3021 Grays Ferry Ave	215-551-7275	5
Pathmark	330 E Oregon Ave	215-462-4750	11
ShopRite	29 Snyder Ave	215-271-2711	11

Locksmiths

	Phone
Houdini Lock & Safe	215-336-7233
Adam's Locksmith Service	215-423-6868
Adam's Locksmith Service	215-837-3779
B&W Locksmith	215-229-9439
Locksmith	215-242-6260

Garage Door Service

	Phone
Garage Doors	215-487-3443

Plumbing

	Phone
Goodman Plumbing	215-455-1000
Philadelphia's Local Plumber	215-739-4343
Plumbing	215-329-8008
Plumbing	215-333-8780
Plumbing	215-545-7330
Plumbing	215-612-0500
Plumbing	215-743-1755
Plumbing	215-745-9552
Plumbing	215-878-8280
Plumbing (Emergency Service)	215-425-4737
Plumbing Works	215-329-4993
Plumbing Works	215-473-1610
Roto-Rooter	215-535-7644
Roto-Rooter	215-545-4509
Roto-Rooter	215-744-4207
Roto-Rooter	215-763-2021
Roto-Rooter	215-849-5067
Roto-Rooter	215-925-3079
Sam Wexler Plumbing	215-922-5555
Sam Wexler Plumbing	215-934-7811
VJC Mechanical	267-467-1676

Arts & Entertainment • **Movie Theaters**

In Center City, most of your options fall into two categories. 1. The art house Bermuda triangle of **Ritz Theaters (Bourse, Five,** and **East)(Map 4)**. 2. The insidious, stadium-seating caverns of **The Riverview** multiplex **(Map 8)**, which we heartily encourage you to avoid, especially on weekends, unless you truly enjoy loud audiences of fifteen-year-olds hurling gummi concessions at your head. For variety, check out the **Roxy Theatre (Map 1)**, showing independent and bigger-name fare in hugely uncomfortable seats. And if you can ignore that someone got shot out front two days after the theater opened, there's the otherwise beautiful seven-screen Pearl Theater (1600 N Broad St, 215-763-7700) north o' Market.

A welcome addition to the Philly film scene has been **The Bridge (Map 13)** in University City. They also allow you to buy your (pricey!) tix in advance and reserve your seat, which is perfect for big summer movie openings, if that's your thing. And when the Bridge is sold out, you can always see if anything's playing at the International House (3701 Chestnut Street, 215-387-5125), an international-student housing building with a year-round film program.

You can find plenty of big corporate theaters if you're willing to drive or take the bus a ways. In Manayunk there's the **UA Main Street (Map 22)**, and if you go to Franklin Mills (1149 Franklin Mills Cir), you can take advantage of $5 Tuesday if you don't mind the bratty crowds.

Movie Theater	Address	Phone	Map
Roxy Theatre Philadelphia	2023 Sansom St	215-923-6699	1
Tuttleman IMAX Theater-Franklin Institute	222 N 20th St	215-448-1111	1
Ritz 5	214 Walnut St	215-925-7900	4
Ritz at the Bourse	400 Ranstead St	215-925-7900	4
Ritz East	125 S 2nd St	215-925-7900	4
United Artists Riverview Stadium 17	1400 S Columbus Blvd	215-755-2219	8
The Bridge: Cinema de Lux	S 40th St & Walnut St	215-386-3300	13
United Artists Main St Theatre	3720 Main St	215-482-6230	22

Overview

The Philly bookstore scene has radically changed for the much better of late—after all, even one or two new institutions can make a difference. With the slaying of Borders, we now only have one giant behemoth store downtown that you may have heard of that's called **Barnes & Noble (Map 2)**. But there are plenty of independents vying for your business—and, heck, they deserve it already.

General New/Used

Joseph Fox (Map 2), selling literary fiction, nonfiction, poetry, art and children's books, is an excellent place to start. Tucked several streets behind behemoth number 1 (Barnes & Noble), this nook o' wonder has existed for over fifty years, and the original proprietor, Madeline Fox, can be found here with her son, Michael, who now runs the place. At Joseph Fox, there is a real mind behind the selection, and the shelves are packed tightly with books you get the sense you really must read—and the booksellers employed have read that book twice already, which makes for a useful conversation—or two. **Robin's (Map 2)** is one-stop shopping for all literary, art, and periodical needs. The poetry selection here is possibly the best in the city, and the left-bending reading events are worth checking out. Penn students flock to **House of Our Own (Map 13)** to get slightly off-campus—hell, they don't do it that often, so that's really saying something. Newcomer **Head House Books (Map 8)** has already made a giant splash in its Society Hill community. Idealist-

minded proprietor Richard de Wyngaert hosts readings, a chess club for kids, story hours, and book groups. Any new literary title can be found here, plus an awesome children's selection. Head House also sells plenty of that kind of five-pounder coffee-table slab, many of which can be really quite beautiful, and make a lovely gift. Two of our favorite used spots are Last Word Bookshop (Map 13) and the Book Trader (Map 4), where we get great satisfaction from trading in our old books for ones that are new to us.

Specialty

You can get caught up on all of your anarchy manifestos at **Wooden Shoe (Map 4)** and then learn to love one another again at **Garland of Letters (Map 8)**, which also provides a wafting aroma of fine incense. Design mavens can't get enough of **AIA (Map 2)**, which has a giant array of architecture and urban planning tomes including anything by or about our city hero, Edmund Bacon. The gay/lesbian scene is neatly served by **Giovanni's Room (Map 3)**, which also offers a hugely popular reading series. For un-translated Asian authors, **WJ Bookstore (Map 3)** in Chinatown has thousands of titles, primarily in Mandarin. To find out who really did do it, **Whodunit (Map 2)** has all the answers. **Big Blue Marble Books (Map 25)** in Mount Airy sells progressive and multi-cultural titles for both adults and children—and those Mount Airy neo-cons (yeah f***in' right) can't get enough of. And, finally, newcomer **Bookspace (Map 19)** is an inspiring, massive space filled with cool art and tons of books.

Map 1 · Center City West

Book Corner	311 N 20th St	215-567-0527	New, rare, and good used books in all genres.
Famulus Books	244 S 22nd St	215-732-9509	Used books.
Fat Jack's Comicrypt	2006 Sansom St	215-963-0788	Comic books.

Map 2 · Rittenhouse / Logan Circle

AIA Book Store	117 S 17th St	215-569-3188	Architecture and design.
Barnes & Noble	1805 Walnut St	215-665-0716	Chain.
Barnes & Noble	1805 Walnut St	215-665-0716	Chain.
Bauman Rare Books	1608 Walnut St	215-546-6466	Rare books.
MCP Hahnemann University Bookstore	1505 Race St	215-762-7629	Drugs, diseases & more. We challenge you to find denser reading.
Joseph Fox Book Shop	1724 Sansom St	215-563-4184	Independent.
Whodunit Used & Rare Books	1931 Chestnut St	215-567-1478	Used, more than just mysteries & thrillers.

Map 3 · Center City East

AIA Bookstore & Design Center	1218 Arch St	215-569-3188	Architecture and design.
Atlantic Books	920 South St	215-592-1275	Bookstore chain from the shore forays into the city.
Chinese Culture & Arts	126 N 10th St	215-928-1616	Chinese books.
CLC Bookcenters	730 Chestnut St	215-922-6868	Bibles & Christian books.
Cookbook Stall	12th St & Arch St	215-923-3170	Cookbooks.
Giovanni's Room	345 S 12th St	215-923-2960	Lesbian, gay, bisexual, and transgender.
Horizon Books	901 Market St	215-625-7955	African-American.
Jefferson Bookstore	1009 Chestnut St	215-955-7922	Medical and health science.
Russakoff's Books and Records	259 S 10th St	215-592-8380	Used Books.
WJ Bookstore	1017 Arch St	215-592-9666	Chinese book store.

Map 4 · Old City / Society Hill

The Book Trader	7 N 2nd St	215-925-0517	Discounted used, first editions, and out-of-print books.

Map 8 · Bella Vista / Queen Village

Atomic City Comics	642 South St	215-625-9613	Comics, Japanese animation, cult films and beyond.
Brickbat Books	709 S 4th St	215-592-1207	Great used books, occasionally chilly staff.
Garland of Letters	527 South St	215-923-5946	New-age books, trinkets, and many, many types of candles.
Head House Books	619 S 2nd St	215-923-9525	General bookstore.
Mostly Books	529 Bainbridge St	215-238-9838	Used.
Pilothouse Charts	1600 S Columbus Blvd	215-336-6414	Maritime.
Wooden Shoe Books	704 South St	215-413-0999	For those who'd call *The Nation* a conservative rag.

Map 9 · Point Breeze / West Passyunk

Prosperity Bookstore	2059 Snyder Ave	215-755-1225	General bookstore.

Map 13 · West Philly

House of Our Own	3920 Spruce St	215-222-1576	Politics, history, sociology, and multi-cultural topics.
Last Word Bookshop	220 S 40th St	215-386-7750	Used.
Marvelous Records Comics & Books	208 S 40th St	215-386-6110	Comics, graphic novels.

Map 14 · University City

Dolbey's Medical Bookstore	3734 Spruce St	215-222-6020	Textbooks, medical, and health and science reference.
Drexel University Bookstore	S 33rd St & Chestnut St	215-895-2860	College bookstore.
First District Bookstore	3801 Market St	215-662-5110	General.
Penn Book Center	130 S 34th St	215-222-7600	College bookstore.
Penn Bookstore	3601 Walnut St	215-898-7595	Used and new textbooks.

Map 17 · Fairmount

Bookhaven	2202 Fairmount Ave	215-235-3226	Used.

Map 18 · Spring Garden / Francisville

Community College of Philadelphia Book Store	1700 Spring Garden St	215-751-8152	Textbooks, reference, and more.

Map 19 · Northern Liberties

Bookspace	1113 Frankford Ave	215-291-5880	An emotionally warm atmosphere within a voluminous physical space.
That's the Book	1113 Frankford Ave	215-291-5880	That's the book!

Map 25 · Germantown North

Big Blue Marble Bookstore	551 Carpenter Ln	215-844-1870	Specializing in progressive and multicultural books

Map 26 · Mt Airy

Walk a Crooked Mile Books	7423 Devon St	215-242-0854	Used.

Museums

The **Philadelphia Museum of Art (Map 17)** stands proudly as one of the five best art museums in the country; allow yourself several days to peruse their permanent collection. While you're in the area, you should definitely hit up the **Rodin Museum (Map 17)**, which is filled with sculpture from one of the 20th-century's most prominent artists. For the more literary-inclined, the **Rosenbach (Map 1)** has the original manuscript of Joyce's *Ulysses* as well as art by Maurice Sendak, author of the beloved *Where The Wild Things Are*. The Rosenbach is so fond of Joyce, in fact, that every June they host a Bloomsday festival, named after Leopold Bloom, the main character in *Ulysses*. Local volunteers read passages from the book to onlookers throughout the day. If you're up for the weird world of science and the macabre, **Mütter Museum (Map 1)** is brimming with biological specimens. For a mental twist, the **Museum of the American Philosophical Society (Map 4)** mounts intellectual, engaging exhibits about things that maybe you never thought you'd care about (the history of natural history, anyone?), and yet you really do while you're there. For a museum that is a museum piece on museums, go to **Franklin Court (Map 4)**, under the sculptural outline of Ben Franklin's house—there, you'll receive old-school telephone calls from even older-school ghosts. On the more modern tip, the **Institute of Contemporary Art (Map 14)**, while small, uses space inventively to show up-to-the-minute art grabbed with curatory aplomb from an international pool. And if you're a cartographic junkie (like the entire staff of NFT), make sure to check out the largest map of Philadelphia in the world at the **Atwater Kent Musuem (Map 3)**.

Museum	Address	Phone	Map
The Academy of Natural Sciences	1900 Benjamin Franklin Pkwy	215-299-1000	2
The African American Museum in Philadelphia	701 Arch St	215-574-0380	3
American Philosophical Society	104 S 5th St	215-440-3400	4
American Swedish Historical Museum	1900 Pattison Ave	215-389-1776	n/a
The Athenaeum	219 S 6th St	215-925-2688	4
Philadelphia History Museum	15 S 7th St	215-685-4830	3
Elfreth's Alley Museum	126 Elfreth's Aly	215-574-0560	4
The Fabric Workshop and Museum	1214 Arch St	215-561-8888	3
The Fairmount Water Works Interpretive Center	640 Waterworks Dr	215-685-0723	n/a
Fireman's Hall Museum	147 N 2nd St	215-923-1438	4
The Franklin Institute	222 N 20th St	215-448-1200	1
Germantown Historical Society	5501 Germantown Ave	215-844-1683	24
Grand Army of the Republic Museum and Library	4278 Griscom St	215-289-6484	n/a
The Historical Society of Pennsylvania	1300 Locust St	215-732-6200	3
Independence Seaport Museum	211 S Columbus Blvd	215-413-8655	4
Insectarium	8046 Frankford Ave	215-335-9500	n/a
Institute of Contemporary Art	118 S 36th St	215-898-7108	14
Johnson House	6306 Germantown Ave	215-438-1768	25
La Salle University Art Museum	1900 W Olney Ave	215-951-1000	n/a
The Mario Lanza Museum	712 Montrose St	215-238-9691	8
Masonic Temple	1 N Broad St	215-988-1900	2
Mummers Museum	1100 S 2nd St	215-336-3050	8
Mütter Museum	19 S 22nd St	215-563-3737 ext. 211	1
National Constitution Center	525 Arch St	215-409-6600	4
National Liberty Museum	321 Chestnut St	215-925-2800	4
National Museum of American Jewish History	101 S Independence Mall East	215-923-3811	4
New Hall Military Museum	320 Chestnut St	215-965-2305	4
Philadelphia Doll Museum	2253 N Broad St	215-787-0220	n/a
Philadelphia Museum of Art	2600 Benjamin Franklin Pkwy	215-763-8100	17
The Philadelphia Ship Preservation Guild	801 S Columbus Blvd	215-238-0280	4
Please Touch Museum	4231 Avenue of the Republic	215-963-0667	1
Polish American Cultural Center	308 Walnut St	215-922-1700	4
Rodin Museum	N 22nd St & Benjamin Franklin Pkwy	215-568-6026	17
Romanian Museum	1606 Spruce St	215-732-6780	2
The Rosenbach Museum & Library	2008 DeLancey Pl	215-732-1600	1
Stenton: A Historic House Museum	4601 N 18th St	215-329-7312	n/a
Shoe Museum	810 Race St	215-625-5243	3
Shofuso Japanese House & Garden	4301 Lansdowne Dr	215-878-5097	n/a
United States Mint	151 N Independence Mall E	215-408-0110	4
University of Pennsylvania Museum of Archaeology and Anthropology	3260 South St	215-898-4001	14
The Wagner Free Institute of Science	1700 W Montgomery Ave	215-763-6529	n/a
Woodmere Art Museum	9201 Germantown Ave	215-247-0476	27

Pennsylvania Academy of the Fine Arts

General Information

NFT Map: 2
Address: 118-128 N Broad St (Galleries)
Philadelphia, PA 19102
1301 Cherry St (School)
Philadelphia, PA 19107
Phone: 215-972-7600
Website: www.pafa.org
Hours: Tues–Sat 10 am–5 pm,
Sun 11 am–5 pm,
Closed Mon and legal holidays

Overview

The Pennsylvania Academy of the Fine Arts is an old and much-venerated institution: in 2005 it celebrated its 200th anniversary. This stunning architectural space is renowned for collecting, exhibiting, teaching, and promoting American fine art. The Academy is made up of a fine arts school, a public programs facility, various art galleries, and the country's oldest museum.

School of Fine Arts

The school has nearly 300 full-time students presently enrolled. The educational program includes a certificate course (painting, sculpture, and printmaking), a Bachelor of Fine Arts program (in conjunction with UPenn), and a one-year post-baccalaureate program (that allows students to work towards the two-year Masters of Fine Arts degree). Notable alumni include Philadelphia-born photographer Charles Sheeler, master painter Thomas Eakins, and oddball filmmaker David Lynch—who was so inspired by Philly's blighted glumness in the mid-'70s, he created *Eraserhead* as an homage.

The Galleries

Throughout its history, the gallery has held over 1,000 shows of artists such as Edgar Degas, Judith Rothschild, and Andy Warhol. The gallery is also renowned for exhibiting the work of new and emerging local talents. Opening hours are Tuesday through Saturday, 10 am-5 pm, and Sunday, 11 am-5 pm. Admission to the gallery is $10 for adults, $8 for students and seniors, and $6 for youth (aged 5-18), Museum tours are given at 12:30 am and 1:15 pm during the week, and at 1 pm and 2:45 pm on weekends. Tours are free with admission.

How to Get There—Driving

From I-95 S, follow signs to I-676. Take I-676 to the Broad Street exit, which will put you on 15th Street. Turn left onto Race Street, then right onto Broad Street. The Academy is one block down on the right.

From I-95 N and I-76 (Schuylkill Expressway), take I-76 W, and exit at I-676/Central Philadelphia. Follow directions above.

Parking

There are three pay lots on Academy grounds. Two are between 16th and Broad Street—one on Cherry Street and one on Race Street. The third is located at the northeast corner of Broad Street and Cherry Street.

How to Get There—Mass Transit

Ride the Market/Frankford Line to the 15th Street Station. Walk one block north to Arch Street, then one block east to Broad Street. Make a left on Broad Street. The Pennsylvania Academy is one block north.

Take the Broad Street line to the Race/Vine stop. Exit the station on Race and Broad Streets. Walk one block south (toward City Hall) on Broad Street. The Museum is at the northeast corner of Broad and Cherry Streets.

By Regional Rail, take any one of the lines to the Market East Train Station. Exit the station on Market Street and walk west (toward City Hall) until you reach Broad Street, then turn right. The Museum is one block along on the left.

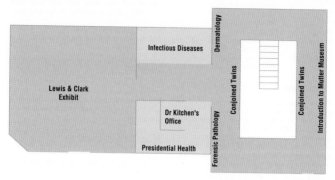

Infectious Diseases

Dermatology

Conjoined Twins

Introduction to Mutter Museum

Conjoined Twins

Lewis & Clark
Exhibit

Dr Kitchen's
Office

Forensic Pathology

Presidential Health

UPPER LEVEL

MAP
1

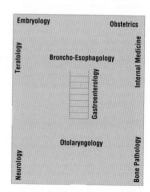

Embryology

Obstetrics

Teratology

Broncho-Esophagology

Internal Medicine

Gastroenterology

Neurology

Otolaryngology

Bone Pathology

LOWER LEVEL

General Information

NFT Map: 1
Address: 19 S 22nd St
Philadelphia, PA 19103
Phone: 215-563-3737
Website: www.muttermuseum.org
Hours: Mon–Sun: 10 am–5 pm, every day of the year except for Thanksgiving, Christmas Eve, Christmas, and New Year's Day.
Admission: General Admission $14, Children, Seniors, & Students w/ ID $10, Free for Children under 6.

Overview

In the early 1800s in the US, medical students were lectured for two years then sent out to try their newly acquired knowledge on patients. In Europe at the time, medical students worked with trained physicians and surgeons throughout their education, and Thomas Mütter decided that he wanted to bring European teaching pedagogies to the US. Mütter spent $20,000 of his own money to build a teaching collection of anatomical specimens, medical instruments, and pathological models that were used by generations of medical students as part of their training. Now run by the College of Physicians of Philadelphia, the museum has become an offbeat attraction for ordinary visitors.

The most popular exhibit remains the stomach-churning five-foot long colon, which was removed from a man who lived (and died) around the turn of the century (the colon contained over forty pounds of feces when removed—grossed out yet?). Other attractions include the cast of Chang and Eng, the famous Siamese twins attached at the liver, and a collection of more than 2,000 objects that have been swallowed and removed. Did you ever wonder where Grover Cleveland's secret cheek tumor ended up? It's in a jar on the first floor.

As a warning, you'd be wise to forego that second helping of goulash before you visit, as some of the exhibited collection is definitely not for the weak-stomached. The display of diseased skin springs to mind, for example. A key goal of the museum is to provide a look at the world of health and medicine as it existed in the 19th century, some of which can be very uncomfortable for contemporary visitors to behold. But if you keep an open scientific mind, you'll likely learn a great deal about the modern history of medicine in the US.

How to Get There—Driving

Follow I-76 E (Schuylkill Expressway) to Exit 344 (I-676 E/Central Philadelphia—formerly Exit 38) and the stay in the middle lane in order to get on I-676 E. Merge right and take the first (quick) right hand exit, which is the Benjamin Franklin Parkway/23rd Street exit.

Follow the ramp to the second light and turn right on 21st Street. Stay on 21st Street for about seven blocks and then turn right on Chestnut Street and proceed one block to 22nd Street. The museum is located at 19 S 22nd Street, on the right-hand side of the street.

Parking

Good luck. Trawl the streets and keep your eyes peeled!

How to Get There— Mass Transit

Take the Green Line trolley to 22nd and Market Streets. From the stop, walk down 22nd Street (against the traffic), and the museum will be on your left. Eastbound bus routes 21 and 42 stop at 22nd and Chestnut Streets. Westbound bus routes 21, 42, and 12 stop at 22nd and Walnut Streets.

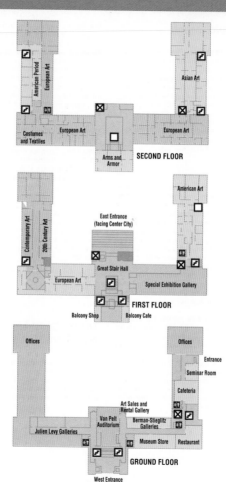

MAP
16

American Period
European Art

Asian Art

Costumes
and Textiles

European Art

European Art

Arms and
Armor

SECOND FLOOR

Contemporary Art

20th Century Art

American Art

East Entrance
(facing Center City)

Great Stair Hall

European Art

Special Exhibition Gallery

FIRST FLOOR

Balcony Shop

Balcony Cafe

Offices

Offices

Entrance

Seminar Room

Cafeteria

Art Sales and
Rental Gallery

Van Pelt
Auditorium

Berman-Stieglitz
Galleries

Julien Levy Galleries

Museum Store

Restaurant

GROUND FLOOR

West Entrance
(facing Fairmont Park)

General Information

NFT Map: 16
Address: 26th St & Benjamin Franklin Pkwy
Philadelphia, PA 19130
Phone: 215-763-8100
Recorded
Information: 215-684-7500
Website: www.philamuseum.org
Hours: Tues–Sun 10 am–5 pm, extended
hours on Friday till 8:45 pm.
Closed Mondays, Thanksgiving,
Christmas, New Years, and July 4th.
Admission: Admission $16, Seniors $14,
Students (with valid ID) and
Kids (aged 13–18) $12,
Children under 12 are free,
first Sundays of the month: pay-
what-you-wish.

Overview

We understand that it's difficult for tourists to resist running up the stairs in front of the Philadelphia Museum of Art and prancing around in a tight circle at the top with their fists raised in the air. Not every city has such a far-reaching pop culture icon. But as a Philly resident, you absolutely CANNOT do it (you are, however, welcome to dress the Rocky statue in pink underwear). You lose that privilege the second you move here. Besides, the main purpose of your visit to PMA should be to view the 300,000 splendid art works inside the museum.

Founded in 1876, the Philly Museum of Art is a world-renowned art institution recognized for its vast permanent collections of East Asian, American, European, and contemporary art. As with many things in this city, our museum is regularly given short shrift compared to New York's incredible facilities, but the PMA stands on its own. The impressive permanent collections are ably supplemented by the museum's visiting exhibitions in fashion, contemporary art, photography, impressionism, pop art, sculpture, and Old Masters. What's more, just down the parkway sits the fabulous Rodin Sculpture garden, which is free to visit.

Special events take place throughout the week at the PMA. On Friday evenings, the austere Great Stair Hall is transformed into a pseudo-jazz club, with musicians beginning their sets at 5 pm while visitors enjoy wine and finger food to ease them into the weekend. The museum also offers lectures, classes, art classes for children, tours of the surrounding historic houses in Fairmount Park, trolley rides, and a guided Schuylkill stroll to picturesque Boathouse Row. Check the PMA website for a calendar of events.

How to Get There—Driving

From the west, take I-76 E and exit at Spring Garden Street. At end of exit ramp go left. Continue past the side of the museum, through the first traffic light and around Eakins Oval, staying in the far left lane. Turn left at the second traffic light and then bear right. Follow the sign for the Art Museum. After the sign, get in the far left lane and turn left at the first traffic light (Art Museum Drive). This will take you to the west entrance of the museum, where limited parking is available.

From I-676 (Vine Street Expressway), take the Benjamin Franklin Parkway exit on your right. At the end of the exit ramp, turn right onto 22nd Street and get into the far left lane. Turn left onto the outside lanes of the Benjamin Franklin Parkway. Follow the sign for the Art Museum. After the sign, turn left onto Art Museum Drive. This will take you to the west entrance of the museum, where limited parking is available.

Parking

Free museum parking does exist, but in such a limited capacity that you might as well forget about it. Parking at the Eakins Oval is a flat rate of $10 from 10 am – 5 pm. Upper Terrace parking is $8 for museum members and $10 for non-members. Parking in the museum parking garage is $8 for museum members and $10 for non-members for four hours, then $2 for each additional hour. For more information call Visitor Services at (215) 763-8100.

How to Get There—
Mass Transit

The PHLASH bus (215-925-TOUR) provides direct transportation from Center City and Penn's Landing to the Museum of Art between 10 am and 6 pm, May through November for only $2. SEPTA bus routes 7, 32, 38, 43, and 48 all serve the museum area.

The party is always in Philly, legally till 2 am, but usually much later. We love to drink, as evidenced by our freakish restrictions about buying booze. State liquor stores close by 10 pm, having collected adequate war cash for the day, leaving us with two options: go to a bar, or go to Jersey—and we often can be seen with swooshy fingers, taking out no-service-charge twenties at Wawa, having chosen (with all our might) not Jersey. Unfortunately, when Jersey is faced with the same dire choice, they choose not themselves, and can be spotted living, er, trashing, it up in certain special locales where spray-tans glisten with the metal sheen of the Camden side of the river. But this is just the drink talking.

Beer

The **Standard Tap (Map 19)** and **Johnny Brenda's (Map 20)** are favorites for local beers on tap. Known as hipster enclaves, the two (especially the Standard Tap) are now catering to more varied crowds. Down south is **Devil's Den (Map 7)**, a beer geek's paradise with lots of unique beers on tap. If you're looking more for exotic beer than a night out, though, you should really just make your own six pack at **The Foodery (Shopping, Map 19)**. For a more Irish perspective, go to **Fergie's (Map 3)**; please be aware that there really is a Fergie and he is, in fact, quite Irish. The scene here is multifarious and seems to shift with each new wave of clientele, from music lovers on floor 2 to bonding med students, and then, of course, friends of Fergie. **The Nodding Head (Map 2)** isn't bad at all if **Monk's (Map 2)** won't let you in. If it's on the menu, we recommend the Monkey Knife Fight—that's the name of a beer, not an unfortunate form of entertainment.

Sports

O'Neal's (Map 8) is relatively low-key as sports bars go, and you can even stay after the game to get your groove going. **DiNic's Tavern (Map 9)** is the sort of place that you want to leave before the riot. **Liberties (Map 19)** is pretty hard-core—not the place to take your kids. **Tir Na Nog (Map 2)**, with its league of brash devotees, continues to host athletic adventures in athletic voyeurism. We hesitate to mention it because it's both small and one of our favorite spots, but when it comes to game time, **Murph's (Map 20)** is, as the sign promises, a comfortable place to be.

Swank

The **Ritz-Carlton Rotunda (Map 2)** is the end all be all of places to be seen. **Washington Square (Map 3)**, with its civilized park view, helps you get eased into nature if you're feeling a little stiff, while **Haru (Map 4)** feeds you fresh raw fish, while. **Red Sky (Map 4)** glows magenta on Market with dessert martinis. **Tria (Map 2)**, from its knowledgeable servers, voluminous menu, anally chosen glassware, and artful food pairings, is wine perfect. **Franklin Mortage & Investment Co. (Map 2)** makes the fanciest vintage cocktails this side of 1908, and its bartenders are walking liquor encyclopedias. The latest **Continental (Map 2)** in Center City is impressive for its swinging chairs and batshit roofdeck (which features terribly annoying clientele on the weekends). **The Black Sheep (Map 2)**, meanwhile, will help you wind down in style, and **L'Étage (Map 8)** will transport you to a French haven in, of all places, here.

Dive

We're not sure if a bar can still technically be a dive after being voted "Best Dive," but **Oscars' (Map 2)** $3, 22 oz. lagers certainly count for something. Neighborhood obsession, **Doobie's (Map 1)** is good pretty much always. And anything goes—smoking, anything—at **Dirty Frank's (Map 3)**. If you find yourself stuck on South Street, beeline it to **Tattooed Mom's (Map 8)**, which has a smoking room and great drink specials—$1 PBR pounders, anyone? Similarly, if you're stuck in Old City, get to **Sugar Mom's (Map 4)**, Tattooed Mom's sister that offers the same deals with a slightly creepier cave-like atmosphere. **Bob and Barbara's (Map 7)** will do you whiskey for 3 bucks, and if the amazingly jazzy house band isn't putting your head back together as you systematically drink it apart, the juke box can rock, too. It seems pertinent to mention **The Dive (Map 8)**, which, in a newly booming location, is the zest of the neighborhood—but don't miss Saturday night karaoke with a mix of dirty hipsters and old neighborhood men at **Ray's Happy Birthday Bar (Map 8)** down the street. And we'll leave it at this: you can't smoke at **The Fire (Map 19)**, but depending on the evening you can either get in a fight or listen to bluegrass. Hope for the bluegrass.

Dance

Most of the big clubs in Philly (including **Shampoo (Map 19)**, and anything on Delaware Ave.) are filled with Jersey kids and suburbanites. For some truer getting down, how about a little **700 Club (Map 19)**? Also known as "Seven Hundies," this once-bastion of hipster dancing has lost a little of its edge, but it's still fun. If you're looking for the next big thing, though, try **The Barbary (Map 19)**. While the 700 Club is mostly spinning hip-hop on the weekends now, The Barbary holds strong on Fridays with Michael Madonna Prince. **Medusa's (Map 1)** basement of rank delight is a trip alright. Drum n' Bass beats fill this dungeon of E enthusiasts who perform nice dance moves with athletic dedication. Five cop cars aren't pulled up beside **McFadden's (Map 19)** on a weekend for nothing—there's a party inside, and it's trashy as hell—good for a joke night that turns black-eye serious.

Gay/Lesbian

Most of the alternative bars are in roughly the same area of Center City (lovingly referred to as the "Gaybor-hood"). The **12th Air Command (Map 3)** has multiple floors of dancing fools getting up and getting down. The **Bike Stop (Map 3)** is not so dainty, and has whips to boot. **Woody's (Map 3)** is the mainstay of the gay community, and is large and welcoming for all. The oft grumbled-over **Sisters (Map 3)** is not hated but loved, the way you might love a stray dog that keeps showing up at your door, or a bar that is sadly the only lesbian bar in the entire city. The annually (or so it seems) renamed, cosmopolitan **Bump (Map 3)** seems to have caught hold with those who take their drinks pink. **Stir (Map 2)** serves up tasty cocktails with images of grinding packages on LCD TVs. And to venture out every once and a while (we mean from the gayborhood, silly) check out the weekly Thursday-night drag show at **Bob & Barbara's (Map 7)**.

Music Venues

Philly's music scene is as varied and wide-open as you could hope for. For down and dirty indie bands, check out R5 Productions' (www.r5productions.com) (occasionally all-ages) shows at the **First Unitarian Church (Map 1)**, **The Barbary (Map 19)** and more. For the over-21 contingent there's **Johnny Brenda's (Map 20)** and **The Tritone (Map 7)**, the former of which also regularly holds comedy shows. **The Electric Factory (Map 19)** is a larger venue in No-Libs but not as big (or as obnoxious) as the **Wells Fargo Center (Map 12)**, which gets many of the big touring bands. For a more gentle vibe, the **North Star (Map 16)** remains a great space to check out up-and-comers, and The Filmore at the **TLA (Map 8)** on South Street is like a white canvas (ok, but black and a little used) where mid-level music acts make the space and crowd their own. If you want some cred, refuse to call it "The Filmore." Quickly losing its luster is the **Trocadero (Map 3)**, legendary for its titty show days, now home of acts from the Insane Clown Posse to Clap Your Hands Say Yeah.

Map 1 • Center City West

The Bards	2013 Walnut St	215-569-9585	Laid-back watering hole.
Doobie's	2201 Lombard St	215-546-0316	Smoky and intimate, you'll become friends with everyone in the place.
Helium Comedy Club	2031 Sansom St	215-496-9001	Top-rated comics haggle for laughs in an uninspired, basement-like room.
Irish Pub	2007 Walnut St	215-568-5603	Rowdy student hang-out unsafe for morally mature.
Medusa	27 S 21st	215-557-1981	A "write your name on the ceiling when the bartender's not looking," kind of place.
Mix	2101 Chestnut St	215-568-3355	Beer. And pretty decent pizza.
Roosevelt Pub	2220 Walnut St	215-569-8879	Penn fave and with good reason: best drink deals in the city.
Tank Bar	261 S 21st St	215-546-4232	Giant fish tank highlights this sultry joint.

Map 2 • Rittenhouse / Logan Circle

The Black Sheep	247 S 17th St	215-545-9473	Pricey but authentic English pub atmosphere rules.
Boathouse Row Bar	210 W Rittenhouse Sq	215-546-9000	Swanky Rittenhouse Hotel bar the place to be for wannabe trophy wives.

Map 2 · Rittenhouse / Logan Circle—*continued*

Cadence	300 S Broad St	215-670-2388	The resplendent Kimmel Center's house bar. Black tie optional.
Denim Lounge	1712 Walnut St	215-735-6700	Jeans' mogul opens trend-setting lounge/eatery. Acid-washed.
Drinker's Pub	1903 Chestnut St	215-564-0914	At the door you'll find Weaver--the best bouncer in Philly.
The Franklin Mortgage & Investment Co	112 S 18th St	267-467-3277	A bit pretentious, but totally amazing cocktails.
Good Dog	224 S 15th St	215-985-9600	Yumalicious local brews are featured in their draught pulls.
Happy Rooster	118 S 16th St	215-963-9311	The Passion of the Cristal: Mel's fave bar in Philly.
Mace's Crossing	1714 Cherry St	215-564-5203	Where Tad and Kitty unwind from grueling regatta-cheering.
McGlinchey's	259 S 15th St	215-735-1259	Brilliantly low-end Uarts joint has cheap pints and Ms. Pac Man.
Misconduct Tavern	1511 Locust St	215-732-5797	Giant flatscreens make for some excellent sports watching.
Monk's Café	264 S 16th St	215-545-7005	Possibly the best beer list in the city. Long wait, though.
Noche	1901 Chestnut St	215-568-0551	Is cowprint fur on the walls sassy? Or just weird?
Nodding Head	1516 Sansom St	215-569-9525	Monk's much-less-annoying alter ego has good home brew.
Oscar's Tavern	1524 Sansom St	215-972-9938	Beers so big you need two hands to hold 'em.
Raven Lounge	1718 Sansom St	215-840-3577	It's all fun and games at this funky hot spot.
Ritz-Carlton Rotunda	10 S Broad St	215-523-8000	They say your first million is the hardest. Well worth a toast.
Rouge	205 S 18th St	215-732-6622	Rittenhouse fave is resurrected under Starr's careful guidance.
Stir	1705 Chancellor St	215-732-2700	Fun gay friendly dance club. With cheap drinks!
Tangier Café	1801 Lombard St	215-732-5006	Sparkling little oasis reaches back to North Africa, circa 1932.
Tavern on Broad	200 S Broad St	215-546-2290	"Upscale casual" sports bar open 7 days a week; no luck gettin' hip with any dolled-up sheik daddy at this here Stephen Starr gin mill.
Tequila's Bar	1602 Locust St	215-546-0181	When you want to sober up, there's also decent, upscale Mex waiting for you.
Time Restaurant	1315 Sansom St	215-985-4800	Did someone say Absinthe?
Tir Na Nog	1600 Arch St	267-514-1700	Sports-themed Irish bar panders to the City Hall set.
VIP Lounge	38 S 19th St	215-636-9901	Two floors of rich Euros and wannabes finding their groove.
The Walnut Room	1709 Walnut St	215-751-0201	No sign out front and Elderflower Martinis. Status symbol crowd, hold the pretentiousness.
Whistle Bar	40 S 19th St	215-636-9901	About as traditional as a Quentin Tarantino movie.

Map 3 · Center City East

12th Air Command	254 S 12th St	215-545-8088	Three floors and hot male bods at every stop.
Bike Stop Inc	206 S Quince St	215-627-1662	Play pool; get ogled by gay men. Not that there's anything wrong with that.
Bump	1234 Locust St	215-732-1800	What joint is it this week? Bump? Okay, then, it's bump.
Dirty Frank's	347 S 13th St	215-732-5010	City's premier dive.
The Field House	1150 Filbert St	215-629-1520	TVs at your table...you won't miss a single play.
El Vez	121 S 13th St	215-928-9800	Features fancy, dopey cocktails but many of them still rock.
Fergie's Pub	1214 Sansom St	215-928-8118	Great pulled pints, excellent chow, and no TVs of any kind. Go for pub quiz night.
The Irish Pub	1123 Walnut St	215-925-3311	Simple place with solid pints and great daily specials.
Las Vegas Lounge	704 Chestnut St	215-592-9533	Well, they get the seedy, paying-with-your-last-dollar feel right.
Locust Bar	235 S 10th St	215-925-2191	Not the place to go if you want to quit smoking; otherwise, it's fun.
Lucky Strikes	1336 Chestnut St	215-545-2471	The first bowling alley with a dress code, they keep the hoodlums out and the celebrities in.
McGillin's Old Ale House	1310 Drury St	215-735-5562	One of Philly's oldest saloons has historical charm.
Moriarty's Restaurant	1116 Walnut St	215-627-7676	Theater crowd-pleaser has dramatic license to serve.
Sal's on 12th	200 S 12th St	215-731-9930	Tiny hipster dancing spot.
Sisters	1320 Chancellor St	215-735-0735	Where the sisters go to check out other sisters and grab a bite.

Tavern on Camac	243 S Camac St	215-545-0900	Flaming gay piano bar cum discotheque.
Tenth Street Pour House	262 S 10th St	215-922-5626	Wake up and smell the espresso. Home of the $2.75 brunch.
Trocadero	1003 Arch St	215-922-6888	Former titty show palace now hosts a wild eclectica of music acts.
Vintage	129 S 13th St	215-922-3095	Being wine-giddy is more attractive than getting Jager-Bomb hammered.
Westbury Bar & Restaurant	261 S 13th St	215-546-5170	Gay respite from the throbbing beats of surrounding clubs.
Woody's	202 S 13th St	215-545-1893	For nearly 30 years, a Philly gay institution.

Map 4 · Old City / Society Hill

32 Degrees	16 S 2nd St	215-627-3132	Ice shots and fine champagne attract assorted VIPs.
Beneluxx	33 S 3rd St	267-318-7269	Wash your own glass between beers to preserve savory flavors.
Bleu Martini	24 S 2nd St	215-940-7900	Yet another trendy OC watering hole. Wear complicated shoes.
Buffalo Billiards	118 Chestnut St	215-574-7665	Poolhall has much to recommend it, including strong drinks.
The Continental	138 Market St	215-923-6069	Lavish drinks and mostly shallow conversation.
Cuba Libre	10 S 2nd St	215-627-0666	Known for its pretty rollicking mojitos.
Dark Horse	421 S 2nd St	215-928-9307	A rabbit-warren of rooms, bars, and mystery alcoves.
Downey's	526 S Front St	215-625-9500	Weekend karaoke great, all else meh.
Eulogy Belgian Tavern	136 Chestnut St	215-413-1918	Trappist ales have a way of kicking your ass, so be careful.
Haru	241 Chestnut St	215-861-8990	Raw fish, sake, and dancing equate to vomit in OC.
The Irish Pol	45 S 3rd St	215-238-9353	Free beer AND air conditioning!
The Khyber Pass	56 S 2nd St	215-238-5888	Former music venue now mostly food and drink.
LoungeOneTwoFive	125 S 2nd St	215-351-9026	Stationed under a parking garage, the joint has an intimate feel.
Mac's Tavern	226 Market St	267-324-5507	Owned by Mac (well, Rob McElhenney) from *It's Always Sunny*.
National Mechanics Bar and Restaurant	22 S 3rd St	215-701-4883	Beetlejuice-like. Excellent.
Paddy Whacks Pub	150 South St	215-464-7544	Share in the joy (but mostly pain) of being a Philly sports fan.
Paradigm	239 Chestnut St	215-238-6900	Overpriced and trying too hard, but the bathrooms are a marvel.
The Plough and the Stars	123 Chestnut St	215-733-0300	Fight through the Jersey crowd to the bar, then expect to wait.
Race Street Café	208 Race St	215-627-6181	Lots of polished wood makes your buzz more noteworthy.
Red Sky	224 Market St	215-925-8080	Let me get this straight: an ultra-trendy bar? In OC? Really?
Rotten Ralph's	201 Chestnut St	215-925-2440	Upstairs: chow. Downstairs: rollicking bar with decent prices for the area.
Sassafras	48 S 2nd St	215-925-2317	The place that launched a thousand martinis.
Society Hill Hotel Bar	301 Chestnut St	215-925-1919	An elegant throwback.
Sugar Mom's	225 Church St	215-925-8219	Underground grotto bar has pool, video games (including Erotic Photo Hunt!), and a rocking juke.
Swanky Bubbles	10 S Front St	215-928-1200	We can think of at least two things wrong with their name.
Triumph Brewing Company	117 Chestnut St	215-625-0855	Hoppy fun time.
Woolly Mammoth	430 South St	215-923-8780	Take-out beer. Loud and grimy.

Map 6 · Graduate Hospital / Gray's Ferry

Grace Tavern	2229 Grays Ferry Ave	215-893-9580	Dark, but not dingy bar for a casual night out.
L2	2201 South St	215-732-7878	Torchy jazz club has the right feel to it.
Ten Stone Bar & Restaurant	2063 South St	215-735-9939	English pub has darts, billiards, and a stone fireplace.

Arts & Entertainment · **Nightlife**

Map 7 · Southwark West

Bob & Barbara's Lounge	1509 South St	215-545-4511	Perhaps the city's best boozy entertainment center. PBR, ping pong, and drag queens.
Devil's Den	1148 S 11th St	215-339-0855	A spacious South Philly beer snob paradise.
Dolphin Tavern	1539 S Broad St	215-467-1752	Cheap beer and strippers. NFT pick.
Fiso Lounge	1437 South St	215-735-2220	Get your freak up on high—check the rooftop deck.
Pub on Passyunk East (P.O.P.E.)	1501 E Passyunk Ave	215-755-5125	Hipsters unite.
Triangle Tavern	1338 Reed St	215-467-8693	F-ing cheap, triangle-shaped bar, we love you.
Tritone	1508 South St	215-545-0475	Hip live music, happening scene, and deep fried candy bars.

Map 8 · Bella Vista / Queen Village

12 Steps Down	831 Christian St	215-238-0379	South Philly's esoteric basement booze hall.
Bridget Foy's	200 South St	215-922-1813	South Street people-watching from an upscale environment.
Cheers to You	430 South St	215-923-8780	Unpretentious sports bar has decent beer, many TVs.
Copabanana	344 South St	215-923-6180	Classiest place on South Street.
Connie's Ric Rac	1132 S 9th St	215-279-7587	Grungy, black and fit for a show.
The Dive	947 E Passyunk Ave	215-465-5505	Former old man bar repopulated with hipsters.
Fluid	613 S 4th St	215-629-3686	One of the better DJ spots in the city.
For Pete's Sake	900 S Front St	215-462-2230	Typified eatery, bar has good taps.
Friendly Lounge	1039 S 8th St	215-627-9798	Corner tavern with old tables and Highlife. Who needs more?
Jon's Bar and Grille	300 South St	215-592-1390	Good outdoor seating area allows you to see South in full regalia.
L'Etage	624 S 6th St	215-592-0656	Classy French-themed lounge, with wine and cheese platters to match.
Laff House	221 South St	215-440-4242	Status quo comedy club.
Lyon's Den	848 S 2nd St	215-467-0100	Neighborhood boozeria conveniently across from Wawa.
Mako's	301 South St	215-625-3677	Supposed to be for retired surfers, but the $2 PBR's just attract poor posers.
New Wave Café	784 S 3rd St	215-922-8484	Rock solid food and a swinging booze crowd. Plus, Quizzo.
O'Neal's	611 S 3rd St	215-574-9495	A sports bar with a DJ? It works, but makes for some strange crossovers.
Ray's Happy Birthday Bar	1200 E Passyunk Ave	215-365-1169	The quintessential dark corner bar.
Reef Restaurant and Lounge	605 S 3rd St	215-629-0102	A real life Margaritaville.
Royal Tavern	937 E Passyunk Ave	215-389-6694	Standard Tap South: great menu and beer choice.
Saloon	750 S 7th St	215-627-1811	Reportedly where Tony Bennett eats when he's in town.
Tattooed Mom	530 South St	215-238-9880	Regulars pack into the one major bar on South that isn't for tourists.
Teri's	1126 S 9th St	267-761-9154	Get the tater tots, always.
Theatre of the Living Arts	334 South St	215-922-1011	Indie-band paradise, right down to the crappy bathrooms.
Vesuvio	736 S 8th St	n/a 215-922-8380	Rehearsal dinner joint with romance trappings.

Map 9 · Point Breeze / West Passyunk

Brew/Ultimo	1900 S 15th St	215-339-5177	Coffee and beer together, so you never need to leave.
DiNic's Tavern	1528 Snyder Ave	215-336-2333	Flyers-centric bar has decades of history and dust.
JR's Bar	2327 S Croskey St		Punk music. Cheap beer. Sign up.
South Philly Tap Room	1509 Mifflin St	215-271-7787	Stylish gastropub in South Philly.

Map 10 · Moyamensing / East Passyunk

Cantina Los Cabalitos	1651 E Passyunk Ave	215-755-3550	Tequila shooters + pork empanadas = A good night out.
Le Virtu	1927 E Passyunk Ave	215-271-5626	Restaurant industry folks get 20% off at the bar. Word.

Map 11 · South Philly East

Penn's Port Pub	1920 S Columbus Blvd	215-336-7033	Strip club where "auditions are always welcome."

Map 12 · Stadiums

McFadden's at Citizen's Bank Ball Park	1 Citizens Bank Wy	215-952-0300	Beer and beer tub girls.

Map 13 · West Philly

Cavanaugh's	119 S 39th St	215-386-4889	College party scene offering more than kegs of Busch Lite.
Fiume	229 S 45th St	n/a	Tiny little hipster bar.
Local 44	4333 Spruce St	215-222-2337	Lotsa draft beer and decent enough gastropub vittles.
The New Angle	3901 Lancaster Ave	215-387-5147	Where punk kids, college kids, and local winos converge.
Smokey Joe's	210 S 40th St	215-222-0770	Penn's unofficial watering hole has seen many a fine academian fall to ruin.
University Pinball	4008 Spruce St	215-387-9523	No drinks, but lots of 18+ arcade fun after curfew.
Watutsi II	232 S 45th St	215-243-9389	Dive bar with a solid group of regulars.

Map 14 · University City

Biba Wine Bar	3131 Walnut St	215-222-2422	Tria's less-expensive little sibling. Wine/beer/cheese/etc.
Bridgewater's Pub	2951 Market St	215-387-4787	For getting drunk before getting on the R5. Good beer.
Mad Mex	3401 Walnut St	215-382-2221	Big college hang-out has decent grub and plenty of booze.
Mikey's American Grill & Sports Bar	3180 Chestnut St	215-222-3226	A sports bar on a college campus. Meh.
New Deck Tavern	3408 Sansom St	215-386-4600	Sports and students congregate in high volume.

Map 15 · Strawberry Mansion

St Stephen's Green	1701 Green St	215-769-5000	A great addition to the 'hood.
Urban Saloon	2120 Fairmount Ave	215-232-5359	Pretty sharp place to watch the Phillies.

Map 16 · Brewerytown

North Star Bar	2639 Poplar St	215-787-0488	Cool live music most nights, damn fine drinks every night.

Map 17 · Fairmount

The Bishop's Collar	2349 Fairmount Ave	215-765-1616	Neighborhood fave. Come for the beer. Stay for the beer.

Map 18 · Spring Garden / Francisville

The Institute	549 N 12th St	267-318-7772	Their catchphrase? "Beer is fun." We agree.
J & J Trestle Inn	339 N 11th St	215-925-3343	Grime and go-go girls. Awesome.
Prohibition Taproom	501 N 13th St	215-238-1818	Often changing beer list, plus early and late happy hours.

Map 19 · Northern Liberties

700 Club	700 N 2nd St	215-413-3181	Crowded, smoky lower bar; extremely crowded, smoky dance floor upstairs.
The Abbaye	637 N 3rd St	215-627-6711	Belgian bistro uses good beer liberally throughout menu.
The Barbary	951 Frankford Ave	215-634-7400	Hipster dance parties, plus occasional all-ages shows.
Bar Ferdinand	1030 N 2nd St	215-923-1313	Delicious libations that will make you forget you're in Philly.
Club Ozz	1155 N Front St	215-203-7201	Stripping under the El for the utterly wasted.
Electric Factory	421 N 7th St	215-627-1332	Large venue for bigger rock shows: stick to the balcony.
Finnigan's Wake	547 N 3rd St	215-574-9317	Slam a Miller Lite while listening to a cover band jam Puddle of Mudd tunes.
The Fire	412 W Girard Ave	267-671-9298	Good rock shows, minimal amounts of hipsters.
The Foodery	837 N 2nd St	215-238-6077	Sandwiches and legendary make-your-own six pack.
Johnny Brenda's	1201 Frankford Ave	215-739-9684	Fishtown hipster hang.
Liberties	705 N 2nd St	215-238-0660	Food plus beer equals fooooodbeeeer.
The Manhattan Room	15 W Girard Ave	215-739-5577	Rocking Fishtown with live preformances and hipster art shows.

Map 19 · Northern Liberties—continued

McFadden's	461 N 3rd St	215-928-0630	Great spot to drink shooters with 21-year olds.
North 3rd	801 N 3rd St	215-413-3666	A blood-orange margarita, under the right circumstances, can be life-altering.
Palmer Social Club	601 Spring Garden St	215-925-5000	After-hours joint keeps on pourin' until 3:30 AM.
Shampoo	417 N 8th St	215-922-7500	Where the Real Worlders got down and nasty. And terribly annoying.
Silk City Diner	435 Spring Garden St	215-592-8838	Energetic crowd.
Standard Tap	901 N 2nd St	215-238-0630	The legend grows about this trend-setting No-Libs marvel.

Map 20 · Fishtown / Port Richmond

Atlantis the Lost Bar	2442 Frankford Ave	215-739-4929	Perfect neighborhood pub.
Kraftwork	541 E Girard Ave	215-739-1700	Good beer available in lots of different sizes!
Les & Doreen's Happy Tap Kitchen	1301 E Susquehanna Ave	215-634-1123	Maybe someday the hip kids will like it here. The karaoke night'll likely get 'em.
Memphis Taproom	2331 E Cumberland St	215-425-4460	Affordable, amazing beer? We approve.
Murph's Bar	202 E Girard Ave	215-425-1847	Comfortable place to be? The jury is still out.
Yards Brewery	901 N Delaware Ave	215-634-2600	Philly's best home brew.

Map 21 · Roxborough / Manayunk

Agiato	4359 Main St	215-482-9700	Get classy with a...er, glassy of wine.
Bayou Bar and Grill	4245 Main St	215-482-2560	All you can eat crab nights and frat party feel.
Bourbon Blue	2 Rector St	215-508-3360	An upscale rock n' roll joint in the mighty 'Yunk.
Castle Roxx Café	105 Shurs Ln	215-482-9000	Relaxed out-of-the-way joint.
Flat Rock Saloon	4301 Main St	215-483-3722	One of the biggest Belgian beer selections in all of Philly.
The Grape Room	105 Grape St	215-930-0321	Live music in the Yunk.
Kildare's	4417 Main St	215-482-7242	The new hot spot in the 'Yunk. Recommended: the Dirty Hoe.
Manyunk Brewery and Restaurant	4120 Main St	215-482-8220	A multitude of home-brews highlights this popular hangout.
Pitchers Pub	4326 Main St	215-487-1370	Divey. Guess what you should order your beer in?
Tonic	4421 Main St	215-509-6005	New martini/cosmo bar. Lounge feel.

Map 22 · Manayunk

Dawson Street Pub	100 Dawson St	215-482-5677	A small escape from the normal Manayunk crowd.
Old Eagle Tavern	3938 Terrace St	215-483-5535	A great oasis in a mostly residential desert.
Vaccarelli's East End Tavern	4001 Cresson St	215-482-4944	Cozy neighborhood joint with rocking prices.

Map 23 · East Falls

Falls Taproom	3749 Midvale Ave	215-849-1222	A solid gastropub. Good beer and food.

Map 27 · Chestnut Hill

McNally's Tavern	8634 Germantown Ave	215-247-9736	Don't try to avoid it: Eat the Schmitter.

Northeast Philly

Chickie and Pete's	11000 Roosevelt Blvd	215-856-9890	Incredible crab fries inspiring the hilarious "Got Crabs?" T-shirt.
Dave & Buster's	1995 Franklin Mills Cir, Franklin Mills Mall	215-632-0333	Another dateless Friday night...
The Grey Lounge	6235 Frankford Ave	215-624-2969	Yards on tap, good pub grub, and—dare we say—the occasional hipster.
Sweeney's Station Saloon	13639 Philmont Ave	215-677-3177	You might run into a high school friend you haven't seen in a while here.
Whiskey Tango Tavern	14000 Bustleton Ave	215-671-9234	A 3-floor bar with live music, pool tables, and a dance

Philly has the kind of restaurant-to-person ratio we could only dream about for teacher-to-student in our public schools—the kind that allows us to sample new flavors in new seating scenarios as often as we please. And we're a lot smarter for it. From our slew of exposed brick BYOBs, our pizza meccas and cheesesteak musts, to a whole galaxy of Starr's, there isn't one good reason to eat where you pay the rent.

Italian

Man, where to begin? The mega-hyped **Vetri (Map 3)** lives up to its reputation and has prices to match, just in case you'd rather eat than send your future kids to college—maybe try Mark Vetri's more casual, but still pricey, **Osteria (Map 18)**. **La Viola (Map 2)**, right across the street from the always mega-busy **Monk's (Map 2)**, is a fine example of opportunism, but it also happens to be aw-fully good. For purists, **Villa di Roma (Map 8)** provides absolutely kick-ass pasta dishes in an atmosphere reminiscent of the house in All in the Family. **L'Angolo (Map 9)** is perhaps the best pure Italian joint in the city, and their desserts are bliss. **Melograno (Map 2)**, the always buzzing BYOB, provides a hip milieu some of us might require. BYOB **Modo Mio (Map 19)** gets our vote for date night though—the menu turista gets you four courses for $33, plus the chance to sight real celebrities like Georges Perrier—yeah, the guy who opened Philly's top French restaurant, **Le Bec-Fin (Map 2)**.

Asian

Besides the people getting on the bus to New York, everybody else is in Chinatown for the food, and with excellent reason. **Vietnam (Map 3)** is the unconquerable champion here—and its West Philly sister site, the **Vietnam Café (814 S 47th St)** is pretty wonderful as well.

Moving on from Vietnam (as if that were possible), other Chinatown greats include the hipster-discovered **Rangoon (Map 3)**, serving Burmese food with unflinching quality, not to mention oomph—try the calamari salad. **Lee How Fook (Map 3)**—which, right next to Vietnam, is a wonderful Plan B if Plan A has a two-hour wait—has a sophisticated Chinese menu and the dishes come large enough to share.

Our sushi awards go to **Hikari (Map 19)** and **Vic Sushi Bar (Map 1)**—both small, relatively inexpensive, and stocked with beautifully fresh fish. If we catch you at nearby **Mizu (Map 1)** instead of Vic...well, we'd make a threat to you, but your dissatisfaction with your meal will probably be punishment enough.

If you're looking for upscale, foodies flock to **Morimoto (Map 3)**, for reasons having to do with lobster.

Pizza

We don't want no trouble, we just want to share some of our favorite slices. Perhaps the most famous spot in Philly is out in Port Richmond, **Tacconelli's (just off the edge of Map 20)**, which is so popular, they require you to reserve your dough in advance. Not good at planning in advance? Grab a huge slice from **Lazaro's (Map 7)**. **Marra's (Map 10)** is a South Philly legend, and you can't get that kind of

exalted status unless you know how to twirl some dough. **Lazaro's (Map 8)** has the Italian Market wrapped around its finger, and **Lorenzo and Son (Map 8)** has good reason for attracting the South Street crowd. Also, we give it up to **Mama Palma's (Map 1)** for having the most variety—while not for purists, try the Peking Duck pizza.

Breakfast

For the best breakfasts in Philly, you have no choice but to buck up and wait—and the four places that'll make you wait the longest, **Sam's Morning Glory Diner (Map 7)**, **Sabrina's Café (Maps 8 & 17)**, **Café Estelle (Map 19)**, and **Honey's Sit 'n' Eat (Map 19)** are where you should plant yourself along with the rest of us. At Morning Glory, the bright, homey feel gives way to creations no one's willing to execute at home—packed pancakes, exquisite frittatas. **Sabrina's** delivers similarly with a possible advantage of being in the vibrant Italian Market—or the advantage of a slightly shorter wait if you go to the Callowhill location. The newest of the group, Café Estelle, is weirdly placed in a fancy apartment building, but has breakfasts that sing. Honey's, meanwhile, combines Southern comfort food with Jewish fare for a result that'll leave you longing for latkes days after you've left. For a quieter, cheaper morning, **Ida Mae's (Map 20)** still has the right idea.

Luxe

Le Bec-Fin (Map 2) remains Philly's most prominent fine dining experience and will occasionally deliver meals like two dinners for $50. **Lacroix (Map 2)** provides yet another fine French dining experience. Guests (and gawkers) of the Four Seasons enjoy the all-encompassing luxury of **Fountain (Map 2)**. The ubiquitous Stephen Starr's ritzy meat establishment **Barclay Prime (Map 2)** out-steaks some of the more stern (GOP Incorporated) competition. Vegans, don't worry, there's fanciness a-plenty for you too at **Horizons (Map 8)**. Oh, and despite the name, avoid **Swanky Bubbles (Map 4)**—it's a lot of attitude and bathroom attendants without good food to match.

BYOB

One of Philly's most engaging traditions is its affinity for the inexpensive fine dining experience. Stop by a good wine store (say, in Jersey) and head over to one of these beauties. **Lolita (Map 3)** shoots to the top of our list, with its sultry fusion fare—meat and tofu cooked to smoldering perfection—terribly sexy (not to mention kind) waitstaff, and house-made margarita mixes, provided you bring the tequila (which we suggest you do) Old City's **Chloe (Map 4)** continues to be a perennial favorite amongst foodies and those trying to dodge Old City while in Old City. **Audrey Claire (Map 1)** is a professed favorite of the Rittenhouse crowd. Other NFT faves include seasonal fare at **Pumpkin (Map 2)** and gourmet Italian at **Melograno (Map 1)**. The awesome Sicilian spot **Monsu (Map 8)** is amazing. Make a reservation and go this weekend. Finally, what would life be like without **Dmitri's (Map 8)** loving Mediterranean fare? We shudder to think.

Time refers to kitchen closing time on Friday night.
Key: $: Under $10 / $$: $10–$20 / $$$: $20–$30 / $$$$: $30–$40 / $$$$$: $40+
* : Does not accept credit cards. / † : Accepts only American Express / †† : Accepts only Visa and Mastercard.

Map 1 · Center City West

Audrey Claire	276 S 20th St	215-731-1222	$$$$*	10:30 pm	Simple, classic dishes done with suitable aplomb.
The Bards	2013 Walnut St	215-569-9585	$$	12 am	Fries and curry sauce a must.
Bistro St Tropez	2400 Market St, 4th Fl	215-569-9269	$$$	10:30 pm	Way-upscale French bistro has style to spare.
Café Lutecia	2301 Lombard St	215-790-9557	$*	3 pm	Baguette or croissant sandwiches, simple, delicious soup, and the best lemonade in the city.
Dmitri's	2227 Pine St	215-985-3680	$$	10pm	Great for small dishes with big drinks.
Erawan Thai Cuisine	123 S 23rd St	215-567-2542	$$	10:30 pm	Not a looker, but the dishes (esp. the glass noodles) are solid.
Friday Saturday Sunday	261 S 21st St	215-546-4232	$$$	10:30 pm	The Tank Bar on the second floor is a great place to get lit.
Fuji Mountain	2030 Chestnut St	215-751-0939	$$$$	11 pm	Thoughtful and cozy, belly up to the sushi bar and do a shot of fish.
Mama Palma's	2229 Spruce St	215-735-7357	$*	11 pm	Wood-fired, thin-crust pie in variations unthinkable—so you thought.
Mama's Vegetarian	18 S 20th St	215-751-0477	$*	3 pm	Cheap, tasty, healthy, and they'll even deliver. Try the falafel.
Melograno	2012 Sansom St	215-875-8116	$$$$	9 pm	Sophisticated yet unpretentious Italian joint packs 'em in.
Porcini	2048 Sansom St	215-751-1175	$$$	10 pm	Tiny but amazingly endearing. The ravishing food helps.
Primo Hoagies	2043 Chestnut St	215-496-0540	$	8 pm	One of the premier hoagie experiences in the city.
Roosevelt Pub	2220 Walnut St	215-569-8879	$	11 pm	Have some fine pub fare in an FDR-inspired setting.
Tampoo	104 S 21st St	215-557-9593	$	9:30 pm	Inexpensive and speedy sushi, with lots of veggie options.
Thai Singha House to Go	106 S 20th St	215-568-2390	$	11 pm	Tasty Thai food to-go in a tiny space.
Tinto	114 S 20th St	215-665-9150	$$$$	12 am	Upscale wine bar inspired by Basque country. No need to look at the menu—every decadent thing you could think of is already on it.
Twenty Manning	261 S 20th St	215-731-0900	$$$$	11 pm	Hipster haute with a solid bar scene.
Vic Sushi Bar	2035 Sansom St	215-564-4339	$$	11 pm	Get down and dirty with the cheap and fresh.

Map 2 · Rittenhouse / Logan Circle

Alfa	1709 Walnut St	215-751-0201	$$$	1 am	Betas, get the f*** out.
Alma de Cuba	1623 Walnut St	215-988-1799	$$$$$	12 am	Cuban soul food without all that annoying Communism.
Barclay Prime	237 S 18th St	215-732-7560	$$$$$	11 pm	Starr, well done.
Bliss	224 S Broad St	215-731-1100	$$$	11 pm	Unpronounceably delicious dishes, but don't let the chef's yelling get to you.
Byblos	114 S 18th St	215-568-3050	$$$	2 am	Hookahs and a euro-sheik menu, with the collared-shirt, gold-chain crowd to match.
Cadence	300 S Broad St	215-670-2388	$$$$	8 pm	The Kimmel Center's auspicious fine-dining option.
Capital Grille	1338 Chestnut St	215-545-9588	$$$$	11 pm	Steakhouse for the Masters of the Expense Account.
Chez Collette	120 S 17th St	215-569-8300	$$$$	11 pm	The Sofitel Hotel's unflinching French, the brunch is very fluent.
Chris' Jazz Café	1421 Sansom St	215-563-3131	$$$	2 am	Where Jimmy Bruno and other jazz allstars play.
Continental Mid-town	1801 Chestnut St	215-567-1800	$$	12 am	With such cool design, it's a shame such uninspired preps attend.
Davio's	111 S 17th St	215-563-4810	$$$	11 pm	The calamari, for one, is pretty special.
Devon Seafood Grill	225 S 18th St	215-546-5940	$$$	11 pm	Swanky, but you definitely pay the price.
Di Bruno Brothers	1730 Chestnut st	215-665-9220	$	7 pm	Pricey gourmet to go—or stay and eat in the freon.
Dolce Carini	1929 Chestnut St	215-567-8892	$	9 pm	Unadulterated NY-style pies & Philly cheesesteaks.
Fountain Restaurant	1 Logan Sq	215-963-1500	$$$$$	10 pm	When money is no object.
Good Dog	224 S 15th St	215-985-9600	$	2 am	Bark up a good dog burger (presumably still made of cow).
Il Portico	1519 Walnut St	215-587-7000	$$$	11 pm	Fine Jewish-Italian in the heart of Restaurant Row.
Jake's Pizza	201 N Broad St	215-587-0447	$	11 pm	Pizza and cheesesteak.
Tavern on Broad	200 S Broad St	215-546-2290	$$	2 am	"Upscale casual" sports bar open 7 days a week; no luck gettin' hip with any dolled-up sheik daddy at this here Stephen Starr gin mill.
Jean's Cafe	1334 Walnut St	215-546-5353	$	6 pm	Cheap and tasty breakfast sandwiches. All the art kids like 'em.
Joe's Pizza	122 S 16th St	215-569-0898	$	7:30 pm	Some of the best 'za in the city. Weird hours.
Jose Pistola's	263 S 15th St	215-545-4101	$$$	2 am	Best nachos in Philly? No doubt!

Name	Address	Phone	Price	Hours	Description
La Creperie	1722 Sansom St	215-564-6460	$$††	9:30 pm	Pizza crepes? Believe it, pilgrim.
La Viola	253 S 16th St	215-735-8630	$$$*	11 pm	Sweet, cozy BYOB; perfect for when you can't stand waiting in line at Monk's anymore.
Lacroix at the Rittenhouse	210 W Rittenhouse Sq	215-546-9000	$$$$$	10:30 pm	Luxe out at the Rittenhouse Hotel. Make a night of it.
Le Bec-Fin	1523 Walnut St	215-567-1000	$$$$$	9:30 pm	Philly's premier (now slightly soiled) snoot-o-rama. Point your nose up.
Le Castagne	1920 Chestnut St	215-751-9913	$$$	10 pm	Lots of insalatas amidst the rain of pesces, pastas, and carnes.
Little Pete's	219 S 17th St	215-545-5508	$$*	24 hrs	A greasy spoon with no apologies.
Marathon Grill	121 S 16th St	215-569-3278	$$$	12 am	Amidst class-action lawsuits, the grub still has class.
Marathon Grill	1339 Chestnut St	215-561-4460	$$$	10 pm	Amidst class-action lawsuits, the grub still has class.
Marathon Grill	1818 Market St	215-561-1818	$$$	8 pm	Amidst class-action lawsuits, the grub still has class.
Matyson	37 S 19th St	215-564-2925	$$$$$	10 pm	The food is great, but the desserts are sublime. dickheads.
Miel Patisserie	204 S 17th St	215-731-9191	$$	6 pm	Stunning French desserts and fine chocolates. Ooh la la.
Monk's Café	264 S 16th St	215-545-7005	$$	1 am	Great beer list and monster fries, Belgian-style. Plan to wait.
Moshi Moshi	108 S 18th St	215-496-9950	$	10:30 pm	Mimamalist setting provides many happy tempura memories.
Nodding Head Brewery & Restaurant	1516 Sansom St	215-569-9525	$	1:30 am	Almost as good as Monk's and no wait.
Paolo's Pizza	1334 Pine St	215-545-2482	$*	12 pm	Salty as a codfish, but a nice hand-tossed crust.
Parc	227 S 18th St	215-545-2262	$$$$	12 am	Fancy French bistro. Lobster cocktails.
Philly Falafel	1740 Sansom St	215-569-8999	$	10 pm	Falafel in Philly?!
Pietro's Coal Oven Pizzeria	1714 Walnut St	215-735-8090	$$	11 pm	Delicious thin-crust pies and solid salads.
Prime Rib	1701 Locust St	215-772-1701	$$$$$	11:30 pm	Tasteful and elegant steakhouse in the Warwick.
Pumpkin	1713 South St	215-545-4448	$$	12 am	The Sunday tasting menu is "the jam."
Rick's Steaks	200 S Broad St	267-519-9253	$*	6 pm	New location downstairs at the Bellevue.
Rouge	205 S 18th St	215-732-6622	$$$$	11 pm	French/Asian foo foo that will not be ignored.
Roy's	124 S 15th St	215-988-1814	$$$$	11 pm	Rocking the Hawaiian fusion. Surf's up, Kahuna.
Sahara Grill	1334 Walnut St	215-985-4155	$$	10 pm	Middle Eastern; no eye contact. crowd.
Shank's Original	120 S 15th St	215-629-1093	$*	5 pm	The roast beef could be enshrined in the Meat Hall of Fame.
Shiroi Hana	222 S 15th St	215-735-4444	$$	10:30 pm	Contemporary sushi house caters to tuna lovers.
Sotto Varalli	231 S Broad St	215-546-6800	$$$$	11 pm	Soak in the atmosphere—and stick to the wine.
Swann Lounge	1 Logan Sq	215-567-5309	$$$	12 am	Get your blue-blood on and order a crustless watercress sandwich.
Tequilas	1602 Locust St	215-546-0181	$$$	11 pm	Upscale Mex has beautiful, open ceilings and fine offerings.
Tria	123 S 18th St	215-972-8742	$$	1:30 am	Artfully-appointed food tailored to fit serious wine.
Tuscany Café	222 W Rittenhouse Sq	215-772-0605	$	8 pm	Your number one reason to skip La Colombe.
Upstares & Sotto Varalli	1345 Locust St	215-546-4200	$$$	11:30 pm	Grammatically challenged, but fine Italian cuisine.
Warsaw Café	306 S 16th St	215-546-0204	$$	10:30 pm	Load up on the pierogis and wiener schnitzel, then try to stand up.
XIX (nineteen)	200 S Broad St, 19th floor	215-790-1919	$$$$	11 pm	19 floors up to dine on the deep.

Map 3 • Center City East

Name	Address	Phone	Price	Hours	Description
Aqua	705 Chestnut St	215-928-2838	$	10 pm	Thai food and a sexy setting. Date night, anyone?
Banana Leaf	1009 Arch St	215-592-8288	$$	2 am	New Malaysian cuisine Penang competitor; open late for no one.
Basic Four Vegetarian	1136 Arch St	215-440-0991	$*	5 pm	Chock full of veggie love in Reading Terminal.
Bassett's Ice Cream	45 N 12th St	215-925-4315	$*	6 pm	Perfect happy ending to your Reading Terminal experience.
Bindi	105 S 13th St	215-922-6061	$$$*	11 pm	Fresh Indian fusion cuisine for the terminally trendy.
Capogiro Gelateria	119 S 13th St	215-351-0900	$	11 pm	Some of the best gelato in the city—pricey, though.
Caribou Café	1126 Walnut St	215-625-9535	$$$	11:30 pm	Euroville in CC. Drink in the atmosphere.
Charles Plaza	234 N 10th St	215-829-4383	$	12 am	Cool mood lighting sets up a fabulous veggie cornucopia of delights.
Chickpeas	630 South St	215-922-0300	$	11 pm	Perfect pitas. Delivery a bonus.
Delilah's at the Terminal	12th St & Arch St	215-574-0929	$	7 pm	Not that Delilah's, you perv. This soul food joint has got bounce.
Down Home Diner	51 N 12th St	215-627-1955	$$*	7 pm	Reading's sit-down joint where Amish bumpkins in overalls serve ok stuff for cheap.
Dutch Eating Place	1136 Arch St	215-922-0425	$*	5 pm	Hot turkey sandwiches smothered in gravy. And scrapple.

Effie's	1127 Pine St	215-592-8333	$$*	11 pm	Simple Greek fare in an adorable setting.
El Fuego	723 Walnut St	215-592-1901	$	9 pm	Fresh, made-to-order burros, but heavy on the rice.
House of Chen	932 Race St	215-923-9797	$$	4 am	Perfect if you suddenly need lo mein at 4 am.
Imperial Inn	146 N 10th St	215-627-5588	$$$	2 am	Just chow down on the dim sum. Leave the rest behind.
Jones	700 Chestnut St	215-238-9600	$$$	1 am	Comfort food in a Brady Bunch-like setting.
Kanella	266 S 10th St	215-922-1773	$$	10:30 pm	Pricey and tasty.
Kingdom of Vegetarians	129 N 11th St	215-413-2290	$	11 pm	You up for a mock duck that will curl your toes?
Knock Restaurant	225 S 12th St	215-925-1166	$	11 pm	Will Bill overcome the curse of this corner?
La Buca	711 Locust St	215-928-0556	$$$	11 pm	Get dressed up real nice and enjoy fine Italian cuisine.
Lee How Fook	219 N 11th St	215-925-7266	$$	10 pm	Low-key and casual, and great hot pots.
Little Thai Market in Reading Terminal	51 N 12th St	215-873-0231	$*	5:30 pm	The line wraps around the corner for a reason.
Lolita	106 S 13th St	215-546-7100	$$*	11 pm	In this scenario, you are Humbert Humbert. The food is you know who.
Maccabeam	128 S 12th St	215-922-5922	$*	8 pm	Its ambiance is sort of "old church kitchen" but it smells holy hella delicious in there. Glatt kosher (no dairy).
Maoz	1115 Walnut St	215-922-3409	$	-	Dutch falafel chain with all-u-can eat toppings.
Mercato	1216 Spruce St	215-985-2962	$$*	11 pm	Don't spill the homemade pasta on the rosewood floor.
Mixto	1141 Pine St	215-592-0363	$$	12 am	Can you say ceviche?
More Than Just Ice Cream	1119 Locust St	215-574-0586	$††	11:30 pm	Succulent desserts don't overshadow the delectable comfort food.
Moriarty's	1116 Walnut St	215-627-7676	$$	1 am	Huge theater crowd enlivens the place.
Morimoto	723 Chestnut St	215-413-9070	$$$	12 am	The best shrimp tempura ever. Anywhere.
Nan Zhou Hand Drawn Noodle House	927 Race St	215-923-1550	$*	9 pm	Home-made noodles go into every bowl of delicious soup.
New Harmony Vegetarian Restaurant	135 N 9th St	215-627-4520	$	10 pm	Mock if you must, but the meat here is unreal.
New Samosa	1214 Walnut St	215-546-2009	$$	10:30 pm	All-vegetarian Indian.
Pho Xe Lua	907 Race St	215-627-8883	$	11 pm	The fresh mango lassi should be more than enough inducement.
Rangoon	112 N 9th St	215-829-8939	$$	9 pm	An in-the-know Burmese spot.
Sang Kee Peking Duck House	238 N 9th St	215-925-7532	$$*	12 am	From obscure to titillating. And back.
Santa Fe Burrito Company	212 S 11th St	215-413-2378	$	9 pm	Not bad for beans out of a can, but pricier than necessary.
Shiao Lan Kung	930 Race St	215-928-0282	$$$	12 am	South Cantonese joint has good veggie options.
Singapore Kosher Vegetarian	1006 Race St	215-922-3288	$	11 pm	Great for Rabbis with PETA memberships.
Spruce Rana	1034 Spruce St	215-238-1223	$	4 pm	Gourmet grub from paninis to sushi. Skinny jeans suck, anyway.
Tai Lake	134 N 10th St	215-922-0698	$$	3 am	When you must have live frogs and lobster at 1 am.
Tenth Street Pour House	262 S 10th St	215-922-5626	$*	3 pm	Wake up and smell the espresso. Home of the $2.75 brunch.
Tria	1137 Spruce St	215-629-9200	$$$	12 am	Get your wine and cheese on at this second location.
Union Trust	717 Chestnut St	215-925-6000	$$$$$	11 pm	Trust us...impressive in every way.
Valanni	1229 Spruce St	215-790-9494	$$	1 am	Eclecticism with zero pretentiousness.
Varga Bar	941 Spruce St	215-627-5200	$$	1 am	Pin-up girls, burgers & beer!
Venture Inn	255 S Camac St	215-545-8731	$$	1 am	Classic American food with not so conventional clientele.
Vetri	1312 Spruce St	215-732-3478	$$$$	9 pm	Intimate and romantic, one of Philly's best.
Vietnam	221 N 11th St	215-592-1163	$	10:30 pm	One of the best restaurants in Philly. Be prepared to wait.
Vietnam Palace	222 N 11th St	215-592-9596	$	10 pm	Good, but way outclassed by Vietnam across the street.
Zio's Pizza	115 S 13th St	215-627-1615	$$	11 pm	Warm, cheesy, delicious.

Map 4 · Old City / Society Hill

Amada	217 Chestnut St	215-625-2450	$$$	1 am	Authentic tapas is superb, and homemade sangria makes it even better.
Anjou	206-08 Market St	215-923-1600	$$$	12:30 am	Global fusion ain't just an economist's dream.
Beneluxx	33 S 3rd St	267-318-7269	$	2 am	Cheese, chocolate, fondu, and crepes. Oh, my!
Bistro 7	7 N 3rd St	215-931-1560	$$$	10:30 pm	Spendy, contemporary BYOB French stuff.
Bistro Romano	120 Lombard St	215-925-8880	$$$	11 pm	Eat heavy Italian under dim candlelight.
Bookbinder's	125 Walnut St	215-925-7027	$$$$	11 pm	Everything old except the fish.

Arts & Entertainment · **Restaurants**

Name	Address	Phone	$	Time	Notes
Campo's Deli	214 Market St	215-923-1000	$*	10 pm	Over-stuffed sandwiches served by underfed sandwich makers.
Chloe	232 Arch St	215-629-2337	$$$	9:30 pm	Excellent food in an intimate setting.
The Continental	138 Market St	215-923-6069	$$	1 am	Starr's biggest success, the drinks and food are hip, and consumed hungrily by Jersey.
Cuba Libre	10 S 2nd St	215-627-0666	$$$$	1 am	Fine mojitos, great atmosphere. Food? Um, we guess.
Dark Horse	421 S 2nd St	215-928-9307	$$$	12 am	Oy, gov, fancy some bangers 'n mash?
DiNardo's Famous Seafood	312 Race St	215-925-5115	$$	11 pm	Gulf-coast soft shells are the major draw.
Dolce	241 Chestnut St	215-238-9983	$$	11 pm	Fancy-pants OC-style Italian joint flaunts it nightly.
Eulogy Belgian Tavern	136 Chestnut St	215-413-1918	$$	1:30 am	Great beer selection highlights a so-so menu.
European Republic	213 Chestnut St	215-627-5500	$	10 pm	Uber-good fries with a variety of dipping sauces.
Farmicia	15 S 3rd St	215-627-6274	$$	4 pm	Adjoining Metro Cafe makes bagels like whoa.
Fork	306 Market St	215-625-9425	$$	11:30 pm	Upscale without being obnoxious.
The Franklin Fountain	116 Market St	215-627-1899	$*	12 am	1920's ice cream parlor, a true Old City gem.
Gianfranco Pizza Rustica	6 N 3rd St	215-592-0048	$	10 pm	Some think it's the best. It's not, but it ain't bad.
Karma	114 Chestnut St	215-925-1444	$$	11 pm	High-end Indian fare but still veggie-friendly.
Kisso Sushi Bar	205 N 4th St	215-922-1770	$$	11 pm	Service with a never ending smile.
Konak	228 Vine St	215-592-1212	$$$	12 am	Authentic Turkish abounds, and wonderful feta, too.
La Famiglia	8 S Front St	215-922-2803	$$$	9:30 pm	Impeccable high-end Italian fare.
La Locanda del Ghiottone	130 N 3rd St	215-829-1465	$$*	11 pm	Gluttonously huge portions. Not that there's anything wrong with that.
Margherita Pizzeria	60 S 2nd St	215-922-7053	$*	3 am	Flamboyant toppings, by the slice.
Marrakesh	517 S Leithgow St	215-925-5929	$$*	11 pm	Sit on circular sofas and stuff your face with phyllo.
Mexican Post	104 Chestnut St	215-923-5233	$	11 pm	Average chow but solid margaritas.
Mizu Sushi Bar	220 Market St	215-238-0966	$$	11 pm	Creative little BYOB.
Moshulu	401 S Columbus Blvd	215-923-2500	$$$$	10:30 pm	Elegant food in a century-old sailing vessel. Avast ye matey.
Mrs. K's Koffee Shop	325 Chestnut St	215-627-7991	$	3.30 pm	Breakfast all day, bottomless coffee.
National Mechanics Bar and Restaurant	22 S 3rd St	215-701-4883	$$	2 am	"It's gourmet food, and it's drunk food."
Old City Cheese Shop	160 N 3rd St	215-238-1716	$	-	No cheese, just good sandwiches and baked goods.
Old City Coffee	221 Church St	215-629-9292	$	7pm	Good vibes lunch spot with serious coffee.
Pagoda Noodle Café	125 Sansom St	215-928-2320	$$	11:30 pm	Grab a bite on your way to the Ritz East.
Paradigm	239 Chestnut St	215-238-6900	$$$$$	11 pm	Overpriced and trying too hard, but the bathrooms are a marvel!
Patou	312 Market St	215-928-2987	$$$	11:30 pm	Masts, sails, and portholes. Oh, and the food is fine, too.
Philadelphia Java Co	518 S 4th St	215-928-1811	$*	10 pm	Woody and hipster quaint, like hanging out in the Berenstein Bears house, but with your laptop.
Pizzicato	248 Market St	215-629-5527	$$	11 pm	Stunning—and that's just the waitstaff.
The Plough & the Stars	123 Chestnut St	215-733-0300	$$	10:30 pm	If you can fight off the NJ scenesters, the food is fine.
Race Street Café	208 Race St	215-627-6181	$$	2 am	Decent burgers, great brew selection.
Restorante Panorama	14 N Front St	215-922-7800	$$$	11 pm	Along with Spasso and Famiglia, the murderer's row of high-end Italian fare.
Sassafras	48 S 2nd St	215-925-2317	$$	1 am	Snag an ostrich burger and don't spare the cheese.
Serrano	20 S 2nd St	215-928-0770	$$$	11:30 pm	Worth braving Old City on the weekend for their pumpkin gnocchi.
Sonny's Famous Steaks	228 Market St	215-629-5760	$*	3 am	Cheesesteaks like no other cheesesteak, considering you'll be drunk when you eat these ones.
Spasso	34 S Front St	215-592-7661	$$	11 pm	Affordable Italian and their clams have earned them a rep.
Swanky Bubbles	10 S Front St	215-928-1200	$$$$	2 am	Score some Dom with your sushi. Come loaded.
Xochitl	408 S 2nd St	215-238-7280	$$$	1 am	Like *anyone* can pronounce the name after a few margaritas.
Zahav	237 St James Pl	215-625-8800	$$$	11 pm	Culinary greatness from the Middle East.

Map 5 · Gray's Ferry

Name	Address	Phone	$	Time	Notes
D'ambrosio's Bakery	1401 S 31st St	215-389-8368	$*	7 pm	Get your rolls on in this South Philly enclave.
La Rosa's Café	1300 S Warfield St	215-339-1740	$*	4 pm	If you ever need a breakfast pizza, this is the joint to hit up.
Moe's Hot Dog House	2601 Washington Ave	215-465-6637	$*	3 pm	Dog toppings galore, plus veggie & turkey options.

Map 6 · Graduate Hospital / Gray's Ferry

Ants Pants Cafe	2212 South St	215-875-8002	$	4 pm	Brunch and lunch with an Australian flair.
Betty's Speakeasy	2241 Grays Ferry Ave	215-735-9060	$	7 pm	Cupcakes, lunch bits, and fabulous fudge. Chocolate and balsamic vinegar!
Divan Turkish Kitchen & Bar	918 S 22nd St	215-545-5790	$$	11 pm	Turkish delights.
Grace Tavern	2229 Grays Ferry Rd	215-893-9580	$	12 am	The best green beans you'll ever eat.
L2	2201 South St	215-732-7878	$$$	11 pm	Great bar and solid food choices.
My Thai	2200 South St	215-985-1878	$	10:45 pm	Cozy and casual, with just the right amount of sass to its cooking.
Phoebe's Bar-B-Q	2214 South St	215-546-4811	$	10 pm	Take-out only, but worth the mess.
Sidecar Bar & Grille	2201 Christian St	215-732-3429	$$††	1 am	Subtle gentrification amidst the unsubtle sound of the gun.
Ten Stone Bar & Restaurant	2063 South St	215-735-9939	$$	1 am	Traditional British pub with American food. Go figure.

Map 7 · Southwark West

August	1247 S 13th St	215-468-5926	$$*	10 pm	Downtown style across from Passyunk Square.
Bitar's	947 Federal St	215-755-1121	$	7 pm	Baked—not fried—falafel, plus lots of gyros.
Carmen's Country Kitchen	1301 S 11th St	215-339-9613	$*	2 pm	Tiny and quirky, but avant garde food is sublime.
Chiarella's Ristorante	1600 S 11th St	215-334-6404	$$	10 pm	Italian food...just like grandma used to make.
Dante & Luigi's	762 S 10th St	215-922-9501	$$*	10:30 pm	Heaping out the gravies since 1899.
Da Vinci Ristorante	1533 S 11th St	215-336-3636	$$	-	Unique Italian with great desserts.
Devil's Den	1148 S 11th St	215-339-0855	$$	2 am	Mediocre food, but the beers are delish.
Fiso Lounge	1437 South St	215-735-2220	$$	1 am	Fine dining that comes with a whole lot of ass-grinding.
Franco's & Luigi's	1549 S 13th St	215-755-8903	$	11 pm	Huge-portioned BYOB packs in the locals. Lots of singing.
Govinda's	1408 South St	215-985-9303	$$	12 am	Excellent whole-food eats from vegan hypnotherapists.
Green Eggs Cafe	1306 Dickinson St	215-226-3447	$	-	Light and sweet, it's time to eat.
Isgro Pastries	1009 Christian St	215-923-3092	$	6 pm	Fattening you up since 1904. Just order cakes in advance.
Jamaican Jerk Hut	1436 South St	215-545-8644	$	12 am	Check out their Caribbean-inspired outdoor space.
JNA Institute of Culinary Arts	1212 S Broad St	215-468-8800	$$$	11 pm	Four course, $25 prix-fixe dinners? Yes please!
Lazaro's Pizza House	1743 South St	215-545-2775	$*	11 pm	You like slices the size of Bangladesh? This is the joint for you.
Morning Glory Diner	735 S 10th St	215-413-3999	$$*	4 pm	Huge lines, but pancakes will make you weep.
Ms. Tootsie's	1314 South St	215-731-9045	$$	9:30 pm	Catfish, collards, mac & cheese.
Nam Phuong	1100 Washington Ave	215-468-0410	$	10 pm	Tasty pho and avocado shakes.
Pico de Gallo	1501 South St	215-772-2710	$	12 am	Cozy Mex joint offers fine margarita mixes.
Ricci Brothers	1165 S 11th St	215-334-6910	$*	3 pm	Old-school deli stuffs the hoagies with charm.
Ron's Ribs	1627 South St	215-732-3561	$	11 pm	In the middle of BBQ row.
Tritone	1508 South St	215-545-0475	$$	12 am	Find your groove while supping on mac and cheese.

Map 8 · Bella Vista / Queen Village

Anni Cent'	770 S 7th St	215-925-5558	$$††	10 pm	Italian food for less.
Beau Monde	624 S 6th St	215-592-0656	$$$	11 pm	Elegant French creperie. Comment charmont!
Brauhaus Schmitz	718 South St	267-909-8814	$$$	2 am	Beer hall with solid German food and lotsa soccer.
Bridget Foy's	200 South St	215-922-1813	$$	11:30 pm	Strong drinks and a nice spot to survey the crowd.
Café Huong Lan	1037 S 8th St	215-629-9966	$*	10 pm	Vietnamese hoagies done with flair.
Café Nhuy	802 Christian St	215-629-6544	$*	7 pm	A Vietnamese veggie hoagie that will slap your ass and call you sonny.
Caffe Valentino	1245 S 3rd St	215-336-3033	$$$	11 pm	For a nice meal before a shitty UA Theatre film.
Catahoula	775 S Front St	215-271-9300	$$	11 pm	Get your po boys here. Don't miss dessert.
Copabanana	344 South St	215-923-6180	$	1 am	Decent Tex-Mex in a busy bar atmosphere.
Crescent City	900 South St	215-627-6780	$$$	1 am	Delectable cajun charm and hospitality right on South St.
Cucina Forte	768 S 8th St	215-238-0778	$$	11 pm	A creepy little place with nothing going for it.
Dmitri's	795 S 3rd St	215-625-0556	$*	11 pm	Popular neighborhood BYOB; be prepared to wait.
Famous 4th Street Deli	700 S 4th St	215-922-3274	$	5 pm	Great cookies, and the largest order of eggs you have ever seen.
Fitzwater Café	728 S 7th St	215-629-0428	$*	9:30 pm	Blissful eggs and great pancakes.

Geno's Steaks	1219 S 9th St	215-389-0659	$*	24 hrs	Spanish speakers beware. Geno is a goddamn patriot so he doesn't want your f***ing business. Vamos to Pat's.
Gnocchi	613 E Passyunk Ave	215-592-8300	$$*	10 pm	Their eponymous dish does them justice.
Golden Empress Garden	610 S 5th St	215-627-7666	$$*	12 am	Ho-hum Chinese with many veggie options.
Hikaru	607 S 2nd St	215-627-7110	$$	11:30 pm	Delicate specialty rolls in keeping with the low-key atmosphere.
Horizons	611 S 7th St	215-923-6117	$$$	11 pm	Vegan fare puts on its fancy pants.
Hosteria Da Elio	615 S 3rd St	215-925-0930	$$	11 pm	There really is an Elio, and he's a magician with a whisk.
Ishkabibble's Eatery	337 South St	215-923-4337	$*	2 am	Fast, late night chow at its finest.
James	824 S 8th St	215-629-4980	$$$	11 pm	Romantic BYOB for people who are into that kind of thing.
Jim's Steaks	400 South St	215-928-1911	$*	3 am	For those who love smelling of onions while standing in line.
Johnny Rockets	443 South St	215-829-9222	$	2 am	If you like your burgers served with '50s-style doo-wop, be our guest.
La Fourno Trattoria	636 South St	215-627-9000	$	11 pm	Good pastas, solid wood-fired 'za.
La Lupe	1201 S 9th St	215-551-9920	$	1 am	Traditional Mex in the heart of Cheesesteak Central.
Latest Dish	613 S 4th St	215-629-0565	$$$$	1:30 am	DJ spins tunes as you throw down irresistible chow.
Lovash	236 South St	215-925-3881	$$	11 pm	Decent Indian with a bit of fire in its loins.
Lorenzo Pizza	900 Christian St	215-922-2540	$*	8 pm	Very garm-heavy but it definitely sticks to your ribs.
Lorenzo & Son Pizza	305 South St	215-627-4110	$*	4 am	Philly's most famous (not necessarily best) pie.
Lovash	236 South St	215-925-3881	$$	11 pm	Decent Indian with a bit of fire in its loins.
Monsu	901 Christian St	215-440-0495	$$$	10 pm	Spectacular Sicilian. Affordable and BYOB under one roof!
Mustard Greens	622 S 2nd St	215-627-0833	$$	10 pm	You must try the garlic noodles. Trust us.
Napoli Pizzeria	944 E Passyunk Ave	215-336-3833	$*	2 am	Panzerotti: a pizza, deep fried. This is so good, it's worth the heart attack.
New Wave Café	784 S 3rd St	215-922-8484	$$	1 am	Locals pub with elegant chow.
Pat's King of Steaks	1237 E Passyunk Ave	215-468-1546	$*	24 hrs	When you've gotta have a cheesesteak at 5 am.
Ralph's	760 S 9th St	215-627-6011	$$*	11 pm	Serving up pasta for more than a century.
Rita's	239 South St	215-629-3910	$		Great spot for tasty custard.
The Royal Tavern	937 E Passyunk	215-389-6694	$	1 am	Mellowed hipsters drink like kings.
Sabrina's Café	910 Christian St	215-574-1599	$$	10 pm	Brunch specials and great décor, plus polenta fries.
Saloon	750 S 7th St	215-627-1811	$$$$$	11 pm	Reportedly where Tony Bennett eats when he's in town.
Sarcone's Deli	734 S 9th St	215-922-1717	$		Hoagie fixins live up to the bread.
Snockey's	1020 S 2nd St	215-339-9578	$$	11:30 pm	Down and dirty oyster house.
South Street Diner	140 South St	215-627-5258	$$	24 hrs	24 hours of cheap, reliable grub.
Supper	926 South St	215-545-2860	$$$$	11:30 pm	Locally focused, highly delicious. Great date-night spot.
Taco Loco	Jefferson Square Park	215-883-9191	$	9 pm	Brutally good taco truck parked on Washington Ave.
Tamarind	117 South St	215-925-2764	$$	11 pm	Dutiful Thai in casual atmosphere.
Taqueria La Veracruzana	908 Washington Ave	215-465-1440	$	12 am	Not much to look at, but authentic and delicious.
Termini Brothers Bakery	1523 S 8th St	215-334-1816	$	7 pm	The cannoli is legend. Spoken of in whispers.
Trattoria Alla Costiera	769 E Passyunk Ave	267-861-4640	$$††	11 pm	Quaint and cozy Italian nook.
The Ugly American	1100 S Front St	215-336-1100	$$	2 am	Only place we know of for a "classy" garbage plate.
Vesuvio	736 S 8th St	215-922-8380	$$$	11 pm	Put it this way: This would be Paulie Walnuts' favorite joint.
Villa di Roma	936 S 9th St	215-592-1295	$*	11 pm	If loving their ricotta/mozzarella pasta is wrong, then we don't want to be right.

Map 9 · Point Breeze / West Passyunk

Barrel's	1725 Wolf St	215-389-6010	$$	9:30 pm	No-frills Italian joint, popular for lunch.
Hardena Restaurant	1754 S Hicks St	215-271-9442	$$	11 pm	Delicious, tiny, unpretentious Indonesian hole in the wall.
L'Angolo	1415 Porter St	215-389-4252	$$	11 pm	Homemade Italian. Ravioli. To. Die. For.
La Stanza	2001 Oregon Ave	215-271-0801	$$$	10:30 pm	Standard Italian, but the theme's on stilts.
Melrose Diner	1501 Snyder Ave	215-467-6644	$	24 hrs	A breakfast institution 24 hours a day.
Plenty	1710 E Passyunk Ave	267-909-8033	$	8 pm	"Artisanal sandwiches" sound douchey, but the goods deliver.
Royal Villa Café	1700 Jackson St	215-462-4488	$$	10 pm	Plenty of clams from which to choose.
Tap Room	1509 Mifflin St	215-271-7787	$$	1 am	Stylish gastropub in South Philly.
Valanni	1229 Spruce St	215-790-9494	$$$	11 pm	In the heart of the gayborhood, it's eclecticism with zero pretentiousness.

Map 10 · Moyamensing / East Passyunk

Name	Address	Phone	$	Time	Description
10th Street Café	1000 Snyder Ave	215-463-2097	$	2 pm	Banana pancakes and formica tabletops for the foodies on the cheap.
Artisan Boulanger Patissier	1648 S 12th St	215-271-4688	$*	2 pm	French baked goods that will make you feel sinful for indulging.
Bomb Bomb Bar-B-Que Grill	1026 Wolf St	215-463-1311	$$	11 pm	BBQ is expected here, but the quality Italian food is something only locals know about.
Cantina Los Cabalitos	1651 E Passyunk Ave	215-755-3550	$	1 am	Tequila shooters + pork empanadas = A good night out.
Criniti Restaurant	2611 S Broad St	215-465-7750	$	10:30 pm	Unpretentious, inexpensive spaghetti house.
Fond	1617 E Passyunk Ave	215-551-5000	$$$$	10 pm	Lovely fine French in more casual (but crowded) space. BYOB.
Izumi	1601 E Passyunk Ave	215-271-1222	$$	10 pm	Your best South Philly sushi fix.
Le Virtu	1927 E Passyunk Ave	215-271-5626	$$$	11 pm	Dine in a garden? In South Philly? For real!
Mamma Maria	1637 E Passyunk Ave	215-463-6884	$$$$	11 pm	Seven-course prix fixe varies from evening to evening.
Marra's	1734 E Passyunk Ave	215-463-9249	$*	11 pm	Zounds! The thin crust pie is heavenly.
Mazza Mediteranean Takeout	1100 Jackson St	215-952-2600	$$*	10 pm	Amazing hummus, falafel, etc.
Mr Martino's Trattoria	1646 E Passyunk Ave	215-755-0663	$$*	11 pm	Elegant, understated, and the food is bliss.
Paradiso	1627 E Passyunk Ave	215-271-2066	$$$	11 pm	Fine contemporary dining with waiters who compare the gnocchi to "angel pillows."
Pop's Water Ice	1337 W Oregon Ave	215-551-7677	$*	1 pm	Water Ice from a non-chain, taste the difference.
Scannicchio's	2500 S Broad St	215-468-3900	$$	10 pm	NJ legend finally opens branch in Philly.
Tre Scalini	1915 E Passyunk Ave	215-551-3870	$$$	10 pm	The food is extraordinary, the décor, horrendous.
El Zarape	1527 E Passyunk Ave	215-336-1293	$$	10 pm	Authentic Mexican cusine great for take-out.

Map 11 · South Philly East

Name	Address	Phone	$	Time	Description
Chic-Fil-A	2204 S Columbus Blvd	215-271-2313	$	10 pm	The crème-de-la-crème of fast food branches out beyond the mall.
Chuck E Cheeses	9 Snyder Ave	215-551-4080	$	11 pm	Some would find the visage of a giant rat hovering over your food disconcerting.
Gooey Looie's	231 McClellan St	215-334-7668	$	8:30 pm	Giant, cheap, and amazing cheesesteaks without the tourists.
Langostino	100 Morris St	215-551-7709	$$*	12 am	Another yummy crustacean from the folks who brought you stone crabs.
Tony Luke's	39 E Oregon Ave	215-551-5725	$*	2 am	No higher honor amongst the various sandwich

Map 12 · Stadiums

Name	Address	Phone	$	Time	Description
McFadden's	1 Citizens Bank Wy	215-952-0300	$$	11 pm	Sports bar in the Phillies Citizen's Bank Park.
Medora's Mecca	3101 S 13th St	215-336-1655	$$$$	11 pm	Quiet place, amazing tiramisu.
Talk of the Town	3020 S Broad St	215-551-7277	$$*	1 am	Stop by for a breakfast'wich on your way to the game.

Map 13 · West Philly

Name	Address	Phone	$	Time	Description
Abyssinia Ethiopian Restaurant	229 S 45th St	215-387-2424	$	12 am	Casual African restaurant; veggie/vegan-friendly.
Allegro Pizza	3942 Spruce St	215-382-8158	$	2 am	Good pizza! Beer! Good pizza and beer!
Colonial Pizza	400 S 43rd St	215-387-7702	$	12 am	Some people swear by it, others don't. Serves beer.
Distrito	3945 Chestnut St	215-222-1657	$$$	12 am	Big, expensive, campy, fun.
Ethio Cafe & Carry O Out	4400 Chestnut St	215-222-2104	$$	11 pm	Tasty, inexpensive Ethiopian eats.
Evan's Varsity Pizza	4311 Locust St	215-386-8881	$	3 am	Get your 40's here, but not your pizza.
The Greek Lady	222 S 40th St	215-382-2600	$	11 pm	Began as a lunch truck, now popular enough for a building.
Izzy and Zoe's	224 S 40th St	215-382-2328	$	4 pm	Classic deli fare.
Kaboobeesh	4201 Chestnut St	215-386-8081	$††	11 pm	Tasty kabobs of many varieties.
Kaffa Crossing	4423 Chestnut St	215-386-0504	$	9 pm	Fair Trade coffee and Ethiopian grub at this café with a mission.
Kilimanjaro Restaurant	4317 Chestnut St	215-387-1970	$$	11 pm	Large-portioned, African goodness.
Koch's Deli	4309 Locust St	215-222-8662	$$	8 pm	Seriously good sandwiches, and sometimes they feed you pickles.
Lee's Hoagie House	4034 Walnut St	217-387-0905	$$	10 pm	Greasy. Decent if you're already in the neighborhood.
Local 44	4333 Spruce St	215-222-2337	$$	12 am	Lotsa draft beers and decent enough gastropub vittles.
Marathon Grill and MarBar	200 S 40th St	215-222-0100	$$	1 am	Get served by Penn students before they never have a service job again.

Marigold Kitchen	501 S 45th St	215-222-3699	$$$	10 pm	Extremely fine dining frequented by the university crowd.
Mexicali Café	110 S 40th St	215-222-2667	$	8 pm	Kind of crappy. Want good Mexican food? Leave West Philly.
Nan	4000 Chestnut St	215-382-0818	$$$	10 pm	Slower service, but specials are worth the wait.
Pasquali's Pizza & Pasta	200 S 43rd St	215-387-6100	$	12 am	Food? Meh. Beer? Oh yes.
Pattaya Grill	4006 Chestnut St	215-387-8533	$	11 pm	Not your father's Thai restaurant: exotic and challenging.
Philly Diner	3901 Walnut St	215-382-3400	$	24 hrs	It's a diner!
Pho & Café Saigon	4248 Sruce St	215-222-6800	$	9 pm	Lychee milkshake? Yes please! Tasty, tasty place.
Rx	4443 Spruce St	215-222-9590	$$	10 pm	Ivy League-style BYOB has the goods.
Saad's Halal Place	4500 Walnut St	215-222-7223	$$††	10 pm	Friendly, funny, delicious, and cheap as hell.
Tandoor India	106 S 40th St	215-222-7122	$$	10:30 pm	Good, but go for the buffet, not the menu.
Thai Singha House	3939 Chestnut St	215-382-8001	$$	10:45 pm	Another in the long line of superior Thai joints in the 'hood.

Map 14 • University City

Abner's Cheesesteaks	3813 Chestnut St	215-662-0100	$	3 am	Or you can just have them FedEx you a sandwich.
Ed's/Rana	3513 Lancaster Ave	215-222-4000	$$*	2 am	Great for those in the mood for both hummus and wings.
Lemon Grass Thai	3626 Lancaster Ave	215-222-8042	$$	10 pm	Charming Thai cuisine. Order extra corn fritters.
Mad Mex	3401 Walnut St	215-382-2221	$$	1 am	Student-friendly joint has edible burritos, good beer.
New Deck Tavern	3408 Sansom St	215-386-4600	$$	2 am	Bar food of a standard order, but whiskey selection is a plus.
Paris Cafe Creperie	3417 Spruce St	215-222-6500	$	11 pm	Real men eat crepes.
Penne	3600 Sansom S	215-832-6222	$$$	11 pm	The Hilton's pasta emporium has abundance of wine.
Picnic	3131 Walnut St	215-222-1608	$$	10:30 pm	Gourmet deli has the goods to go.
Pod	3636 Sansom St	215-387-1803	$$$	12 am	If Kubrick had opened a sushi bar…
Powelton Pizza	3651 Lancaster Ave	215-387-1213	$	10:30 pm	Decent pizza in University City. Try the pesto.
Sitar India	60 S 38th St	215-662-0818	$$	10 pm	Don't miss their great buffet.
Slainte	3000 Market St	215-222-7400	$	2 am	Less scary than the pub that was there before.
White Dog Café	3420 Sansom St	215-386-9224	$$$	11 pm	Progressive liberal idealists served locally-sourced organica and tasty cocktails.
Zocalo	3600 Lancaster Ave	215-895-0139	$$	10 pm	Fine Mexican flava: No tacos or chimichangas for miles.

Map 15 • Strawberry Mansion

The Belgian Café	2047 Green St	215-235-3500	$$$	1 am	New addition to the Monk's family.
Dominics Fish Market	2842 Cecil B Moore Ave	215-232-7120	$*	10 pm	All the fresh seafood you might expect—only cheaper.
Umai Umai	533 N 22nd St	215-988-0707	$$	10:30 pm	Sushi with BYO Sake.
Yuri Deli	1618 N 29th St	215-763-7395	$*	12 am	Small spot filled with bunly goodness.

Map 16 • Brewerytown

Butter's Soul Food	2821 W Girard Ave	215-235-4724	$	11 pm	Take-out soul food—fried chicken, ribs, greens, etc.
Era	2743 Poplar St	215-769-7008	$$	11 pm	Cheap Ethiopian food & drinks.
Granite Hill	2600 Benjamin Franklin Pkwy	215-684-7990	$$$	2:30 pm	The Museum of Art's requisite fancy restaurant.
Trio	2624 Brown St	215-232-8176	$$	11 pm	Thai BYOB.
Water Works Restaurant and Lounge	640 Water Works Dr	215-236-9000	$$$$	9 pm	Because you wanted to pay $50 for bottled water.

Map 17 • Fairmount

Angelino's Restaurant & Pizzeria	849 N 25th St	215-787-9945	$	10 pm	It's pizza! Nothing that wild about it.
The Bishop's Collar	2349 Fairmount Ave	215-765-1616	$$	1 am	Sandwiches and good barfood highlight this AM staple.
Bridgid's	726 N 24th St	215-232-3232	$$	11 pm	Popular neighborhood joint has good chow and great beer.
Doma	1822 Callowhill St	215-564-1114	$$	10:30 pm	A resounding "hell yes!" for this Japanese joint.
Figs	2501 Meredith St	215-978-8440	$$*	11 pm	Mediterranean BYOB hot spot has charm to spare.
Illuminare	2321 Fairmount Ave	215-765-0202	$$	10 pm	Rocking the brick-oven pizzas for all a youse.
Jack's Firehouse	2130 Fairmount Ave	215-232-9000	$$	10:30 pm	Former fire station still brings the BBQ heat.
Little Pete's	2401 Pennsylvania Ave	215-232-5001	$	11 pm	A greasy spoon with no apologies.

L'Oca Italian Bistro	2025 Fairmount Ave	215-769-0316	$$	10 pm	BYOB Italian.
Little Pete's	2401 Pennsylvania Ave	215-545-5508	$	11 pm	A greasy spoon with no apologies.
London Grill	2301 Fairmount Ave	215-978-4545	$$$	10:30 pm	Weirdly enough, expect Asian, Latin, AND Mediterranean chow.
Rembrandt's	741 N 23rd St	215-763-2228	$$	1 am	Perhaps the best plate of calamari in the city.
Rose Tattoo Café	1847 Callowhill St	215-569-8939	$$$	11 pm	Like being on the set of a Tennessee Williams opus.
Rybread	2319 Fairmount Ave	215-769-0603	$$	-	Killer sandwiches and a nice outdoor patio.
Sabrina's Cafe	1804 Callowhill St	215-636-9061	$$$	10 pm	New location. Same great food and long wait.
Tavern On Green	2047 Green St	215-235-6767	$$	11 pm	Bang-for-your-buck food. Great drink selection and specials.

Map 18 · Spring Garden / Francisville

Café Lift	428 N 13th St	215-922-3031	$$	3 pm	No line and super-luscious brunch foods.
City Line Pizza	1547 Spring Garden St	215-564-1910	$*	12 am	Standard-issue pizza joint, big with CCP students.
Jose's Tacos	469 N 10th St	215-765-2369	$	11 pm	Ignore the gourmet Mexican explosion: Jose's has the goods.
Osteria	640 N Broad St	215-763-0920	$$$	11 pm	More tasty (and a little cheaper) Italian grub by Mr Vetri.
Sazon	941 Spring Garden St	215-763-2500	$$	11 pm	Venezuelan for the show-off man-on-a-budget.
Westy's Tavern & Restaurant	1440 Callowhill St	215-563-6134	$*	2 am	Old-man joint that reeks of smoke, grease, and greatness.

Map 19 · Northern Liberties

The Abbaye	637 N 3rd St	215-627-6711	$$	1 am	Belgian bistro uses good beer liberally throughout menu.
A Full Plate	1009 N Bodine St	215-627-4068	$$	10 pm	We swear, all Philadelphians do is go to brunch.
Bar Ferdinand	1030 N 2nd St	215-923-1313	$$	2 am	Yummy tapas brunches and dinners. Ole!
Cafe Estelle	444 N 4th St	215-925-5080	$$	4 pm	Worth getting up for brunch and homemade pastries.
El Camino Real	1040 N 2nd St	215-925-1110	$$	11 pm	Three words: Fried pickle chips.
Darling's	1033 N 2nd St	267-239-5775	$	12 am	Famous cheesecake at a mediocre, neo-retro diner.
The Foodery	837 N 2nd St	215-238-6077	$††	12 am	Sandwiches and legendary make-your-own six pack.
Green Eggs Cafe	719 N 2nd St	215-922-3447	$$		Tasty "eco-concious" brunch.
Hikari	1040 N American St	215-923-2654	$$$	11 pm	Good sushi. BYO sake.
Home Slice	1040 N American St	215-627-2726	$	12 am	Whole wheat crust, vegan cheese by request; slow service variable.
Honey's Sit 'n Eat	800 N 4th St	215-925-1150	$	4 pm	The wait for brunch just goes on and on.
Il Cantuccio	701 N 3rd St	215-627-6573	$$*	11:30 pm	Small, trend-setting trattoria, simple but effective.
Johnny Brenda's	1201 Frankford Ave	215-739-9684	$	1 am	Hipster hang has the best food in Fishtown!
Koo Zee Doo	614 N 2nd St	215-923-8080	$$$	11 pm	Bitchin' Portuguese BYOB, served family style.
Las Cazuelas	426 Girard Ave	215-351-9144	$$	10 pm	Mexican seafood that will knock your calcetines off.
Liberties	705 N 2nd St	215-238-0660	$$$$	12 am	Food plus beer equals fooooobeeeer.
Modo Mio	161 W Girard Ave	215-203-8707	$$$*	11 pm	Pros: delicious. Cons: full of themselves, not of large portions.
North 3rd	801 N 3rd St	215-413-3666	$$	1 am	Yummy chalkboard specials abound in this busy bar/bistro.
The New Acropolis	1200 Frankford Ave	215-634-2211	$*	10 pm	Diner-style food, featuring infamous omelet on a hoagie roll.
Paesano's	152 W Girard Ave	267-866-9566	$	3 pm	Real talk: The city's best sandwiches are here.
Pura Vida	527 Fairmount Ave	215-922-6433	$	10 pm	Guatemalan, cheap, and so good.
PYT	1050 N Hancock St	215-964-9009	$$	2 am	Hip central. A party promoter opened a burger joint.
Radicchio	314 York Ave	215-627-6850	$$	11 pm	Old City's version of a simple little BYOB with updated Italian cuisine.
Rustica Pizza	903 N 2nd St	215-627-1393	$*	2 am	Gianfranco's No-Libs extension: good and salty.
Soy Café	630 N 2nd St	215-922-1003	$*	9 pm	Homemade fake cheese will make you scream, "I-can't-believe-it's-VEGAN!"
Standard Tap	901 N 2nd St	215-238-0630	$$$	1 am	Flagship joint with sumptuous dinners and brunches.
Tiffin	710 W Girard Ave	215-922-1297	$$	10 pm	Indian delivery.

Map 20 · Fishtown / Port Richmond

Best Deli & Pizza	2616 E Lehigh Ave	215-291-9310	$	11 pm	Fine, but perhaps a bit of an inflated self-image.
Ekta	250 E Girard Ave	215-426-2277	$	10 pm	Hot, tiny, well-priced Indian/Pakistani.
Father & Sons Pizza & Pasta	2500 Frankford Ave	215-634-7982	$*	11 pm	This might be the best pizza in Fishtown.
Fathom Seafood House	200 E Girard Ave	267-761-9343	$$	2 am	A pretty decent fish house in the Fishtown.

Ida Mae's Bruncherie	2302 E Norris St	215-426-4209	$*	3 pm	Traditional Irish breakfast or tofu scramble. You decide.
Jovan's Place	2327 E York St	215-634-3330	$$	10 pm	Super legit Eastern European food with heaping huge portions.
Les & Doreen's Happy Tap Kitchen	1301 E Susquehanna Ave	215-634-1123	$$	2 am	Two fryers, a cash register, and a lady.
Sketch	413 E Girard Ave	215-634-3466	$$*	11 pm	Very tasty, if you leave the hype at home.
Stock's Bakery	2614 E Lehigh Ave	215-634-7344	$*	5:30 pm	Stock up on all your baked goods needs. Forgive us.
Sulimay's Restaurant	632 E Girard Ave	215-423-1773	$*	3 pm	High-class eggs and wondrous pancakes.
Tacconelli's Pizza	2604 E Somerset St	215-425-4983	$*	11 pm	So good you need to call ahead to reserve your dough. No joke.

Map 21 · Roxborough / Manayunk

Adobe Cafe	4550 Mitchell St	215-483-3947	$$	11 pm	Southwestern-style steakhouse offers seitan options.
Chabaa Thai Bistro	4371 Main St	215-483-1979	$$	10 pm	Pad thai to tha max.
Couch Tomato Café	102 Rector St	215-483-2233	$	9 pm	Worth a slice if you're in the neighborhood.
Dairyland	4409 Main St	215-482-6806	$	7 pm	Crazy good ice cream & knock-off "Blizzardos" from locals.
Hikaru	4348 Main St	215-487-3500	$$$	10 pm	OK if you really need your sushi and hibachi fix.
Il Tartufo	4341 Main St	215-4822-1999	$$$$	11 pm	Lovely Italian spot despite the annoying Manayunk location.
Jake's	4365 Main St	215-483-0444	$$$$	10:30 pm	Pricey Manayunk flagship that got the ball rolling.
Kildare's	4417 Main St	215-482-7242	$$$	11 pm	Fine Irish Food. Recommend the Boxys.
La Colombe Torrefaction	4360 Main St	215-483-4580	$*	6 pm	The good twin to Center City's Israeli trash evil twin.
Le Bus	4266 Main St	215-487-2663	$	11 pm	Continental style with top-shelf baguettes.
Manayunk Brewery & Restaurant	4120 Main St	215-482-8220	$$	2 am	Lots of outdoor space and solid sushi.
Mom's Bake at Home	4452 Main St	215-487-2440	$	9 pm	Grab a slice, or order a pie & cook at home.
Mugshots Coffeehouse & Café	110 Cotton St	215-482-3964	$††	4 pm	I'll have avacado in my sandwich.
Zesty's	4382 Main St	215-438-6226	$$	11 pm	Nice Greek spot.

Map 22 · Manayunk

| Terrace Street Bistro | 3989 Terrace St | 215-508-2775 | $$$$ | 9 pm | Utterly lovely food at this French BYOB. |
| Urban Cafe | 5109 Rochelle Ave | 215-254-9557 | $$$ | 9 pm | Another worthwhile BYOB, this one serving "American" cuisine. |

Map 23 · East Falls

Brothers Old Style Deli	3492 Tilden St	215-713-0541	$	6 pm	OMG, these sandwiches. Go.
Epicure Cafe	3401 Conrad St	215-438-8566	$	7 pm	East Falls' badly needed coffee and sandwich shop.
Frank's Pizza	3600 Fisk Ave	215-848-6433	$	10 pm	Cheap, decent pizza for when you want to order in.
Johnny Manana's	4201 Ridge Ave	215-843-0499	$$	11 pm	Unusual Mexican, but forget that and check the tequila shelf.

Map 24 · Germantown South

Aprons	5946 Germantown Ave	215-843-5080	$$	9 pm	Southern and Italian food. Cornbread and spaghetti, yup.
Dahlak	5547 Germantown Ave	215-849-0788	$$	10 pm	Ethiopian imported from West Philly.
House of Jin	234-36 W Chelten Ave	215-848-7700	$$	11 pm	Fusing Chinese, Japanese, and American jazz? Whatever.
K&J Caribbean and American Diner	5603 Greene St	215-849-0242	$*	11 pm	Have some red beans with your french toast.
The Urban Cafe	5815 Wayne Ave	215-844-0296	$$*	10 pm	Cute cafe open for three square meals.

Map 25 · Germantown North

Bacio	311 W Mt Pleasant Ave	215-248-2740	$$$	9 pm	Germantown date spot.
Chef Ken's Café	7135 Germantown Ave	215-242-2495	$$	10 pm	OMG BBQ. Good Southern cooking.
Earth Bread + Brewery	7136 Germantown Ave	215-242-6666	$$	12 am	By "Earth Bread" they mean "Pizza."
Geechee Girl Rice Cafe	6825 Germantown Ave	215-843-8113	$$*	9 pm	Try a Southern specialty from the Low Country of South Carolina & Georgia.
Golden Crust Pizza	7155 Germantown Ave	215-248-2929	$	11 pm	Pedestrian, uninspired. Kids love it.

High Point Café	602 Carpenter Ln	215-849-5153	$$$	5 pm	A wholesome chill spot.
Lincoln Pizzeria	277 W Mt Pleasant Ave	215-248-2233	$$	11 pm	Much-loved pizza.
Mi Puebla Restaurant	7157 Germantown Ave	215-247-1779	$$	9 pm	Decent! Mexican! Food!
Rib Crib	6333 Germantown Ave	215-438-6793	$*	1 am	Meaty joint has cult following.
Tiffin	7105 Emlen St	215-242-3656	$$	9:30 pm	The famous Indian delivery expands to the northern regions.
Toto's Pizzeria	6555 Greene St	215-848-4550	$$	9 pm	Good time for Pizza? Have a good pizza this time.
Umbria	7131 Germantown Ave	215-242-6470	$$*	9 pm	Cozy little BYOB that remains a hit with locals.

Map 26 · Mt Airy

Bredenbeck's Bakery & Ice Cream Parlor	8126 Germantown Ave	215-247-7374	$	10 pm	Fight through the line to score sweet ice cream treats.
Cafette	8136 Ardleigh St	215-242-4220	$$*	9:30 pm	Bohemian bistro shows off its (mismatched) colors.
CinCin	7838 Germantown Ave	215-242-8800	$$	11 pm	Highly-rated Chinese in a largely non-Asian community.
North by Northwest	7165 Germantown Ave	215-248-1000	$$	11 pm	Soul-food and jazz roll off the tongue, cats.
Roller's Restaurant at Flying Fish	8142 Germantown Ave	215-242-0707	$$*	10 pm	Gourmet international cuisine, prepared by masters.
Trolley Car Diner	7619 Germantown Ave	215-753-1500	$	10 pm	Classic food, classic look. Ice cream served on an old trolley.

Map 27 · Chestnut Hill

Campbell's Place	8337 Germantown Ave	215-242-2066	$$	11 pm	Pub fare in a busy neighborhood joint.
Chestnut Grill & Sidewalk Cafe	8229 Germantown Ave	215-247-7570	$$	11 pm	Cajun-flavored fare with Asian accents.
Chestnut Hill Coffee Co	8620 Germantown Ave	215-242-8600	$	6 pm	Prim desserts match thoroughly-crafted espresso drinks.
Metropolitan Bakery	8607 Germantown Ave	215-753-9001	$	6 pm	Great breads, rolls, soups—and brownies to die for.
Thai Kuu	35 Bethlehem Pike	267-297-5715	$$	9 pm	Recommendable Thai food on the city outskirts.

Northeast Philly

Benny the Bum's	9991 Bustleton Ave	215-673-3000	$$	11:30 pm	Try the buffalo shrimp.
Chink's Steaks	6030 Torresdale Ave	215-535-9405	$	9 pm	A less than PC name, but a delicious cheesesteak for over fifty years. Cute retro interior, too.
Dining Car	8826 Frankford Ave	215-338-5113	$$*	24 hrs	As the name indicates, a former working sidecar turned purveyor of above-average diner chow.
Guido's Restaurant	3545 Welsh Rd	215-335-1850	$$††	10 pm	BYOB Red sauce Italian overflowing with portions and flavor.
Hinge Cafe	2652 E Somerset St	215-425-6614	$$	10 pm	Nice breakfast and lunch options.
Joseph's Pizza	7947 Oxford Ave	215-722-7000	$	12 am	Good pizza and cheesesteaks.
Macaroni's Restaurant	9315 Old Bustleton Ave	215-464-3040	$$	12 am	Pedestrian name with cooking like Momma used to make.
Mayfair Diner	7353 Frankford Ave	215-624-4447	$$	24 hrs	Philly's answer to the New York Diner ego trip.
Moe's Deli	7360 Frankford Ave	215-338-6637	$	5 pm	Solid sandwiches and pickles worth seeking out.
Moonstruck	7955 Oxford Ave	215-725-6000	$$$	10 pm	Upscaling in Northeast. Wear a tie with your brass knuckles.
Nick's Roast Beef	2212 Cottman Ave	215-745-1292	$$	2 am	Get your roast beef sandwiches here. Period.
Nifty Fifty's	2491 Grant Ave	215-676-1950	$*	1 am	Glorious diner chow and the best milkshakes in the city.
Santucci's Square Pizza	4010 Cottman Ave	215-332-4333	$	11 pm	Generations of Santuccis have made these square pie classics since 1960.
Steve's Prince of Steaks	7200 Bustleton Ave	215-338-0985	$*	3 am	Try their signature steak with melted white American cheese on top.
Sweet Lucy's Smokehouse	7500 State Rd	215-331-3112	$$	9 pm	Philly's best BBQ, hands down.
Tiffany Diner	9010 Roosevelt Blvd	215-677-3916	$$	24 hrs	Don't miss the smoked fish platter!

It must be humbly admitted: We're still catching on to the fashion thing. Macy's is a sad department store, and Walnut Street, supposedly our fanciest offering, is still offering Ann Taylor Loft and other duds. But you know what? Screw it. If you really want a day of big-name shopping (or an Apple store), drive out to the King of Prussia Mall. For the funky, the used, or (fine, if you really want 'em) a $200 pair of jeans, read on!

Beauty

For sophisticates whose hair is of the utmost importance, **Giovanni & Pileggi (Map 2)** will lovingly apply their brand of follicle therapy and **Liquid (Map 2)**, also quite chic, will turn you out perfect. For tired and aching muscles, make an appointment at the **Massage Arts Center of Philadelphia (Map 3)**, where you can get a sumner massage for super-cheap. Crave an edgy 'do from a man who makes sculptures out of human hair? Check out **Julius Scissor (Map 1)**.

Clothing

Always start with the shoes! **Head Start Shoes (Map 2)** is hands and feet down the most deliriously euro-hip place for women's shoes—starting at 200 bucks, it's ok if you just want to look . . . or try on . . . or . . . Men and women alike must see **Daffy's (Map 2)** assorted suedes and snake skins, discounted downwards. Speaking of, Daffy's is the place in general for fine Italian threads and a multitudinous miscellany of what might best be described as clothing concoctions. **Vagabond (Map 4)** sells elegantly artsy, flowing designs for women. **Mathew Izzo (Map 3)**, good for men and women, sells urban clothing with a dash of refinement. For the men folk only, if **Boyd's (Map 2)** is good enough for NBA 'ballers, it's probably okay for you too. Sports fan who has (nearly) everything? **Mitchell & Ness (Map 3)** sells the unique throwback jerseys that can't be out of style. For a slightly (and just slightly) cheaper take on **Urban Outfitters (Maps 2, 14)**, go by **Retrospect (Map 8)** on South Street for a chance to buy the Salvation Army's best, plucked from those racks and brought to you here. Oh, and if you crave the skintight, designed-by-a-perv look, don't worry: we have a couple of **American Apparels (Map 14 & 2)** too.

Home and Gift

For the kitchen, **Fante's (Map 8)** offers every conceivable kind of appliance, device, and gadget, and **Philadelphia Bar & Restaurant Supply (Map 8)** can get you all your pots, pans, and glasses for cheap. If you're a student trying to fill an empty apartment, fine deals can be had at **Uhuru (Map 3)**, although one should be prepared for Free Mumia indoctrination before, during, and after all purchases. For people who are the opposite of Uhuru shoppers, there's the ironically named **Design Within Reach (Map 2)**. The delight-ful **PHAG (Map 3)** sells hip vinyl furniture, kooky martini glasses, and more. Owing to the owner's pitch-perfect taste, it's impossible to go wrong at **Open House (Map 3)**, which sells furniture that swerves at you, geometric lamps, clever espresso cups, and even body products with subtle, ever-so-coy scents. If you don't like anything here, it means you should go to Pottery Barn and buy a beige lump to hide under (you freak). If you're not quite sure what you're looking for, check out the handmade grab-bag known as **Art Star (Map 19)**, where you can feel good for supporting independent artists. Finally, after a long day of hitting the pavement, stop by the **Random Tea Room (Map 19)** and score a bag of something entirely soothing.

Accessories

Chunky is in, and **De Village (Map 3)** in Reading Terminal Market sells some pretty heavy pieces—wood, gems, or shells, there's something big and bold to be found here. Another notable place to pick up chunk is at the **Philadelphia Flea Market** (various locations), which comes around in the spring, summer, and fall months, and where vendors display box after box of the stuff. We'd talk about diamonds but we don't want to. Your status quo, status-driven engagement is not our problem.

Walnut Street (Map 2)

Shopping is a dangerous addiction for some. When you don't have money to make a purchase, that **Coach** print can haunt you, redundantly, in your dreams. Sometimes you just need a new necklace to make it through the day. The businesses on Walnut Street understand. They know you'll drop your last dime at **Urban Outfitters** or, for a sexy breed of biz-casual, at **Zara**—even if that means you have to eat Easy Mac every day for a week. **H&M** has most of us addicted—but if you're repulsed by cheap fashion, at least take advantage of the freon dumping zone out front during a hot day. Anthropologie, for the mature outfit-wearer, resides in a building that outshines the clothes. It's always amusing when a t-shirt costs $200, which is where **Ubiq**, quite unabashedly, pops in its ugly, rave-chic head. **Knit Wit and Danielle Scott** give rise to original design amidst the branding madness that, at least on this stretch of golden road, rules.

Mall

Yep, singular. There's only one mall in the heart of the city—**The Gallery at Market East (Map 3)**. Chaotic, crowded, kids screaming on the escalators, and teenagers ruefully sucking lollipops, Market East has always seemed reminiscent of that scene in the educational film about Free Market Capitalism, shot in the eighties, that you watched in Applied Economics class. This "bustling economy" has got the usual roundup of stores like **Victoria's Secret, Gap, Sunglass Hut,** and **Old Navy**, where consumers can choose at their leisure what they most totally need to have based on, of course, the laws of supply and demand. It also has the conven-ience of being a convergence of all main bus and train lines, not to mention being nice and close to the Greyhound Bus Terminal (If ever there was a sign of swank . . .).

Department Store

Macy's (Map 3), our only department store unless you count K-Mart...exists. Its window displays are more depressing than seeing somebody's run-over cat in the street and they haven't come home yet and they're about to find out. Or like Russian orphans. Sad, sad mannequins. So sad.

Vintage/Resale

You can deck yourself in Versace circa 1992 or dig for even earlier finds at stores like **Sophisticated Seconds (Map 2)**, and snag some one-of-a-kind furniture for your digs at **Uhuru (Map 3)**. **Retrospect (Map 8)** gets a bad rap for marking up cool stuff they found at the Salvation Army by about 1000%—but, just like on the playground, rules are rules, and they found it first!

Electronics

If you're the next Bill Gates-in-training, head over to **Bundy (Map 2)** or **Springboard Media (Map 1)** to fuel your PC needs. The closest Apple stores are in the King of Prussia Mall and the Cherry Hill Mall. Approach both locations with caution.

Music

Whether you're a Butch Walker fan or a Lady Gaga junkie, **Sound of Market Street (Map 3)** has the biggest selection since Tower Records went out of business.. The staff is incredibly knowledgeable and helpful at **AKA Music (Map 4)**, and can turn you on to underground artists. You must be in-the-know to graze at **Repo (Map 8)**. Nearby **Philadelphia Record Exchange (Map 8)** and **Revelations (Map 8)** are also well-worth a browse..

Map 1 · Center City West

Bilt Well Furniture Showroom	2317 Chestnut St	215-568-4600	You hope there merchendize is beter then there speling.
Rejuvalux Body Klinic Day Spa	2012 Walnut St	215-563-8888	Enjoy all their various transdermal services.
Classical Guitar Store	2038 Sansom St	215-567-2972	Dude, where do you keep your Strats?
Dahlia	2003 Walnut St	215-568-6878	Unique jewelry pieces in a refreshingly Israeli atmosphere.
Dollar General	520 S 23rd St	215-732-3079	Save Time. Save Money.
Home Sweet Homebrew	2008 Sansom St	215-569-9469	Friendly folks & brew supplies galore.
Julius Scissor	2045 Locust St	215-567-7222	A hair artiste, with various hair-crafted sculptures on display.
Long In The Tooth	2027 Sansom St	215-569-1994	Big space selling cds, records, and movies into late-nite when you're drunk and ready.
Pleasure Chest	2039 Walnut St	215-561-7480	Honey, where are my dang nipple clips?
Salvation Army Family Store	2140 Market St	215-561-0178	One of many. Deals, deals and crap.
Springboard Media	2212 Walnut St	215-988-7777	Best Mac store in the city.
Trader Joes	2121 Market St	215-569-9282	It's not just for cheap yuppies anymore.
Wonderland	2037 Walnut St	215-561-1071	Pipes, bongs, hookahs—strangely, all just for tobacco!

Map 2 · Rittenhouse / Logan Circle

Adresse	1706 Locust St	215-985-3161	You know you can't afford it if they only have three items for sale.
AIA Bookstore & Design Center	117 S 17th St	215-569-3188	Architectural specialists have lots of amazing design books and portfolios.
Anthropologie	1801 Walnut St	215-568-2114	UO-owned, but this one's for the ladies and femmes.
Apple Store	1607 Walnut St	215-861-6400	Finally, our very own bar of geniuses.
Barnes & Noble	1805 Walnut St	215-665-0716	Ho-hum, just another behemoth of a bookstore with all the usual trimmings.
Benjamin Lovell Shoes	119 S 18th St	215-564-4655	Tasteful Euro-wear with a conservative bent.

Boyd's	1818 Chestnut St	215-564-9000	Where visiting NBA players score sweet suits.
Buffalo Exchange	1713 Chestnut St	215-557-9850	On a good day, some great finds.
Bundy	1809 Chestnut St	215-567-2500	Mac specialists have somewhat limited selection but solid service.
City Sports	1608 Walnut St	215-985-5860	Full-service from sneaks to parkas.
Coach	1703 Walnut St	215-564-4558	I surrender, here's the deed to my house.
Daffy's	1700 Chestnut St	215-963-9996	Either you'll find a Versace shirt for $8 or nothing at all.
David Michie Violins	1714 Locust St	215-545-5006	Exquisite, tuneful, and strung with cat guts.
Design Within Reach	1710 Walnut St	215-735-3195	Put an Eileen Gray table next to a Wassily chair—voila!
Frankinstein Bike Worx	1529 Spruce St	215-893-0415	If you're really lucky, one of the Dead Milkmen will stop by.
Giovanni & Pileggi	256 S 16th St	215-568-3040	Fancy-pants folks love to have their follicle paradigm shifts here.
Greenhouse Market	1324 Chestnut St	215-545-2306	Ultra-fresh salad bar.
H&M	1725 Walnut St	215-563-2221	Urban Outfitters is shaking in its purple cowboy boots.
Halloween	1329 Pine St	215-732-7711	Gothic jewelry and really tasteful.
Head Start Shoes	126 S 17th St	215-567-3247	If you can't afford anything, treat it like a musuem of hip.
International Salon	1714 Sansom St	215-563-1141	Smileless Slavs give good, cheap spa treatments.
Jacob's Music	1718 Chestnut St	215-568-7800	If you ask, they'll play you "Piano Man" on any of their models. Please don't ask.
Jos. A. Bank Clothiers	1650 Market St	215-563-5990	High-end Tory-wear for today's neoconservatives.
Joseph Fox Bookshop	1724 Sansom St	215-563-4184	Strong-minded independent.
Knit Wit	1718 Walnut St	215-564-4760	Despite the awful pun, an evening wear store for 'mature' ladies.
Liquid Hair Salon	112 S 18th St	215-564-6410	Expect perfection from this friendly yet chic salon.
Loop	1914 South St	215-893-9939	Gorgeous, high-end yarns for when AC Moore won't do.
Lucky Brand Jeans	1634 Walnut St	215-732-8934	When $150 feels about right for a pair of miner-pants.
Maron Chocolates	1734 Chestnut St	215-988-9992	Candy, ice cream, chocolate—what's not to love?
Motherhood Maternity	1615 Walnut St	215-567-1425	Casual, comfy clothes for moms-to-be.
Nicole Miller	200 S Broad St	215-546-5007	Manayunk's own designer gone big-time.
OMOI	1608 Pine St	215-545-0963	Coolness from Japan and beyond.
Pearl of the East	1720 Chestnut St	215-563-1563	Asian-themed furnishings; plenty of kimonos.
Ritz Camera	1330 Walnut St	215-563-8803	Practical camera chainstore.
Scoop DeVille	3417 Spruce St	215-222-3417	Tasty, awe-inspiring concoctions.
Sophisticated Seconds	2019 Sansom St	215-561-6740	Upscale consignmentorium also has wedding dresses.
Spool	1912 South St	215-545-0755	Designer fabrics for the young and fashion-minded, plus classses.
Sue's Produce Market	114 S 18th St	215-241-0102	Fruits and veggies.
TLA Movies	1520 Locust St	215-735-7887	Several locations of city's fave DVD rentals—auteur/foreign heaven.
UBIQ	1509 Walnut St	215-988-0194	Colorful whimsy that costs.
Urban Outfitters	1627 Walnut St	215-564-2313	Started right here and still too flashy and over-priced.
Vigant Inc	200 S Broad St	215-735-5057	More cow-based products than a butcher shop.
VIP Food & Produce	1314 Walnut St	215-735-1977	Pretty sweet grocery spot. Lots of unique choices.
Zara	1715 Walnut St	215-557-0911	Business-casual. Pretty... pretty... pretty... expensive!

Map 3 • Center City East

Afficial	658 South St	215-627-3001	Hard-to-find sneakers.
After Hours Formalwear	1205 Walnut St	215-923-1130	Tuxes from Dick Cheney to Liberace.
AIA Bookstore & Design Center	1218 Arch St	215-569-3188	Architectural specialists have lots of amazing design books and portfolios.
Aldo Liquidation	901 Market St	215-625-9854	Reasonably priced footwear haven for both genders.
Armand Records	1108 Chestnut St	215-592-7973	Hip-hop DJs do all their significant shopping here.
Baum's	106 S 11th St	215-923-2244	Selling Philly dancers tutus and tapshoes for over a century.
Beaux Arts Video	1000 Spruce St	215-923-1714	Small, independent video rental store has helpful staff and solid picks.
Bike Line	1028 Arch St	215-923-1310	Decent chain of stores offering fair service.
Black Tie Formal Attire	1120 Walnut St	215-925-4404	Family-owned shop rents styles ranging from princely to Prince. Great service.
Bridals by Danielle	203 S 13th St	215-670-9500	Looking good on the big day ain't cheap.
Burlington Coat Factory	1001 Market St	215-627-6933	Seven hundred million coats and no one to help you.
Chartreuse	1200 Spruce St	215-545-7111	Wanna be mom's favorite child? Shop for her here!
Children's Place	Market St & 9th St	215-627-8187	From infants to adolescents, plus kid beauty products.
Claire's Boutique	Market St & 9th St	215-592-8507	Accessorize, accessorize, accessorize. Quite cheaply.
DeCarlo Salon	1210 Sansom St	215-923-5806	Monster assortment of hair products, including 'poos, gels and sprays.
De Village in Reading Terminal	12th St & Arch St	215-923-9860	African jewelry, hippo-sized.
Downtown Cheese	N 12th St & Arch St	215-351-7412	We say "Downtown", you say "Cheese"! Downtown Cheese! Downtown Cheese!
Dudes Boutique	646 South St	215-928-0661	Suede and leather shoes for the special dude in your life.
Duross & Langel	117 S 13th St	215-592-7627	Naked, Mojitos and Vegan...and we're talking about SOAPS.

(247)

Map 3 • Center City East—*continued*

Giovanni's Room	345 S 12th St	215-923-2960	Gay/lesbian themed tomes, plus visiting writers and readings.
Greene Street Consignment Shop	700 South St	215-733-9261	Good deals on good clothes.
Grocery 13 Inc.	105 S 13th St	215-922-5252	Premade gourmet meals for the luxurious and the lazy.
I Goldburg Army & Navy	1300 Chestnut St	215-925-9393	Army/Navy surplus store with plenty of other goodies.
M Finkel and Daughter	936 Pine St	215-627-7797	Daughter is always there to help you out.
Macy's	1300 Market St	215-241-9000	Apparently, all that 6th borough hype worked. Look what we got!
Massage Arts Center of Philadelphia	519 S 4th St	267-321-0200	Massages and a massage school. Revitalizing all around.
Mitchell & Ness	1318 Chestnut St	267-765-0613	Where the whole retro-Jersey craze started.
Modern Eye	145 S 13th St	215-922-3300	Insane collection of eclectic, fashionable, and smart-looking frames.
Old Navy	1001 Market St	215-413-7012	Fashion for overweight families, and more.
Old Nelson Food Company	701 Chestnut St	215-627-7090	Sandwiches and snacks not for tourists.
Open House	107 S 13th St	215-922-1415	Good taste spreads thick on minamilistic, funky, and modern home furnishings.
PHAG	1225 Walnut St	215-627-0461	Bi-level, gay kitsch.
R. E. Load Bags	608 N 2nd St	215-922-2018	Custom designed messenger bags.
Rustic Music	333 S 13th St	215-732-7805	Sweet little guitar shop also has a collection of CDs and vinyl.
Sailor Jerry	116 S 13th St	215-531-6380	Old-school tattooed t-shirts.
Septa Transit Store	1234 Market St	215-580-7168	Transit junkie heaven.
Sound of Market Street	15 S 11th St	215-925-3150	The largest independent music store in the city. Huge amounts of jazz.
Spruce Street Video	252 S 12th St	215-985-2955	The largest selection of gay porn in the country.
Uhuru Furniture & Collectibles	1220 Spruce St	215-546-9616	Politically-minded used furniture store.
Wawa Food Market	1038 Arch St	215-627-4121	Common coffee stop-along for the Chinatown bus travelers.
Wawa Food Market	912 Walnut St	215-923-1404	A godsend for 3 am munchies.

Map 4 • Old City / Society Hill

AKA Music	27 N 2nd St	215-922-3855	A music buff's dream: hard-to-find CDs and LPs.
Brave New World Comics	45 N 2nd St	215-925-6525	Secret den of comictude.
Cappelli Hobbies	313 Market St	215-629-1757	Scale models of all kinds of crap: check out the WWI bombers.
Charlie's Jeans	233 Market St	215-627-3390	If you have to ask the price, set your face on stun.
Friedman Umbrellas	20 S 3rd St	215-922-4877	Big selection and ingratiating sales force.
Gourmet of Olde City	26 N 3rd St	215-627-8890	Bricks'o chocolate.
Matthew Izzo	151 N 3rd St	215-829-0606	Urban splendor, in gift, home, or clothing form.
Nike Samsun	324 South St	215-829-1160	Affordable! Sneakers!
Olde City Tattoo	44 S 2nd St	215-627-6271	Display all of your life's major accomplishments.
The Papery Of Philadelphia	57 N 3rd St	215-922-1500	Super cute.
Pierre's Costumes	211 N 3rd St	215-925-7121	Well over 100,000 costumes.
Red Red Red Hair Salon	222 Church St	215-923-4042	Colorings and much teasing.
Sugarcube	124 N 3rd St	215-238-0805	Vintage and contemporary fashions.
Tartes	212 Arch St	215-625-2510	Tartes cupcakes bring all the old, fur-swathed society ladies to the yard.
Topstitch Boutique	54 N 3rd St	215-238-8877	The buzz is rampant. Check it out for yourself, up on the 2nd floor.
Triune	325 Cherry St	215-627-6279	From yoga to chiropractors, all things posturing.
Vagabond	37 N 3rd St	267-671-0737	Seasonal fashions and original designs.
Viv Pickle	21 N 3rd St	215-922-5904	Pickle party in handbag.
Wawa Food Market	518 S 2nd St	215-629-1050	A godsend for 3 am munchies.
Zeke's Fifth Street Deli Bakery	318 S 5th St	215-627-1001	Mmmm...bacon, ham, tomato and grilled cheese sandwiches.

Map 6 • Graduate Hospital / Gray's Ferry

Bicycle Therapy	2211 South St	215-735-7849	The best bike-repair joint in the city.

Map 7 • Southwark West

Anvil Iron Works	1022 Washington Ave	215-468-8300	Gates, grates and everything in between!
Harry's Occult Shop	1238 South St	215-735-8262	Sorry black arts enthusiasts—White Magic only at Harry's.

Map 8 • Bella Vista / Queen Village

Adidas	436 South St	267-514-1952	For meatheads and fashionistas alike.
Anastacia's Antiques	617 Bainbridge St	215-928-9111	Yeah, we bought an antique speculum here; wanna fight about it?

Atomic City Comics	642 South St	215-625-9613	Comics, Japanese animation, cult films and beyond.
Bella Boutique	527 S 4th St	215-923-8174	Pre-worn designer wear ain't cheap, apparently.
Center City Pretzel Co	816 Washington Ave	215-463-5664	Opens at midnight. Gourmet and cheap.
Cohen Hardware	615 E Passyunk Ave	215-922-3493	Friendly, slightly odd staff make it worthwhile.
Crash Bang Boom	528 S 4th St	215-928-1123	Where all today's punks score combat boots and eye shadow. Formerly Zipperhead.
EB Games	505 South St	215-625-0795	Everything from Scrabble to GTA.
Essene	719 S 4th St	215-922-1146	Organic, vegan market and cafeteria. Plus lots of vitamins.
Fante's Kitchen Wares Shop	1006 S 9th St	215-922-5557	Exhaustive inventory of all kitchen goodies.
Garland of Letters	527 South St	215-923-5946	New-age books, trinkets, and many, many types of candles.
Goldstein's Boy's & Men's Wear	811 S 6th St	215-468-0564	Italian imports since 1902. Loads of suspenders, too.
Hats in the Belfry	S 3rd St & South St	215-922-6770	Grab a cool Gandalf hat and be the envy of your D&D club.
Headhouse Books	619 S 2nd St	215-923-9525	An independent running on integrity fuel, not to mention huge, glossy gift books.
House of Moore	739 S 4th St	215-668-9694	Trust April for all your prom/med school formal/hot night out needs.
House of Tea	720 S 4th St	215-923-8327	Some varieties more expensive than good hashish.
Kroungold's Better Furniture	710 S 5th St	215-925-2483	No-pressure sales and a range of selection.
Masquerade	1100 S Columbus Ave	215-952-0980	Basically a Wal-Mart of costuming.
Maxie's Daughter	724 S 4th St	215-829-2226	The heart of fabric row.
Mostly Books	529 Bainbridge St	215-238-9838	Books, furniture, and "20th Century Artifacts."
Nocturnal Skateshop	610 S 3rd St	215-922-3177	X-Games street champ Kerry Getz is the owner.
PAT (Philadelphia AIDS Thrift)	514 Bainbridge St	215-922-3186	Buy vintage stuff, support a great cause.
Pearl of Africa Gates of Zion	624 South St	215-413-8995	Um, that is burning incense, right?
Philadelphia Bar & Restaurant Supply	629 E Passyunk Ave	215-925-7649	From non-stick ladles to sweet wine keys.
Philadelphia Eddie's Tattoo	621 S 4th St	215-922-7384	Ask for Tony.
Philadelphia Record Exchange	618 S 5th St	215-925-7892	Excellent jazz and rock stuff, plus tons of vinyl.
Repo Records	538 South St	215-627-3775	Joke: How many indie kids does it take to screw in a lightbulb? Answer: You don't know?
Retrospect	534 South St	267-671-0116	Clothes, knick-knacks and furniture—though handily cheap.
Rode'o Designs	721 S 4th St	215-625-9530	Frilly and whacked-out clothes for disturbed children.
South Street Antique Market	615 S 6th St	215-592-0256	Converted synagogue houses many treasures.
Triple Play Sporting Goods	827 S 4th St	215-627-4898	Customized fan-ware and lots of USA pride.
Via Bicycle	606 S 9th St	215-627-3370	Unpretentious and nothing fancy—but cheap.

Map 9 • Bella Vista / Queen Village

Indonesia Store	1701 S Bancroft St	215-755-3100	Indonesian food and more. Mmmm.
RKO Video & South Philly Comics	1621 Passyunk Ave	267-318-7855	Comic geeks love that it's open late.

Map 10 • Moyamensing / East Passyunk

Beautiful World Syndicate	1619 E Passyunk Ave	215-467-0401	Hit or miss record shop—give yourself plenty of time to rifle.
Fabulous Finds Boutique	1535 S Broad St	215-336-5226	From evening gowns to baby booties.
Interior Concepts Furniture	1701 E Passyunk Ave	215-468-6226	Leather furniture, beds, and salesmen.
Mia	1748 E Passyunk Ave	215-465-2913	Rodeo-Drive-style upscale boutique in South Philly.
Mike's Bikes	1901 S 13th St	215-334-9100	New bikes and repairs for all you bikers who've been doored.
Nice Things Handmade	1731 E Passyunk Ave	267-455-0256	The name says it. Handicrafts here!
Shoe Barrel	1812 E Passyunk Ave	215-755-0942	Affordable shoes for every occasion, not that you need an excuse.
St Jude Shop	1807 E Passyunk Ave	215-389-7694	Known for its religious artifacts.

Map 11 • South Philly East

Barry's Home Brew	101 Snyder Ave	215-755-4556	Instead of wasting money at the bar, waste it making your own booze.
Forman Mills	22 E Wolf St	215-389-5353	Lots of bargains, but be prepared to hunt for them.
Ikea	2206 S Columbus Blvd	215-551-4532	Have a handy friend or hammer ready.
Lowe's	2106 S Columbus Blvd	215-982-5391	Hardware for your inner construction worker.
Schafer's Brakes & Mufflers	1924 S Columbus Blvd	215-755-1270	Friendly service for sad cars.

Map 13 · West Philly

Donut Plus	4325 Chestnut St	215-222-0811	"Donut" miss it! See? See what we did there?
Eak Chuong Grocery	4421 Chestnut St	215-386-1254	For all your rice flour and black bean sauce needs.
The Fresh Grocer	4001 Walnut St	215-222-9200	Fresh? Yes. Overpriced? Also yes.
International Foods and Spices	4203 Walnut St	215-222-4480	Inidan-Pakistani grocery.
The Last Word Bookshop	220 S 40th S	215-386-7750	Good and funky selection of second hand books.
Makkah Market	4249 Walnut St	215-382-0909	Hot foods (falafel!!!) and awesome groceries.
The Marvelous	208 S 40th St	215-386-6110	CDs and comics: living together as god meant them to.
Metropolitan Bakery	4013 Walnut St	215-222-1492	The people who make bread for half the city.
The Natural Shoe Store Inc.	220 S 40th St	215-382-9899	Expansive array of shoes at disparate prices.
P&P Grocery	4307 Locust St	215-387-3509	Asian grocery! Always a pleasure.
The Second Mile Center Thrift Stores	214 S 45th St	215-662-1663	HUGE thrift store. Watch for occasional Saturday half-off sales.
Toviah Thrift Shop	4211 Chestnut St	215-382-7251	Come for the needles in the haystack of crap. Stay to talk to proprietor Larry.
Food Market	3744 Spruce St	215-387-0029	A godsend for 3 am munchies.

Map 14 · University City

American Apparel	3661 Walnut St	215-222-2091	Get the "crazy waif in a leotard-thong" look.
Eastern Mountain Sports	3401 Chestnut St	215-382-0930	Decent selection of camping gear, wait for the sales.
Philadelphia Runner	3621 Walnut St	215-662-5100	Everything you need to try and make running actually enjoyable.
Trophy Bikes	3131 Walnut St	215-222-2020	Best place in town for a folding bike.
Urban Outfitters	110 S 36th St	215-387-6990	Meeting ground of hipsters and UPenn students.
Wawa Food Market	3604 Chestnut St	215-222-6422	A godsend for 3 am munchies.

Map 15 · Strawberry Mansion

The Beehive	2319 Fairmount Ave	215-235-4483	Sweet little hair salon.
Wawa Food Market	2040 Hamilton St	215-988-0648	A godsend for 3 am munchies.

Map 17 · Fairmount

The Beehive	2323 Fairmount Ave	215-235-4483	Sweet little hair salon.
Bookhaven	2202 Fairmount Ave	215-235-3226	Haven of books.
JK Market	2001 Green St	215-236-2788	Nice little corner store.
Oliver's Antiques	2052 Fairmount Ave	215-232-8377	Antiques. Clothes. Nice owners.
Philly Flavors	2004 Fairmount Ave	215-232-7748	Small means huge.

Map 18 · Spring Garden / Francisville

Diving Bell Scuba Shop	681 N Broad St	215-763-6868	Just don't watch *Open Water* first.
Philadelphia Tire & Auto	545 N Broad St	215-829-1640	They don't rob you blind.

Map 19 · Northern Liberties

Almanac Market	900 N 4th St	215-625-6611	Buy fresh, buy local, buy here.
Art Star Gallery	623 N 2nd St	215-238-1557	Gallery and crafty boutique. Get your handmade here.
Brown Betty Dessert Boutique	1030 N 2nd St	215-629-0999	Desserts aren't just baked; theyre nurtured.
City Planter	814 N 4th St	215-627-6169	Garden pots (planters), but no plants. But what a collection it is!
Delicious Boutique & & Corseterie	1040 N American St #901	215-413-0375	Because it's always time for a $500 corset.
Euphoria	1001 N 2nd St	215-238-9209	Smoothies.
The Foodery	837 N 2nd St	215-238-6077	Mix and match your brewskis.
Hanusey Music & Gifts	244 W Girard Ave	215-627-3093	For all of your Ukrainian egg-decorating needs.
Jerusalem	115 W Girard Ave	215-634-1991	Middle Eastern culinary delights.
The Little Candy Shoppe	1030 N American St	215-667-8567	Hundreds of delicious ways to rot your teeth.
Northern Liberties Mailbox Store	630 N 3rd St	215-627-6215	Cute mail supplies and all sorts of shipping.
Palm Tree Market	717 N 2nd St	215-925-4707	Upscale corner store for when you're out of fresh mozzarella.
Quince Fine Foods	209 W Girard Ave	215-232-3425	Pair your cave aged gouda with a 40 from across the street.
Random Tea Room	713 N 4th St	267-639-2442	Delicious tea and delicious wifi.
Reverie	205 W Girard Ave	215-769-2302	Annoying hours but great clothes and homewares.
Spring Garden Market	400 Spring Garden St	215-928-1288	New market with fruits, fish and all things fresh.

Tequila Sunrise Records	525 W Girard Ave	212-965-9616	Highly curated, mostly vinyl, also a label; awesome.
Trax Foods	1204 N Front St	215-423-5801	Deli and small grocery in an area that needed it.
Very Bad Horse	1050 N Hancock St	267-455-0449	Where Steven Tyler would shop if he were 22 and cool.

Map 20 · Fishtown / Port Richmond

Circle Thrift	2007 Frankford Ave	215-423-1222	Thrift store with weird church space upstairs.
DiPinto Guitars	407 E Girard Ave	215-427-7805	Guitars for real.
Dollar Plus Party Fair	2415 E Lehigh Ave	215-634-2760	Screw Dollar Tree.
Jay's Pedal Power	512 E Girard Ave # 12	215-425-5111	Strange bikes and regular bikes from a well-established shop.
Little Shop of Treasures	419 E Girard Ave	267-446-5574	Hooray for junk shops.
Scoops	812 E Thompson St	215-634-7629	Ice cream window with the works; namely, pizza nuggets and happy patrons.
Stocks Bakery	2614 E Lehigh Ave	215-634-7344	Port Richmond's pride rocks the best poundcake around.
Thrift Fair	2403 Aramingo Ave	215-426-5204	Buy stuff that belonged to people who are now dead.
Thriftway	2497 Aramingo Ave	215-425-5690	They don't care about data. And that's how it should be.

Map 21 · Roxborough / Manayunk

Main St Music	4444 Main St	215-487-7732	Indy music store.
Pompanoosuc Mills	4120 Main St	215-508-3263	Great high-end furniture.
Potery Barn	4230 Main St	215-508-6778	Pottery Barn... What can you say.
Restoration Hardware	4130 Main St	215-930-0330	See Pottery Barn.
VAMP Consignment	4231 Main St	215-487-2340	Boutique fashion for ladies that you can actually afford.
Worn Yesterday	4235 Main St	215-482-3316	Your youngsters will be natty with the help of this Manayunk staple.

Map 25 · Germantown North

Big Blue Marble Bookstore	551 Carpenter Ln	215-844-1870	An independent with lots of events for progressive parents and their wannabe kids.
Joa Mart	361 W Hortter St	215-438-2802	Awesome small grocery.
Weaver's Way Co-op	559 Carpenter Ln	215-843-2350	Become a member and save money on high quality food.

Map 27 · Chestnut Hill

Cake	184 E Evergreen Ave	215-247-6887	Sweets in a former greenhouse.
Chestnut Hill Cheese Shop	8509 Germantown Ave	888-343-3327	Family-owned cheese bazaar.
Hideaway Music	8612 Germantown Ave	215-248-4434	Nice collection of high quality vinyl and posters.
Kitchen Kapers	8530 Germantown Ave	215-242-2866	Cove of all things culinary.
Mango	8622 Germantown Ave	215-248-9299	Hempy clothing, endless incense, and crafty gifts.

Northeast Philly

Contempo Cuts	2857 Holme Ave	215-676-1900	An all in one salon, spa, hair, and nail boutique.
Dutch Country Farmers' Market	2031 Cottman Ave	215-745-6008	Vendors selling pretzels, produce, and rotisserie meats year round.
Harry's Natural Food Store	1805 Cottman Ave	215-742-3807	After 25 years, Harry still sells herbs, vitamins, and specialty natural foods.
International Coins Unlimited	1825 Cottman Ave	215-745-4900	Rare and new coins for sale or trade.
Lipkin's Bakery	8013 Castor Ave	215-722-2848	Excellent rye, amazing rugalach.
Roosevelt Mall	2311 Cottman Ave	215-331-2000	A shopping bonanza.
Philadelphia Flea Market	Various Locations	215-625-3532	Unimaginable loads of not-quite junk, mixed in with fabulous treasure. Call for current location.

With each year, Philly's burgeoning art scene continues to push boundaries and make a name for itself. Between long-time traditional artists and recent graduates from the city's three highly-regarded art schools, there's literally something for everyone.

A great way to become acquainted with some of the galleries, at least in Old City, is to regularly attend Philly's First Friday gatherings. On the first Friday of each month, the OC galleries stay open late, launch lots of new exhibits, and pander to guests with cheap wine and bites to eat. Check out the works at **Pentimenti (Map 4)**, **Artists' House (Map 4)**, **Hot Soup (Map 4)**. For performance space as well as fine arts exhibits, **Painted Bride (Map 4)** has long been a Philly stalwart. In May and June, local arts students hold their senior shows in

many galleries, which results in quite a few surprisingly professional, avant-garde works. And for the younger, DIY set, plenty of starving artists without access to studios make and sell their art right on the sidewalks in front of the galleries. In the warmer weather, the scene becomes a veritable open-air market, complete with live music and impromptu dancing.

There are of couse also plenty of worthwhile galleries outside of the Old City boundaries. Check out **Space 1026 (Map 3)**, the **Fabric Workshop and Museum (Map 3)**, the **Highwire Gallery (Map 3)** or the **Esther M. Klein Art Gallery (Map 14)**. If you have money to burn for art, you can hit the big leagues at **Locks (Map 4)** or, for considerably less, purchase a world-class piece from **The Clay Studio (Map 4)**.

Map 1 · Center City West

Dolan/Maxwell	2046 Rittenhouse Sq	215-732-7787
The Galleries at Moore College of Art & Design	N 20th St & Benjamin Franklin Pkwy	215-965-4045
Gallery 339	339 S 21st St	215-731-1530
Sande Webster	2006 Walnut St	215-636-9003

Map 2 · Rittenhouse / Logan Circle

The Center for Emerging Visual Artists	237 S 18th St	215-546-7775
Calderwood Gallery	1622 Spruce St	215-546-5357
Fleisher/Ollman Gallery	1616 Walnut St	215-545-7562
Gross McCleaf	127 S 16th St	215-665-8138
Highwire Gallery	1315 Cherry St	215-829-1255
Makler Gallery	225 S 18th St	215-735-2540
Mangel Gallery	1714 Rittenhouse Sq	215-545-4343
Newman Galleries	1625 Walnut St	215-563-1779
Pennsylvania Academy of the Fine Arts	118 N Broad St	215-972-7600
Philadelphia Art Alliance	251 S 18th St	215-545-4302
The Print Center	1614 Latimer St	215-735-6090
Rosenwald-Wolf Gallery	333 S Broad St	215-717-6480
Schmidt/Dean Gallery	1710 Sansom St	215-569-9433
Schwarz Gallery	1806 Chestnut St	215-563-4887

Map 3 · Center City East

African American Museum in Philadelphia	701 Arch St	215-574-0380 ext. 235
Bridgette Mayer Gallery	709 Walnut St	215-413-8893
The Fabric Workshop and Museum	1222 Arch St	215-568-1111
Gallery Space 1026	1026 Arch St	215-574-7630
M Finkel and Daughter	936 Pine St	215-627-7797
The Philadelphia Sketch Club	235 S Camac St	215-545-9298
Seraphin Gallery	1108 Pine St	215-923-7000
Vox Populi	319 N 11th St	215-238-1236

Map 4 · Old City / Society Hill

3rd Street Gallery	58 N 2nd St	215-625-0993
Artists' House	57 N 2nd St	215-923-8440
ArtJaz	53 N 2nd St	215-922-4800
The Clay Studio	139 N 2nd St	215-925-3453
FAN Gallery	221 Arch St	215-922-5155
The FUEL Collection	249 Arch St	215-592-8400
Gallery Joe	302 Arch St	215-922-7752
Hot Soup	26 S Strawberry St	215-922-2232
Indigo	151 N 3rd St	215-922-4041
The Knapp Gallery	162 N 3rd St	267-455-0279
Larry Becker	43 N 2nd St	215-925-5389
Locks Gallery	600 Washington Sq S	215-629-1000
Muse Gallery	52 N 2nd St	215-627-5310
Painted Bride	230 Vine St	215-925-9914
Peng Gallery	35 S 3rd St	215-280-5753
Pentimenti	145 N 2nd St	215-625-9990
Qbix Art Gallery	211 Arch St	215-625-2521
Rodger LaPelle Galleries	122 N 3rd St	215-592-0232

Rosenfeld Gallery	113 Arch St	215-922-1376
Snyderman-Works Gallery	303 Cherry St	215-238-9576
Wexler Gallery	201 N 3rd St	215-923-7030
Wood Turning Center	501 Vine St	215-923-8000

Map 7 · Southwark West

Mew Gallery	906 Christian St	215-625-2424

Map 8 · Bella Vista / Queen Village

Da Vinci Art Alliance	704 Catharine St	215-829-0466
Eye's Gallery	402 South St	215-925-0193
Fleisher Art Memorial	719 Catharine St	215-922-3456 ext. 318
SoulPurl 77	1138 S 9th St	215-528-1367

Map 14 · University City

Arthur Ross Gallery/ University of Pennsylvania	220 S 34th St	215-898-2083
Esther M Klein Art Gallery	3701 Market St	215-966-6188
Institute of Contemporary Art	118 S 36th St	215-898-7108

Map 17 · Fairmount

Philadelphia Museum of Art	2600 Benjamin Franklin Pkwy	215-763-8100
Rodin Museum	N 22nd St & Benjamin Franklin Pkwy	215-568-6026

Map 18 · Spring Garden / Francisville

Cerulean Arts	1355 Ridge Ave	267-514-8647
Khmer Art Gallery	319 N 11th St	215-922-5600

Map 19 · Northern Liberties

Art Star Gallery	623 N 2nd St	215-238-1557
Projects Gallery	629 N 2nd St	267-303-9652
Rebekah Templeton Contemporary Art	173 W Girard Ave	267-519-3884
Tower Gallery	969 N 2nd St	215-253-9874

Map 20 · Fishtown / Port Richmond

Highwire Gallery	2040 Frankford Ave	215-426-2685

Map 27 · Chestnut Hill

The Carol Schwartz Gallery	101 Bethlehem Pike	215-242-4510
JMS Gallery	8236 Germantown Ave	215-248-4649
Woodmere Art Musuem	9201 Germantown Ave	215-247-0476

General Information

NFT Map: 2
Address: 1729 Mt Vernon St
                  Philadelphia, PA 19130
Phone: 215-685-0750
Website: www.muralarts.org

Overview

If graffiti-covered buildings and dreary gray walls can look ominous and depressing on the most vibrant blocks, one can only imagine their effect on the psyche of poverty-stricken neighborhoods. But like concealer that hides facial blemishes, the Mural Arts Program covers up blights on the cityscape; more than 2,400 indoor and outdoor murals have been commissioned across the city since 1984. Philadelphia has quickly become the mural capital of the country, and the Mural Arts Program continues to commission up to 100 murals each year in neighborhoods that request their help.

This same public art program now offers bi-weekly trolley tours that guide participants to some of the more obscure mural sites. Often led by mural artists, the tours explore different neighborhoods each week and provide a "behind-the-scenes" look at the making of the intricate paintings.

There's also a free Mural Arts Program map with a walking route and a driving route that you can follow in your own time at your own pace. The walking tour is approximately 3.3 miles long and takes at least an hour and a half to complete. The driving tour also takes about an hour and a half and covers 10.5 miles of territory. Pick up a map at the Independence Visitor Center on 6th and Market Streets.

Regular Tours

Weekly tours (Wednesdays, Saturdays, and Sundays) depart from the Market Visitor Center on the corner of 6th and Market Streets at 11 am from April to October on Saturdays, and May to October on Wednesdays. Tour tickets are $25 for adults, $23 for seniors 65 and older, $15 for children 3–10, and free for children under 2.

1st Sat and Wed of each month: Center City
2nd Sat and Wed of each month: North Philly
3rd Sat and Wed of each month: South Philly
4th Sat and Wed of each month: West Philly
If there is a 5th Sat or Wed, the tour features Broad Street highlights.

Murals and Meals

"Murals and Meals" is a combined tour/restaurant program that couples mural-viewing with neighborhood dining, so you can chomp down on a greasy cheesesteak from Pat's and/or Geno's in South Philly while gazing at the mural of the infamous Italian mayor Frank Rizzo. You'll definitely need to make reservations (215-685-0754), as tours are limited to just 35 people per trip. Tours are held on different Saturdays and Sundays each month, so check the website for schedules and pricing.

Winter Tours

There are no regularly scheduled winter tours, but the Mural Arts program does offer specific programs and lectures between October and April. Check the website for events.

A little-known fact about Philadelphia: it has a pretty vibrant theater community. Sure, you don't think of us in the same league as Chicago or that rinky-dink city to our immediate north, but the truth is that theater is huge here. Every September, the **Philadelphia Live Arts Festival** and **Philly Fringe** (seperate, but concurrent) are occasions to sample the best of the local scene alongside emerging artists from around the world. You can always rely on the local **Pig Iron Theatre Company** (www.pigiron.org) for thought-provoking, original work. Ever since 2006's production of *Killer Joe*, **Theatre Exile (Map 4)** has been on a rampage, producing some of the best emotionally driven work around. **Philadelphia Theatre Company (Map 2)**, with its new move to the Avenue of the Arts, is set to rival the **Wilma (Map 2)** and the **Arden (Map 4)** in its caliber of performances, with, of course, its own wacky and sometimes lyrical flavoring.

History-lovers will know that the venerated **Walnut Street Theater (Map 3)** is, in fact, the oldest in the country. **The Arden Theater (Map 4)**, in Old City, backs local playwrights Michael Hollinger and Bruce Graham, puts on Sondheim for the subscription crowd, and offers some of the most fanciful children's theatre in town. For those who enjoy the puppetry arts, there's Spiral Q (Map 14), whose biggest annual event is a parade and pageant called Peoplehood. Broadway enthusiasts should head to the **Academy of Music (Map 2)**, which runs the Broadway at the Academy series, drawing touring shows of the hottest musicals to befall the great white way. The **Forrest (Map 3)** and the **Merriam (Map 2)** also provide plenty of high notes and shoe-tapping.

Philadelphia also has a small (but growing!) comedy scene. To start, we've got the stand-up clubs **Laff House (Map 8)** and **Helium (Map 1)**. Short form improv groups The N Crowd (www.phillyncrowd.com) and ComedySportz (www.comedysportzphilly.com) both perform weekly. The Philly Improv Theater puts on sketch and longform improv shows at **The Shubin (Map 8)**, and the **Walking Fish Theatre (Map 20)** and **Connie Ric Rac (Map 8)** both occasionally host comedy as well. The best place to find out about the local scene, though, is the Comic vs. Audience website at www.comicvsaudience.com.

Theater	Address	Phone	Map
941 Theater	941 N Front St	215-235-5603	19
Academy of Music	S Broad St & Locust St	215-893-1999	2
Arden Theater	40 N 2nd St	215-922-1122	4
Bistro Romano Mystery Dinner Theatre	120 Lombard St	215-925-8880	4
Forrest Theatre	1114 Walnut St	215-923-1515	3
The Gershman Y	401 S Broad St	215-446-3027	2
The Harold Prince Theatre	3680 Walnut St	215-898-6701	14
International House Theater	3701 Chestnut St	215-895-6546	14
Irvine Auditorium	3401 Spruce St	215-898-6701	14
Kimmel Center	260 S Broad St	215-790-5800	2
Merriam Theater	250 S Broad St	215-732-5997	2
Mum Puppettheatre	115 Arch St	215-925-7686	4
Philadelphia Arts Bank	601 S Broad St	215-545-0590	7
Philadelphia Theatre Company	480 S Broad St	215-985-0420	2
Plays & Players	1714 Delancey St	215-735-0630	2
Prince Music Theater	1412 Chestnut St	215-569-9700	2
Shubin Theatre	407 Bainbridge St	215-592-0119	8
Society Hill Playhouse	507 S 8th St	215-923-0210	3
Spiral Q Puppet Theater	3114 Spring Garden St	215-222-6979	14
Theater Catalyst	2030 Sansom St	215-563-4330	1
Theatre Exile	525 S 4th St	215-922-4462	4
Theatre of Living Art	334 South St	215-922-1011	8
UArts Drake Dance Theater	1512 Spruce St	215-717-6110	2
Walking Fish Theatre	2509 Frankford Ave	215-427-9255	20
Walnut Street Theatre	825 Walnut St	215-574-3550	3
The Wilma Theater	265 S Broad St	215-546-7824	2
The Zellerbach Theatre	3680 Walnut St	215-898-6701	14

General Information

NFT Map: 2
Address: 260 S Broad St
Philadelphia, PA 19102
Phone: 215-670-2321
Website: www.kimmelcenter.org
Tele-charge: 215-893-1999
Hours: Mon–Sun 10 am–6 pm, and later during evening performances.

Overview

The Kimmel Center occupies a full city block on Broad Street's southern side and is considered the crown jewel in the refurbished Avenue of the Arts. Fifteen million dollars of the $265 million project came from philanthropist Sidney Kimmel, the most generous individual donor. Playing home to the Philadelphia Orchestra, the Chamber Orchestra of Philadelphia, PHILADANCO, American Theater Arts for Youth, the Philadelphia Chamber Music Society, the Opera Company of Philadelphia, the Pennsylvania Ballet, and Philly Pops, the place oozes culture.

The 2,500-seat **Verizon Hall** was custom-built by acoustician Russell Johnson to enhance the orchestral sound of the Philadelphia Orchestra. The architectural design of the hall, with its wood paneling and curves, makes it look like the inside of a violin or cello. Despite pre-construction hoopla about the hall's planned world-class acoustics, classical music connoisseurs found the sound to be less than exceptional; the average, untrained concert-goer will find little to complain about, though. And in May 2006, the world's largest concert hall organ was unveiled, complete with 7000 pipes, the largest of which extend 32 feet high, enough to please both size and sound queens alike.

The smaller **Perelman Theater** has 650 seats and is used for chamber music and dance performances. The 2,893-seat **Philadelphia Academy of Music** is owned by The Philadelphia Orchestra Association, managed by the Kimmel Center, and hosts performances by the Opera Company of Philadelphia, the Pennsylvania Ballet, and Philly Pops with Peter Nero. The Academy of Music also runs the Broadway at the Academy series, which features touring Broadway shows like Wicked, The Lion King, and Spamalot, giving Philadelphians a little more breathing room in the pecking order battle with New York.

In addition to a pretty cool eatery and gift shop, the Kimmel Center has a gallery showcasing works from nearby Moore College of Art and Design.

How to Get There—Driving

From the north, follow Broad Street around City Hall and you'll find the Kimmel Center on the southwest corner of Broad and Spruce Streets. The Vine Street Expressway (I-676) will get you to Broad Street, and either I-95 or I-76 will get you to the Vine Street Expressway. From the Ben Franklin Bridge, take the first exit on 8th Street to Spruce Street and continue west to Broad Street. From the Walt Whitman Bridge, take the Broad Street exit and go north.

Parking

Entrance to the Kimmel Center parking garage is south of the Broad Street entrance to the center and can only be accessed by cars traveling south on Broad Street. Garage hours change seasonally, but regular hours are Monday through Friday 6 am until 10 pm, Friday from 7 am until midnight, and weekends the garage opens two hours prior to all matinees. If you're in by noon and out by 6 pm, you'll pay $21 on weekdays. If you arrive after noon, expect to pay $16, and if you arrive after 6 pm you'll have to pay $20. Weekends are a flat rate of $16. If that seems expensive, you can try your luck with street parking or check the rates of the local lots that surround the area.

How to Get There— Mass Transit

Take the subway. The Broad Street line's Walnut-Locust Station is two blocks from the Kimmel Center. Make a free transfer from the Market-Frankford line and the trolleys to the Broad Street Line at the 15th & Market stop. Regional Rail is also an option, with Suburban Station a 15-minute walk away from the Kimmel Center. The PHLASH makes a stop near the Kimmel Center and bus routes C, 27, 32, 12, 9, 21 and 42 all stop at the center.

How to Get Tickets

The only way to avoid the $5 service charge per ticket is by purchasing tickets at the Kimmel Center box office, which is open Monday-Sunday 10 am-6 pm. Tickets are also sold online at www.philorch.org or by phone on 215-893-1999. Tickets to Broadway at the Academy can be bought online at www.kimmelcenter.org/broadway or at the Academy of Music box office.

If you're on a limited budget, shoot for the $10 tickets to "Kimmel Center Presents" performances. The $10 tickets are up for grabs at the box office starting at 5:30 pm for evening performances and 11:30 am for matinees. "Citizens Bank Broadway" performances offer $25 tickets on a show-to-show basis. Tickets are available two hours before curtain time, must be paid for in cash, and are limited to one per person. Student rush tickets are also available with a student ID (also $10).

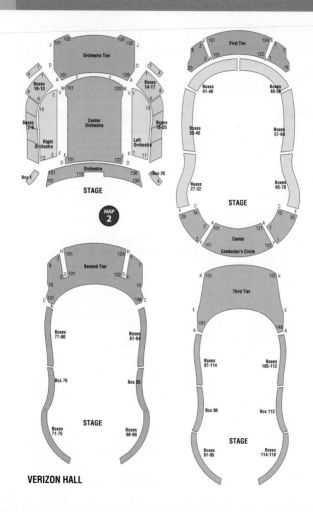

MAP 2

STAGE

STAGE

STAGE

STAGE

VERIZON HALL

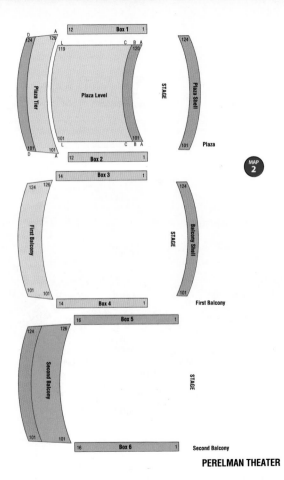

MAP
2

PERELMAN THEATER

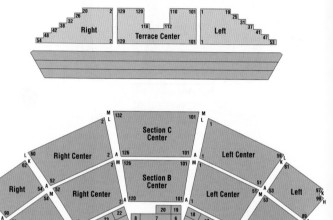

General Information

Address:	5201 Parkside Ave
	52nd St & Parkside Ave
	Philadelphia, PA 19131
Phone:	215-893-1999
Website:	www.manncenter.org

Overview

Every major city in America has a big outdoor concert space on its outskirts; the venerable Mann Center is Philly's. The venue is ideal for picnicking on the grass with family and friends while concerts serve as background music to more pertinent social activity. It's also a great place to watch the Fourth of July fireworks.

The Mann Center was originally built to serve as the summer home of the Philadelphia Orchestra. It now boasts an eclectic concert schedule including mainstream rock bands, operas, stand-up comedians, children's programs, and popular classical music selections, as well as the occasional Christian Night Out.

For most events, lawn tickets are cheap and still in sight of the stage, and pavilion tickets are affordable. All tickets are non-refundable. (meaning you'll be expected to plop down on the grass, rain or shine.) You're allowed to take lawn chairs and food with you (you can also buy food there) and, depending on the event, you can also take alcohol (make sure you check before your six-pack is confiscated at the door). The formerly-confusing eating facilities have undergone a reorientation of sorts, but we recommend booking in advance if you want a sit-down meal.

How to Get There—Driving

From Center City, take the Benjamin Franklin Parkway to the Art Museum Circle. Follow the signs to West River Drive. Once you're on West River Drive, turn left at the first traffic light (Sweet Briar Cut-Off). Turn right at the stop sign to Lansdowne Drive and proceed on Lansdowne to the parking areas.

Parking

Parking costs $7. Parking areas, as well as the center itself, open two hours before any event, so you can arrive early for dinner before the show.

How to Get There— Mass Transit

SEPTA bus lines 38, 40, and 43 deliver you within walking distance of the Mann Center. The Center City Loop Bus provides service between certain stops in the city and the Mann (one-way fare is $4.50). Check the bus schedule online on the Mann Center website: www.manncenter.org

How to Get Tickets

You can purchase tickets on the Mann Center website or on the phone, but be ready to pay a service charge of $5.50 per ticket and $3 per order. Tickets purchased online can only be picked up at the Mann Center box office will-call window at 52nd Street and Parkside Drive. To avoid service charges, you can buy tickets in person from the Mann Center box office, which is open Monday-Saturday from 10 am to 5 pm. You can also purchase tickets from the Center City box office, located at the Kimmel Center (Broad St & Spruce St), for a $2 service charge per order.

THERE'S NO FASTER WAY TO THE AIRPORT. THE R1 AIRPORT TRAIN.

SEPTA

215-580-7800 www.SEPTA.org

Street Index

Street / Range	Page	Grid
100 Steps	22	B2
N 2nd St		
(1-310)	4	A2
(311-1248)	19	A2/B2
S 2nd St		
(1-554)	4	A2/B2
(555-1612)	8	A2/B2
(1613-2699)	11	A1/B1
N 3rd St		
(1-307)	4	A1
(308-1299)	19	A1/B1
S 3rd St		
(1-558)	4	A1/B1
(559-1399)	8	A2/B2
(1900-2899)	11	A1/B1
(3100-3699)	12	B2
N 4th St		
(1-336)	4	A1
(321-1299)	19	A1/B1
S 4th St		
(1-558)	4	A1/B1
(559-1649)	8	A2/B2
(1650-2699)	11	A1/B1
N 4th Street Rear	4	A1
N 5th St		
(100-311)	4	A1
(312-1299)	19	A1/B1
S 5th St		
(2-570)	4	A1/B1
(571-1615)	8	A1/B1
(1616-2699)	10	A2/B2
N 6th St		
(1-308)	4	A1
(309-1299)	19	A1/B1
S 6th St		
(1-556)	4	A1/B1
(557-1606)	8	A1/B1
(1607-2699)	10	A2/B2
N 7th St		
(1-306)	3	A2
(307-1299)	19	A1/B1
S 7th St		
(1-560)	3	A2/B2
(561-1615)	8	A1/B1
(1615-2749)	10	A2/B2
(2750-3699)	12	A2/B2
N 8th St		
(1-308)	3	A2
(307-1299)	19	A1/B1
S 8th St		
(1-558)	3	A2/B2
(559-1606)	8	A1/B1
(1607-2710)	10	A2/B2
(2711-2899)	12	A2
N 9th St		
(1-307)	3	A2
(308-599)	18	B2
(800-1299)	19	A1
S 9th St		
(1-556)	3	A2/B2
(557-1606)	8	A1/B1
(1607-2749)	10	A2/B2
(2750-2899)	12	A1
N 10th St		
(1-308)	3	A1
(309-1299)	18	A2/B2
S 10th St		
(1-557)	3	A1/B1
(558-1606)	7	A2/B2
(1607-2749)	10	A1/B1
(2750-3599)	12	A1
N 11th St		
(1-306)	3	A1
(307-1249)	18	A2/B2
S 11th St		
(1-557)	3	A1/B1
(558-1615)	7	A2/B2
(1615-2710)	10	A1/B1
(2711-3999)	12	A1/B1
N 12th St		
(1-309)	3	A1
(310-1226)	18	A2/B2
S 12th St		
(1-554)	3	A1/B1
(555-1649)	7	A2/B2
(1650-2714)	10	A1/B1
(2715-2899)	12	A1
N 13th St		
(1-309)	3	A1
(310-1213)	18	A2/B2
S 13th St		
(1-560)	3	A1/B1
(561-1649)	7	A2/B2
(1650-2749)	10	A1/B1
(2750-3299)	12	A1/B1
N 15th St		
(1-315)	2	A2
(314-1217)	18	A1/B1
S 15th St		
(2-561)	2	A2/B2
(562-1649)	7	A1/B1
(1650-2799)	9	A2/B2
N 16th St		
(1-307)	2	A2
(304-1219)	18	A1/B1
S 16th St		
(1-561)	2	A2/B2
(562-1649)	7	A1/B1
(1650-2799)	9	A2/B2
N 17th St		
(1-307)	2	A1
(308-1222)	18	A1/B1
S 17th St		
(1-562)	2	A1/B1
(563-1624)	7	A1/B1
(1618-2798)	9	A2/B2
N 18th St		
(1-313)	2	A1
(310-1431)	17	A2/B2
S 18th St		
(1-565)	2	A1/B1
(566-1609)	6	A2/B2
(1610-2799)	9	A2/B2
N 19th St		
(1-304)	2	A1
(305-1415)	17	A2/B2
S 19th St		
(1-560)	2	A1/B1
(561-1606)	6	A2/B2
(1607-2799)	9	A2/B2
N 20th St		
(1-305)	1	A2
(306-1430)	17	A2/B2
S 20th St		
(1-563)	1	A2/B2
(564-1606)	6	A2/B2
(1607-2898)	9	A1/B1
N 21st St		
(1-299)	1	A2
(306-1414)	17	A1/A2/B2
S 21st St		
(2-559)	1	A2/B2
(560-1606)	6	A2/B2
(1607-2699)	9	A1/B1
N 22nd St		
(1-306)	1	A2
(305-1428)	17	A1/A2/B1
S 22nd St		
(1-558)	1	A2/B2
(559-1615)	6	A1/B1
(1615-2699)	9	A1/B1
N 23rd St		
(1-2348)	1	A2
(500-1418)	17	A2/B1
S 23rd St		
(1-555)	1	A2/B2
(556-1606)	6	A2/B2
(1607-2499)	9	A1/B1
N 24th St	17	A1/B1
S 24th St		
(1-599)	1	A1/A2/B1/B2
(600-1630)	6	
N 25th St	17	A1/B1
S 25th St		
(200-557)	1	B1
(558-1699)	5	A2/B2
N 26th St		
(700-1668)	16	A2/B2
(1669-2999)	15	A2/B2
S 26th St		
(300-558)	1	B1
(559-699)	6	A1
(800-1699)	5	A2/B2
N 27th St		
(700-1649)	16	A2/B2
(1650-2999)	15	A2/B2
S 27th St	5	A2/B2
N 28th St		
(700-1649)	16	A2/B2
(1650-2998)	15	A2/B2
S 28th St	5	B2
N 29th St		
	14	A2/B2
(800-1665)	16	A2/B2
(1666-3099)	15	A2/B2
S 29th St		
	14	B2
(1100-1699)	5	A2/B2
N 30th St		
(1-99)	14	B2
(800-1666)	16	A1/B1
(1667-2699)	15	A2/B2
S 30th St		
(1-299)	14	B2
(1200-1699)	5	B1
N 31st St		
(300-698)	14	A2
(1200-1599)	16	A1

Street Index

Street Index